Butterflies of Europe
vol. 8

# Butterflies of Europe

## Edited by Otakar Kudrna

Vol. 1

**Concise Bibliography of European Butterflies**

Vol. 2

**Introduction to Lepidopterology**

Vol. 3

**Papilionidae; Pieridae**

Vol. 4

**Lycaenidae (incl. Riodininae)**

Vol. 5

**Nymphalidae: Satyrinae**

Vol. 6

**Nymphalidae: Nymphalinae; Danainae; Libytheinae**

Vol. 7

**Ecology of European Butterflies**

Vol. 8

**Aspects of the Conservation of Butterflies
in Europe**

If necessary–depending on the quantity of material–volumes
may be divided into two parts.

# Butterflies of Europe

Edited by OTAKAR KUDRNA

## Volume 8

### OTAKAR KUDRNA

## Aspects of the Conservation
## of Butterflies in Europe

AULA-Verlag Wiesbaden

Dr. Otakar Kudrna
Rhenusallee 32
D-5300 Bonn 3
(Federal Republic of Germany)

or: Universita di Genova
Instituto di Zoologia
Via Balbi 5
I-16126 Genova
(Italy)

CIP-Kurztitelaufnahme der Deutschen Bibliothek

**Butterflies of Europe** / ed. by Otakar Kudrna. –
Wiesbaden : Aula Verlag
NE: Kudrna, Otakar [Hrsg.]
Vol. 8. Kudrna, Otakar: Aspects of the conservation
of butterflies in Europe. – 1986

**Kudrna, Otakar:**
Aspects of the conservation of butterflies in
Europe / Otakar Kudrna. – Wiesbaden : Aula Verlag, 1986
   (Butterflies of Europe; Vol. 8)
   ISBN 3-89104-039-3


© 1986, AULA-Verlag GmbH, Wiesbaden
Verlag für Wissenschaft und Forschung

Illustrations: E. M. Wolfram
Fotos: O. Kudrna
Coverdesign: Klaus Neumann
Typeset by Maschinensetzerei Janß, Pfungstadt
Printed and bound in Federal Republic of Germany
Druck- und Buchbinderei-Werkstätten
May + Co, Darmstadt

ISBN 3-89104-039-3 D5

# Contents

# Preface

There are some 1,400,000 described animal species in the World, with perhaps another three to five milion species as yet to be described. Some 80% of these are insects. Only a small fraction of the known animal species are large mammals, birds and reptiles. Of the unknown species, many will probably become extinct owing to human agency before they are even discovered. More than two thirds of the described and named animal species are known only from preserved specimens deposited in a museum or other similar institution. We know the names of such species, we know how they differ from their allies, we know their type-locality, some specialists can identify them in their adult stage, but we know nothing of their biology or ecology, except perhaps that in some cases it is possible to make a judgement based upon analogies, that one species is probably a parasite and another possibly phytophagous, or related to a certain major geographical or ecological unit, such as high mountains or the steppes. Such animal species are recognized purely by their morphological characters, which do not always correspond with their biological properties: it has been shown time and time again, that one morphological species can consist of more than one biological species. Naturally, in view of this, not all insect species are of the same value for the conservation of nature: it is practically impossible to undertake anything for the conservation of a taxonomic species known only from a few specimens deposited in a museum collection, and it is impossible to use it as a tool in more complex conservation efforts.

The butterflies (Lepidoptera: Papilionoidea), with their about 20,000 known species worldwide, are better known than any other large invertebrate animal group. In Europe, there are some 450 known butterfly species; it is safe to estimate that this represents some 90% of the total number of extant European butterfly species. Further more, the great majority of European butterfly species are defined both morphologically and biologically. They have been extensively studied for more than 200 years and are immensely suitable as estimators of environmental changes, forming a comprehensive group of bioindicator organisms.

This group, consisting in Europe of some 450 butterfly species, facilitates as a whole effective conservation of perhaps as many as 30,000 insect species, which could not be effectively protected by any other means. This amounts to between one quarter and one third of the whole European fauna.

Bonn, March 1986                                                     Otakar Kudrna

The editor gratefully acknowledges the support received from the following companies:
Agfa-Gevaert AG, D-5090 Leverkusen, West Germany
Ilford GmbH, D-6078 Neu-Isenburg, West Germany
Carl Zeiss, D-7082 Oberkochen, West Germany
Without their generous assistance the preparation of this volume would have been much more difficult.

# 1 Introduction

## 1.1 Aims and scope

The aim of this work is to outline rational pragmatic principles for the construction of a long term comprehensive concept for the conservation of indigenous butterflies in Europe, scientifically based on the introduction of extensive preventive measures and the utilization of butterflies as a bioindicator group for the relevant animal communities and ecosystems. The task is divided methodically into four major units:

1. A critical survey of anthropogenic reasons responsible for the decline of butterflies in Europe and conservation measures including an evaluation of sources of information relevant to the conservation of our butterflies; an evaluation of "red data books" and information contained therein by means of selected examples; and a review of the anthropogenically influenced evolution of European butterfly fauna during the holocene.

2. The application of taxonomy in the conservation of butterflies including rationalization of taxonomic categories and their consistent application; clarification of tasks of lepidopterological taxonomy in Europe; and a critical annotated list of European butterflies, with a synonymic list and recommendations for the stabilization of their nomenclature.

3. The application of biogeography in the service of the conservation of butterflies including a critical survey of the distribution of butterflies in Europe based on the evaluation and classification of their colonies; and the biogeographic evaluation of nominal species on the disposition/condition principle (as defined therein).

4. An outline of a comprehensive conservation programme for our indigenous butterflies, with an outline of priorities and recommendations regarding the implementation of the whole concept, and giving due care to the safeguarding of particularly susceptible species and further applied research.

Methodic reasons behind this course of research are explained, if specifically necessary, in the chapters relevant to each individual topic (usually in the introductory paragraph).

Butterflies are identical with the superfamily Papilionoidea (i.e.
Rhopalocera), containing families Papilionidae, Pieridae, Lycaenidae,
Riodinidae, Libytheidae, Danaidae, Nymphalidae and Satyridae, as defined by WARREN (1947). The family Hesperiidae (superfamily Hesperioidea, i.g. Grypocera) is specifically excluded.

Europe is defined as the westernmost extremity of the Euroasiatic landmass bordered to the west by the Atlantic Ocean (and "tributary" seas) and
including the Azores, Madeira and the Canary Islands and by the Mediterranean Sea to the south. The (very arbitrary) eastern border runs as follows: Ural Mts. and river–Volga river–Caspian Sea coast–Manych river
and tributary canals–Sea of Azov (western coast)–Crimean coast (inland
included)–Black Sea coast–European Turkey (eastern coast). Included
are all Greek islands regardless of how close to Asiatic Turkey, and Cyprus.

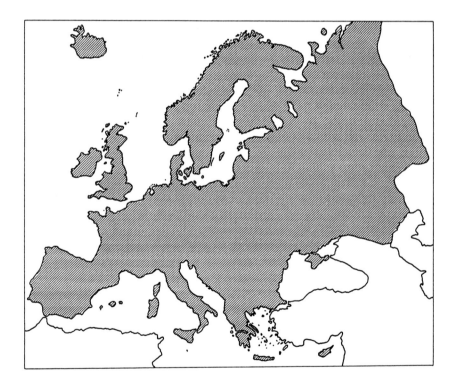

Fig. 1. Europe (hatched) is the westernmost extremety of the Eurasiatic landmass;
included are also all Greek islands regardless of how close to the the Turkish coast
they may be, Cyprus, Madeira and the Canary islands.

Excluded are Asiatic Turkey and all African territories politically under the administration of European countries. (Fig. 1).

If necessary, to avoid any possible confusion, further limits are imposed and defined in the text. So far as I am aware, the term "comprehensive conservation programme" has never been used or defined for any one animal group and/or continent.

## 1.2 Material and methods

Most of the taxonomic research necessary for this work had been carried out at the time of working on the revision of the butterflies named by R. VERITY (KUDRNA 1983) and is, in some ways, a byproduct of that work. The necessity to formulate a conservation programme for European butterflies was first recognized while I was working on a similar project concerning German butterflies (BLAB & KUDRNA 1982). Published information used in the course of this research has been fully cited and apparently unpublished data are acknowledged in the text as personal communications, with reference the author's name. Extensive use has been made of the bibliography of European butterflies (Volume 1 of the series "Butterflies of Europe") unpublished at the time of writing this book (KUDRNA 1985). Specific applications with regard to the stabilization of certain species-group names will be made and addressed to the International Commission on Zoological Nomenclature (London) in due course.

Hidden wing pattern (figs. 31 & 32) was photographed with the same camera, but using Planar f. 1,7/50 mm; additional supporting flash units; Hoya U360 filter and Ilford FP4 film. Illustrations of habitats are reproductions of colour slides, taken at various times with different equipment. All line drawings were done by Dr. E. WOLFRAM (Bonn).

This volume of the "Butterflies of Europe" series differs from all the other volumes in that it can stand on its own, quite independently from the rest of the series. It is intended not only for scientists but also for naturalists and conservationists unlikely to subscribe to the whole series. It was therefore decided to include an extensive bibliography and to repeat references cited also in the first volume of the series, as long as they are mentioned in the text. (In all future volumes, references already cited in the first volume will not be repeated, but referred to by the serial number in the bibliography). There was an unforeseen delay in the production of this volume, caused neither by the present publishers nor by the author. The manuscript was completed in 1984 and planned as a supplement to "Butterflies of Europe"; following the decision to produce this book as a "full" volume of the series, additional new material was added in 1986. The introduction in 1985 of new rules of zoological nomenclature presented some additional problems; they could not have been overcome to perfection.

## 1.3 Acknowledgements.

I would like to acknowledge the help and support received from a number of colleagues and friends.

Prof. Dr. E. BALLETTO (Genova) read almost the whole manuscript and made valuable critical comments and suggestions; he also made available some of his unpublished results of his research, especially on Lycaenidae.

Dr. E. M. WOLFRAM (Bonn) produced all the line drawings and his technical assistance proved invaluable.

Prof. Dr. G. KNEITZ and Prof. Dr. W. KLOFT (both Bonn) read parts of the manuscript and made helpful comments and suggestions of a general nature.

Miss E. J. M. WARREN (Folkestone) corrected both the manuscript and the proofs and made many helpful comments and suggestions.

I have great pleasure in expressing my sincere thanks to all of them.

I further thank for suggestions, encouragement, material, data, information and useful criticism the following colleagues and friends:

Dr. E. M. ANTONOVA, W. ARNSCHEID, L. BIEBER, Dr. J. BLAB, Dr. W. BÖHME, G. C. BOZZANO, R. F. BRETHERTON, L. A. CASSULO, J. G. COUTSIS, J. A. DILS, Dr. W. DIERL, K. M. DOMINKE, Dr. J. GANEV, W. H. J. M. GERAEDTS, Prof. Dr. H. J. HANNEMANN, P. JAKSIC, Dr. F. KASY, Dr. A. O. KOCAK, Dr. Y. P. KORSHUNOV, Dr. J. C. KÜHLE, F. A. LADDA, Prof. Dr. G. LEIGHEB, S. MASCHERINI, R. V. MELVILLE, Dr. R. H. T. MATTONI, Prof. Dr. E. V. NICULESCU, S. OEHMIG, E. PALIK, Dr. H. PIEPER, D. VAN DER POORTEN, W. DE PRINS, L. RAKOSY, R. REINHARDT, Prof. Dr. K. ROSE, P. SCHAIDER, Dr. R. SCHMIEDER, K. G. SCHURIAN, K. F. SEDYKH, D. SIEDE, Dr. R. SIJARIC, A. B. DE SOUSA, V. STERBA, W. G. TREMEWAN, U. WOLF and Dr. K. WOLLMANN.

# 2 Considerations on the significance of native butterflies for the conservation of nature in Europe*

The decline in numbers of native butterflies has been observed all over Europe, more in some regions than in others, increasingly so over the last fifty years and accelerating to alarming proportions in some countries over the last two or three decades. The reasons for the decline are (almost) exclusively anthropogenic; they are discussed elsewhere.

Nationally, regionally and locally motivated efforts to halt the decline of some butterfly species have been carried out with increasing sophistication in some European countries–particularly in those countries where the decline of butterflies has reached the most alarming proportions. The success of these efforts cannot be described as better than mixed. The leading role in the conservation of butterflies has probably been played by Great Britain, a country with a very poor butterfly fauna both in the number of species and their abundance, if judged from the European point of view. It was probably the natural rarity of butterflies and the past record of their regional and national extinction of the colonies and species that raised the „awareness" of butterflies in that country. In England for example, *Lycaena dispar* became extinct in the middle of the last century following extensive drainage of the fens in Cambridgeshire and their subsequent intensive cultivation. An introduced population has been successfully maintained at the national nature reserve Woodwalton Fen by supplementing the wild population with releases of laboratory bred stocks at times of need (DUFFEY 1977). All efforts to prevent the extinction in Great Britain of *Maculinea arion* failed (THOMAS 1982) as well as the attempts to reintroduce *Papilio machaon* to Wicken Fen (DEMPSTER & HALL 1980) where the species became extinct earlier in this century. The primary outcome of these experiments are ecological observations which, most probably, would not otherwise have been made. In Germany *Iphiclides podalirius, Parnassius apollo, P. mnemosyne* and *P. phoebus* have been given legal protection against collecting since 1936–and their decline continues. None the less, the example was followed by other European countries (e.g. Czechoslovakia, Poland)–with the same results, needless to say. The use of such legal means alone cannot halt the decline of any species threatened by more than one cause of decline. The chief requirement in halting the de-

---

* European butterflies play an exceptional role in the conservation of nature; their significance remains undervalued.

cline of any nominal species is the identification of the main causes of decline (i.e. harmful factors) and their subsequent exclusion.

All national, regional and local conservation efforts have one common
denominator: they are usually last minute attempts to save from extinction
national (regional, local) rarities, and they are usually carried out
haphazardly in the race against time. Any chance for success depends
largely on circumstances beyond the control of the conservationists, such
as the size of the remaining stocks, the long term suitability of the remaining sites, the availability of resources including financial means, the help of
successive favourable seasons, the speed in discovering the "bottleneck",
its causes and how to overcome them. In other words the factor of good
luck plays by no means a negligible part in the saving of endangered (rare)
species from extinction and some of them are saved only at the cost of the
introduction of conditions not unlike those in intensive care units or safari
parks (e.g. the reintroduced population of *Lycaena dispar* mentioned
above). The total contribution of all such efforts to the conservation of nature as a whole is negligible, particularly if the same nominal species are
relatively widespread and regionally common elsewhere (e.g. *Maculinea
arion* is widespread from Europe to Japan!). The scientific contribution of
all such attempts is chiefly the advancement of our understanding of the
ecology of the species concerned and, perhaps, of butterflies as a whole.

None the less, all these efforts to save last colonies of rare and regionally
endangered species, even if objectively successful, entirely miss some
essential issues of nature conservation:

- They totally fail to realize the exceptional value of butterflies as
  indispensible bioindicators;
- They fail to take into consideration natural communities and overall
  disposition of the species protected;
- They may sacrifice the habitat ecosystem for the protection of a single
  species (and that even if the long term success depends on its being
  maintained by semiartificial means);
- They are governed by national (regional, local) wishes instead of being
  based on objective judgements and real needs.

It would be unreasonable to pretend that either the present or any future
political reality would be able to produce and carry out an individual conservation programme for each animal species, not to mention the fact that
their preparation would hardly be feasible, at present or in the forseeable
future. Apart from the securing of a sound financial basis for such an extensive programme, we must appreciate that there are not enough trained
zoologists and research facilities, and that more than two thirds of these

species are known only from preserved specimens (as already mentioned), i.e. not backed up by even the minimal biological information necessary for such an undertaking. Additionally, according to our experience derived from numerous observations of the conservation of nature in central and northern Europe, the "single species" approach rarely achieves the desired goal, apart from some very special cases mostly concerning the vertebrates. These rare cases of success were made possible through the activities of, for instance, enthusiastic bird-watchers willing to provide unpaid work for the creating and maintaining of semiartificial "biotopes" for selected species. Similar activities have often proved in the long run to be rather harmful to the other members of the ecosystem concerned. For example the artificially induced overabundance of the Great Tit *(Parus major)* in the wooded parts of the Moseltal (in Germany) significantly contributes to the already existing anthropogenical threats endangering the rare local population of *Parnassius apollo* (competition between intensive vine growing and the colonies of *P. apollo* inhabiting old abandoned vineyards; the butterfly species is considered seriously threatened).

Nonetheless, these critical remarks must not be understood as a total rejection of regional conservation programmes as such. A comprehensive regional conservation programme for butterflies is fully justified if its priorities are determined by and coordinated with larger scale (e.g. European) conservation programmes, if the region is large and diverse enough to accommodate a rich butterfly fauna capable of serving as a bioindicator group. The advantage of regional conservation programmes must be seen in the fact, that their execution does not suffer from political barriers dividing the region. Such regional conservation programmes also enable close cooperation between the nature conservation authorities and individual lepidopterists, as long as adequate supervision of the programme by highly qualified specialists on the staff of the nature conservation authorities ensures proper permanent supervision and can provide ready advice in the execution and implementation of the programme (KUDRNA 1986).

The decline of indigenous butterflies is surely not more than the tip of the iceberg: the decline of other invertebrate groups in Europe has escaped unnoticed by all but a few specialists, and perhaps only in a few countries. The vertebrates, particularly the birds and some larger mammals, have caused much greater concern among the general public, perhaps because they are more conspicuous and therefore better known. This division of attention is quite unjustified. The Invertebrata represent the overwhelming majority of all animal species: from every ten known animal species nine are invertebrates, eight are insects (Fig. 2). This fact seems to have been ignored by all planners of the conservation of nature so far: although there are numerous national parks and nature reserves in Europe, only a negligi-

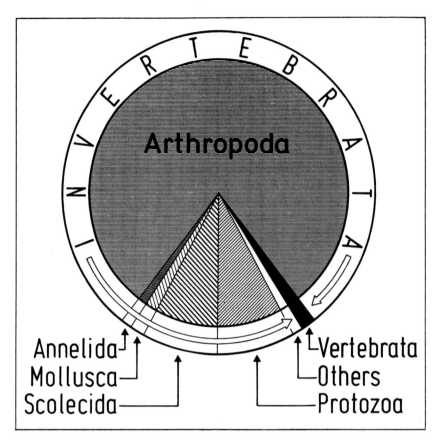

Fig. 2. Composition of German fauna. Some 90% of Arthropoda are insects, some 10% of insects are Lepidoptera. The butterflies constitute about 0,5% of the whole fauna.

ble proportion are intended to serve also for invertebrates, and the management methods used in some of them are adverse to insects, tailored solely for the protection of certain vertebrates (HEATH 1981).

Whereas it may be possible to provide for the conservation of the individual threatened species of birds, mammals or reptiles, it would be very difficult, indeed practically impossible, to plan and carry out individual protection measures for every insect species, or even for every lepidopterous species, of which there are in Europe probably "only" around 8,000 (estimate)–owing to their sheer numbers alone. The survival of the diverse fauna of European invertebrates depends, therefore, by and large on the development of a novel approach towards their conservation: it is the conservation of natural communities based upon extensive preventive conservation measures and represented by selected (bio)indicator groups, which are both manageable in their size and adequately ecologically diverse enough to be "representative" and which are well documented and whose study does not require the use of inconvenient methods (e.g. traps).

The butterflies form from this point of view an ideal indicator group, surely the most important invertebrate bioindicator group of heliophilous phytophagous species, because:

● Butterflies are represented in Europe by about 450 indigenous species: this amount is on the one hand representative and on the other still manageable.
● Butterflies inhabit almost all major types of terrestrial habitats: their ecological diversity is exceptionally broad.
● Butterflies are doubtless better taxonomically and ecologically known than any other (similar) group of invertebrates.
● Butterflies are phytophagous (both larvae and adults) but the availability of their hostplants alone is inadequate to secure their continuous occurrence.
● Butterflies are important pollinators of wild flowers, hosts to numerous parasites and prey to various predators.
● Butterflies have much greater ecological requirements, particularly in space, than most invertebrate species.
● Butterflies are conspicuous enough and diurnal (heliophilous) so that they can be (by and large) recorded and studied without the use of traps and unnecessary killing.
● Butterflies are beautiful and harmless: it is therefore easier to win the support of the general public for their conservation, taking into account their unique aesthetic value.

It should be mentioned here that European Hesperiids (i.e. superfamily Hesperioidea, a taxonomic "sister" group of the Papilionoidea) and, above all, the Zygaenids (Zygaenidae is a family taxonomically very distrinct from but ecologically very close to the Papilionoidea) also exhibit similar properties as indicator groups. Purely technical reasons, and above all the adequacy of butterflies for the purpose, led to their exclusion from this study.

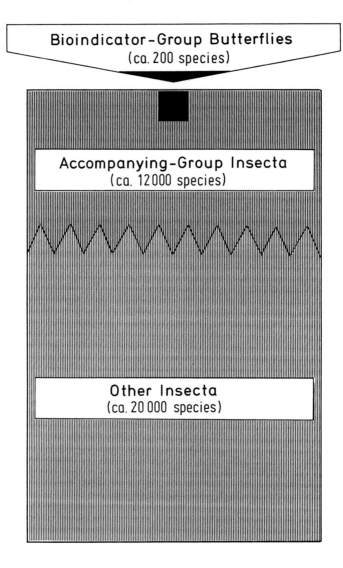

Fig. 3. The butterflies, with their less than 200 German species, constitute an ecologically dominating bioindicator group; the conservation of butterfly habitats through indirect preventive measures can protect all ecological accompanying groups of insects, in all about 12,000 species in Germany, which could not be effectively protected by any other means.

The significance of butterflies for the conservation of European insects can be demonstrated by the example of the Federal Republic of Germany. The German fauna is estimated to consist of between 40,000 (BROHMER 1977) and 45,000 (NOWAK 1982) species (Fig. 2). From this amount only about 2% are Vertebrata and the "rest" – some 98% – are Invertebrata, of which over 30,000 (over 75%) are insects. The taxonomic diversity of insects is well known; there are not enough specialists to study them, their species group taxa are usually based on the morphospecies concept because the information on their biology (s.l.) is inadequate; even identification keys are few and far between, often completely out of date. For the conservation of nature this clearly means, that it is impossible at present to devise effective conservation programmes for European insects. It must be noted that the insects are in central Europe much better known than in countries like Spain or Greece, not to mention those of really remote areas.

The only practical approach to the conservation of insects anywhere in Europe is through the conservation of ecologically dominating bioindicator groups ("Oekologische Leitgruppe"), such as the butterflies (as a whole), whose ecological requirements are greater, than those of the "rest" of the community they dominate.

● An ecologically dominating bioindicator group is an assemblage of taxonomically relatively closely related and well known organisms whose ecological and biogeographical requirements are much greater than those of the accompanying ecological groups which share the same habitat with them (Fig. 3).

It can be assumed that the ecological factors required by the species of the ecologically dominating bioindicator group include by and large those of the accompanying groups. It is therefore safe to assume that the conservation of the bioindicator group (as a whole) facilitates automatically the conservation of the accompanying group in any given habitat, as long as the habitat and its community is kept in the balance. The ecological balance of the biocenosis concerned could be disturbed for instance by the introduction of some species specific measures intended to "improve" its conditions.

The accompanying ecological groups can be divided into two subgroups according to their relationship to the dominating group:

– The first subgroup consists of consumers, the occurrence of which depends directly of the presence of the dominating group. The consumers of butterflies include their predators and parasitoids.
– The second subgroup consists of species which are not directly dependent on the presence of the butterflies, but which are well known from

experience to occur parallel with butterflies and to share with them their habitat and its biotopes.

It is safe to assume that the less than 200 German butterfly species are accompanied by (conservatively estimated) about 12,000 accompanying insect species–other groups of invertebrates are excluded from these considerations (Fig. 3).

The systematic composition of insects accompanying the butterflies in Germany can be outlined as follows:

Coleoptera (D. SIEDE pers. comm.):
About 2000 accompanying species from ca. 6000 species of German Coleoptera. The consumers are chiefly the predators of butterfly larvae (e.g. Carabidae, esp. *Calosoma* spp., occasionally also some Staphilinidae. The parallel companions are

- species whose larvae feed on same of similar foodplants as those utilized by the butterflies (Scarabaeidae, esp. Melolontinae; Cerambycidae; Chrysomelidae; Curculionidae; Bruchidae) and

- species frequenting flowers (Staphilinidae, esp. Omatiinae; Malacodermata, esp. Cantharidae, Malachiidae, Cleridae and Melyridae; Elateridae; Buprestidae; Dermestidae; Byturidae; Coccinelidae; Oedomeridae; Pyrochoridae; Anthycidae; Meloidae; Scarabaeidae; Cerambycidae; Bruchidae).

Diptera:
Over 1000 accompanying species from ca. 6000 German Diptera include Syrphidae, Bombilidae, Tachinidae, Nematocera etc. (exact information not available at present).

Heteroptera (E. WOLFRAM pers. com.):
About 600 accompanying species from ca. 800 German species: all families except aquatic bugs and some ecological specialists, Auchenorrhyncha not taken into consideration.

Hymenoptera (K. WOLLMANN pers. com.):
Over 6000 accompanying species from well over 10,000 species of Hymenoptera represented in Germany, including Aculeata and the majority of the families of parasitoids, such as Braconidae, Ichneumonidae, Chalcidoidea, and others.

Lepidoptera:
Over 2000 accompanying species, from about 3000 species recorded from Germany, from practically all families with the exception of some ecological specialists.

Practically all the accompanying groups of insects mentioned above cannot be conserved efficiently by any other means than the protection of butterfly habitats.

The final aim of the bioindicator concept outlined above is to safeguard the continuity of complicated natural animal communities and ecosystems by means of "neutral" management of the animal group selected. The "neutral" or "moderating" management practice must protect the community and its site from adverse anthropogenic pressures and, if the circumstances so dictate (e.g. seminatural habitats, small isolated sites, seral communities and habitats) to help to maintain its identity. Quite contrary to this concept are efforts which try to make everything subordinate to a single species or a small group. HEATH (1981) demanded that new methods of management propagating butterflies by introducing changes favourable to them should be developed for certain nature reserves. MORTON (1983) went as far as demanding the establishment of a "captive breeding institute" to breed endangered species for reintroduction to strengthen their existing colonies. Mass production of threatened species becomes totally unrealistic as soon as one takes into consideration the number of species that would have to be bred alone. Also NIKUSCH's (1981) proposals concerning *Parnassius apollo* must be rejected. All such and similar "conservation measures" disregard at least the carying capacity of the site concerned and have surely more in common with adverse anthropogenic pressures.

Europe is covered by six different main biomes (MARCUZZI 1979, RILEY & YOUNG 1966), each of which is particular to a certain geographical area characterized by a specific climax vegetational type. These biomes (Fig. 4) are:

Sclerophylous forest: This biome occupies in Europe the northern coast of the Mediterranean Sea, most of Iberian Peninsula and a narrow strip along the coast of southern and southeastern Crimea. There are four major vegetational types:

– In the areas dominated by dry climate, the typical vegetation consists of shrubs and/or tree pseudosteppe and open forests, not rarely with garrigue undergrowth.
– In the areas dominated by somewhat "cooler" climates, especially with relatively cold winters, there is mainly grassland ("high steppe") with or without trees or shrubs, such as in parts of inland Spain and the Crimea.
– In the areas dominated by "Mediterranean-maritime" climate, such as in coastal districts, the typical trees of the sclerophylous forest are evergreen oaks, frequently replaced by "maquis" – a product of degradation.

– In subhumid parts of Mediterranean basin, e.g. in Cyprus and in some restricted localities dominated by insubrian climate in northern Italy, the sclerophylous forest is replaced by the domination of deciduous trees.

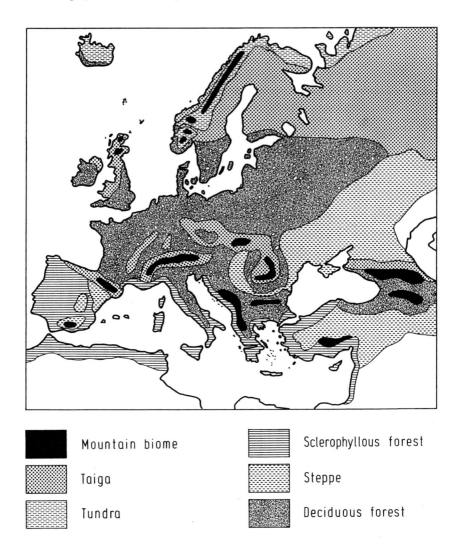

| | Mountain biome | | Sclerophyllous forest |
|---|---|---|---|
| | Taiga | | Steppe |
| | Tundra | | Deciduous forest |

Fig. 4. Main European biomes (after Marcuzzi 1979). Note: The steppe includes relict steppe-like habitats in Hungary and the so called "high steppe" in Spain and the Crimea).

Because of the favourable climatic conditions, the human impact on the sclerophylous forest has a long history–above all in Greece and Italy, especially in coastal districts.

Deciduous forest: This biome occupies the most conspicuous part of Europe and dominates its central latitudes at low levels, usually below 500 m. Its climate ranges from the attenuated oceanic zone through the transitional zone of central Europe to the continental climate. Without the influence of human culture, the deciduous forest would cover more or less continuously the whole of western and central Europe, except localities where trees cannot grow, such as rocks, screes, marshes, peat-bogs etc.). At present, the areas covered by natural climax deciduous forest are in western and central Europe quite small. Butterfly species inhabiting deciduous forest are in their majority linked to various seral stages and the undergrowth which offers them numerous larval and adult hostplants as well as shelter.

Mountain biome: This biome is difficult to define precisely from the geographical point of view; some authors maintain that every habitat situated at an altitude of 500 m and higher belongs to this biome. In Europe, there are essentially two major vegetational types within this biome:
– Woodland, ranging from deciduous forest through mixed forest to coniferous forest (at higher altitudes), which is often compared to the taiga.
– Alpine tundra occupying the higher levels above the upper tree line, it can be compared with the arctic tundra.
Southern slopes of the Alps are characterized by butterfly communities extremely rich in both their species diversity and abundance, possibly unmatched by any other European region.

Taiga: This biome, also often called coniferous forest, covers an extensive area of northern Europe, situated approximately between the latitudes of 58° and 70° N. In the south, it merges into the deciduous forest and in the north into the arctic tundra. Taiga is dominated by cold continental climates. The vegetation consists predominantly of coniferous trees (e.g. *Abies* spp. and *Pinus* spp.), often mixed with some deciduous trees (e.g. *Betula* spp.). The European taiga is only the western extremity of the Asiatic taiga, which stretches across Siberia to the Far East. The European taiga is much more continuous than the deciduous woodland, but not as uninterrupted as tundra. There are no European butterflies linked directly or ex-

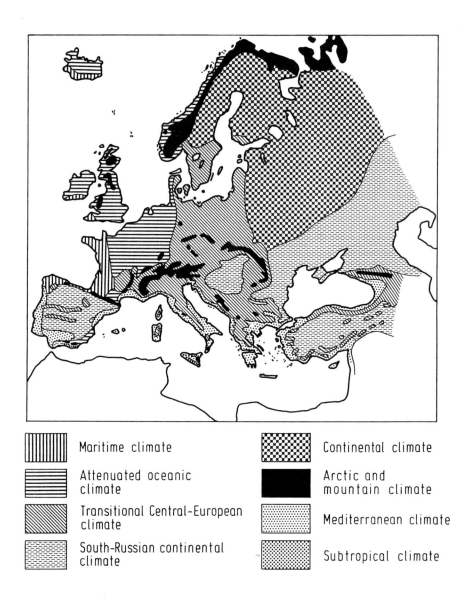

| | Maritime climate | | Continental climate |
| --- | --- | --- | --- |
| | Attenuated oceanic climate | | Arctic and mountain climate |
| | Transitional Central-European climate | | Mediterranean climate |
| | South-Russian continental climate | | Subtropical climate |

Fig. 5. Major European climatic zones (after MARCUZZI 1979).

clusively to coniferous trees, but there are many species inhabiting clearings and in the north also swamps and bogs, i.e. more or less treeless open spaces within the taiga.

Tundra: This biome covers the semi-frozen landscape of northernmost Europe, north of taiga. Also tundra stretches across the whole of Eurasia. The climate of tundra is arctic and allows only a short summer; the flight period of butterflies lasts usually only four to five weeks and culminates mostly during the second half of June, coinciding with the longest day. Although butterfly larvae probably can feed a little longer, many species cannot complete their development in one season and have an essentially biennial life-cycle. The butterfly fauna of the European tundra is not rich in species, but most of them do not live anywhere else in Europe; only some of them also inhabit high altitudes in the Alps or elsewhere.

Steppe: This biome occuppies southern and south-eastern Russia and the Ukraine; a small enclave–the Puszta–is in Hungary (now mostly used for agriculture). The steppe is a vast lowland grassland with only occasional trees or shrubs; the specific wetness of the soil on the one hand prevents the steppe becoming a desert or semidesert and on the other does not facilitate the growth of trees. The climate is distinctly continental, with cold winters, during which the steppe is covered by a thick layer of snow, short spring and autumn and long, dry, hot summers. It is the water from melting snow that during the short spring provides the moisture necessary for the growth of permanent thick grassland on deep chernozem soil. The relatively monotonous character of the steppe does not allow the development of a butterfly fauna rich in species, but provides conditions for ecological specialists, a few of which reach their western limit in central Europe, isolated relict populations of e.g. *Colias chrysotheme* and *C. myrmidone* among them.

Some authors consider also the western European heaths and moors (marshes, peatbogs; "Flachmoore" and "Hochmoore") to form distinct biomes. It is true that Flachmoore and Hochmoore are climax communities and have a specific distinct flora and fauna, with many tyrphophilous butterfly species; however, these species usually live outside peatbogs at higher altitudes and in northern Europe. From the lepidopterological point of view, Flachmoore and Hochmoore are somewhat analogous to screes, rocks and similar habitats within deciduous forests, inhabited by xerothermophilous species otherwise not directly linked to deciduous trees.

European biomes coincide by and large with climatic zones of Europe (Fig. 5). The following climatic zones are recognized (MARCUZZI 1979):

Arctic climate: Extreme fluctuations between summer and winter; permanent snow and ice at higher altitudes; permafrost at lower altitudes; similar conditions are at high altitudes in C. Europe.

Continental climate: Stable conditions; long summers, cold winters; short spring and autum transitions.

South-Russian continental climate: Hot sunny summers; cold winters; wet springs; short autumns (similar to the above).

Transitional Central-European climate: Transition between the continental climate and the attenuated oceanic (atlantic) climate.

Attenuated oceanic climate: Similar to maritime climate, but with greater differences between winter and summer temperatures, gradually merging into the transitional climate of central Europe.

Maritime climate: True oceanic climate in coastal areas influenced mainly by the Atlantic Ocean and partly by the Gulf Stream.

Mediterranean climate: Hot, dry, sunny summers; dry autumn; warm usually wet springs; short, usually mild, moist winters (very long vegetation period).

Subtropical climate: In Europe only small enclaves along the coast of southern Spain and southern Sicily, characterized by mean monthly temperatures never lower than 6° C and the lack of frost in winter months.


This implies that after an absolute withdrawal of "management", all Europe would eventually become dominated by the area specific climax biome. This means that, for instance, the area of deciduous woodlands would be covered by deciduous trees unless adverse natural conditions locally prevented their growth. For this reason two different forms of habitat (site) conservation are suggested:

● "Unmanaged" natural habitats either in their climax biome or left to proceed through the seral stages of natural succession. Such habitats and sites must form the backbone of any conservation programme because they are natural and most economical to run: all they need are preventive measures safeguarding their continuous undisturbed existence. The precondition of their indefinite existence may be their adequate size, this being particularly important for the sites undergoing continuous natural succession (of their plant and animal communities) in relative isolation from other such sites, to prevent accidental extinctions. Some species, e.g. *Coenonympha oedippus,* the most endangered European butterfly species, can apparently only survive in such natural habitats (BISCHOF 1968).

● "Managed" secondary habitats which have been produced indirectly by human activities and have become inhabited by valuable diverse animal communities from their vicinity. Such habitats include above all some traditionally managed meadows and pastures; some old orchards; some woodland clearings, rides and verges. These habitats must be maintained by the application of "neutral management" by the "arresting" of the site in its present "status quo" (e.g. the grassland habitats by cutting in a mosaic pattern once, in some cases twice a year, or grazing) or by provisions for their continuous existence in an area not separated by barriers (e.g. in case of woodland clearings by the use of rational coppicing, and maintaining of connecting rides to channel the butterfly communities accordingly). Some principles concerning management methods of various central european habitats have already been described (BLAB & KUDRNA 1982).

It must be made abundantly clear that the significance of secondary habitats in comparison to natural habitats is really "secondary". From the puristic view of nature conservation all managed habitats must be rejected: the species inhabiting these habitats lived here in Europe long before human activities helped to provide for them. In Great Britain, where advanced agriculture and high population have destroyed secondary habitats of most species, common butterflies are now local rarities. With the progressing denaturalization of European countryside, the abandonment of secondary habitats from a conservation concept would probably lead to heavy losses and regional extinction of many species, which may become too isolated in some areas, to survive indefinitely outside nature reserves. The extinction in Great Britain of a widespread Palaearctic species *Maculinea arion,* although in principle "unimportant", is a good example to show the relative significance of secondary habitats: the species became wide spread in England during the last century apparently owing to overgrazing; its decline and subsequent isolation led finally to its extinction there (MUGGEL-TON & BENHAM 1975).

It has become à custom in some official circles of conservationists to produce from time to time new statistics demonstrating how intensive forms of above all agriculture and forestry are responsible for the decline of certain species and the destruction of certain habitats and sites. This activity is usually combined with reissue of "red lists", not necessarily based on better basic information, and the publication of distant theoretical papers. It is hardly surprising that "red lists" have been growing in such circumstances. It must be at last realized that agriculture and forestry are industries responsible primarily for the production of food and wood, not for the conservation of nature, and they are most unlikely to follow repeated general requests to introduce management techniques favourable to this or that animal group. Although it is necessary to describe the anthropogenic factors harmful to butterflies and to identify their causes, it is incomparably more important to show efficient ways of preventing them and their repercussions. This can be demonstrated by two examples:

- A general request by the conservationists to abandon further wetland drainage or further intensification of grassland management would certainly contribute to the safeguarding of butterfly species concerned, but would be unlikely to be put into operation by farmers and authorities concerned.
- A general request to abandon further afforestation of xerothermic grassland and seminemoral habitats would certainly help the conservation of the species concerned, but would be unlikely to be followed by the authorities responsible for the planning of forestry expansion.

It is much easier for the nature conservation authorities to issue from time to time similar calls than to carry out detailed mapping of indicator groups so that the requests can be specified to prevent possible, perhaps unwanted, destruction of valuable habitats. Specific requests concerning specific sites would certainly have a much better chance of being fulfilled, particularly if concerning the forestry authorities and supported by concrete suggestions, than general ones. A statement announcing the destruction of a site or the extinction of a species, and denouncing the causers, is of little help for conservation unless it shows the way how to prevent and therefore avoid its repetition. This can only be done if the sites and nominal species are recorded and mapped. The existence of such documentation is absolutely essential for all conservation efforts. (Strictly speaking, it is often very difficult to demonstrate the decline of a nominal species owing to the lack of such most basic data). It is more than absurd that the only European country running a rational mapping scheme (combined with other related research) is the Netherlands. It is possible that two reasons are responsible for the refusal by most nature conservation authorities to carry out rational mapping programmes:

- General belief that the task is being carried out by the European Invertebrate Survey (which is not the case); and
- Dominance of "generalists" holding the decisive positions among the conservationists (who cannot be bothered with "details").

It is not surprising that in such circumstances rational scientific conservation concepts are few and far between.

However, the success of the conservation of nature depends on the implementation, by politicians, of relevant rational concepts developed by scientists. The failure of this cooperation has been responsible for numerous absurdities in the conservation of European butterflies, and nature as a whole. A few of them may serve as typical examples:

- The European Parliament (of the European Community) has no committee or similar body responsible for the conservation of nature within the EC.
- In spite of the failure of the 1936 legislation, the federal government introduced during 1981 a new law imposing an almost total ban on the collecting of butterflies (and other groups) as a form of their "protection" in Germany.
- The relevant department of the ministry responsible for the conservation of nature in the Federal Republic of Germany does not employ permanently a single biologist (lawyers are preferred).
- Among the six (only!) scientists employed by the institute advising the above ministry on questions of animal conservation there is not a single entomologist (yet some 80% of German animal species are insects: BLAB & KUDRNA 1982, NOWAK 1983).

In these circumstances it is hardly surprising that governments so often arrive at most amazing actions purporting to be specific conservation measures. For instance, the German federal government decided recently to introduce lead-free petrol for motor vehicles from 1986 as the measure to bring under control advanced acidification causing extensive dying-out of woodland in central Europe, as if it was not quite clear that the causes of the so called acid rain are industrial emissions containing above all sulphur dioxide, and also nitrogen oxides, produced in the first place by some power stations and private households, tolerated owing to low standards of antipollution control, which are to stay (PERSSON 1982). This approach to the conservation of nature leads to another typical missjudgement: conservation of nature is seen as a regulating mechanism of economic utilization; the value of woodland is seen as equal to that of wood the it produces, and not as of an ecosystem.

Everywhere throughout civilized Europe products of human genius are valued and protected. Nobody would ever dream about destroying architectural or historical monuments. None the less, everything once built, made, or painted can be reproduced again, if necessary elsewhere in a more convenient location, better erected. Natural ecosystems, species communities and, indeed, also individual nominal species resulted from thousands of years of evolution, they are not man made and they cannot be man made. They have at least the same value as the products of human inventiveness. Butterflies as other organisms are such irreplaceable treasures, too.

Obviously the greatest decline of butterfly populations has taken place in the most industrialized, and therefore richest, countries of central Europe. It seems that the most important single factor responsible for the decline of butterflies is agricultural overproduction. Perhaps it is up to the most developed countries to show the way in new attitudes to those of our "neighbours" who have the same right to live even if they are not eligible to vote for representatives to look after their interests, such as the butterflies.

If this work contributes positively towards safeguarding the survival of butterflies in Europe, before their time has run out,—and to the conservation of European nature in general—its purpose will be fulfilled.

# 3 The decline of European butterflies, its anthropogenic causes and present countermeasures: survey and analysis

A decline of butterflies has been observed almost everywhere in Europe and can be documented for a period of over one hundred years, attributed almost exclusively to anthropogenic pressures of the modern civilized industrial society. Lack of subfossil material makes it difficult to trace anthropogenic influences further back, although they must have existed since early man began to "rule" the Earth. A survey and analysis of both the reasons for the decline of butterflies and the – relatively unsuccessful – present countermeasures enables a new pan-European view of the complex problems surrounding the conservation of nature and protection of butterflies in Europe and helps to show new methods to master it.

## 3.1 Outline of biogeographic history of European butterflies during the holocene

The general biogeographic history of Europe is reasonably well known (e.g. COX, HEALEY & MOORE 1973, LATTIN 1968, WOLDSTEDT 1954, 1958) and provides some interesting data for the reconstruction of the probable evolution of the European butterfly fauna since the last glaciation.

The last glacial period, the Weichselian glaciation, lasted some 110,000 years. It was interrupted by at least six warmer interstadials, two of which occurred towards the end of the period; the Allerod interstadial was the most significant of the two. After the Allerod, the last period of glaciation lasted only about 500 years and the ice cap did not reach as far south as during the all time maximum glaciation, when the ice covered Europe southwards as far as the 50th parallel. During the cold periods most of ice free Europe was covered by subarctic tundra and frozen soil, temperate woodland being confined chiefly to the northern Mediterranean. During the somewhat warmer interstadials various plant and animal species had the opportunity to penetrate the lowland areas north of the Alps, chiefly along the coast with its milder climate. This enabled boreal forest to develop over large stretches in a rapid outburst of life, yet it was inadequate to support temperate woodland. The Allerod interstadial lasted over 1000 years, being thus more than twice as long as the subsequent last cooling of the climate. At the end of the last glacial period, i.e. ca. 8300 B.C., all northern Europe and the higher altitudes of central and–to a lesser degree–southern Europe were covered by a thick cap of permanent ice, being totally devoid of butterflies. The lower levels of central Europe were inhabited by species similar to those restricted today to high altitudes and/or to the European Arctic. Some of these species, such as *Colias palaeno,* also survived locally to the present time in the lowland areas of raised bogs but have their main distribution centres (i.e. "headquarters") at higher altitudes and in the far north of Europe. Other dominant species presumably widespread over ice-free central Europe were probably various *Oeneis* spp., *Erebia* spp., some *Boloria* spp. (e.g. *B. eunomia, B. freija, B. frigga, B. polaris, B. chariclea, B. pales, B. thore, B. titania* etc.), *Colias hecla, C. nastes, Vacciniina optilete* and other species with similar ecological requirements and biogeographic history. At low and moderate altitudes of southern Europe the temperate species found their glacial refugia, and were the dominant element of such areas; the majority of them would probably be classified as nemoral and subnemoral mesophils at present. The true thermophilous and xerothermophilous species inhabited above all parts of northern Africa, with only limited refugial distribution along the northern Mediterranean coast at low altitudes. (Fig. 6).

The invasion of Europe by butterfly species from the south, south-east and east probably progressed rather slowly. Great Britain, separated from the Continent by water from the melting ice-cap since about 5500 B.C. was reached by very few xerothermophilous species as well as by relatively few immigrants from the east. The main period of the invasion of Europe by the xerothermophilous species certainly took place between ca. 5000 and 3000 B.C., i.e. during the postglacial climatic optimum. During this period some xerothermophils were able to reach as far north as at least the southern coast of Scandinavia (e.g. *Hipparchia hermione* survived to the present time as a relict in its refugium in southern Norway; it must have penetrated into Scandinavia before multiple land and sea movements finally separated Denmark from Sweden and Norway). The climax biome spread over most of Europe north of the Pyrenees. the Alps and the Balkan Peninsula was deciduous woodland; it reached further north and much higher up in the mountains than today and contained a significant proportion of xerothermophilous species. Although this thick woodland was at least in some areas impenetrable to early man, it was structurally much less inconvenient to butterflies: beech woodland with natural clearings rich in undergrowth in central Europe (ELLENBERG 1978), chiefly oak woodland (with *Quercus ilex*) over most wooded parts of southern Europe. This period of some 2000 years of warm climate probably played the most significant role in the for-

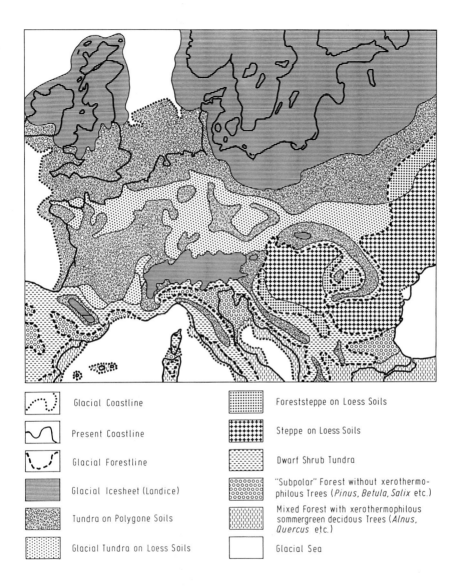

| | |
|---|---|
| Glacial Coastline | Foreststeppe on Loess Soils |
| Present Coastline | Steppe on Loess Soils |
| Glacial Forestline | Dwarf Shrub Tundra |
| Glacial Icesheet (Landice) | "Subpolar" Forest without xerothermo-philous Trees (*Pinus, Betula, Salix* etc.) |
| Tundra on Polygone Soils | Mixed Forest with xerothermophilous sommergreen decidous Trees (*Alnus, Quercus* etc.) |
| Glacial Tundra on Loess Soils | Glacial Sea |

Fig. 6. Main types of vegetation in central Europe towards the end of the pleis-tocene–Weichselian (Würm) glaciation.

mation of the contemporary ranges of the majority of European butterfly species, and not only the inhabitants of nemoral and subnemoral habitats. The somewhat skiophilous inclination of most mesophilous grassland species certainly seems to indicate their past affinity to woodland.

Europe is inhabited by relatively few truly nemoral species of Papilionoidea that are directly associated with woodland and widespread. They are usually species of Euro-Sibirian faunal type and their larvae feed mostly on trees or bushes, some also on herbaceous nemoral plants. Their characteristic wing-pattern is black or dark ground-colour with whitish transverse stripes on the upperside, but some are quite uniform blackish-brown or „spotted“; their underside is usually more colourful. A most characteristic habit of the majority of nemoral species is their spending much time in the canopy, usually sunbathing for thermo regulation. The following mostly widespread species must be mentioned: *Argynnis pandora, A. paphia, Apatura ilia, A. iris, A. metis, Limenitis camilla, L. populi, L. reducta* (all NY), *Lasiommata maera* (SA), *Neptis sappho, N. rivularis* (both NY), *Pararge aegeria* (SA), *Quercusia quercus* and *Thecla betulae* (both LY). It must be noted that two nemoral species probably never use the canopy: *Erebia aethiops* and *E. ligea* (SA).

Most of the European butterflies, especially the species inhabiting seminemoral and grassland habitats, particularly north of the Mediterranean, could have spread in the relatively thickly wooded regions only owing to their remarkable ability to utilize specific seral stages in the plant succession in natural clearings. The distribution of such species must remain dynamic, consisting of unstable colonies: while some colonies become extinct, new ones are established elsewhere. Among the 17 most widespread European butterfly species (cd. fig. 47) eight to ten used (or could have used) this form of extending their ranges. These species are: *Anthocharis cardamines* (PI), *Callophrys rubi, Celastrina argiolus* (both LY), *Gonepteryx rhamni* (PI), *Issoria lathonia* (NY), *Lycaena phlaeas* (LY), *Maniola jurtina* (SA), *Pararge aegeria* (SA) and *Pieris napi* (PI). Of course, the same mode of range dynamics is utilized by numerous other species which for various reasons could not spread so far as the above. For example, *Zerynthia polyxena* (PA) is at present expanding its range in Italy as the result of the spreading of its larval hostplant (*Aristolochia* spp.) which is linked to the recolonization seres of natural mesophilous woodland and following the withdrawal of cultivation from some montane environments (E. BALLETTO pers. comm). At the same time, the species *Z. polyxena* is believed to be declining owing to coniferans afforestation towards its northern biogeographical limit. Likewise the mode of range expansion of grassland species now inhabiting meadows must have followed very similar patterns.

Little is known of the speed of dispersal of species attempting an invasion of new land, previously uninhabited by them, where a free ecological niche already exists. HRUBY (1956) examined the mode of dispersal of *Araschnia levana* during its expansive phase in Bohemia (Czechoslovakia) and concluded that the fastest ways of dispersal of that species were along rivers and streams, at least in southern Bohemia. this corresponds also with the ecological requirements of the species. Only once HRUBY (1956) came across reliable data regarding the actual speed of dispersal measured over a period of four years in an area not particularly suitable, and hardly representative, for the species: wetlands and peat-bogs north-west of the market-town of Veseli nad Luznici (some 40 km north of Ceske Budejovice); the species extended its range over 20 km in a period of four years, using stretches of reclaimed land on predominantly sandy soils and usually covered by pine woodland. This suggests that the annual progress made by *A. levana* was on average 5 km. Taking *A. levana* as a species possessing an average dispersal potential and the conditions and habitat as representative, an average nominal species can extend its range by 500 km in a hundred years. Of course, there are numerous other ecological factors which have not been taken into this consideration simply because they are not known; further the reasons for the fluctuation of the *A. levana* populations examined by HRUBY (1956) have not been determined except that the influence of climatical cycles on the short term range dynamics of this particular species (SLABY 1951) have been ruled out.

Nothing precise can be said with regard of the contracting of ranges of most thermophilous (xerothermophilous) species that must have followed the rather sudden cooling of the climate in Europe which took place in several stages at about 3000 B.C. and later. During Roman times the mean temperatures rose again allowing new penetrations or reestablishments of the xerothermophilous species northwards; the following optimum was reached between the years 1000 and 1300 A.D. It is safe to presume that during this time the conditions were slightly more favourable for the expansion of the species inhabiting open grassland (i.e. xerophils, xerothermophils, etc.) without causing a real hindrance to the subnemoral and nemoral species: human activities had probably already achieved some not entirely insignificant increase in the overall amount of partly "cultivated" grassland, so very important for the agriculture of the growing human population, against some relatively unimportant reduction of natural woodlands. The weather was so stable and favourable that vine growing flourished during Roman times even as far north as southern England. This period of relative stability was followed by further cooling resulting in the growth of pack-ice in the Arctic and at higher altitudes in central Europe, particularly of the alpine glaciers. Poor summers and cold winters after

1315 A.D. led to crop failures, causing later famine especially in central Europe. The subsequent climatic deterioration culminated, between the years 1550 and 1850 A.D., in the so called "Little Ice Age" (Cox, HEADLEY & MOORE 1973). Despite this development at least some populations of xerothermophilous species survived in certain parts of northern and central Europe, perhaps well beyond their contemporary northernmost limits. This can be documented by the example of *Hipparchia statilinus*, an essentially Mediterranean species, which was described from the vicinity of Berlin (Germany) in 1766. The stocks of the xerophilous and xerothermophilous species more suitable to survive cold inactive periods (i.e. diapause) probably originated from eastern and south-eastern Europe and Asia and retained their tolerance of cold winters, perhaps developing additionally a further tolerance of shorter and cooler summers. The now possibly extinct colony of *Hipparchia hermione* from the Lüneburger Heide (northern Germany) shows a certain affinity to the specimens from western Russia rather than to those of southern-central Europe, although they are slightly smaller and in size similar to the populations of *H. hermione* from southern Norway, which exhibit certain morphological likenesses (e.g. male genitalia) to those from Spain and Portugal, in spite of being much smaller in size (KUDRNA 1977). Obviously, such species were confined exclusively to habitats of refugial character in northern and northern parts of central Europe. On a smaller scale, an expansion and subsequent retraction of ranges of some xerothermophilous species in central Europe took place during recent years between about 1940 and 1950, when species such as *Colias chrysotheme, Argynnis pandora, Zerynthia polyxena* and particularly the burnet *Zygaena laeta* established new, and strengthened their already existing, colonies in the area (north of the Alps). Also the two single (never satisfactorily explained) records of *Argynnis pandora* in the Vltava river valley south of Ceske Budejovice (Czechoslovakia) reported by SCHACK (1936) could possibly be better understood in the light of short term climatical changes. The subsequent decline of these species after about 1950 can only partly be explained by climatic change as the supplementary, and perhaps locally decisive, factor in some localities must be attributed to adverse human activities, such as above all afforestation and, locally, to the successful expansion of the introduced false acacia tree *(Robinia pseudacacia)*.

Many changes inflicted by early man upon the environment could have proved rather advantageous to the butterflies: they increased the open spaces within woodlands and provided better opportunities for all heliophilous species inhabiting open grassland, without substantially reducing the habitats of nemoral and subnemoral species. This increased the continuity of the distribution of butterflies and thus provided better conditions for their natural dispersal. Only much later did human activities become contrary to the needs of butterflies, as the human population gradually grew and started to destroy nature without mercy.

It is mostly believed, but untrue, that the first regional extinction of a European butterfly species took place in England around 1850 when *Lycaena dispar* was extirpated after the extensive draining of fenland in East Anglia, chiefly north of Cambridge. In fact, the first regional extinctions due entirely to human activities took place elsewhere and much earlier; they were even more extensive and concerned more than one species.

Until the latter part of the second half of the 16th century a large part of South Bohemia (present south-western Czechoslovakia: a large region surrounding the city of Ceske Budejovice) was covered by marshes and fens, with a good proportion of raised peat bogs (particularly in the valleys) and swamps (particularly along rivers). These areas, usually called locally "Blata" were situated in three partly separated basins estimated to total well over 150 km²: (Fig. 7)

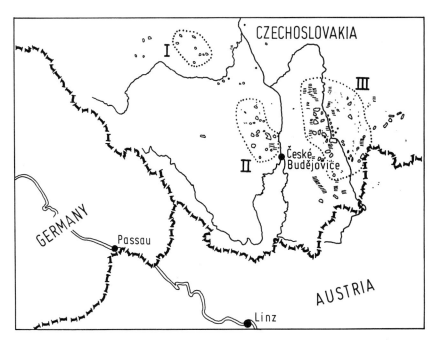

Fig. 7. Extensive draining of wetlands took place in South Bohemia (Czechoslovakia) towards the end of the 16th century; it was combined with creation of new waterways and artificial lakes. Roman I indicates the "Western Basin"; II the "Central Basin" and III the "Eastern Basin".

- The "Eastern Basin" was situated east of Ceske Budejovice and centered perhaps around the small town of Trebon, reaching northwards as far as Veseli and Luznici, eastwards as far as Jindrichuv Hradec and southwards chiefly along the rivers Luznice and Nezarka about to the present border with Austria; the "Eastern Basin" covered an area of over 100 km² and was only partly separated from the "Central Basin".

- The "Central Basin" was situated just west of Ceske Budejovice; it was much smaller than the "Eastern Basin" and extended over an area of about 35 km².

- The "Western Basin" was situated well over 50 km north-west of the "Central Basin" in the vicinity of a town of Blatna; it was much smaller, stretching over less than 15 km², and isolated from the other two.


Towards the end of the 16th century it became evident to the Duke of Rozmberg, and to some other landowners, that large scale drainage of the "Blata" could provide both reclaimed land suitable for agricultural crops and immense new opportunities for fresh water fisheries. Therefore, after successful completion of experiments carried out earlier, it was decided to build a system of, for that time, most sophisticated canals draining the "Blata" (sinking water tables) to a network of small and medium sized ponds joined by canals and rivers to large artificial lakes and reservoirs, leading subsequently to larger rivers and finally mainly to the river Vltava. The earthworks required to accomplish the project must have been enormous, as the largest lake in the "Eastern Basin" (Rozmberk, near Trebon) stretches over 721 ha and the largest lake in the "Central Basin" (Bezdrev, betwen Hluboka and Vltavou and Ceske Budejovice) covers 520 ha; there are a further eight lakes of more than 330 ha each and 40 lakes and larger ponds of over 50 ha each, the smaller ponds not being counted.

The draining of the wetlands in South Bohemia was one of the most complex and largest destructions of habitats of hygrophilous and tyrphophilous butterfly and other animal species in Europe, at any one time. There are, of course, no authentic old records of butterflies originally inhabiting the drained land, yet it is quite possible to reconstruct a faunal check-list of hygrophils of the territory at the critical time (i.e. late 16th century). A good judgement can be made, without much speculation, from the ecological requirements and contemporary ranges of the "candidate" species. The following table lists left names of twelve hygrophils/tyrphophils believed present in the above described parts of South Bohemia before the "Blata" water tables were reduced towards the end of the 16th century.

| Species (family) | Present status |
|---|---|
| *Boloria aquilonaris* (NY) | Extinct in the area; a few small colonies in Sumava (Böhmerwald) Mts. and elsewhere in the country. |
| *Boloria eunomia* (NY) | Extinct in the area; a few small colonies in Sumava (Böhmerwald) Mts. |
| *Brenthis ino* (NY) | Extinct in the area but later discovered elsewhere in the province (KUDRNA 1957, 1970–71), possibly extending its range at that time from an unknown centre of dispersal. |
| *Coenonympha hero* (SA) | Extinct in the area and absent from the province. |
| *Coenonympha oedippus* (SA) | Extinct in the area and absent in the province (apparently extinct in the whole country). |
| *Coenonympha tullia* (SA) | A few residual colonies in the "Eastern Basin" and elsewhere in the province (e.g. at higher altitudes in Sumava Mts.). |
| *Colias palaeno* (PI) | Isolated colonies in the remaining undisturbed areas of peat bogs in the "Eastern Basin" and much less localized at higher altitudes of Sumava Mts. |
| *Euphydryas aurinia* (NY) | Extinct in the area and absent from the province. |
| *Lycaena dispar* (LY) | Extinct in the area, now absent from the province; two single specimens were found some 45 and 60 years ago and never again (KUDRNA 1970–71). |
| *Lycaena helle* (LY) | Extinct in the area and absent from the province, now apparently extinct in the country. |
| *Minois dryas* (SA) | Extinct in the area; another ecotype possibly still inhabits a few small localities elsewhere in the province. |
| *Vacciniina optilete* (LY) | Isolated colonies still present in the "Eastern Basin" and at higher altitudes elsewhere in the province (Sumava Mts.). |

All true hygrophils are now absent from both the "Central Basin" and the "Western Basin". The last habitats suitable for hygrophils and tyrphophils are still found (as nature reserves) in some less accessible areas of the "Eastern Basin", where they were unattractive for exploitation. Only three hygrophilous butterfly species are now present in the area having survived the massive drainage which took place some 400 years ago. The extinct species were already absent at the end of the last century: they were not listed from the area in reliable faunistic publications (e.g. BATA 1929–31, BINDER 1910, STERNECK 1929).

It is interesting to observe that of the three species still present in the "Eastern Basin" at least two are tyrphophils, the third species also inhabits peat bogs in South Bohemia (BRCAK 1948). It is chiefly because the drainage of peat bogs presented greater technical problems than that of marshes, where the soil could have been directly utilized for agriculture. It was otherwise necessary first to remove the layer of peat, not an easy task at that time. It is particulary noteworthy that the four most acutely threatened European butterfly species are hygrophils unable to inhabit peat bogs and which depend upon lowland marshes, such as those destroyed in South Bohemia.

It was the continuous growth and expansion of human population in Europe that necessitated a steady enlargement of cultivated land. This development contributed to the creation of a new environment exceptionally favourable to butterflies: the extensive traditionally managed meadows (and pastures), at moderate altitudes, such as they existed and to some extent still exist, particularly in central Europe. This development, more than any other human agency must have contributed to the spread of many butterfly species. It provided a new secondary habitat for the butterfly species so far restricted to certain seral stages in woodlands which allowed only small populations on a rather instable basis, apart from geographically limited natural highland and alpine grassland. The most characteristic butterfly group inhabiting meadows are the species of the lycaenid tribe Polyommatini (e.g. *Polyommatus icarus*) and various satyrids (e.g. *Coenonympha pamhilus*); both species belong to the most successful European butterflies. A characteristic ecological feature of all European species living in meadows (and analogical forms of permanent cultivated grassland) is their ability to inhabit other, often quite distinct habitats: *Aricia eumedon* lives in wet meadows and sparse woodlands closely bound to its hostlants *Geranium palustre*, *G. pratense* and *G. sylvaticum* respectively, and *Plebejus argus* inhabits mesophilic meadows and heathlands, etc. and *Maniola jurtina* lives almost exclusively in meadows and similar permanent grasslands north of the Alps and inhabits predominantly woodlands in southern Europe. Also the present central European distribution of

*Papilio machaon* is closely related to the mode of land use (small fields and meadows with many balks and a good proportion of clover cultivation; the species is known to have disappeared regionally or become rare after extensive land consolidation). Meadows are important for two types of species: (1) those living in meadows throughout their life cycle and (2) those using meadows as adults because they offer desired nectar, so far as they are not separated by impassable barriers from their breeding sites. As traditional meadows contributed positively to the spread of essentially mesophilous species, the spread of essentially xerothermophilous species in central Europe must have been assisted by the expansion of old-fashioned orchards: the expansion and decline in many areas of *Aporia crataegi* and *Iphiclides podalirius*, as well as of other species, may well be closely connected with orchard management.

The present distribution patterns of a vast majority of European butterfly species are due to long term effects of two distinct phenomena. They are the

- natural factors, and
- human agencies.

Exempted from the influence of the latter phenomenon are, perhaps, only some species confined to the far north of Europe (i.e. northern Fennoscandia and Russia), and to some rather remote localities at high altitudes (this applies particularly to extremely stenochoric species). It has been shown that up to a certain point the needs of butterflies coincided by and large with the needs of man; during this period – terminating perhaps at the beginning of this century – the optimal effect of the combined natural factors and human agencies facilitated the all-time maximum of the abundance and distribution of butterflies in Europe.

Further sustained growth of human population and the ever increasing standard of living made it necessary to keep the food production adjusted to new requirements, without opportunities for a corresponding enlargement of land available for cultivation, indeed with reductions in some regions. The resulting intensification and modernization of agriculture, particularly its industrialization after the second world war, not only led to the withdrawal of its earlier positive effects on the butterflies, but to the introduction of new destructive elements. Previously uncultivated land was utilized for intensive production and the changes in management of cultivated land made it uninhabitable to butterflies. A return of butterflies to their natural environment became in the meantime impossible in many parts of Europe because these ceased to exist or were substantially reduced and isolated. A similar process of industrialization of forestry taking place at about the same time contributed substantially to this development.

## 3.2 Anthropogenic factors harmful to butterflies, their causes and control

Every nominal butterfly species is exposed to certain specific and general environmental pressures. These are partly of natural and partly of anthropogenic origin, the latter being an additional burden upon the species, as shown in the following diagram (Fig. 8).

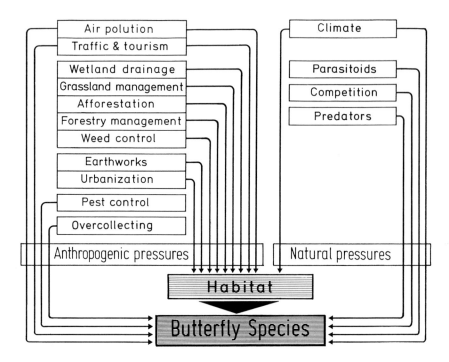

Fig. 8. Environmental pressures on any butterfly species consists of a combination of natural and anthropogenic factors; most of them affect the colony indirectly, through its habitat.

BLAB & KUDRNA (1982) carried out detailed analysis of factors harmful to butterflies in the Federal Republic of Germany, which are applicable anywhere in central Europe, and with some qualifications well beyond that area; they also pointed out causers responsible for them. Also HEATH (1981) listed and outlined some of the reasons for the decline of butterflies in Europe. Nevertheless, it is thought useful to present here a short survey of the main groups of factors harmful to butterflies at European level, based partly on the analysis mentioned above (BLAB & KUDRNA 1982), with some chiefly non-German and general groups of factors added (e.g. air pollution, tourism, bacteriological pest control), with brief data regarding the causers and possible protection measures, as well as selected examples of the better known and characteristic nominal species threatened.

Natural factors (cf. Fig. 8), such a climatical changes, are considered irreversible and therefore not dealt with here; apart from this reason, they appear to be of small or even negligible significance in most countries, "threatening" only 3.3% of native species in the Federal Republic of Germany (BLAB & KUDRNA 1982). Climatical cycles are a natural phenomenon and all changes attributed to them are of both positive and negative effect if judged against the background of range dynamics of the nominal species concerned: a species that has lost some of its colonies purely as the result of negative development has probably been able to establish them during– and as the result of–the positive development of the climatical cycle. It is often all too easy to attribute a certain sudden or drastic change in the distribution of a nominal species to adverse climatical changes (SLABY 1951) but this can only be done if all other possible factors have been considered and excluded (HRUBY 1956). It is important to examine also all anthropogenic factors that could contribute to the negative or positive development of the species' range. It is perhaps worth mentioning that it would be pointless and wasteful to concentrate resources on the protection of any nominal species changing its range because of purely natural causes.

Owing to the prevailing contradictory views on the negative influence of collecting on the stability of butterfly colonies, it is also thought necessary to deal with various negative and positive aspects of the subject elsewhere.

Wetland drainage (Fig. 9)

**Description:** All kinds of measures aimed at the draining of natural and seminatural wetlands (i.e. sinking of water tables), regardless of the type of habitat (e.g. moor, peat bog, meadow, woodland, etc.) and the subsequent utilization.

**Examples:** Drainage of wet meadows before subsequent management intensifictaion; drainage of moors for their subsequent utilization as agricultural land; draining of wet woodlands before subsequent intensification of forestry management; reclaiming of land for urbanization or industrial development.

Fig. 9. A typical habitat of hygrophilous species *Brenthis ino* near Salzburg (Austria), with *Filipendula ulmaria*, which is here accompanied by another essentially hygrophilous butterfly *Minois dryas* and other species. (Photo O. KUDRNA, 1985).

**Effect:** Microclimatic changes; quantitative and qualitative changes of the composition of flora, with extinction or drastic reduction of habitat dependant stenotopic hygrophilous hostplants; changes of abiotic ecofactors.

**Causers:** Land owners and developers, predominantly agriculture.

**Species affected:** All hygrophilous und tyrphophilous species, such as *Boloria aquilonaris, B. eunomia, Coenonympha hero, C. oedippus, C. tullia, Colias palaeno, Euphydryas aurinia, Lycaena dispar, L. helle, Vacciniina optilete,* etc.; additionally affected may be some relatively widespread eurytopic butterflies inhabiting a broad spectrum of habitats and able to adapt to certain wetland conditions (BLAB & KUDRNA 1982, BRCAK 1948) but unable to survive subsequent developments following the drainage of the site.

**Protection measures:** Careful planning taking into account valuable sites rich in stenotopic hygrophilous (and tyrphophilous) butterfly species before granting permission to begin any kind of work that could result in the lowering of water tables. A site and area specific buffer zone must be maintained between the site (habitat) and surrounding agriculturally (or otherwise) utilized land. Improvement of sites damaged by sinking of natural watertables is not a realistic remedy once the habitat specific species have become extinct owing to their limited dispersal potential and subsequent reinvasion of isolated habitats. The most important countermeasure is, therefore, a site register and mapping.

## Intensification of grassland management

**Description:** All kinds of site and area melioration, agricultural land consolidation; artificial fertilization; large scale mechanization; and any other kind of grassland management rationalization including introduction of new crops and varieties; land use change.

**Examples:** Consolidation of farm grassland in few larger units; introduction of high quality forage grass varieties (to replace native permanent grassland); use of artificial fertilizers; intensified cutting of hay in shorter intervals; eutrophication of wet (acid) meadows and pastures; overgrazing by domestic animals.

**Effect:** Reduction of natural ever-green meadows with permanent turf specific plant formations and associations; destruction of natural cycle between the hostplant and host butterfly species (larva and/or adult); reduction of actually flowering wild herbaceous plants ("weeds") in meadows and pastures; extinction or reduction of all plants intolerant of increased amounts of nitrogen and increase of nitrogen tolerant species; destruction of natural, varied mosaics of biotopes in the open countryside; turning meadows into fields; breaking of hostlant/host synchronization; etc.

**Causers:** Agriculture.

**Species affected:** All species inhabiting open grassland, ranging from moderate hygrophils to moderate xerophils (and xerothermophils), above all eurychroic "widespread and common" mesophils, according to altitude, latitude and habitat type, such as *Coenonympha glycerion, Cyaniris semiargus, Erebia medusa, Lycaena hippothoe, L. virgaureae, Maculinea nausithous, M. teleius, Melanargia galathea, Melitaea cinxia, Papilio machaon* and numerous other species.

**Protection measures:** Maintaining of traditional grassland management with varied "natural" meadows and pastures in areas rich in butterflies (chiefly grassland mesophils), particularly in areas of less productive agriculture, if necessary at the cost of direct or indirect subsidies to farmers concerned. Introduction of substitute habitats in nature parks, recreation areas, in and around towns and cities (e.g. replacement of the "English lawn" by ecologically diverse meadows generally cut only once a year in the autumn in all suitable localities within the reach of potential invading colonies of butterflies). To encourage and if necessary support by direct or indirect subsidies various forms of "ecological farming" in areas still inhabited by diverse butterfly species, including "ecological cells" (KLOFT 1978).

Afforestation (Fig. 10–12)

**Description:** All kinds of planting with (chiefly coniferous) trees of natural and seminatural areas of open country inhabited by valuable colonies of butterflies, particularly in mountainous districts.

**Examples:** Afforestation of above all south-west to south to south-east facing slopes covered with natural or seminatural agriculturally unused grassland and semi-nemoral scrubland, usually unsuitable for any other kind of exploitation by man.

**Effect:** Drastic change in the flora and fauna of the site, including the microclimate, resulting eventually in the extinction of most of the butterfly species inhabiting the site, as it gradually becomes uninhabitable to them.

**Species affected:** Above all numerous xerothermophilous and xerophilous grassland and semi-nemoral butterfly species, differing in their faunal composition according to region and altitude. *Parnassius apollo* is threatened by afforestation schemes in most parts of its European range, in some regions (e.g. southern Spain: Sierra de los Filabres, Sierra Nevada) at altitudes as high as around 2000 m. In certain habitats at moderate altitudes also *Parnassius mnemosyne* is threatened by afforestation, although natural succession of sparse woodland is quite advantageous. In central Europe afforestation is especially dangerous for all expansive Mediterranean species reaching their northernmost limit there.

**Causers:** Forestry.

Fig. 10. Large scale afforestation in Sierra Nevada (eastern part) near Puerto de la Ragua at about 2000 m (S. Spain: Guadix). Among the species threatened by afforestation in this locality are *Parnassius apollo, Melanargia ines, Pseudochazara hippolyte, Erebia hispania* and others. (Photo O. KUDRNA, 1973).

Fig. 11. A part of a habitat of *Parnassius apollo* and *Pseudochazara hippolyte* in original condition: South-eastern Spain: Prov. Almeria: Sierra de los Filabres: Calar Alto: ca. 2000 m. This site probably no longer exists. (O. KUDRNA, 1972).

Fig. 12. Another part of Calar Alto, to the west of the highest plateau, almost entirely destroyed by large scale afforestation; *Parnassius apollo* and *Pseudochazara hippolyte* could at the time of taking this photograph have lived in a part of the locality, now both colonies can be considered extinct (cf. fig. 11). (Photo O. KUDRNA, 1972).

**Protection measures:** Preventive protection of the sites is the only effective form of conservation of the habitat. Sites which do not have status of nature reserves and are inhabited by valuable colonies of butterflies should be protected by agreements drawn between local (regional) nature conservation authorities and forestry commissions, if necessary with the help of the relevant government. Precondition here is a site register and their mapping and comprehensive evaluation according to principles set out in section 6. Leaving of a buffer zone around certain sites may prove necessary for their long term protection.

Intensification of forestry management

**Description:** All kinds of changes in traditional woodland management practice aimed solely at streamlining and rationalization of wood (and game) production, e.g. gradual turning of essentially mixed seminatural woodlands into commercially more viable essentially dense coniferous "tree plantations".

**Examples:** Abandonment of natural woodland edges and ecotones (with transitional zone connecting woodland with the adjacent grassland, especially along the south-western to southern to south-eastern edge); reduction of plant diversity including control of "weed" trees and shrubs (e.g. various species of *Populus, Rubus* or *Salix,* etc.); widening and tarring of service roads and paths in place of glades; introduction of exotic trees resistant to pests; abandonment of coppicing; changing of traditionally managed woodland meadows and pastures (German "Waldwiesen") into fields, and all similar measures in areas rich in butterfly species.

**Effect:** Mainly destruction of one or more ecoelements required by any one nominal species concerned, thus making the completion of its full life cycle impossible and consequently the biotope uninhabitable (cf. ecoelements required by *Argynnis paphia:* see fig. 16, p. 58).

**Causers:** Forestry.

**Species affected:** By and large all mesophils inhabiting subnemoral and nemoral habitats, also some mesophils and to a lesser degree also xerophils inhabiting open grassland and shrubland with strong preference for sites sheltered from wind by the adjacent woodland or in them. Characteristic nominal species are: *Apatura ilia, A. iris, Argynnis adippe, A. niobe, A. paphia, Erebia aethiops, Hipparchia fagi, H. hermione, Limenitis camilla, L. populi,* and many others owing to the great diversity of biotopes provided by the various woodland types according to character, latitude and altitude. None of these species is seriously threatened in Europe although some have suffered regionally, particularly in central Europe. The unusually high proportion of species threatened by intensification of forestry (incl. afforestation) in Germany, being 43.9% (BLAB & KUDRNA 1982), must be seen in the light of the unusually rich composition of butterfly fauna in this type of habitat.

**Protection measures:** Retaining and maintaining of various ecological cells in woodlands, selected according to their diversity and representative composition of species. Conservation and management of such sites should be carried out by the forestry authorities according to the local (regional) agreements with nature conservation authorities. Woodlands in nature parks and similar recreation areas may prove particularly suitable and, in the long term, could also be utilized as substitute habitats.

Urbanization (Fig. 13)

**Description:** All kinds of building-over of natural and seminatural sites inhabited by butterfly colonies, regardless of causers and/or final purpose.

**Examples:** Expansion of towns and cities, industrial development, building of roads, airports, facilities for sport and recreations, etc.

**Effect:** Destruction of sites.

**Causers:** Nonspecific.

**Species affected:** Nonspecific, particularly susceptible are colonies of butterflies living in the immediate neighbourhood of large cities and in industrial areas.

**Protection measures:** Withholding planning/building permission to all developers (including the owners) of sites inhabited by especially valuable colonies of butterflies, terminating if necessary by compulsory purchase of the land concerned. Only preventive measures based on a site register and mapping can protect the sites concerned.


Earthworks

**Description:** All kinds of open-pit mining (regardless of extent) and all other anthropogenic changes of the countryside involving extensive moving and/or removing of soil or minerals.

**Examples:** Mines; stone, sand and peat pits; refuse tips, building of dams; filling-in, covering-over of areas and sites containing valuable natural and seminatural habitats inhabited by butterflies.

**Effect:** Destruction of the site.

**Causers:** Nonspecific, but mainly mining and building industries, land developers, etc.

**Species affected:** Any ecological group of species may be affected, mainly according to the type of the site or habitat and region. For example tyrphophilous *Colias palaeno* is affected at lower altitudes by the extraction of peat and various xerothermophilous species inhabiting regionally calcare-

Fig 13. Valuable habitats are being destroyed by urbanization everywhere; here a development on the slopes of the Sierra de Gudar in a remote part of east-central Spain (Prov. Teruel). (Photo O. KUDRNA, 1976).

ous habitats (e.g. in some parts of central Europe) are locally threatened by extraction of limestone (i.e. limestone pits): *Chazara briseis, Melitaea didyma, Parnassius apollo,* and other species.

**Protection measures:** In principle only a full legal protection of the site may prevent its destruction: only preventive measures can save the most valuable sites, based upon a site register, mapping and refusal of planning permission. Some abandoned (lime)stone pits have become valuable secondary seminatural habitats for xerothermophilous grassland and subnemoral species; this suggests that partial exploitation of some sites is possible and provides valuable substitute habitats.

Weed control

**Description:** All kinds of chemical defoliators used to destroy unwanted wild plants usually called "weeds"; in forestry also mechanical extraction of "weeds" (e. g. *Rubus,* etc.).

**Examples:** Herbicides, often specialized to control certain plant species, are used in agriculture to suppress certain "weeds" particularly in growing of special products (e.g. vine growing, rice growing, etc.), along roads and dams, often just to keep an area "clean and tidy".

**Effect:** Herbicides defoliate (i.e. destroy) vegetation suddenly, for a period long enough to exterminate butterfly colonies by lack of food. Isolated habitats cannot be reinvaded and the colony is lost for ever. Drift of herbicides can affect colonies situated far away from the locality treated.

**Causers:** Above all agriculture, particularly farming of special crops, and various nonspecific causers.

**Species affected:** Nonspecific groups so far as their colonies live within the area treated or its critical vicinity. *Lycaena dispar* inhabits in northern Italy (Piedmonte: river Po basin) certain secondary habitats within rice fields where it became established along (chiefly) main irrigation ditches; as the smaller ditches and the fields are regularly treated with defoliators, also the colonies established along larger more natural old ditches are under threat.

**Protection measures:** To minimize the use of herbicides, to ban their use completely in areas of valuable habitats unless their drift can be totally eliminated. Precondition: site and habitat register and an agreement between the nature conservation and agricultural local/regional authorities, if necessary supported by subsidies for the farmers concerned. The above mentioned sites of *Lycaena dispar* are of European significance and require special arrangements to safeguard the species, if necessary with the help of the regional government.

Pest control

**Description:** All kinds of chemicals used to control pests and diseases as well as certain biological (bacteriological) means.

**Examples:** Application of chemicals and bacteria (e.g. *Bacillus thuringiensis*) to control pests, particularly in work intensive special projects such as vine growing or (bacteriological control) in forestry.

**Effect:** The application of chemicals causes either chronic or acute toxicity and kills effectively not only the pest but also any other species living with the range of the drift which can reach as much as 30–40 km with the assistance of wind, if chemicals are applied from an aircraft or a helicopter; young larvae are particularly susceptible. *Bacillus thuringiensis* kills any lepidopterous larva within its radius and is capable of exterminating colonies of any nominal species at the time of application.

**Causers:** Agriculture and forestry.

**Species affected:** Nonspecific: any one ecological group of species can be affected, particularly xerothermophilous species in central Europe so far as their colonies live in the vicinity of cultivation of special agricultural crops or in the areas of application of *Bacillus thuringiensis*.

**Protection measures:** Minimizing of the use of insecticides and their ban, if necessary, in the areas inhabited by valuable colonies of butterflies, natural reserves, etc.; limiting of the application of insecticides from the air in susceptible areas, particularly if the prevailing wind can cause drifts. Complete ban on the use of *Bacillus thuringiensis* in areas inhabited by valuable colonies of butterflies. In both cases a broad safety belt must be maintained. Only a site register can serve as a basis for protection measures.

**Note:** The use of fungicides to control diseases has not been investigated; it is possible that their drift causes adjacent hostplants to become unpalatable to lepidopterous larvae.


Air pollution

**Description:** All kinds of toxic chemical substances contained in air and distributed by wind, except for pesticides drift.

**Examples:** Acid rain; industrial emissions; exhaust fumes; distribution of sulphur dioxide, nitrate oxides, heavy metals, carbon monoxide, transported by wind and deposited far away from the source.

**Effect:** The direct effect of atmospheric pollutants on the butterflies has never been properly investigated; nevertheless they are known to form a substantial part of the so called acid rain which in certain areas (e.g. northwestern Czechoslovakia, Germany) destroys woodlands to such an extent that survival of butterflies is most unlikely owing to adverse changes of the habitat and probable destruction of some of their hostplants.

**Causers:** Industry, above all coal/oil fired power stations, private households (oil/coal heating), chemical plants, locally also traffic.

Fig. 14. Road verges and banks are usually rich in ruderal vegetation flowers; they are often frequented by butterflies in search of nectar. Many of them are killed by passing traffic. The road shown does not threaten butterflies visiting the flowers, among them a rare European endemic species *Hipparchia ballettoi*, because cars there are few and far between. It is in southern Italy: Isola Ischia: vic. Fontana. (Photo O. KUDRNA, 1985).

**Species affected:** Particularly nemoral and subnemoral species in areas affected by acid rain fall.

**Protection measures:** The only effective protective measure is much stricter control of emissions. The effect of liming on the butterfly populations in areas affected has not been investigated.

Tourism and transport (Fig. 14, 15)

**Description:** Development and running of centres of tourism and recreation and all activities related thereto, including all forms of transport, whether related or not.

**Examples:** Building of new and expansion of existing centres of tourism, chiefly in the mountains and along sea coasts, and above all in countries

Fig. 15. An extreme high altitude habitat in southern Spain: Sierra Nevada: nr. Pico Veleta: ca. 3000 m inhabited by a colony of *Aricia morronensis*. Although species inhabiting such localities are not (yet) threatened, the presence of a road suitable for cars and an observatory indicates that they are not outside the sphere of human interests. (Photo O. KUDRNA, 1973).

bordering the Mediterranean Sea; all forms of traffic regardless of purpose; building of hotels, camping sites, ski lifts, marinas, playing fields, etc.

**Effect:** Area specific: destruction of an alarming proportion of natural and seminatural habitats along the Mediterranean coast (e.g. in Spain, France, Italy, Yugoslavia and Greece), lesser yet by no means negligible damage to habitats in mountainous areas and around winter resorts.

**Causers:** Nonspecific groups such as holidaymakers, developers and tourist boards and authorities, etc., all travellers.

**Species affected:** Mainly species distributed along the Mediterranean Sea coast (i.e. directly in coastal districts), such as *Charaxes jasius*; to a lesser degree some alpine species, especially if very local and confined to sites in the vicinity of major tourist centres.

**Protection measures:** Concentration of new development in established centres rather than the creation of new ones; direct protection of selected habitats (site register) in coastal districts, and wherever necessary also elsewhere, especially in the mountains; careful planning and protection of unique sites.

## Overcollecting

**Description:** Repeated heavy collecting of selected species for commercial and related purposes.

**Examples:** Collecting of above all panoramic species; collecting for commercial purposes; collecting for any other than purely scientific aims.

**Effect:** Thinning of populations in localities popular with collectors and of certain panoramic species.

**Causers:** Collectors and traders.

**Species affected:** Chiefly all spectacular species, particularly those commercially most attractive, and rare species confined to isolated localities.

**Protection measures:** Restrictions, if necessary ban on collecting of species threatened by overcollecting for any other than strictly defined scientific purposes; if necessary total ban on trade in such species; patrolling of selected sites by rangers during critical times. Encouragement of captive breeding by dealers as a legal source of specimens by licence.

## Evaluation and discussion

It has been shown that certain human activities have a negative effect on the trend of development of numerous butterfly species. Only two groups of harmful factors affect the butterflies directly: overcollecting (that is a form of direct persecution mostly with the aim to kill selected individuals) and pest control (which is never intended against butterflies themselves, perhaps with the exception of the only two pests among European butterflies: *Pieris brassicae* and *P. rapae*. Also tourism, traffic and air pollution could affect directly butterflies but their effect has not been adequately studied or even investigated on samples of representative material (GEPP 1981) to allow conclusions to be drawn. The remaining anthropogenic factors harmful to butterflies are indirect and can be characterized as follows:

- all groups of factors are side effects of various human activities not directed against butterflies, and
- all groups of factors affect butterflies indirectly through the destruction of their habitats and/or biotopes.

Also tourism, traffic and air pollution certainly belong to the latter group being also side effects of otherwise motivated human activities and damaging primarily butterfly habitats and biotopes.

Since the main threat to any one nominal butterfly species in Europe comes through the in principle unwanted destruction of the species' habitat (biotope), the most important step in the conservation of that species is the safeguarding of its habitat (biotopes) against all possible (potential) forms of destruction. Without the fulfilling of this precondition–conservation (protection) of habitats (biotopes)–all other attempts are nonsensical and all such efforts are doomed to failure. It is unfortunate that this simple condition is not fully appreciated, as shown by various forms of the legal protection of selected species against collectors (i.e. ban on all collecting of butterflies imposed in the Federal Republic of Germany) although all earlier attempts are well known as failures.

The destruction of habitats takes on, in principle, two distinct forms which both amount to the same effect:

- drastic, sudden change of the habitat, such as building over, extracting of certain abiotic elements, etc., and
- breaking the species' life cycle by extracting certain ecoelements vital for the species.

Both forms may occur together or followed by each other, such as in case of wetland drainage followed by intensification of grassland management. The second form, the breaking of a nominal species' life cycle is responsible for the decline of numerous eurychoric species, such as *Argynnis paphia*.

*Argynnis paphia* is a eurychoric species widespread throughout most of Europe and abundant in some countries and regions (chorological index = 5). The world range of *A. paphia* stretches from Europe across most of temperate Asia to Japan, with small distribution in northern Africa (Algeria). In Europe the species is absent only from most of southern Spain, Crete and the extreme north, it being absent from about 64°N northwards, becoming very local and rare north of 62°N (BRETHERTON 1968, HIGGINS & RILEY 1980, KORSHUNOV 1972, KUDRNA 1974, KURENTZOV 1970,

MANLEY & ALLCARD 1970, NORDSTRÖM 1955, etc.). The extensive distribution and the density of colonies show the success of the ecological strategy of *A. paphia* over a very long period of time *(Fig. 16)*.

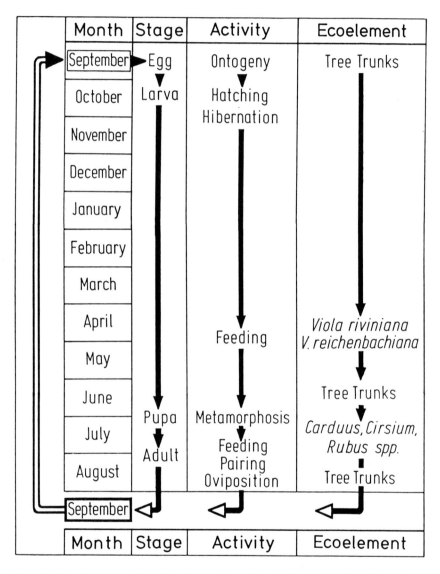

| Month | Stage | Activity | Ecoelement |
|---|---|---|---|
| September | Egg | Ontogeny | Tree Trunks |
| October | Larva | Hatching Hibernation | |
| November | | | |
| December | | | |
| January | | | |
| February | | | |
| March | | | |
| April | | Feeding | *Viola riviniana* *V. reichenbachiana* |
| May | | | |
| June | Pupa | Metamorphosis | Tree Trunks |
| July | Adult | Feeding | *Carduus, Cirsium, Rubus spp.* |
| August | | Pairing Oviposition | Tree Trunks |
| September | | | |
| Month | Stage | Activity | Ecoelement |

Fig. 16. Ecoelements utilized by *Argynnis paphia* during the species life-cycle. A withdrawal of any one ecoelement can cause the extinction of the colony.

The habitat of *Argynnis paphia* is woodland, originally sparse natural woodlands with rich undergrowth. In seminatural woodlands *A. paphia* inhabits woodland edges containing in adequate quality and quantity all basic ecoelements required by the species (Fig. 16); in certain circumstances *A. paphia* can inhabit localities where regulated coppicing provides permanent presence of certain seral stages of vegetation development in areas without barriers for the dispersal of the species. *A. paphia* cannot inhabit forests unless their edges are similar to a natural woodland.

The eggs of *Argynnis paphia* hatch in the autumn, some already during late August, and the first instar larva enters immediately into hibernation (taking no food) in small crevices in the bark of the tree trunk (close to the empty egg shell). In spring the overwintered larva descends from the tree and starts feeding on *Viola reichenbachiana* and *V. riviniana,* possibly (in some regions) also on *V. canina.* The identity of the larval hostplant of *A. paphia* is a little confused. FROHAWK (1934) states that *A. paphia* is a monophag on *V. canina* after observations made by himself in the New Forest in southern England. *V. canina* is also mentioned in most of standard lepidopterological works as the only (or one of the) larval hostplant(s) of *A. paphia,* without any reference to the original source or actual observation; bearing in mind the difficulties with the identification of the majority of *Viola* spp., such statements are worthless (BLAB & KUDRNA 1982) regardless of how many times they have been copied. *Viola canina* is generally rare or absent from most of the European habitats of *A. paphia* whereas *V. reichenbachiana* and *V. riviniana* are usually common there. In captivity the larva seems to prefer *V. riviniana* but takes also other *Viola* species (S. OEHMIG pers. comm.). Fully grown larva pupates attached by the cremastral hooks to any convenient object, often at the bottom of tree trunks. The adults feed on flowers, with preference for *Carduus* spp., *Cirsium* spp. and particularly during the latter part of their lives (ovipositing females) on *Rubus* spp. (there are slight variations of habits according to the type of habitat). The ovipositing female flies low above the ground until she finds a convenient tree trunk surrounded by an abundance of *Viola reichenbachiana* and/or *V. riviniana* – according to FROHAWK (1934) also *V. canina.* Eggs are deposited singly onto the bark of the selected tree trunk, from less than one meter above ground to as high as about three to four meters, starting near the bottom of the tree and following it in a spiral. There is a marked preference for pine trees but also oak and spruce trees are used. Most of this description is based on my own observations made chiefly in Czechoslovakia and Spain; apart from the source already cited also P. PRETSCHER (pers. com.) and SCHWARZ (1949) made some authentic observations of the species' life history.

The presence of this species, and any other butterfly species, depends of the existence in adequate quantity and quality of certain species specific ecoelements in the habitat, synchronized with the species life cycle (fig. 16). Extraction or destruction of any one of these ecoelements results in the extinction of the species in the habitat (locality) concerned, negative reduction of one or more ecoelements in their quality and/or quantity results in the creation of a "bottleneck" in the species life cycle, which can be successfully completed only by a limited number of individuals and weakens the whole population, in the case of the larval hostplant shortage possibly additionally affecting the sex ratio (males usually complete their development earlier). The individual ecoelements are not of the same value for the species. Whereas the extraction of all trees after the oviposition has been completed is likely to cause the extinction of *Argynnis paphia* in the locality because it breaks the life cycle, the extraction of *Rubus* spp. would probably only bring about reduction of population density as particularly the late females unable to find another adequate source of nutrition to substitute for the lost one, would either die prematurely or more likely disperse in search of another habitat. The weakened population is more susceptible to both anthropogenic and natural pressures and much less likely to survive the next natural distress. There is nothing like a safe minimum size of a butterfly population outside purely theoretical thinking; recovery of a population is possible only if the original conditions are restored and the slow dying out prevented.

*Argynnis paphia* is a convenient example of an "average" butterfly species, adequately known and in spite of a certain decline still quite common in most regions. The present decline of this and some other similar species is discussed elsewhere.

It is probably quite impossible to produce a consistent detailed classification of anthropogenic factors harmful to butterflies, and their causers from all over Europe at present: the data concerning many countries and species would be inadequate and incomplete. As the butterflies of central Europe are exposed to anthropogenic threats more than anywhere else in western Europe, it is convenient to use the recently provided data concerning the butterflies, skippers and burnets (Papilionoidea, Hesperiidae and Zygaenidae) of the Federal Republic of Germany (BLAB & KUDRNA 1982):

● From the total of 200 indigenous species inhabiting the Federal Republic of Germany 91 species (i.e. 45%) are considered to be under anthropogenic threat.

● Of the total of 91 threatened species (i.e. 100%) 69.2% are threatened by agriculture; 43.9% are threatened by forestry; 36.9% are threatened by earthworks. Overcollecting constitutes a threat to 21.9 % of species, but each and every species threatened by collectors is also threatened by other groups of factors.

Among the various anthropogenic causes of the decline of butterflies the two following affect the largest number of species (including some formerly widespread taxa):

- Intensification of grassland management as a collective term for all kinds of intensification of meadow and pasture uses, site and area melioration and consolidation, mechanization, increased artificial fertilization, introduction of resistant forage grass varieties, etc., affects 49.5 % of threatened species.

- Forestry management intensification as a collective term for all kinds of measures aimed at increased production, such as abandonment of transitional zones and ecotones along woodland edges, extraction of "weed trees", widening of service roads, replacement of seminatural woodlands by forests, etc., affects 41.8 % of species.

The degree of threat depends by and large upon the type of habitat inhabited by the species; of all ecological formations represented in Germany only the ubiquists are not threatened at present. The ratio of the total of German native butterfly species placed in each ecological formation to the number of species considered threatened in Germany, with the amount expressed in % given in parenthesis, is as follows:

- Xerothermophils 60 : 55 (91 % threatened species): inhabitants of grassland 40:38 (95 % threatened species); inhabitants of subnemoral and nemoral habitats 20:17 (85 % threatened species).
- Hygrophils 25:21 (84 % threatened species): inhabitants of marshes, fens and peat bogs 12:12 (100 % threatened species); inhabitants of wet grassland 13:9 (69 % threatened species).
- Mesophils 73:15 (21 % threatened species): inhabitants of grassland 30:1 (3 % threatened species); inhabitants of subnemoral habitats 23:3 (13 % threatened species); inhabitants of nemoral habitats 20:11 (55 % threatened species).
- Alpicols 34:5 (15 % threatened species): montane species 11:2 (18 % threatened species); alpine species 23:3 (13 % threatened species).

**Note:** species threatened by more than one cause are listed under each cause concerned; species inhabiting more than one habitat type are listed only once according to their ecological "headquarters"; species which have declined in numbers but are not considered threatened according to the logical interpretation of the German red data book categories are not taken into consideration here; the high proportion of species threatened by changes in the forestry practice is enhanced by the ecological diversity of natural woodland edges which offer habitats to more butterfly species than any other terrestrial habitat in central Europe; many of the xerothermophils threatened in Germany reach there their ecological and/or zoogeographical limits and are common and widespread in southern Europe. It may be mentioned that MORRIS (1981) estimated that 95 % of British butterflies would become extinct if intensive forms of agriculture were allowed to spread over the remaining uncultivated land.

The evaluation of the provisional list of butterflies threatened in Europe (cf. p. 63 and fig. 24, p. 98) shows that their decline is to be attributed chiefly to the following harmful anthropogenic factors:

| | |
|---|---:|
| – wetland drainage | 13   species |
| – intensification of grassland management | 9 (1) species |
| – afforestation | 4   species |
| – intensification of forestry management | 4   species |
| – overcollecting | 3 (3) species |
| – other (unspecified) factors | 3 (1) species |

(Also in this calculation any species threatened by more than one factor is calculated under each factor concerned; uncertain threats are listed in parenthesis and are not calculated). This evaluation also confirms the very high responsibility of modern agriculture for the decline of butterflies in Europe, concerning particularly central Europe, which is doubtless in a much worse state than any other part of the Continent.

In the following table butterfly species considered threatened in the Federal Republic of Germany (BLAB & KUDRNA 1982) are listed, with reasons for their decline shown according to the system of classification introduced in this work (fig. 17). This analysis also confirms the negative influence of modern agriculture on the butterflies:

| | |
|---|---:|
| – wetland drainage | 16 species |
| – intensification of grassland management | 33 species |
| – afforestation | 22 species |
| – intensification of forestry management | 21 species |
| – overcollecting | 18 species |
| – other (unspecified) factors | 17 species |

This calculation is based on the same principles as the preceeding one; species believed extinct have been excluded from the table and categories of threat have not been listed as they differ from those utilized in this work. Potentially threatened species are excluded.

The last group of species to be discussed are the eurychoric species. None of them could be described as threatened although many of them have declined, particularly in the most heavily populated parts of central Europe. None of these species are threatened by overcollecting and/or wetland drainage. It was, therefore, convenient to utilize different grouping of harmful factors potentially threatening their existence.

| Species (family) | Harmul factors: | | | | | |
|---|---|---|---|---|---|---|
| | (0) | (1) | (2) | (3) | (4) | (5) |
| *Apatura ilia* (NY) | | | | | + | |
| *Apatura iris* (NY) | | | | | + | |
| *Aricia agestis* (LY) | | | + | + | | |
| *Aricia eumedon* (LY) | | + | + | + | | |
| *Boloria aquilonaris* (NY) | | + | | | | + |
| *Boloria eunomia* (NY) | | + | | | | + |
| *Boloria thore* (NY) | | | | | + | + |
| *Boloria titania* (NY) | | | | | + | |
| *Brenthis ino* (NY) | | + | + | | | |
| *Chazara briseis* (SA) | + | | | + | | |
| *Coenonympha hero* (SA) | | + | | | + | + |
| *Coenonympha tullia* (SA) | | + | + | | | |
| *Colias alfacariensis* (PI) | | | + | + | | |
| *Colias myrmidone* (PI) | + | | | + | | + |
| *Colias palaeno* (PI) | | + | | | | + |
| *Cupido minimus* (LY) | | | + | | | |
| *Euphydryas aurinia* (NY) | | + | + | | | |
| *Euphydryas maturna* (NY) | | | | + | + | |
| *Glaucopsyche alexis* (LY) | | | + | + | | |
| *Hamearis lucina* (RI) | | | | | + | |
| *Hipparchia fagi* (SA) | | | | + | + | + |
| *Hipparchia hermione* (SA) | | | | + | + | + |
| *Hipparchia semele* (SA) | | | | + | | |
| *Hyponephele lycaon* (SA) | | | + | + | | |
| *Iphiclides podalirius* (PA) | + | | + | + | | |
| *Kanetisa circe* (SA) | | | + | + | | |
| *Lasiommata achine* (SA) | | | | | + | |
| *Limenitis camilla* (NY) | | | | | + | |
| *Limenitis populi* (NY) | | | | | + | |
| *Limenitis reducta* (NY) | + | | | + | | + |

**Explanation:** (0) other than 1–5; (1) = wetland drainage; (2) = intensification of grassland management; (3) = afforestation; (4) = intensification of forestry management; (5) = overcollecting.

| Species (family) | Harmful factors: | | | | | |
|---|---|---|---|---|---|---|
| | (0) | (1) | (2) | (3) | (4) | (5) |
| *Lycaeides argyrognomon* (LY) | | | | | | |
| *Lycaena alciphron* (LY) | | | + | | | |
| *Lycaena dispar* (LY) | | + | + | | | + |
| *Lyacena helle* (LY) | | + | + | | | + |
| *Maculinea alcon* (LY) | | + | + | | | |
| *Maculinea arion* (LY) | | | + | | + | |
| *Maculinea nausithous* (LY) | | + | + | | | |
| *Maculinea teleius* (LY) | | + | + | | | |
| *Maculinea rebeli* (LY) | + | | | + | • | + |
| *Melitaea aurelia* (Y) | + | | | + | | |
| *Melitaea britomartis* (NY) | | | | + | | |
| *Melitaea diamina* (NY) | | + | + | | | |
| *Melitaea didyma* (NY) | + | | + | + | | |
| *Melitaea phoebe* (NY) | | | + | | | |
| *Minois dryas* (SA) | | + | + | | | + |
| *Nordmannia acaciae* (LY) | | | + | | | |
| *Nordmannia ilicis* (LY) | | | + | | | |
| *Nordmannia spini* (LY) | | | + | | | |
| *Nordmannia w-album* (LY) | | | + | | | |
| *Nymphalis antiopa* (NY) | | | + | + | | |
| *Nymphalis polychloros* | + | | + | + | | |
| *Papilio machaon* (PA) | | | + | | | |
| *Parnassius apollo* (PA) | + | | | + | | + |
| *Parnassius mnemosyne* (PAP) | | | | + | + | + |
| *Polyommatus bellargus* (LY) | + | | + | | | |
| *Polyommatus coridon* (LY) | + | | + | | | |
| *Polyommatus damon* (LY) | + | | + | | | |
| *Polyommatus daphnis* (LY) | + | | + | | | |
| *Polyommatus dorylas* (LY) | + | | + | | | |
| *Polyommatus thersites* (LY) | + | | + | | | |
| *Pseudophilotes baton* (LY) | + | | + | | | |
| *Pyronia tithonus* (SA) | | | | | + | |
| *Scolitantides orion* (LY) | + | | + | | + | |
| *Vacciniina optilete* (LY) | | + | + | | | |

**Explanation:** (0) other than 1–5; (1) = wetland drainage; (2) = intensification of grassland management; (3) = afforestation; (4) = intensification of forestry management; (5) = over-collecting.

Fig. 17: Butterfly species threatened in Germany (BLAB & KUDRNA 1982), with reasons for their decline.

- Intensification of agriculture, particularly of grassland management, affects the following species:
  *Anthocharis cardamines* (PI), *Aporia crataegi* (PI), *Boloria dia* (NY), *Coenonympha glycerion* (SA), *Cyaniris semiargus* (LY), *Erebia medusa* (SA), *Lycaeides idas* (LY), *Lycaena hippothoe* (LY), *L. tityrus* (LY), *L. virgaureae* (LY), *Melanargia galathea* (SA), *Melitaea athalia* (NY), *M. cinxia* (NY), *Plebejus argus* (LY), *Polyommatus amandus* (LY).

- Intensification of forestry practice, particulary all forms of rationalization resulting in the simplification of ecological diversity of woodlands, affects the following species:
  *Araschnia levana* (NY), *Argynnis adippe* (NY), *A. aglaja*, *A. niobe* (NY), *A. paphia* (NY), *Boloria dia* (NY), *B. euphrosyne* (NY), *B. selene* (NY), *Celastrina argiolus* (LY), *Coenonympha arcania* (SA), *Cupido argiades* (LY), *Erebia aethiops* (SA), *E. ligea* (SA), *Issoria lathonia* (NY), *Lasiommata maera* (SA), *Melitaea athalia* (NY), *Pararge aegeria* (SA), *Plebejus argus* (LY), *Polygonia c-album* (NY), *Quercusia quercus* (LY), *Thecla betulae* (LY).

In a few cases *(Melitaea althalia, Boloria dia)* the same species is threatened by both agriculture and forestry: this is because they inhabit the transitional zone between woodland and grassland or often use vulnerable ecoelements distributed in both habitat types. Otherwise 21 species are potentially threatened by forestry and 15 by agriculture in central Europe; outside central Europe there is apparently no significant decline of any of these species owing to anthropogenic factors. The degree of decline of any of the 15 species threatened by agriculture is appreciably greater than of those threatened by forestry. The higher number of species threatened by forestry corresponds with the overall affinity of European butterflies to open spaces within woodland complexes and certainly not to the significance of the potential threats. Conservation proposals are discussed elsewhere.

Changes of climate, both in short and long term, are known to have played a considerable role in the formation of the present ranges of butterfly species. On some occasions, climatical changes were mentioned as one of the causes of decline of certain butterfly species in given areas (BLAB & KUDRNA 1982, HEATH 1981). They have been excluded from these considerations because they are natural and therefore cannot be compared or considered together with anthropogenic factors.

Last, but not least, it is necessary to consider certain drastic forms of anthropogenic intervention purporting to be genuine conservation measures and usually justified as "necessary" in order to protect a nominal species from regional extinction: they are artificial introductions and reintroductions.

Many attempts to introduce a butterfly species artificially to new site/s have taken place in Great Britain and were reported upon by FORD (1962), who also mentioned a spectacular introduction into Ireland of the continental bivoltine stocks of *Lycaena dispar*:

– An introduction of a foreign species *Lycaena dispar* into Ireland: Tipperary: Greenfields took place in 1913 and 1914. The site, a snipe-bog was especially prepared for the species. The introduction was successful and the colony still flourished in 1928 when it was last examined by an entomologist (cf. BAYNES 1970, 1973).

– *Araschnia levana*, a species foreign to Great Britain, was introduced into England (Monmoutshire: Forest of Dean; Herefordshire: Symond's Yat) about 1912; it not only survived but increased in numbers for several years until it was exterminated by an entomologist opposed to the introduction of foreign species.

Outside Great Britain *Erebia epiphron* was introduced to the Riesengebirge shortly before the second world war and was found there well established some 30 years later (SOFFNER 1967). Not all artificial introductions are successful. It seems that the preconditions are the availability of a suitable habitat, if necessary especially prepared for the species, and a massive stock of fertile females released (DEMPSTER & HALL 1980, FORD 1962): artificial introductions and reintroductions are extremely intensive research and work tasks. They amount to drastic changes inflicted upon the already strained environment. It must be remembered that extinctions of species, and whole faunas, have taken place in course of evolution for perfectly natural causes. Without the extinction of species evolution would not have been possible.

Artificial introductions are drastic measures and must be rejected from the conservationists' point of view (i.e. they have little or nothing to do with the conservation of nature) and all introductions of foreign stock to areas apparently not inhabited by the species, are most deplorable. The only exception that could justify, at least in the eyes of conservationists, an introduction of a nominal species into a site within its natural range but previously not inhabited by it, would be the imminent and irrevocable absolute extinction of that species. This case has apparently never taken place in Europe. Protection of a single nominal species must not be made subordinate to the conservation of nature as a whole.

The state of conservation of European butterflies differs greatly from country to country as well as from region to region within one country. The following review is based on a recent publication on the subject (BALETTO & KUDRNA 1985) and offers a comparison between two industrialised countries: Italy and Germany.

It seems that Italy is at least to some degree an exception among the industrial nations of western Europe, because, the anthropogenically caused endangering of the Italian butterfly fauna is of appreciably less significance than that in, for instance, Great Britain and Germany, two countries with similar area, population and population density. The reasons for this, from the Italian point of view quite fortunate state of affairs, include:

- The physical relief of northern and peninsular Italy, as well as the historical background, limited the high-density agglomerations of human population to a relatively small proportion of the country, confined by and large to the coastal regions and the lowlands along the Po river, leaving the less accessible mountainous areas relatively underpopulated and intact.
- The development of Italian agriculture and forestry over the past hundred or so years was distinctly more favourable to butterflies, than that of central and northern Europe.
- The exceptionally rich and diverse Italian fauna and flora, owing to their greater "reserves" offered a significantly higher degree of "resistance" to the negative anthropogenic pressures, if compared to central and northern Europe.
- Additionally, the greater concentration of large areas of relatively intact environments made these much less susceptible to most types of anthropogenic pressures.

Nonetheless, these fortunate circumstances of natural qualities of the Italian environment are rather counterproductive at least so far as the "awareness" of the necessity for a consistent, scientifically based, conservation of nature and protection of environment is concerned: the underestimation of the need for an environment-oriented strategy by the majority of the population and the neglecting of topics related to the conservation of nature by many leading scientists prove this point.

It has been demonstrated often enough that butterflies, like other animal species, are closely linked to their biotopes, and that the long-term occurrence of any butterfly community or single species depends on the sustained existence of the relevant ecosystem, biotope or site (e.g. Blab & Kudrna 1982). Hand in hand with the progress of civilization and population expansion in Italy (one of the oldest European cultures!), the countryside became gradually more and more influenced by the dominating human agency. In Italy, as in most European countries, the only butterfly species which remained by and large unaffected by athropogenic influences are those inhabiting the alpine vegetational level. At lower altitudes, from the subalpine down to the mediterranean vegetational level, the human agency modified the original, climactic, woodlands to such a degree, that both the flora and fauna of all such areas became gradually transformed into a new, 'unnatural' shape; it would be very difficult to imagine most of Europe in its original state!

Cutting-down large areas of woodlands for farming and stock-raising created many new secondary habitats starting from the very dawn of civilisation. Most butterflies (as well as many other animal species) linked primarily rather to specific seral and ecotonal formations than to climatic conditions, were able to take immediate advantage of this and similar developments.

The historical development of forestry in Italy was characterized above all by the 'chestnut-tree revolution' which dates back to the beginning of the 16th Century: it facilitated a much deeper penetration of man both in the Appennines and in the Alps, as well as a substantial enlargement of many existing and the creation of new permanent settlements. Huge areas of montane woodland were felled, virgin forest land was cut into terraces and stone walls were erected to contain them. In scarcely more than one century, the Italian countryside was subjected to an unprecendented level of changes, the results of which remain clearly visible even today. Although this process resulted in the extinction of large mammals, such as the bear or red-deer, which dates back to those days, the butterflies were certainly less affected, probably as a consequence of the ecotonal nature of their ecological requirements.

As from the middle and late 19th Century, the 'industrial revolution', the importance of chestnuts in human alimentation gradually decreased and finally, after the World War II, became practically negligible. The utilization of natural gas and general availability of electricity also finally put an end to the use of chestnut wood for heating. The spread of bark-cancer sped up the natural succession in the remaining chestnut forests.

Except for groves of poplar trees and some specific local situations, it can be said that Italian woodlands have been left practically unexploited for the last twenty or more years. This allowed on the one hand seral stages of mesophilous woods to succeed the chestnut trees, and on the other it enabled the woodland to spread into the adjacent abandoned fields. This process created new biotopes favourable to many subnemoral species; some of which have already taken advantage of this development. For example *Zerynthia polyxena* is now enjoying an unprecedented period of abundance, at least in northern Italy, following the expansion of its larval hostplant (e.g. *Aristolochia rotundifolia*, etc.). This is because *Aristolochia* spp. are linked to the seral stages that accompany the recolonisation of fields by the native mesophilous woodland.

Fluctuation in abundance and number of colonies is, of course, quite characteristic of many (not only) Italian butterfly species. Expansion, period of abundance, and subsequent decline are three basic stages of a cycle which can be repeated time and time again; each and every one of these stages can be induced by either natural or anthropogenic causes, or by the combination of both. The two following examples are particularly characteristic of the recent evolution of the Italian butterfly fauna:

- *Colias hyale* is a typical example of a group of 'Kulturfolger' among the butterflies, that is among the species which unlike *Zerynthia polyxena* are more or less threatened by the current trend to abandon agriculture in many mountainous districts of Italy. The period of high abundance of *C. hyale* was linked with the extensive cultivation of leguminous fodder plants, such as lucerne and clover, in mesophilous environments. The subsequent rapid withdrawal of the growing of these plants caused the extinction of *C. hyale* in large areas of its former Italian range, particularly in the northern Appennines; in many localities it was replaced by its xerothermophilous sibling *C. alfacariensis*. *C. hyale* is now limited to just a few rather restricted biotopes scattered over the plains of the river Po.

- *Lycaena dispar* (Fig. 18, 19) represents yet another case of the close affinity of a butterfly with an unexpected secondary biotope. The natural biotope of *L. dispar* is marshes, particularly oxbow lakes, in the zone of annual floods along the river Po, covered by Polygono-Bidentetum (BALLETTO *et al.* 1982). The beginning of rice cultivation in the plains of the river Po accompanied by the necessary cutting of many irrigation canals, provided numerous extensive secondary biotopes with *Rumex hydrolapathum* in great profusion (larval hostplant of *L. dispar*). This enabled *L. dispar* to spread and achieve an unprecedented density of colonies and abundance, and to maintain both for a period of several years. The introduction of selective herbicides and their massive application to the Italian rice cultures, as well as their leaking, together with artificial fertilizers, and polluting the water of smaller and medium size irrigation canals are slowly making the life of *L. dispar* in the secondary biotopes impossible. Thus the decades of temporary abundance of *L. dispar* are now followed by its inadvertible decline, both parts of the cycle initiated by human agencies. As the secondary habitats are becoming uninhabitable, the species is regionally in serious danger of extinction.

In principle, both cases mentioned above are comparable to the well known pest *Pieris brassicae* but differ in a single detail: both *Colias hyale* and *Lycaena dispar* profit from certain byproducts of a certain human activity, without disturbing the same in the slightest manner. That is why they are not labelled 'pests' by perfunctory observers, contrary to *P. brassicae*.

Fig 18. In northern Italy *Lycaena dispar* inhabits rice fields where its larval hostplant, *Rumex hydrolapathum*, grows along most of the numerous irrigation ditches; it is abundant along some of the old overgrown canals, as shown, as long as they are free of herbicides. This habitat: N. Italy: Piedmont: Novara district. (Photo O. KUDRNA, 1983).

It is interesting to note that also *P. brassicae* has become rather rare over the last ten or so years, owing to changes in the cultivation of cabbage.

It is clear that there was a different balance between nemoral and sub-nemoral species before man began to shape the European countryside: the former species were much more common, the latter much rarer and confined to semipermanent colonies dependent on natural clearings, initiated probably by an occasional fire or fall of some old trees, and maintained for a time by the grazing of some herbivores (e.g. deer, wild bull, etc.). Also the species inhabiting open herbaceous formations (e.g. meadows, pastures) could only become abundant after human activities had created for them suitable secondary biotopes.

The vulnerability of butterflies is closely linked with their ecological requirements: a butterfly species depending on trivial and widespread ecofactors is less vulnerable than a species depending on rare ecofactors restricted to a small area. In addition to this a species competing for its vital ecoelements with man (i.e. conflict of interests) is always at a disadvantage (i.e. "bottleneck" situations are decisive for the rate of survival) and is

Fig. 19. One of the minor rice field irrigation ditches treated with herbicides, which have destroyed most of *Rumex hydrolapathum*, the larval hostplant of *Lycaena dispar* (cf. fig. 18). Locality: N. Italy: Piedmont: Verceli district. (Photo O. Kudrna, 1981).

more vulnerable than others. This implies that individual nominal species are not of the same "value" and "significance" for conservationists. Generally, two groups of species can be recognized:

– The first group is constituted by rare endemic species, which are particularly vulnerable not only because they live just in Italy, but also because even there they are restricted to only a few suitable localities, and they are often rare even in these. The long term survival of some of them depends on the success of a single colony, their overall stocks being low in absolute terms. The following Italian butterflies belong to this group: *Polyommatus humedasae, P. galloi, Pseudophilotes barbagiae, Melanargia pherusa* and *Hipparchia ballettoi*. Additionally, there are several other endemic species peculiar to Italy, which in spite of their relative rarity are usually abundant in their restricted localities, such as *Hipparchia leighebi, H. sbordonii*, etc.

– The second group is formed by species which have suffered a strong decline over the years, and are considered to be threatened by extinction owing to known anthropogenic pressures, which usually threaten their existence also elsewhere in Europe. In a few cases such species still have strong colonies in Italy. It is in the first place *Coenonympha oedippus*, considered to be the most seriously endangered European butterfly species, and also *Lycaena dispar, Maniola nurag* and *Melanargia arge*. Further species declining at present in Italy are listed in the following table.

Also some so called "panoramic species" are threatened. Panoramic species have become much sought after because of their high and still growing commercial value; they are threatened particularly by overcollecting carried out or initiated by unscrupulous dealers. The most typical species in this respect is surely *Papilio hospiton*, an endemic confined to Sardinia and Corsica, particularly endangered by repeated collecting of the larvae in large numbers every spring. Further panoramic species are listed in the table of butterflies threatened in Italy by anthropogenic factors (Fig. 20).

Only two butterfly species became extinct in Italy during this century:

– *Polyommatus exuberans* disappeared from its few localities in the Susa Valley (Piemonte) in recent years as a consequence of natural afforestation of some xerothermophilous biotopes after the withdrawal of vine growing and is now considered extinct. The species became so closely linked to the biotopes created by human agency that it apparently ceased to live in natural habitats long before its extinction. *P. exuberans* was a typical rare endemic species. Curiously, it is the only European butterfly to have become extinct in this century (in some other similar cases the information available is inadequate to assess the species' status) and its species-rank was established only after its extinction (it is, of course, a morphospecies, its biological relationship can no longer be tested). The case of *P. exuberans* points out the importance of the conservation of both "incipient species" and rare endemic species.

– *Araschnia levana* disappeared from Südtirol already at the beginning of this century and the recently attempted reintroduction of the species' central European stocks to some suitable localities in Piemonte failed completely (G. LEIGHEB: pers.comm.). *A. levana* used to reach in Südtirol a natural limit of its range, but it is a species known for its fluctuation in both range and abundance also in its "headquarters". The extinction of *A. levana* shows the vulnerability of colonies situated on the border of the species range.

The fate of *Polyommatus exuberans* could be repeated at any time of the rare Italian endemic species, which include for instance: *Polyommatus galloi, P. humedasae, Pseudophilotes barbagiae* and *Hipparchia ballettoi*. The species inhabiting restricted localities situated on the natural border of their respective ranges could follow the fate of *Araschnia levana*; they

| Threatened species | Character: | | | | Harmful factors: | | | | | | | | | |
|---|---|---|---|---|---|---|---|---|---|---|---|---|---|---|
| | ES | PS | HQ | TE | OV | WD | SC | GM | BP | AF | FM | OC | TR | SA |
| *Pseudophilotes barbagiae* | ● | | | | | | | | ● | | | | | |
| *Polyommatus humedasae* | ● | | | | | | | | | | | ● | | |
| *Polyommatus galloi* | ● | | | | ● | | | | | | | ? | | |
| *Hipparchia ballettoi* | ● | | | | | | | | | | | ? | ● | |
| *Maniola nurag* | ● | ● | | | ● | | | | | | ● | ● | | |
| *Melanargia pherusa* | ● | ● | | | ? | | | | | ● | | | | |
| *Melanargia arge* | ● | ● | | | ? | | | | | | ● | ● | | |
| *Aglais ichnusa* | | ● | ● | ● | | | | | | | | ● | | ? |
| *Papilio hospiton* | | ● | ● | ● | | | | | ● | | | ● | | |
| *Papilio alexanor* | | ● | ● | ● | | | | | | | | ● | ● | |
| *Coenonympha oedippus* | | ● | ● | ● | | ● | ● | | | ? | | | | |
| *Lycaena dispar* | | ● | ● | ● | | ● | ● | | | | ? | | | |
| *Euphydryas wolfensbergeri* | | ● | ● | ● | ● | | | | | | | ● | ● | |
| *Argynnis elisa* | | ● | ● | ● | ● | | | | ● | | | ● | | |
| *Anthocharis damone* | | ● | ● | | | | | | | | | ● | | |
| *Boloria eunomia* | | | | ● | | ● | | | | | | ? | | ● |
| *Melitaea britomartis* | | | | ● | | ● | | ● | | | | ● | | |
| *Coenonympha tullia* | | | | ● | | ● | | | | | | | | |
| *Libythea celtis* | ● | | | | | | | | | | | ● | | |
| *Apatura iris* | ● | | | | | | | | | | ● | | | |
| *Limenitis populi* | ● | | | | | | | | | | ● | | | |
| *Melanargia occitanica* | ● | | | | | | | | | | | | ● | |
| *Parnassius phoebus* | ● | | | | | | | | | | ? | ● | | |
| *Colias palaeno* | ● | | | | | | | ● | | | | ● | | |
| *Charaxes jasius* | ● | | | | | | | | | | ● | ? | | |

| | | | |
|---|---|---|---|
| ES | = | rare endemic species | |
| PS | = | panoramic species | |
| HQ | = | "headquarters" in Italy | |
| TE | = | threatened in Europe | |
| OV | = | overgrazing | |
| WD | = | wetland drainage | |
| SC | = | special crops | |
| GM | = | intensification of grassland management | |
| BP | = | burning of pastures | |
| AF | = | afforestation | |
| FM | = | intensification of forestry management | |
| OC | = | overcollecting | |
| TR | = | traffic, urbanization, tourism and recreation | |
| SA | = | species and/or area specific causes | |

Fig. 20: Threatened Italian butterflies (BALLEITO & KUDRNA 1985), with biogeographical characteristics and anthropogenic causes of decline.

include in Italy *Boloria thore* (Trentino), *B. graeca* (Piemonte), *Melitaea asteria* (Südtirol), *Neptis sappho* (Veneto), *Erebia flavofasciata, E. christi* (Piemonte), *E. eriphyle* (Veneto), *Nordmannia esculi, Satyrus actaea, Hipparchia fidia, Melanargia occitanica, Polyommatus dolus* (all Liguria) and *Melitaea britomartis* (Piemonte).

## 3.3  Considerations on the significance of collecting for the conservation of European butterflies and lepidopterological research

Collecting of butterflies is at least as old as the science of lepidopterology, probably even older. Without collecting – the basic scientific method of study of butterflies – our present knowledge of butterflies would be rudimentary. Also the trade in butterflies is very old; there were insect dealers already during the life of Charles Darwin. In principle, collecting of butterflies and trade in butterflies are two entirely different topics, except that without collecting there could be no trade and at present the more emotional conservationists seem to see in every collector a dealer killing masses of butterflies and making huge profits. It seems likely that their immagination grows disproportionally with their knowledge of butterflies and understanding their biology.

In Germany the collecting of and trade in butterflies was discussed by PRETSCHER & SCHULT (1978) and briefly mentioned by EBERT, HESSELBARTH & KASY (1978). It is interesting to observe, that neither of the above publications provides an adequate analysis of the market or the proof that collecting of butterflies is an important factor responsible for the decline of butterflies in Germany. It is further interesting to observe that these publications could be linked with the issuing of a decree totally forbidding the collecting of butterflies in the Federal Republic of Germany.

● Collecting is the only reliable method of recording butterflies, which additionally facilitates the revision of identification and the proof of the record.

● In case of subsequent splitting of a species into two or more units, the collected material is the only way which facilitates the study of the former distribution of each newly erected unit.

It is often argued by some conservationists that collecting can be replaced by photography and a notebook. This is absolutely not true! There is no substitute for collecting as a means of permanent recording and identification of butterflies (and other insects). Those conservationsts who argue otherwise probably possess so perfunctory a knowledge of butterflies, that they are unable to fully realize, and therefore learn to appreciate, the value of collected material. Photographs of butterflies cannot always be identified, even if they are good and notebooks tell us what the observer believed he had seen, not what he really saw.

It would seem that the present witchhunt on collectors, as it is now practiced in some European countries by some conservationsts is a convenient political manœuvre that distracts the attention of the public from the real causes of the decline of butterflies and enables the members of certain circles to improve their image.

It is true, that an experienced student of butterflies can often identify butterflies in the field without even catching them. The identification is often possible through the examination, often including the study of certain characters under a stereo microscope, after all similar species have been eliminated as not living in the habitat concerned. Most of conservationsts, who tend to be "generalists" are not adequately familiar with the elements of taxonomy to understand this.

The following butterfly species inhabiting central Europe have been "split" into two specific units each during the past 50 years:
*Colias hyale* produced *C. hyale* and *C. alfacariensis*
*Maculinea alcon* produced *M. alcon* and *M. rebeli*
*Pseudophilotes baton* produced *P. baton* and *P. schiffermuelleri*
*Melitaea athalia* produced *M. athalia* and *M. neglecta*

Similar changes are certain to take place also in the future; in Europe there are at least 10 similar cases, boreo-alpine species with disjunct ranges not counted. The collected and preserved material is the only means to establish the distribution of all such "divided" species.

STUBBS (1985) compiled a list of reasons for and against collecting of butterflies as usually presented by entomologists on the one side and the more extreme "conservationsts" on the other:

| PRO-COLLECTING | ANTI-COLLECTING RESPONSE |
| --- | --- |
| – It is not really possible to identify all butterflies without taking them home. | – There are so few species that even a beginner ought to learn to identify things in the field (as with birds). |
| – Some butterly species may have to be caught to identify them. | – With patience it is possible to find individuals sitting in a position where they can be identified (as with birds). |

PRO-COLLECTING                    ANTI-COLLECTING RESPONSE

– If this really is a significant problem then there may well be ways
round this as regards permissible
activities (*e.g.* catch and immediate release).

– There is no harm in rearing but-          – There is fear as to the real source
terflies in captivity if source stock          of stock.
can be obtained without harming          – There is concern over the sub-
wild populations                                        sequent uncontrolled release of
                                                                 stock (expressed above).

– Cannot schools and individuals          – The pest species can be excluded
have some concession as regards              from protection (small white,
rearing?                                                       large white).

– Butterfly houses are good public-          – Licences can provide for this.
ity for native butterflies, yet they
will be unable to rear and display
livestock.

– It does not matter selling old col-          – Admittedly a problem area, and
lections.                                                       perhaps not beyond solution.
                                                                 – There is a lack of confidence that
                                                                    all old stock is legitimate.
                                                                 – The concept of amassing private
                                                                    collections of dead butterflies is
                                                                    out of date and unjustified.

– Protecting butterflies is ridicu-          – You cannot argue for one without
lous when it is habitat protection            the other.
that is the real requirement.                    – Why should we spend time and
                                                                    effort protecting habitat if en-
                                                                    tomologists are going along to fill
                                                                    up their collections?
                                                                 – What sympathy do you expect
                                                                    when the conservation move-
                                                                    ment is increasingly taking action
                                                                    over habitat?
                                                                 – Don't you realise that it looks bad
                                                                    to see some people collecting but-
                                                                    terflies, of all things, when other

| PRO-COLLECTING | ANTI-COLLECTING RESPONSE |
|---|---|
| – It is reasonable to take unusual varieties. The chance occasion cannot be anticipated. | people are trying to save them in their habitat?<br>– Ornithologists cannot shoot rare varieties of birds.<br>– If you are serious about breeding and the study of genetics, the licences could be obtained in advance by *bona fide* people. |
| – If a legal ban on butterflies were in force, then everyone with a net (even those not collecting butterflies) could find themselves castigated and reported to the police. | – This is one scenario but it may not be the case. It is up to entomologists to present a favourable image to the public. |
| – We are on a slippery slope once more/all butterflies are protected. | – It's up to entomologists, to be convincing why this should not be so. |
| – It does no harm | – Well, entomologists would say that wouldn't they.<br>– Special pleading. |
| – It brings youngsters into entomology; | – Youngsters should be educated to observe, not kill.<br>– Nowadays there are plenty of books, keys, BRC schemes etc. to enable people to start with other groups if they wish to collect. |
| – The study of entomology will shrivel up without the facility to collect butterflies. | – Attitudes must move with the times.<br>– That was said about egg collecting, yet the study of birds is strong. |
| – Butterflies have more young than birds and can recover populations rapidly. | – True, but nowadays in many localities butterflies are in low numbers so the removal of even a few could tip the balance or create fear that this is so.<br>– Well, why aren't butterflies common then? |

| PRO-COLLECTING | ANTI-COLLECTING RESPONSE |
|---|---|
| – The mortality of butterflies is enormous in the wild so collecting a few does not matter. | – We lack your confidence. |
| – Rearing and releasing butterflies is assisting conservation and hence is a positive outcome of collecting. | – What matters is the natural carrying capacity of a site.<br>– Release masks whether site conditions are favourable or deteriorating.<br>– The conservation movement is getting fed up of what has become a widespread cowboy activity.<br>– There are circumstances where the population may be boosted too high for the food supply, causing a population crash.<br>– An excuse for collecting.<br>– There is a fear for local genetics, especially if not released at source site.<br>– BBCS has abandoned this idea as a general policy.<br>– In cases where this is appropriate, it can be done under licence. |
| – Collecting enables the study of genetic and geographic variation. | – Surely there is enough material in collections by now!<br>– Excuse for 'stamp collecting'.<br>– Licensing can permit serious study, including breeding. |
| – The study of the natural history/ecology of butterflies will be halted. | – There is plenty of work relevant to conservation that does not require collecting (monitoring behaviour of adults, location of the early stages).<br>– Licensing can provide for studies that involve handling etc.<br>– Licensing has actually led to increased scientific study of birds and bats because of the kudos of owning a licence. |

It is rather strange to read among the collector's argument that releasing of bred butterflies helps the conservation of the species concerned as well as the reference to the natural carrying capacity of the site as conservationsts' response: it is usually the other way round.

Serious collecting activities are carried out by many private collectors. Their collections are usually well looked after, not rarely better curated than many a museum collection. Both private and public collections must be seen as temprary depositories of material which is permanently a property of science. Normally, a butterfly collection remains long after the collector has gone. The two most important risks butterfly collections are exposed to after the death of their owner are:

- Commercially oriented widows, who look upon a collection as an investment money which must bring a good return.
- Museums which rarely have enough money to offer a reasonable payment for a good collection of butterflies and often lack the interest.

It must be observed that even the best collection of European butterflies can never be sold for the money which the collector had to "invest" while building it (travel expenses, cabinets, storeboxes, setting boards etc.), not to mention his own work (time spent collecting, setting, labelling etc.). Every responsible collector should therefore be seen as a maecenas generously supporting the science of lepidopterology and contributing, if often indirectly, to the conservation of butterflies. It is very sad that the lifelong work of many a collector is jeopardized by those, who do not even understand its purpose and that the collectors must increasingly defend their activities against emotional attacks by those, who have chosen to call themselves conservationsts.

If we look through the collections of butterflies deposited in major European museums of natural history, regardless of their size, significance and history, it will be seen that the richness of deposited material of butterflies originated mostly from private collections and landed in one of those museums after the death of the owner of the collection, either by direct donation or against a small amount of money the museum could offer to pay. It is probable that around 80% of butterflies deposited in European museums originated from private collections. It is interesting that the "witchhunt" on butterfly collectors is conducted by various "general naturalists" and "conservationsts" – who seem to have the say with the officials while the views of scientists familiar with the problems are ignored.

Intensive collecting, that is hcavy and/or successive collecting of one or more species in a given locality (habitat) is considered damaging to the colonies concerned; the definition of the words "intensive" or "heavy" depends largely upon the nominal species concerned. PRETSCHER & SCHULT (1978) compiled an extensive historical survey of the negative influence of overcollecting on the stocks of various insects, particularly butterflies, chiefly in central Europe, and offered some examples concerning particularly panoramic species, such as above all *Parnassius apollo*. PRETSCHER & SCHULT (1978) have also shown that the incentive to overcollect is usually financial and that trade in its various forms is to blame as the main causer. It is therefore astonishing that PYLE, BENTZIEN & OPLER (1981) in their report on insect conservation on a world scale stated that intensive collecting of a butterfly species was followed by an increase of the number of individuals in the population successively overcollected; they thus rejected that heavy collecting may present a danger to the conservation of insects. Surprisingly perhaps that the authors (PYLE, BENTZIEN & OPLER 1981) have not suggested overcollecting as a conservation measure to strengthen colonies of declining and threatened species! Their statement is not entirely new: it is often maintained in collectors' circles that intensive collecting has no adverse effect on the colonies subjected to heavy successive collecting. It is often argued that a predator kills more butterflies than a collector, as if there was any direct comparison between the two. It is perhaps characteristic, that figures regarding the population density and material collected are never offered. It seems that deliberate destruction of selected colonies by overcollecting would be the only means to convince, if all other potentially negative natural and anthropogenic factors were excluded during the tests.

I was able to witness heavy overcollecting of *Argynnis paphia* in Czechoslovakia (South Bohemia: C. Budejovice district) in a large habitat where the species had been common all the previous years before the overcollecting started. For two successive seasons a local collector caught every adult he could get hold of, regardless of whether it was male or female, to obtain a quantity of specimens for decorative purposes. His collecting started rather late in the first season and there was no noticeable decline in the second season, during which apparently well over 1,000 adults were collected. This was followed by a sudden decline in the third season: *A. paphia* was rare in an otherwise unaltered habitat. The colony seemed to recover only slightly in the following years (1957–1962) and the species remained rather rare although the habitat was extensive and by no means isolated by barriers impassable for such a strong flier as *A. paphia*. After 1962 forestry management carried out a series of intensification measures including the almost complete destruction of *Rubus* which probably made the locality uninhabitable for a strong healthy colony of the species.

BLAB & KUDRNA (1982) concluded, that apart from all spectacular species (financial incentive), only species confined to isolated localities can be substantially threatened by overcollecting: this amounts to some 22 % of butterfly species threatened in Germany. To put the collecting in the right perspective, three very important aspects must not be overlooked:

● The destructive effects of overcollecting are not directly comparable with the repercussions of habitat destruction.
● Each species threatened in Germany by overcollecting is also threatened by other harmful anthropogenic factors and causes, usually primarily responsible for its decline.
● None of the species threatened by overcollecting is common or widespread in the country, its rarity being as attractive to collectors as its beauty.

This consideration facilitates the following general conclusion applicable to European butterflies:

● Collecting is unlikely to pose a serious threat to any reasonably widespread and common species but the repercussions of intensive collecting (i.e. "overcollecting") are known to cause lasting damage or even extinction to species confined to isolated habitats (whatever the reason for their isolation).

The term "overcollecting" is of course relative, depending by and large upon the strength of the colony concerned, and probably also on other species specific factors.

In Europe overcollecting threatens particularly strongly all panoramic species and rare species (especially the rare endemic species) which are sought after by collectors and have good commercial (i.e. sale or exchange) value. The danger of being overexploited by intensive successive collecting is probably somewhat less serious if the species is easy to breed in captivity and the adults are rarely found in good condition. The attractivity of any nominal species to a collector grows according to the difficulty of obtaining it in perfect condition (i.e. recognized rarity) and its acknowledged aesthetic value. Relatively less attractive are species which are rather difficult to identify by the means available to an average butterfly collector. The inclination of any one panoramic species to form local ecological or geographical forms ("races"), if possible rather spectacular in their appearance (but in fact in some cases hardly distinguishable) additionally increases the desire of a collector to possess a long series of specimens in his collection. Tastes vary from country to country: some common and widespread Mediterranean butterflies (e.g. males of *Gonepteryx cleopatra, Colias crocea*) are sought after by collectors in northern Europe, and occasionally also vice versa. Only quite exceptionally and perhaps not for a long time a small, unattractive butterfly species becomes something like a panoramic species, as happened to *Polyommatus humedasae,* probably for its great rarity and in spite of its being unidentifiable by those who desire to possess it in their collections (E. BALLETTO pers. comm.). It is convenient to propose a simple definition here:

● "Panoramic" species are conspicuous, usually medium sized to fairly large butterflies, often local or rare but some also widespread, mostly easy to recognize, which for their aesthetic (decorative) value are a praised "must" to every collector, preferably in a long series of specimens.

Panoramic species are often collected by dealers and their agents purely for their high sale value. They are sold at sales and "Insektenbörsen", some of them framed for decorative purposes. Their collecting places an additional strain on their populations, which is absolutely unjustifiable. Many a "subspecies" of *Parnassius apollo* must have been named to justify a higher price tag on its "topotypes". Commercial exploitation of *P. apollo* has been reviewed by PRETSCHER & SCHULT (1978).

Almost all European species of the family Papilionidae are panoramic species, and probably also all *Colias* species. The following list of species includes typical examples of panoramic species but does not pretend to be exhaustive: it is difficult to observe all regionally attractive species. Species which are regionally common so that it is unlikely that their population could suffer from relatively heavy collecting, or could be easily bred in captivity (more economical form of production of perfect specimens) are not included.

**Papilionidae:** *Archon apollinus, Iphiclides feisthamelii, I. podalirius, Papilio alexanor, Papilio hospiton, Papilio machaon, Parnassius apollo, P. mnemosyne, P. phoebus, Zerynthia cerisyi, Z. cretica, Z. polyxena, Z. rumina.*
**Pieridae:** *Colias aurorina, C. balcanica, C. chrysotheme, C. myrmidone, Gonepteryx cleobule, G. cleopatra, G. maderensis.*
**Lycaenidae:** *Iolana iolas, Lycaena dispar, Polyommatus golgus, P. humedasae.*
**Danaidae:** *Danaus chrysippus, D. plexippus.*
**Satyridae:** *Chazara prieuri, Hipparchia neomiris, Lasiommata roxelana.*
**Nymphalidae:** *Apatura ilia, A. iris, A. metis, Argynnis elisa, A. pandora, Charaxes jasius, Limenitis populi, Nymphalis antiopa, N. l-album.*

Most of the species listed above are either declining in some regions or have naturally low stocks (e.g. rare endemic species). The danger of over-collecting increases in the case of species easy to collect in good condition (required by the dealers and collectors) and rather difficult to breed in captivity (e.g. *Parnassius apollo*). Control of trade in these species would be a positive contribution towards their protection, but this is the case only with *Parnassius apollo,* which is listed among the CITES species.

Suggestions have been made that massproduction of panoramic species in captivity for purely commercial purposes, offered at a reasonable price, would help to save the species' stocks (W. H. J. M. GERAEDTS pers. comm., WEIDEMANN 1980). It is fairly easy to massproduce some species, the biology and early stages of others are unknown. The success of the plan may depend on an unlimited supply of specimens and a comprehensive selection of species offered for an indefinite period; otherwise the experiment may play into the hands of speculating dealers.

Nevertheless, panoramic species are not the only species collected. It is, therefore, fully justified to ask whether collecting, which may turn into overcollecting and inflict damage on many species, is necessary and, indeed, morally acceptable at present. Ornithologists, who have always been the forerunners of the nature conservation efforts in Europe, have more or less dispensed with collecting as a scientific method to advance their knowledge of European birds. None the less, our present knowledge of birds is incomparably better than that of butterflies. Bird collecting as an adjunct to research has become less efficient and often inconvenient to provide the information required. Private collectors have almost disappeared over the years, perhaps succeeded by bird watchers keen to protect the objects of their observations. It must also be remembered that a collection of birds is not as easy to store and maintain as an insect collection. A further significant biological difference must be seen in the totally different population dynamics and structure; butterflies are generally much more numerous in numbers and their natural short and long term fluctuation (FORD 1975, FORD & FORD 1930) is unheard of among the vertebrates; adults of butterflies live only a short time (in the great majority of species) to fulfil their function; they have an entirely different natality/mortality relationship. In very simple words: there is no direct comparison between killing of a bird and a butterfly. Furthermore: until our knowledge of butterflies, and other invertebrate groups with rich diversity of species, has reached a certain standard, methodical collecting for purely scientific purposes must remain one of the indispensible sources of information, most important also for the conservation of European fauna.

Collecting can provide (but does not always do so) in the first place indispensible data for the study of taxonomy and distribution of butterflies;

some species can be identified only after examination under the micro-scope and the early stages of many European species are poorly known, often even undescribed (which requires laboratory breeding from wild females), there are still new species to be discovered in Europe; deposition of authentic material enables control of published data even years later. The fact that decades of unlimited free collecting have failed to provide a basis making future collecting unnecessary in spite of numerous large pub-lic (and private) depositories can be logically and historically explained:

● To the collector the collection is the final aim, not the means, and it is, therefore, more efficient for him to obtain material of the species de-sired from easily accessible localities, where success is almost certain: this leads to unrepresentativeness in the material available for the study.

● The material available rarely carries comprehensive data and no Euro-pean museum has ever been concerned to build a comprehensive collec-tion of European butterflies; material scattered over a number of public and private depositories is not really available to scientists, there are no catalogues, data banks, etc.; in other words: those millions of mum-mified *Parnassius apollo* (and any other species) scattered throughout European museums and private collections, often rather lost than depo-sited there, are inadequate to solve the problems concerning the species (this is due above all to the stagnation of European museums in general, to the lack of "sense of purpose" of their staff, which led over the years to the underestimation of the significance and scientific potential of a museum as a research institute with a unique role in society.

● Large areas of Europe have never been methodically investigated, some regions have only been explored for a few rare panoramic species (and to get type-material for the description of a few new "subspecies"). There has never been adequate cooperation and coordination among scientists from various European countries or pooling of resources.

This is caused both by the lack of professionals and professionalism among the students of European butterflies, which can be overcome only by the methodical training of lepidopterists and the creation of working (profes-sional) opportunities for them. It seems that in the past and at present only a negligible proportion of material collected has been scientifically evaluated, as if this were not in the interests of the collector.

Collecting butterflies is, essentially, a highly specialised means of obtain-ing certain basic information. It cannot be substituted for ecological studies, which are of about equal importance and proportionally underre-presented (BLAB & KUDRNA 1982, KUDRNA 1984). The quality of this infor-mation does not necessarily depend on the number of specimens collected.

MORRIS (1976) discussing the role of collecting in the conservation of British butterflies pointed out the dilemma: why should collectors exercise restraint if the progress of civilization destroys habitats and sites much faster than a collector can overcollect the butterflies. In his answer to this dilemma MORRIS (1976) appealed to collectors to curb collecting because it might help to preserve some particularly vulnerable species, and that collectors' care could help to maintain the stocks of such species for future study. To provide guides for collectors, the Joint Committee for the Conservation of British Insects published a new 'Code for Insect Colleting' (MORRIS 1976). The following points concerning collecting of specimens for scientific purposes are based on the above mentioned 'Code':

- Collecting of butterflies for other than research, educational and conservation purposes cannot be justified.
- The same species should not be taken in numbers repeatedly year after year from the same locality to prevent overcollecting.
- Collecting of series of specimens in order to obtain unusual abberations is irresponsible.
- Specimens for exchange or fellow collectors should not be taken except for genuine scientific purposes.
- Butterflies are not to be collected for commercial purposes and as art objects or "jewellery".
- Collectors without scientific aspirations should consider taking up photography of butterflies as their hobby.
- Specimens of rare, local and threatened species should not be collected without special reasons, and even then always with maximum restraint.
- Collectors should attempt to break new ground rather than to work the same localities repeatedly.
- Previously unknown localities of rare and threatenend species are to be reported as soon as possible to the nature conservation authorities concerned.
- Supposed or actual predators and parasitoids of butterflies are not to be destroyed; specimens of parasitoid insects obtained by rearing of butterflies are to be passed on to the specialists concerned (with complete data, incl. locality, host, foodplant).
- Breeding of a species from a fertilised female or pairing in captivity is preferable to taking series of specimens in the field; unwanted surplus livestock may be released in the original site.
- A butterfly collection is a property of science: it is to be responsibly cu-

rated and material deposited therein is to be made available to research workers.

● Collectors are to take precautions to avoid or minimize all such activities that could inflict damage upon the habitat.

● Hostplants of larvae bred in captivity should not be taken in larger quantity than necessary; growing of hostplants and the use of artificial diets should be considered as an alternative.

● Collectors are to seek a formal permission to collect if this is required by law; conditions attached to granting of such permissions are to be obeyed.

● Collectors should publish their observations and make them available to research workers and conservation authorities.

● Collecting of butterflies for any other purpose than legitimate research, educational and conservation purposes is not morally justified.

● Trade in wild-caught butterflies – sales of material to museums and similar public or private research institutions excepted – is deplorable.

● Collectors should care for the indefinite protection of sites and species studied and engage themselves in the conservation of butterflies; they should help to educate the less aware.

Observing these points alone is adequate not only to "neutralize" all harmful aspects of collecting but also to give the collector a brand new, respectable, image, particularly if they remember that a collection of butterflies is a property of science and must never become an object of commercial speculation.

The German federal government passed a law a few years ago forbidding all collecting of butterflies anywhere in the Federal Republic of Germany. Legal protection of butterflies (and any other invertebrate group) can positively contribute towards their conservation (BLAB & KUDRNA 1982) only if it fulfils certain conditions:

● It must protect them and their habitats from the effects of harmful anthropogenic factors primarily responsible for their decline.

● It must facilitate the continuing of genuine research, whether it is carried out by professional or voluntary research workers.

Additionally, like any other law, also this is sensible only if it can be enforced, that is if all relevant areas can be policed by rangers. Bearing in mind that overcollecting is a secondary threat to butterflies in Germany and that without collecting it may become very difficult to obtain even

| Species (family) | A | B | C | D | E | F |
|---|---|---|---|---|---|---|
| *Boloria aquilonaris* (NY) | | | + | + | | |
| *Boloria eunomia* (NY) | | | + | + | | |
| *Boloria thore* (NY) | | + | | | + | |
| *Chazara briseis* (SA) | | + | | | + | |
| *Coenonympha hero* (SA) | | | + | + | | |
| *\*Coenonympha oedippus* (SA) | | | + | + | | |
| *Colias myrmidone* (PI) | | + | | | ? | ? |
| *Colias palaeno* (PI) | | | + | + | | |
| *Hipparchia fagi* (SA) | + | | | | ? | |
| *Hipparchia hermione* (SA) | + | | | | ? | |
| *Iphiclides podalirius* (PA) | | | + | | | + |
| *Limenitis reducta* (NY) | + | | | | ? | |
| *Lycaena dispar* (LY) | + | | + | | + | |
| *Lycaena helle* (LY) | | | + | + | | |
| *Maculinea rebeli* (LY) | + | + | | | | + |
| *Minois dryas* (SA) | | | + | + | | |
| ! *Parnassius apollo* (PA) | | | + | | + | + |
| ! *Parnassius mnemosyne* (PA) | | | + | | + | |
| *Parnassius phoebus* (PA) | + | | | | | ? |

**Explanation:** * species already extinct; **A** = very small total stocks; **B** = small/fluctuating colonies; **C** = extremely isolated colonies; **D** = wetland drainage; **E** = afforestation; **E** = complex of other species or area specific factors; **?** = tentative classification; **!** = species known to have been locally exterminated by overcollecting. (Subsequent and complementary factors are nor considered here.)

Fig. 21: Species threatened by overcollecting in the Federal Republic of Germany: comparison of their biogeographical properties and main harmful anthropogenic factors.

basic data regarding their distribution and, indeed, their decline, the law could possibly be seen as a purely political act designed to cover up disastrous failures of successive governments in the conservation of nature. It is interesting to observe that the ministry responsible for the conservation of nature, including butterflies, is also responsible for its destruction: agriculture and forestry are responsible for the decline of 69 % and 43 % of threatened species respectively whereas overcollecting threatens 22 % of species, each of which is also threatened by at least one of the other two causers (BLAB & KUDRNA 1982). Legally imposed curbs on collecting should be preceded by the setting up of a data collecting centre (i.e. a central data bank) to which all lepidopterists holding an annually issued collecting permit would be obliged to report their results before or with their application for the renewal (extension) of the permit. This would help to obtain records and information useful for the conservation of species and facilitate a consistent site (habitat) conservation programme. The system introduced in Germany serves no useful purpose – there are other means of controlling commercial collecting.

Attempts to protect certain threatened species by imposing a ban on collecting them are not new (e.g. in Bavaria, Czechoslovakia, Poland), but they have never been successful (PALIK 1980) because they have always failed to safeguard the habitats of the hitherto protected species. It is a great pity that the recently introduced German law has not taken into account this simple reality. It is much better to try to win over the collector for conservation by education than to antagonize him and lose his cooperation and interest perhaps for ever.

It may be useful to compare the natural disposition and types of the main anthropogenic threats (i.e. chiefly responsible for the past and present decline) of species susceptible to overcollecting in some parts or the whole of the Federal Republic of Germany (BLAB & KUDRNA 1982) in a simple table (Fig. 21).

## 3.4 Considerations on the significance of the so called "Red Data Books", with an annotated check-list of butterflies threatened in Europe

Red Data Books (or "Red lists") are above all political instruments designed to draw attention to threatened species, and indeed to the fact that certain animal species are threatened. They are also intended to serve both as valuable aids in the hands of decision makers and politicians, and as a memento addressed to the general public, to awake the "awareness" of the necessity to protect nature. So far as the conservation of butterflies is concerned, the political role has been the only one the red data books have been able to fulfil, perhaps with some qualifications. This is unmistakeably implied by the original concept intended to list the last remaining world populations of vertebrate species depleted often down to the minimal residue of their wild breeding stock, chiefly owing to direct exploitation or persecution by man. It is much easier to count or estimate population densities at that level than in the case of butterflies; the fact is that it is always easier to detect a decline from 100 to 50 individuals than from 1,000,000 to 500,000, apart from the much better observation opportunities.

The first red data book concerned with European butterflies appeared in Spain (VIEDMA & GOMEZ BUSTILLO 1976). It was followed by a German list of threatened Lepidoptera (PRETSCHER 1977), with categories adjusted for national/regional application (BLAB, NOWAK, TRAUTMANN & SUKOPP 1977). Over the last few years red lists of threatened butterflies have also been published for some other European countries and in Germany regional and local lists have appeared for some of the federal states and even large cities (e.g. EBERT & FALKNER 1978, GLITZ & STÜBINGER 1981, HAUPT 1982, ROESLER 1980, WAGENER, KINKLER & REHNELT 1977). It appears that the compilation of red data books becomes less and less useful with the decrease in size of the territory represented: the species considered locally endangered may in fact be common and widespread–perhaps with minimal apparent decline–elsewhere outside that area, with massive stocks in various European countries. For example *Anthocharis cardamines* which is considered under threat in the German federal state of Nordrhein-Westfalen (WAGENER, KINKLER & REHNELT 1977) and *Coenonympha arcania* which is considered threatened in the city of Hamburg (GLITZ & STÜBINGER 1981) are both eurychoric species common throughout most of Europe. The explanation is not difficult to find. A significant proportion of the species listed in red data books are those that are naturally rare and local in the country (region) concerned, primarily owing to the rarity of the species' habitat and only secondarily owing to the decline recorded. A nominal species formerly established in a few isolated refugial localities (e.g. relicts) on the border of its biogeographical (i.e. ecological and chorological) limit is much more susceptible to both anthropogenic and natural pressures than a widespread species near the centre of its range; the destruction of two or three colonies of a rare species often represents the destruction of 50% (or even more) of its total regional stocks (and sites), whereas a similar decline is negligible for the widespread species. The additional handicap of the former species against the widespread species is its natural isolation: lost ground cannot be regained at present by reinvasion, i.e. by their means of natural dispersal. It is, therefore, not surprising that at least 29 of the total of 71 butterfly species (Papilionoidea) considered threatened in the Federal Republic of Germany (BLAB & KUDRNA 1982) reach their chorological and ecological limits in central Europe, being confined to restricted extreme habitats; this amounts to fully 40% of all the species threatened in the country. Since such species are usually confined to protected sites such as nature reserves, their inclusion could rather be justified by the character of their distribution and the natural rarity of their habitats–the loss of any one colony is irreversible and irreplaceable owing to the species' negligible dispersal potential–than by the degree and force of the existing anthropogenic threats. A species living solely in nature reserves is "out of danger".

The Council of Europe recently published a report on the threatened butterflies of Europe (HEATH 1981), it being simply a European red data book. The report is intended as a scientific basis and thus the first step in the conservation of European butterflies. HEATH (1981) based the report on the national red lists (and their equivalents) so far as they were available, supplemented by summaries of basic data on each species listed, taken from a standard pocket handbook (HIGGINS & RILEY 1970 – i.e. the first and now outdated edition!), and further simplified. It is necessary to discuss and analyse here some principal and secondary aspects of this work and show some of the numerous errors made by its author, as evidenced by selected examples. The conservation of butterflies in Europe is far too important to tolerate or to overlook misconceptions. Thoughtless acceptance of data provided by other authors is always dangerous, exceptionally so if the subsequent author is not in the position to evaluate them and thus to separate the right from the wrong. To do this amounts to a considerable revisionary work which must be done at one time or another and must always include work with the original material, whatever its nature may be. Experience teaches that there is often something wrong with information included in standard handbooks which is neither original, nor accompanied by references to original sources and authors. Only thorough familiarity with the taxonomic group concerned and profound knowledge of literature helps to recognize the information copied with some ease, to judge it and to discover statements that may be suspect and require further checking. How dangerous the "secondhand" information can become is best shown by the following example selected from HEATH's (1981: 53) work:

"Vulnerable species" *Archon apollinus* is said to have world distribution "Bulgaria, Rumania, Greece and the near East" and the same is repeated for its European range. In Bulgaria subspecies *thracica* is said to be "endangered" and in Greece an unnamed subspecies is said to be "vulnerable", no information is offered on the status of the Rumanian populations. The reasons for the decline of the species are described as "Urbanisation and possibly tourism" and as the remedy the usual "Establishment of suitable nature reserves" is proposed. In fact *A. apollinus* has never been found in Bulgaria (BURESCH & TULESCHKOW 1929, TULESCHKOW 1958; J. GANEV pers. comm.) nor in Rumania (NICULESCU 1961). All data regarding old records of the species from Bulgaria are based on specimens found in Thracia before 1915 (BURESCH 1915) when this territory was briefly occupied and annexed by Bulgaria; also the above mentioned *A. apollinus thracica* BURESCH, 1915, was described from a type-locality outside the present border of Bulgaria. The territory – a part of Thracia – is now a part of European Turkey, and also north-eastern Greece, the type-locality being situated in the former country. The Turkish European distribution is in the Koru Dag Mts., north of the Galibolu peninsula. BURESCH (1915) mentioned also the possibility of the occurrence of this species in the Maric (Evros) river valley on the present border between Greece and European Turkey. Quite recently KOUTSAFTIKIS (1974) recorded apparently well established colonies of *A. apollinus* north of the town of Alexandroupolis in north-eastern Greece; and H. PIEPER (pers. comm.) found the species in the island of Kos. As there is no information regarding long term development of any of these colonies, it is impossible to determine whether they have been declining. Since their habitats are situated well away from larger towns and centres of tourism, it is extremely unlikely that the reasons for decline given by HEATH (1981) can be substantiated by any facts at all. The foodplant is not *Aristolochia hastata* given by HEATH (1981), apparently after HIGGINS & RILEY (1970), but *Aristolochia bodame* (BURESCH 1915). Later KOCAK (1982) confirmed BURESCH's (1915) old information and noted that the species seems to develop an interesting regional monophagy: the larvae of *A. apollinus* are unable to survive on an substitute congeneric foodplant offered to them in captivity (A. KOCAK and S. OEHMIG pers. comm.).

Also the following cases (selected at random) are characteristic of HEATH's (1981) work and abundantly illustrate his approach:

– *Papilio machaon* (p. 47): "Drainage of wetlands" is stated as the first reason for the decline of this species, which, in fact, does not normally inhabit wetlands (outside Norfolk) and their drainage could extend its distribution.
– *Zerynthia rumina* (p. 52) is said to be "endangered by collecting" in Italy; in fact the species does not live in that country.
– *Colias phicomone* (p. 67) is said to be "vulnerable" in Czechoslovakia and Poland, and protected there; in fact the species does not live in either country (HRUBY 1964, KRZYWICKI 1962, KUDRNA 1974, etc.) and is totally absent from the Carpathian Mts. The reason for decline is also said to be "grassland improvement", but *C. phicomone* has not been declining and does not even inhabit grassland that could be "improved".
– *Colias balcanica* (p. 72) is said to be "rare" in Bulgaria, "threatened by tourism", and "vulnerable" in Greece: in fact the species does not occur in those countries. The country called "Balkans" should read Yugoslavia. Similar geographical confusion is also found elsewhere, e.g. *C. aurorina* does not inhabit the country again called "Balkans".
– *Hipparchia statilinus* (p. 103) is classified as "vulnerable" on account of its being endangered in Czechoslovakia, Poland and Germany (it is ap-

parently extinct in the Federal Republic of Germany). *H. statilinus* is a typical Mediterranean species which is common in Portugal, Spain, southern France, Italy, Yugoslavia, Albania, Greece and Bulgaria, and by no means threatened except for some of its instable populations near its biogeographical limits (KUDRNA 1977); thoughtless application of data on untypical colonies does not help to make objective assessment.

– *Coenonympha oedippus* (p. 118) is said to be endangered in Spain; in fact the species was reported from Spain only once, some 100 years ago, and never confirmed (GOMEZ BUSTILLO & FERNANDEZ RUBIO 1974, VIEDMA & GOMEZ BUSTILLO 1976), probably a misidentification.

As conservation measures HEATH (1981) recommends almost exclusively establishing "large", "managed" or just "suitable" nature reserves for each species concerned; since the habitat is usually described in the most perfunctory manner (e.g. *Iphiclides podalirius* is said to inhabit "Open country to 2000 m and above") it is very difficult to imagine what the above adjectives are intended to indicate, to say the least. It would be possible to continue with critical remarks but it is not considered necessary. The publication of reports like HEATH's (1981) is not only waste of valuable resources, it can be downright dangerous to the butterflies if put into operation. None the less, it must be mentioned that this analysis of HEATH's (1981) work differs considerably from the view expressed by EBERT (1983) who described it as outstanding ("herausragend").

The above considerations allow the making of the following conclusions with regard to the significance, compilation and application of red data books for European butterflies;

● A Red data book (red list) should be the result of objective evaluation of the precise information on the long term trend in the development of stocks of a nominal species in a given territory.

● In all cases of inadequate (poor) data availability it is imperative to wait to make conclusions until satisfactory information has been obtained.

● Cumulative evaluation of local (regional) red lists does not produce a reliable red data book for the larger (i.e. cumulative) territory.

● As butterfly populations of numerous nominal species are known to fluctuate in numbers from year to year and over longer periods, precise observations stretching over a representative (adequate) number of years are indispensible.

● If conservation (protection) measures are proposed, these must be based on exact analysis of the reasons for decline and profound knowledge of the species' biotope to neutralize the harmful factors or bottlenecks; these must not cause damage to the habitat and its biocenosis.

- The significance of red data books grows with the size of the territory analyzed as well as with its biogeographical (ecological) diversity; local lists of threatened species are unrepresentative and therefore meaningless.

- Red data books apart from being good political instruments making the general public aware of the necessity to protect the environment can serve as a simple preliminary basis for some extreme "emergency" cases (i.e. protection of species acutely threatened by extinction, and similar).

- Red data books are unsuitable as a basis for a long term comprehensive programme for the conservation of taxonomic groups and communities (that is beyond various single nominal species projects and similar tasks).

It must be remembered that the clear definition of categories of the threatened species is essential for the future success of the list: the precision of the definitions is dictated by the availability of information on the majority of nominal species classified. It is possible that a reduction of categories to two would be advantageous for the representative exactness of the classification. The exclusion of ecologically instable species (i.e. species only temporarily present in the territory) may increase the objectivity of the list. The utilization of sophisticated categories (BLAB, NOWAK, TRAUTMANN & SUKOPP 1977) does not necessarily contribute towards objective classification so long as the data availability remains limited and the interpretation subjective (BLAB & KUDRNA 1982, PRETSCHER 1977, 1983), which surely does not give additional weight to the final result. An inflation of red data books and red list species may produce an adverse effect, particularly if the classification cannot be supported by facts.

The International Union for the Conservation of Nature and Natural Resources (IUCN) recognizes six categories of threatened animal and plant species graded according to the degree of threat:

– Extinct (Ex),

– Endangered (E),

– Vulnerable (V),

– Rare (R),

– Indeterminate (I) and

– Insufficiently known (K).

The limited availability of information concerning invertebrates and certain ambiguity of the official definitions as well as their clear bias towards the world stocks of all nominal species classified do not contribute to their easy and unequivocal application. The German regionally based categories are no better for European butterflies. Until new European categories are agreed upon, the following definitions are proposed for discussion:

● Nominal (butterfly) species that have been declining markedly owing apparently to anthropogenic pressures for a longer period of years over significant part/s of their European range, including their "headquarters" are considered threatened.

Also threatened – and perhaps even more so – are species confined to very restricted ranges, particularly if they inhabit areas suffering from considerable anthropogenic pressures or utilize certain secondary biotopes. This was the case of the only European butterfly species believed extinct (BALLETTO & KUDRNA 1985).

The following categories of threatened butterfly species – based upon the internationally established IUCN categories – can be recognized in Europe (Fig. 22):

### Extinct (X):
The occurrence of the species in Europe in the past is beyond doubt. There are no contemporary records from anywhere in Europe. All known colonies are believed exterminated as the result of direct or indirect anthropogenic pressures. Investigation of old localities and potential new sites produced no new records.

### Missing (M):
The occurrence of the species in Europe in the past is beyond doubt. There are no contemporary records from anywhere in Europe. There are no apparent anthropogenic causes for the disappearance of the species. Investigation of old localities and potential new sites produced no new records. The "reappearance" of the species is not ruled out.

### Endangered (E):
The species is in danger of extinction everywhere in Europe. It has suffered a serious decline in the past and included colonies situated within the "headquarters" of the species' European range. Survival of the species in Europe is unlikely if the causal factors continue to operate. Conservation measures are urgently required.

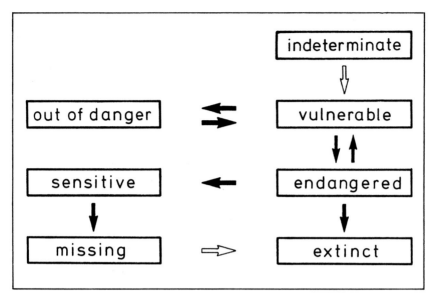

Fig. 22. Categories of threatened species and their "dynamics".

**Vulnerable** (V):
The species has suffered a considerable decline over most of its European range, not only along the edges of the range. There are still strong colonies in the "headquarters" of the species' European range, situated in areas relatively free from adverse anthropogenic pressures. Extinction of the species is unlikely at present, but deterioration feared, unless conservation measures are introduced.

**Indeterminate** (I):
The species is believed threatened, but its status is insufficiently known; it cannot be classified at present.

**Out of danger** (O):
Species formerly included in one of the above categories, usually treated as vulnerable; conservation measures applied proved so successful that the species can no longer be considered threatened.

**Rare** (R):
Endemic and quasi-European species confined to a very small range, usually with a small overall population, either restricted to just one locality or

thinly scattered in small isolated colonies over a larger territory. Their populations, even if not directly threatened at present, are unlikely to withstand much anthropogenic pressure because their stocks are low and habitats small.

It must be noted that the term "rare" is not really suitable for butterflies and other instects. The species considered "rare" are often very common in a restricted locality. In the absence of reliable data on the populations of any "rare" European species, the example of *Apatura iris* must suffice. If the English populations of *A. iris* constituted its whole European population, i.e. if the species were confined in Europe to Great Britain, it would be a sure candidate for the inclusion in the category "rare": it is in Great Britain confined to a small area situated in southern England (Fig. 23). According to ROBERTSON's (1980) very conservative estimate, the English population of *A. iris* consists annually of about 20,000 individuals. This use of the term "rare" is a complete contradiction of its application for mammals or birds and can lead to considerable misunderstandings. KUDRNA (1986) replaced the term "rare" in a German publication with a new term "empfindlich", an equivalent of the English word "sensitive".

The category "missing" was probably introduced for the first time and in slightly different context, as "verschollen" in a German work (BLAB, NOWAK, TRAUTMANN & SUKOPP 1977). It is certainly useful to draw a difference between "missing" and "extinct" in lepidopterology; the category was subsequently redefined and utilized in a German publication by KUDRNA (1986).

Although a short preliminary checklist of threatened European butterfly species is included in this work, it cannot be stressed enough, that the classification of many species is arbitrary. For instance, nearly all rare endemic species are potentially threatened, often more seriously than many a vulnerable species. The compilation of a proper European Red Data book of butterflies appears in this context – and bearing in mind the significance of butterflies for the conservation of nature in general – as an urgent task.

Excluded from the consideration are extra-European populations of the threatened species as well as small, perhaps temporary, colonies of essentially extra-European species. Rare endemic species is the category to replace the plain rare species of IUCN; they are dealt with separately as they are not threatened according to the above criteria, but extremely susceptible because of their rarity: the survival of these species depends on such a small stock that they could not withstand a significant decline. No butterfly species is known to have become extinct in Europe. A short provisional list of butterfly species threatened in Europe, with the main harmful factors marked, is shown in fig. 24; conservation measures are dealt with elsewhere.

Fig. 23. Present distribution of *Apatura iris* in Great Britain (from HEATH, POLLARD & THOMAS 1984, simplified).

| Grade | Species (family) | Harmful factors | | | | | |
|---|---|---|---|---|---|---|---|
| | | (0) | (1) | (2) | (3) | (4) | (5) |
| E | *Coenonympha oedippus* (SA) | | + | + | | | |
| E | *Lycaena dispar* (LY) | | + | + | | | + |
| V | *Coenonympha hero* (SA) | | + | | | + | |
| V | *Lycaena helle* (LY) | | + | + | | | |
| V | *Melanargia arge* (SA) | ? | | + | | | ? |
| E | *Gonepteryx cleobule* (PI) | + | | | | | |
| V | *Boloria aquilonaris* (NY) | | + | | | | |
| V | *Colias palaeno* (PI) | + | + | | | | |
| V | *Parnassius apollo* (PA) | | | | + | | + |
| V | *Maculinea alcon* (LY) | | + | + | | | |
| V | *Vacciniina optilete* (LY) | | + | ? | | | |
| V | *Parnassius mnemosyne* (PA) | | | | + | + | ? |
| V | *Boloria eunomia* (NY) | | + | | | | |
| V | *Coenonympha tullia* (SA) | | + | + | | | |
| V | *Euphydryas aurinia* (NY) | | + | + | | | |
| I | *Zerynthia polyxena* (PA) | | | | + | + | ? |
| V | *Chazara prieuri* (SA) | + | | | | | + |
| V | *Maculinea nausithous* (LY) | | + | + | | | |
| V | *Maculinea teleius* (LY) | | + | + | | | |
| E | *Papilio hospiton* | + | | | | | + |

**Explanation:** Grade of threat: E endangered, V vulnerable, I presumed vulnerable. Harmful factors: **0** = other than 1–5, e.g. general, area specific, etc., incl. urbanization, tourism; **1** = wetland drainage; **2** = intensification of grassland management; **3** = afforestation; **4** = intensification of forestry management; **5** = overcollecting. Species are listed according to the degree of threat and their relative decline; differences between two adjacent species (e.g. *Coenonympha hero* and *Lycaena helle*) are not necessarily very appreciable. Rare species are not considered here.

Fig. 24: A preliminary list of threatened European butterflies, with specific causes of their decline listed.

The following species have been selected as examples for each category because they are typical.

**Extinct:** *Polyommatus exuberans*. This is the only European species known to have become extinct.

**Edangered:** *Coenonympha oedippus*. This species was once widespread in isolated colonies over much of Europe. Drainage of wetlands and intensification of land use caused the extinction of this species in many contries, including Germany, Switzerland and Czechoslovakia. The last strong colonies of *C. oedippus* in western Europe are in N. Italy and W. France (Figs. 52 and 53). The survival of this species in Europe depends, by and large, upon the protection of these colonies, particular of those in northern Italy. The species has no safe "headquarters" anywhere in Europe.

**Vulnerable:** *Parnassius apollo*. This species has become almost a symbol of the conservation of European butterflies; it has also been included – as the only Palaearctic species – in CITES. All this is due to emotions! COLLINS & MORRIS (1985) already drew attention to the situation of *P. apollo*, but it is difficult, indeed impossible, to accept their classification of the species as rare, which it certainly is not. In most European countries, where it lives, *P. apollo* is still locally abundant and probably the major part of its overall population is not threatened. Nonetheless, some of its populations, usually situated near the biogeographical limit of the species and isolated from the main body of the species, are threatened.

**Missing:** Some rare European endemic species have not been recorded for a number of years and their status is uncertain, among them *Cupido carswelli* in the Sierra de Espuna in south-eastern Spain.

**Out of Danger:** None, as conservation measures have so far never been applied on a European scale in order to protect a butterfly species.

**Rare:** *Hipparchia ballettoi*. The species is confined to Monte Faito and Isola Ischia (S. Italy: Napoli district) and even there it is quite rare.

## 3.5 Considerations on the present state of our knowledge of European butterflies

### 3.5.1 Literature on European butterflies

One of the reasons for butterflies (Papilionoidea) being the ideal bioindicator group is that they are certainly the best known and researched taxonomic group (superfamily) of all invertebrates. The best known, however, does not necessarily imply comprehensively or even adequately known.

It is difficult to judge the overall number of publications on the butterflies of Europe, and the estimate is bound to be considerably influenced by the inclusion or exclusion of short notices, descriptive reports from meetings of learned and other relevant societies, and more or less popular papers and books. Nevertheless, it seems quite safe to say that the estimated number of lepidopterological publications concerning at least in part European butterflies, and which appeared since 1758, amounts to (probably well over) 50,000 titles but being well below 100,000 titles (KUDRNA 1985). The rate of increase in numbers of the matter published, whether judged by the number of books, papers and journals or by their size, has been alarming rather than steady. This increase is abundantly illustrated by the chronologically arranged bibliography of the Lepidoptera of Slovakia (HRUBY 1964) from 1772 to 1959: the number of items published in any one year rose from one (e.g. 1772) to 44 in 1959, the total being 889 publications. None the less, the number of individual papers published is not strictly related to the progress of research. It is certain that we owe most of our present knowledge of butterflies to the so called amateur lepidopterists, commonly condemned by most conservationists because of their collecting activities.

The standard of an average contemporary taxonomic or faunistic paper does not depart significantly from those published at the beginning of this century except, perhaps, that fashions have changed over the years and descriptions of new so called subspecies have been substituted for those of individual forms. Characteristically also, very many of the average to better faunistic papers are still modelled on the relevant "standard setting" works of H. REBEL (e.g. REBEL 1903, 1904, 1911, 1913, 1916) which started to appear at the beginning of this century. It seems, therefore, fully justified to remark that the vast increase in quantity has not brought about a proportional increase in quality. The main reason responsible for the present unfortunate state of lepidopterology seems to be the fact, that the majority of publications appear to be a byproduct of collecting activities carried out by their authors as their primary task, instead of this being the other way round. The predominance of amateurs over the professional lepidopterists is certainly not alone to blame, or to be offered as a convenient excuse: there have always been exceptional scientists among the so called "amateurs" and some rather disappointing workers among the so called "professionals", and there are good research opportunities for both groups. The ever increasing number of lepidopterological journals makes it easy to publish both good and substandard papers in transactions of local societies – (as well as in some "central" periodicals) – regardless of the topic being of regional or European interest, even if they are very likely to be subsequently overlooked by all potentially interested parties owing to the obviously poor availability of all such publications in central and institutional libraries, not to mention private libraries of the lepidopterists themselves.

Lepidopterological literature must be judged for this purpose purely according to its applicability to the conservation of butterflies, that is whether and how it answers questions voiced by those active in this field. As all such questions are rather new it is not surprising that they cannot be satisfactorily answered at present.

Analysis of scientific literature on European Papilionidea published in this century (BLAB & KUDRNA 1982, KUDRNA 1985) shows that generally the best information available on European butterflies is that concerning their distribution and taxonomy (in spite of many necessary qualifications), the worst that concerning their ecology, behaviour, early stages and population dynamics. The relative knowledge of butterflies varies greatly from country to country, Great Britain being probably the best researched larger European country, with U.S.S.R. and Albania being safe backmarkers at the other end of the scale. It is necessary to mention here that it was probably the small number of species native to Great Britain that helped to concentrate the interests of some lepidopterists on the biological aspects of the study of butterflies (e.g. FROHAWK 1934), as well as making it much easier to improve faunistic and taxonomic data on the whole butterfly fauna of the country. The rest of western Europe must also be considered reasonably well known, so long as no specific questions are asked and in some respects perfunctory answers are accepted. The term knowledge is rather relative. The conservation relevant aspects of lepidopterology must be discussed separately and judged according to the directly applicable information and its reliability. Certain suggestions are made as to the deficiencies in our present knowledge of butterflies, and how to overcome them.

**Taxonomy.** The overall number of taxonomic (s.l.) papers and works on the butterflies of Europe is astonishingly high, incomprehensible in some popular taxonomic groups. The lack of synoptic and revisionary, not to mention monographic works is alarming. There is a great surplus of descriptive papers (new subspecies, forms, most recently also genera) which are usually based on material selected at random (e.g. specimens from the private collection of the author) which is neither comprehensive enough nor representative enough to enable the author to come to any sound conclusions. There is no up to date work to enable the identification of all European species, and their early stages are neglected by most authors. There is no identification key to the caterpillars of European butterflies at all. There are no catalogues, no synonymic check-lists, no reliable and complete key to genera. (This is even worse in other families of the Lepidoptera). Further priority tasks are discussed in some detail elsewhere.

**Faunistics and distribution.** The majority of faunistic publications are concerned with the positive record of a nominal species from a given locality, negative subsequent records are also occasionally published. Faunistic methods have hardly changed over the last hundred or so years, and nearly all papers are typical byproducts of the author's collecting activities: in order to secure good results well known localities are visited again and again, if by different individual collectors, as long as the butterflies are believed to be plentiful there; this "overexploration" contributes to overcollecting and does not help to advance our knowledge of the distribution of the species. A good proportion of papers are concerned with single records of rare species, particularly if they are new for the country or region. Some published data is vague in order to confuse subsequent collectors. Publication of distribution maps, which have recently become fashionable, is discussed elsewhere although it is primarily relevant to faunistics. There appears to be a total lack of systematic and methodical approach towards the study of distribution supplemented by quantitative information on the dynamics and trends year after year, replaced perhaps by meaningless accounts of males and females deposited in the auther's collection. Butterfly conservation requires primarily accounts of relatively undisturbed sites, their species composition and particular species features (such as rare endemic species); the sites must be clearly defined and described, mapped, suggestions made as to their conservation, management, buffer zone, etc. The (about equal) priority tasks in the faunistic research of European butterflies are:

● Distribution of rare endemic species:
  To revise all known and examine all potential sites; to define and describe the sites inhabited by the species; to map the sites; to identify all site and species specific harmful anthropogenic factors; to propose countermeasures. (Further notes under ecology, below).

● Distribution of endangered species:
  To revise all known and potential sites; to define and describe the sites inhabited by the species at present; to identify all site and/or species specific reasons of the species' decline or extinction; to propose specific countermeasures; to map the sites. Further notes under ecology, below.

● Faunistic synopsis is (a term proposed here for) a preliminary concise up-to-date account of the distribution of a selected taxonomic group in a given (usually larger) territory (cf. e.g. BRETHERTON 1966). Faunistic synopses must compile all species recorded from the territory, exclude false records and extinct species with specific reasons given, provide a comprehensive bibliography, so far as possible ecological and biological data, define species declining, describe principal sites; it is to serve as the basic work to enable/help the most urgent conservation/protection measures to be taken and show the course of further research.

Faunistic synopsis is among the most neglected aspects of faunistic research. Nevertheless, such papers are badly needed for almost all European countries. They have both all-European and regional significance and form an indispensible scientific basis for any form of conservation efforts. Only the availability of such works can help to produce a reasonably comprehensive list of threatened species and to discover specific reasons for their decline.

**Ecology.** None of the European butterfly species are adequately known from the ecological point of view and ecological papers are greatly underrepresented in lepidopterological literature. The simple question 'why does a butterfly species live where it lives' is never fully answered. Ecological terminology is often confused and habitat descriptions so vague and incomplete that they cannot be compared from one work to another: lepidopterological literature is full of useless statements like for example "flies over rough ground" or "lives in open country up to 2000 m and above" which pretend to give a description of habitats of stenotopic species. In many papers ecology is confused with descriptions of how, when and where to collect the species, or to breed it. Names of hostplants are most unreliable with numerous misidentifications or useless statements like "lives on various grasses" and hostplants accepted by the species larvae in captivity are listed as if relevant in natural conditions. Adult hostplant preferences are extremely poorly known and very rarely mentioned, among the few exceptions being SCHWARZ (1948, 1949). It can be said that ecology is for conservation one of the most important aspects of lepidopterology, yet neglected beyond reason. (Perhaps partly because ecology cannot directly assist collecting activities?).

It is almost impossible to compile a short list of ecological tasks relevant for the conservation of European butterflies and classified according to consistently defined priorities, except perhaps for:

● Autecological studies of all rare endemic species.
● Autecological studies of all acutely endangered (and similar) species.
● Compilation of a synopsis of hostplant species on the principles of the one for the butterflies of the Federal Republic of Germany (BLAB & KUDRNA 1982).

Studies of **population biology** and **dispersal** are, strictly speaking, parts of ecology (s.l.) and have also been very neglected in the past, probably because a collector has no time, and little interest, to make pure observations; he must collect. It is perhaps known how many eggs a female can oviposit in captivity but how many she can usually deposit in nature is unknown. The determination of bottlenecks is also important to establish the development of natality and mortality. In spite of all the numerous publication on the migration of butterflies (BAKER 1978, etc.) which are irrelevant to the conservation of butterflies in Europe, observations regarding the natural dispersal of a species are almost nonexistent. It is also unknown which butterfly species in central Europe depend on their colonies being replenished by immigration.

Populations of butterflies are known to fluctuate. There are the sea-sonal fluctuations of bivoltine and polyvoltine species, which can "explode" in summer (usually their second brood) from a scarce or moderately abundant spring brood. This is well exemplified by *Pieris rapae* (Fig. 25). The second type are annual fluctuations, where the abundance changes from year to year, probably substantially influenced for instance by favourable–or unfavourable–dominating weather in the given year (Fig. 26, 27). Practically every butterfly species is subject to such fluctuations.

Published statements concerning the absolute believed abundance of butterflies are not always reliable. Many species fly over a short period of time and reach their peak abundance only for a week or two. Other species

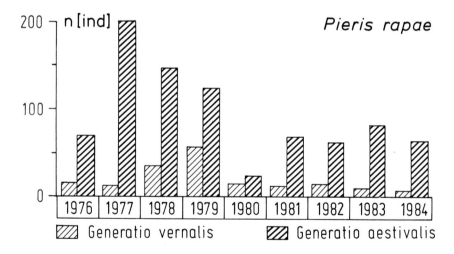

Fig. 25. Seasonal and annual fluctuations of *Pieris rapae* in a monitored English site (Dorset: Swanage) (from THOMAS & WEBB 1985).

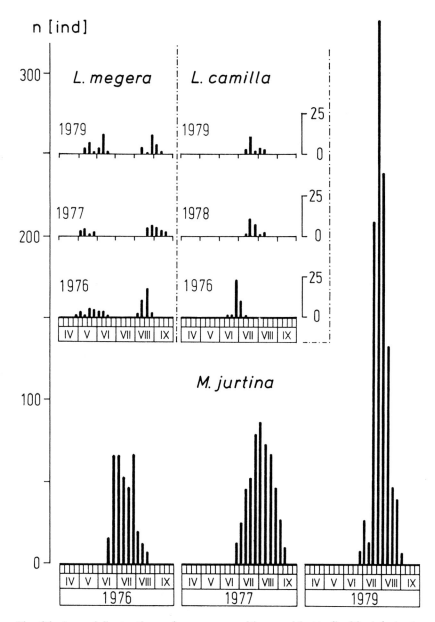

Fig. 26. Annual fluctuations of a common widespread butterfly *Maniola jurtina,*
*Lasiommata megera* and *Limenitis camilla* in three different years in monitored
localities in Great Britain (after HEATH, POLLARD & THOMAS 1984).

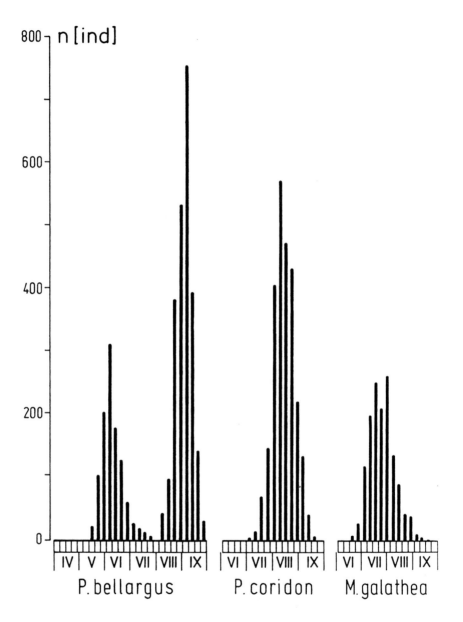

Fig. 27. Examples of typical seasonal fluctuations of some butterfly species in monitored localities in Great Britain (after HEATH, POLLARD & THOMAS 1984).

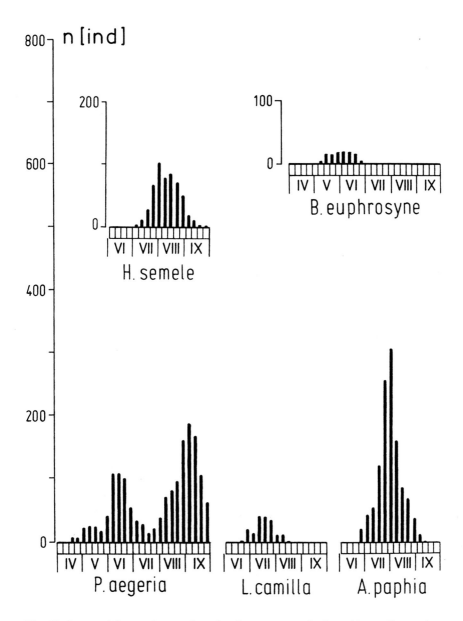

Fig. 28. Seasonal fluctuations and mode of emergence of selected butterfly species in Dorset (after Thomas & Webb 1985).

have a long period of emergence, in some cases they reach their peak abundance for a month or more, but at no time are they quite as common as the former group (Fig. 28).

Our knowledge of **early stages** is particularly incomplete (BLAB & KUDRNA 1982), there is no work to enable the identification of the described taxa; the descriptions, if available are usually quite perfunctory and therefore useless. Although FROHAWKS's (1934) descriptions and illustrations leave something to be desired, it would be a great progress if they could be extended from the relatively few British species to all European butterflies (to say nothing of their geographical or ecological variation and taxonomic significance). Compilation of data on early stages (e.g. MALICKY 1969) would go some way towards the better understanding of larval ecology.

All in all, the lack of quality in lepidopterological literature is made up for by meaningless quantity. Perhaps the worst is, that a good deal of information is copied from one publication to another without bibliographical reference to the original source (making evaluation difficult) and the direct domination of private collecting as the main objective in European lepidopterology, both past and present.

It should be remembered that it is irrelevant whether a specific task is carried out by a professional or an amateur researcher–only the quality of the result is decisive–and there is enough to do for both. Cooperation, particularly interdisciplinary, is in need of much improvement (BLAB & KUDRNA 1982) and coordination of the work by different students on similar topics is badly needed. Research work on the rare endemic species or endangered species does not amount to their overcollecting–this should be noted by both the conservation authorities and the collectors, the cooperation of both could be only to the advantage of their mutual aims. Independent research foundations should support generously projects aimed at the conservation of butterflies and editors of periodical and serial publications should give preference to manuscripts concerned with the conservation of butterflies and indirectly relevant topics. Nature conservation authorities are expected to faciliate research on butterflies, and they should be kept informed of all results published.

### 3.5.2 Mapping the distribution of European butterflies

Ever since their inclusion by HIGGINS & RILEY (1970), distribution maps of butterflies have been fashionable with lepidopterists, and overvalued by most of them. A conventional distribution map is no more than a convenient graphical expression of the distribution described in detail in the text, that is an illustration to accompany–not to replace–the description. Nordström (1955) published distribution maps of the butterflies of Fennoscandia which remain unsurpassed in Europe for their accuracy and reliability in spite of the simple means available to their author. In Great Britain (Heath 1968) a computer aided system of recording was developed for plant species, and utilized for animals, which in due course evolved into the European Invertebrate Survey (EIS) programme. The purpose of the British recording scheme was to show changes in the distribution of the native dragonflies (Odonata) and butterflies as a basis for the introduction of such conservation measures as might be necessary to prevent the extinction of the declining species. The recording is made by marking the UTM grid squares of 10 km² if the nominal species recorded was reported there; a circle indicates an "old" pre-1950/1960 record and a dot shows a "new" post-1950/1960 observation. A record is constituted by the observation/s or capture of the nominal species recorded regardless of instar and number of individuals (i.e. a single "vagrant" adult is valued as much as an established colony). Recording is carried out mainly by volunteers and a record made by an acknowledged scientist has the same value as one made by a child. Individual records are checked only exceptionally and not thoroughly (M. J. Skelton pers. comm.); as there are only some 60 butterfly species (regular migrants included) in Great Britain, nearly all quite easy to identify and rather localized, the proportion of errors can be kept tolerably low. Nevertheless, it took two attempts to produce an acceptable set of distribution maps of the British butterflies (Heath 1970, Skelton & Heath 1975).

The British computer aided system of recording and mapping of distribution ranges has one advantage:

- It is very easy to operate and, with a little diligence, it produces very simple distribution maps which may show spatial decline ("shrinking") of individual nominal species' ranges with reasonable accuracy, provided complete and accurate data have been collected; additionally, it may allow comparison of the range of the butterfly species and its hostplant, should this be needed.

This advantage is outweighed by several methodic disadvantages which become more significant with the increase in size and ecological diversity of the area and number of species recorded:

- 10 km² is an abstract and quite meaningless unit unless the location and identification of the site has been provided separately in the text (this is, of course, not the case; if so, there would be no need for the map!).

- It cannot distinguish between single and repeated observation/s and an established colony of the species, and its strength (i.e. no quantitative recording).
- It does not distinguish between species extinct and not observed since 1950/1960 and species absent or not observed before 1950/1960.
- Recording is not carried out methodically, i.e. distribution maps are much influenced by the distribution of recorders.
- Identification of taxonomically difficult species restricts the circle of potential recorders dramatically.

In day-to-day practice these methodical errors are accompanied by practical ones:

- Existing collections and published data are inadequately–if at all– utilized.
- Territories mapped are not methodically and adequately investigated.

This is abundantly clear from the maps published so far, as evidenced for instance by HEATH & LECLERCQ (1981) and SCHMIDT-KOEHL (1971): in the first case the maps are well behind our present knowledge because the authors have made no use of even the best known standard national faunistic works–e.g. NICULESCU (1961, 1963, 1965) for Romania–and in the second case the recorded distribution of ubiquists (e.g. of widespread migrant species) shows that only about half of the area has been explored for them. Also the progress of mapping has been extremely slow and it is unrealistic to expect either the completion of the programme in the forseeable future (if ever!) or any significant improvements. Although EIS has members from most of European countries, recording centres have been set up only in a few of them, and fewer still are in operation. Only a few countries have produced preliminary maps of some species (e.g. France, Germany) or of a part of the territory (e.g. Spain). Apart from Great Britain and Ireland, distribution maps for Belgium appear to be reasonably complete (VER-STRAETEN 1970, 1971, 1971; VERSTRAETEN & PRINS 1976) and Luxembourg (MEYER & PELLES 1981).

At the European level the EIS maps (UTM grid 50 km² as basic unit) are based upon the completion of all national maps at 10 km², i.e. the utilization of the national recording centres and their data, regardless of whether these exist or not. Only nine (!) European distribution maps have been produced so far–that is about 2 % (!) of the species have been covered by preliminary, incomplete and most unreliable maps. The lack of a competent lepidopterist thoroughly familiar with European butterflies is surely to blame for the errors which have been passed for publication (HEATH &

LECLERCQ 1981): for instance (v. map 1) *Parnassius apollo* has been "re-corded" after 1950 in south-western Bohemia (Czechoslovakia), in the German Democratic Republic and in the north-eastern Netherlands, where there are neither the habitats nor larval foodplant suitable for the species. The remaining eight maps are not much better.

In its present form the EIS does not serve any useful purpose, and it certainly does not provide basic data applicable to the conservation of European butterflies. At least the following principal changes would be necessary to transform the EIS programme into a new scientifically based scheme:

- To dispense with the UTM grid for any other purpose than pure illustration.
- To introduce quantitative recording to distinguish between colonies and single records, where possible.
- To secure professional staff to run the scheme as well as to find an adequate number of trained external recorders on a professional part-time basis.
- To create an official central depository for material collected in the course of recording as well as literature and other data.
- To utilize published information (past and present) as well as all museum and private collections.

This amounts to nothing less than the establishing of at least a medium sized research institute with sound financial backing to carry out the programme. Even then it might be necessary to select priorities in rank and urgency: otherwise the target might prove unrealistic in Europe. Nevertheless, even in the very unlikely event of the finances for such an institute becoming available, the question must be asked whether these cannot be used more effectively than by supporting the reformed EIS programme. In the Netherlands the need to reform the old EIS programme has already been realized (GERAEDTS 1982; TOL 1979). One thing is certain: creation of additional committees (i.e. International Commission for Invertebrate Survey–with by and large identical membership) is certain to be counterproductive, if the production of comprehensive distribution maps is the true objective of the organization.

The only way of mapping the distribution of butterflies which can substantially help in every conservation programme is to map their sites by means of detailed (1:25,000 or similar) maps, concentrating on selected species and sites. For the illustration of the distribution maps of this type, the old excellent system used by NORDSTRÖM (1955) is perhaps even better than the UTM grid in any form.

The unsatisfactory state of mapping of European butterflies can be exemplified by Bavaria, which with about 170 butterfly species is certainly far the richest German federal state (KUDRNA 1986). Fig. 29 shows all localities from which there are records of butterflies, regardless if new or old, extinct or extant, of a single specimen or of a colony, as available to the Bavarian state nature conservation authorities. This example initates a question: Are the so called "well known" or "best known" parts of Europe really adequately researched?

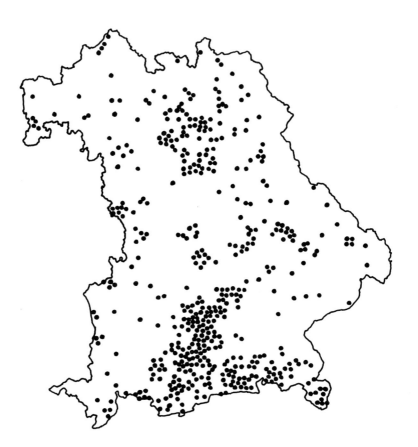

Fig. 29. Mapping of Lepidoptera in Bavaria (Federal Republic of Germany): included are all localities from which records have been received, regardles of time, number or reliability.

# 4 Applied taxonomy of European butterflies

Zoological taxonomy is the first and most important corner stone in every species conservation project: it provides a list of species, defines them, facilitates their correct identification and ensures that their identity is unequivocally understood, using a universal system of distinct names to denote individual nominal species. In this chapter the means of taxonomy are critically discussed and the tasks are outlined.

## 4.1 Taxonomy (s.l.) as an auxiliary biological science

Taxonomy, systematics and classification are terms usually used with more or less synonymous meanings: this is chiefly because each of these three closely interdependant disciplines can hardly exist in isolation from the other two. Although the slight yet significant differences between these disciplines are recognized at least by all taxonomists familiar with the standard textbooks and references, it is appropriate to restate their definitions (MAYR 1969) here:

- Taxonomy is the theory and practice of classifying organisms.
- Systematics is the scientific study of the kinds and diversity of organisms and of any and all relationships among them; or in fewer words: systematics is the science of the diversity of organisms and their relationships.
- Classification makes the organic diversity accessible to the other biological sciences.

CROWSON (1970): pointed out the inadequate differentiation between the "taxonomy" and "classification" as defined above, and criticised the contemporary trend towards abstract terminology where simplicity would positively contribute towards the precision of the statement and its unequivocal understanding. Since "systematics" and "classification" cannot practically exists in isolation from each other, the term "taxonomy" is utilized here as the collective term for the real scientific discipline constituting systematics (MAYR 1969) and classification (sensu CROWSON 1970), this being closer to the original meaning of the word. This meaning of taxonomy will be retained for the rest of the present work.

Additionally, it may be useful to define here the fourth discipline which serves all three branches of biology defined above (or the "compound" taxonomy) as a tool, although not a science in its own right (after MAYR 1969):

● Nomenclature (in zoology) is the theory and practice of application of distinctive names to each of the groups recognized in the zoological classification, according to a code of universal [and presumably] constant rules.

The addition of the adjective "biological" or simply the formation of modern terms like "biosystematics" or "biotaxonomy" stresses the biological nature of these disciplines. The latter two terms are modern, often used at present in the meaning of all four disciplines combined. It certainly is not the purpose of this work to volunteer statements as to the justification and necessity of this usage.

According to its function and objectives, taxonomy can be further divided into three disciplines (MAYR 1969):

● Alpha taxonomy is concerned with the description and meaning of species.
● Beta taxonomy is concerned with the arranging of species into a "natural" system of higher and lower taxa.
● Gamma taxonomy is concerned with biological-evolutionary relationships of taxa.

Also these three disciplines are so closely interrelated that a practicing taxonomist can hardly take up one of them leaving aside the remaining two.

The primary goal of zoological taxonomy is to provide an exhaustive picture of the existing animal diversity of the Earth, classified in a system of higher and lower taxa according to their relationship. Taxonomy is the only science to carry out this task. In order to attain this goal taxonomists utilize information supplied by some of the other branches of biological sciences, such as genetics, ecology, zoogeography, botany, ethology, etc., and even some non-biological disciplines such as geology or palaeontology. Taxonomy is thus both a pure science in its own right, in some respects not unlike pure mathematics, and an auxiliary science serving all disciplines of biological sciences. Indeed, many of them could not exist without a taxonomic basis. In their purest form, the results of taxonomists' work are interesting only to small groups of specialists also working with the taxonomic group concerned. As an auxiliary science – "applied taxonomy" has countless users and its applicable results are sought after both within and outside the sphere of biology. The significance of zootaxonomy within the network of biological sciences depends almost entirely upon the delivered products and services made available and directly applicable outside the ranks of taxonomists. Inadequate awareness of the need for "applied taxonomy" and the little attention paid to the "outside world", led particularly in Europe and America to the degradation of taxonomy in the eyes of many professional biologists. This in turn contributed first to the loss of prestige and later to the loss of financial support for taxonomic research in many countries. The decline of taxonomy in Europe, seen from a rather purist point of view, has caused concern for some time (ESRC Report no. 13 of 1977).

The success of applied taxonomy as an auxiliary science must be judged pragmatically according to the "products" delivered and the "services" rendered directly to the non-taxonomical (predominantly biological) sciences. These products can be divided into the following three groups, not necessarily in order of importance:

● Classification of animals as generally applicable and understandable to all branches of sciences dealing with animals.
● Data and information necessary for the reconstruction of phylogeny and the study of evolution and biogeography (zoogeography, ecology) of animals.
● Catalogues and identification aids of all kinds indispensable to students of ecology, biogeography, phytopathology, physiology, medicine, genetics, behaviour, faunistics, etc., as well as for all those engaged in work and research aimed at the conservation and protection of nature.

The last named user complex, those involved in the conservation and protection of nature is possibly the most important customer of applied taxonomy, whether it receives the "products" and "services" directly or otherwise (e.g. by means of ecologists, etc.) because it is the only discipline that offers the taxonomists an indispensable feedback: the survival in nature of the animal species studied. As this is the only discipline to do so, the needs of the conservation and protection of nature, fully deserve the top priority.

It is the supplier/customer relationship that decides the forms and mode of the "products" and "services" offered, the "applicability" (i.e. usefulness and demand) being the foremost, often the only, criterion. It is almost certain that a taxonomic work dealing with scores of closely related subspecies recognizable only by a few specialists (at best) after a statistical assessment of some minor and usually not entirely constant morphological features, of course with some more subspecies described therein for good measure, will remain for ever inapplicable, while a pragmatic identification aid to a taxonomically difficult group of species, a synonymic catalogue, or a taxonomic revision stabilizing the identity and nomenclature of the group concerned will be most welcome.

## 4.2  Zoological nomenclature, its principles and their application

Zoological nomenclature plays a very significant role in entomological taxonomy as it provides the indispensible language of communication among all those taking a professional interest in animals and their biology. That is, between the group of taxonomists on the one hand, and the non-taxonomists on the other. Since the time of publication of the 10th edition of "Systema Naturae" by C. LINNAEUS, a combination of two zoological names, the generic name and the specific name (epithet), are adequate to denote any one animal species (or phenon), so far as the language remains constant, that is the same taxonomic unit is always referred to by the same combination of names. The identity of zoological names depends in principle on two factors only:

(1) unequivocal objective definition of the name and
(2) rules governing the use of names, their validity and availability.

Both these factors are governed by the International Commission on Zoological Nomenclature and all rules are set out in the International Code of Zoological Nomenclature. This is necessary since a name can only serve as a link of communication if it represents one, and only one, taxon, and its meaning remains stable. The preamble of the International Code of Zoological Nomenclature states: "Priority is the basic principle of zoological nomenclature. Its application" . . . "may be moderated to preserve a long-accepted name in its accustomed meaning".

The Code valid at present is the third, completely revised edition, which was first published in February 1985. It is written in English, with an official traditional French translation incorporated (translations into other languages are not planned because other languages than English (the official means of communication) and French (the traditional second language) are not recognized by the Commission. This is an understandable policy: the translation of the Code presents only difficulties and delays and a – at least basic – knowledge of English language is a necessity for every zoologist. Ever since the appearance of the first "Stricklandian Code" in 1842, every subsequent development has brought about more sophistication, coupled with inevitable growth in size and complexity, has been written in more and more frighteningly legalistic English, and therefore not surprisingly more difficult to use, too. The most convenient was probably the so called "1935 Code", this being an amended third edition of the original "1901 Code", for it was comprehensive and relatively simple to use (BALFOUR-BROWNE 1963). Also the new Code published 1985 has brought about numerous new complications, and thus perhaps confirm the universal applicability of the so called Parkinsons' law (PARKINSON 1977). The present Code requires much study before an experienced taxonomist can put it to work, and is precisely for that reason ignored by some; it is very unlikely that a non-taxonomist will ever make good use of it, for that apparent reason. Priority remains the first principle of the Code, but the provision for moderation in the case of long-accepted names, based on the use of plenary powers, has–as any other form of application to the Commission–the decisive disadvantage that it takes some years, usually perhaps three to five, before a decision is passed. This leaves the zoologist practically without unequivocal names for the taxa concerned during that period. Owing to the general trend towards sophistication, every application intended to bring about some simplifications (KUDRNA 1978) stands a negligible chance of success (HOLLOWAY & ROBINSON 1980).

The development of the Code towards sophistication does not seem to be directly related to the stabilisation of zoological nomenclature. There are at least three principal reasons for the instability of zoological names:

● Some names must change for various reasons following the course of taxonomic research, and there is very little that can be done about this.

● Some changes are due to the subjective application of the Code in certain more complex taxonomically difficult cases without an apparent unequivocal solution. An example is the case of over 1,500 names proposed by R. VERITY. Their availability is subject to interpretation and personal opinion (KUDRNA 1983). The only effective remedy here is the prompt use of the plenary powers by the Commission.

● Some changes are directly induced by alterations made by the Commission to the Code from time to time; they are avoidable, and indeed, deplorable. Example: unnecessary alterations of articles concerning homonymy.

Instable, ambiguous names do not serve as means of communication. it is relatively easy for a specialist to learn by heart a complicated synonymy of a group of taxa he is working on; but the same is impossible for a non-taxonomist. Zoological names must serve as useful tools, otherwise they turn into a burden. Taxonomic problems cannot be settled by changes of names alone.

The only decisive remedy against instability of zoological names is a massive-scale production of nomina conservanda directed by the Commission; every nomen conservandum would have to be objectively defined by a single selected specimen accessible to scientists in a recognized depository, with its name preserved in the original combination, with reference to the current usage. The stability of names is much more important than some formal requirements: a taxonomically unavoidable change of a name once for all, or the loss of priority of a name, is a much lesser evil than lasting ambiguity or instability. All decisions on behalf of the Commission must be swift and an application should be settled in not more than three months. This task could be carried out by a small committee of perhaps three professionals on full time basis. They would have to be obliged to give a ruling within three months from the date of application. Names approved by them would become nomina commendata (based upon the same principles as nomina conservanda mentioned above). After a given period of time these would automatically become nomina conservanda unless a renewed appeal to the Commission made within a set time after the publication of nomen commendatum was received, requesting further changes. Second applications would be refereed by three specialists and the final decision left to the former body. The results would have to be published at regular intervals, and available in zoological libraries, all editors of scientific journals should be requested to follow them. The introduction of this new system should be followed by a drastic simplification of the Code of Zoological Nomenclature.

It must be remembered that, following its preamble, the object of the Commission's work is to promote stability of zoological names. Taxonomy and the International Commission on Zoological Nomenclature would considerably increase their reputation if all their activities concentrated on achieving this goal. (Fig. 30)

In spite of all these critical remarks, it must be remembered, that an imperfect international Code is incomparably better, than several private or national sets of rules.

The following review of principles of zoological nomenclature and their practical application is intended primarily for ecologists, faunists, biogeographers and other lepidopterologists, whose primary interests are not in taxonomy and systematics; the taxonomists must command a much more comprehensive knowledge of the rules contained in the Code. The importance of the basic understanding of the Code is that it enables the nontaxonomist to understand what the zoological nomenclature is all about and how to use it at least in the less complex cases of application.

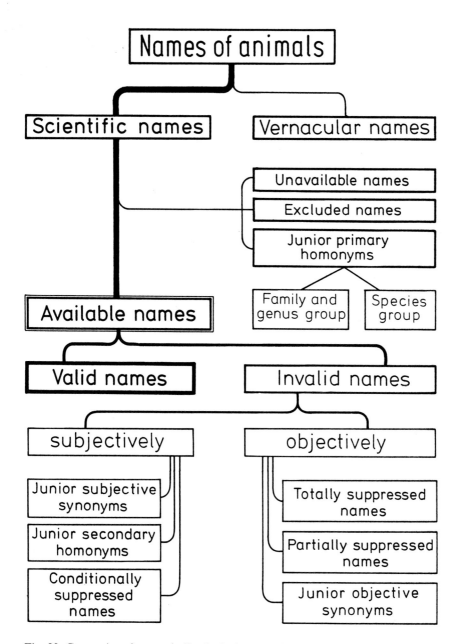

Fig. 30: Categories of names in Zoological nomenclature.

The object of the International Code of Zoological nomenclature–authorized by the International Commission on Zoological Nomenclature–is to promote stability and universality of animal names and to ensure that the name of each taxon is unique and distinct.

The Code provides rules for the naming of animals from the rank of subspecies to the rank of superfamily; all taxa below the subspecies rank and above the superfamily rank are exluded. The most important elements in the structure of the Code are:

- The Code refrains from infringing upon taxonomic judgement, which is not subject to regulations or restrain.
- The Code does not determine the rank to be accorded to any group of animals.
- The Code provides the kind of name that it to be accorded to a taxon at any given rank.
- Every name regulated by the Code is permanently attached to a name-bearing type.

The basic "laws" of zoological nomenclature are contained in the six principles, as outlined below.

The Principle of Priority ensures that the valid name of a taxon is the oldest available name applied to it under the Code, provided that the name is not specifically invalidated by any special provisions or ruling by the Commission (cf. Official Index). The Code incorporates provision for such cases, where rigid application of the Principle of Priority could upset the validity of a long-accepted name in its accustomed meanig, particularly through the validation of little known or unused names, by referring such cases to the Commission. Examples: The species commonly known as *Hipparchia pellucida* was originally named *Satyrus semele pellucida* STAUDER, 1923; it ist deemed identical with a taxon originally named *Satyrus semele cotys* JACHONTOV, 1935; the formerly mentioned name is the oldest and therefore valid name of the taxon–*Hipparchia pellucida* (STAUDER, 1923)–and the latter name is its junior synonym. The generic name *Parnalius* RAFINESQUE, 1815–an almost forgotten name–was rejected by the Commission in favour of the generic name *Zerynthia* OCHSENHEIMER, 1816, because the latter name was the long-accepted name for the taxon.

The Principle of Binominal Nomenclature states, that the scientific name of a species–but not of any other taxon at any other rank–is a combination of two names–a binomen–the first being the generic name (always written with a capital letter at the beginning) and the second is the specific name (always beginning with a small letter). Interpolated names are not inconsistent with this principle. Family-group and genus-group names are always uninominal and names of subspecies are always trinominal (the use of a trinomen for a monotypic species infringes this principle). Genus-group and species-group names are always to be written in italics; family-group names are not to be written in italics. Examples: *Hipparchia semele* (LINNAEUS, 1758) is the name of a species: *Hipparchia semele semele* (LINNAEUS, 1758) is the name of the nominotypical subspecies of a polytypic species *Hipparchia semele*.

The Principle of Homonymy states that an available name that is a junior homonym of another available name within the same rank-group must not be used as a valid name. In simple words this means that there must be no two or more identical names within each of the three rank-groups recognized by the Code: no two family-group names or two genus-group names, nor two identical species-group names within a genus are permitted by the Code.

On the surface, this principle appears to be the most simple of all principles of zoological nomenclature; on closer scrutiny it becomes one of the most complex and confusing principles there are. This is caused partly by the instability of the article concerned, which has been substantially altered three times during the last 50 years and by the additional conditions which are at least in part subjective, i.e. the matter of the author's opinion.

Examples: *Lycaena nevadensis* ZÜLLICH, 1928, is a junior primary homonym of *Lycaena argus nevadensis* OBERTHÜR, 1910; *Papilio jurtina* HUFNAGEL, 1766, is a junior primary homonym of *Papilio jurtina* LINNAEUS, 1758, where the latter name is currently considered a distinct species of the genus *Maniola* SCHRANK 1801, and the former is treated as a junior subjective synonym of *Hipparchia hermione* (LINNAEUS, 1764).

The Principle of the First Reviser implies, that the relative precedence of two or more names or nomenclatural acts published on the same date or two different original spellings for one (and the same) taxon, is determined by the first reviser. The decision made by him, for instance in making the choice between *caerulescens* and *coerulescens* cited together, is binding for all subsequent authors from the nomenclatural point of view.

The Principle of Coordination implies that a scientific name established for any one taxon within each of the three distinct groups of names –the family-group, the genus-group and the species-group–is deemed to be simultaneously established with the same author and date for all taxa based on the same name-bearing type within the group concerned. This means –for instance–that a scientific name established for a subspecies is available, with the same author and date, also for the species, should any subsequent author decide to treat the taxon concerned at the rank of a species, and vice versa. Both such names are objectively defined by the same name-bearing type. Example: Subspecies rank name *Hipparchia semele leighebi* KUDRNA, 1976, coordinates with *Hipparchia leighebi* KUDRNA, 1976; *Hipparchia delattini* KUDRNA, 1975, coordinates with *Hipparchia volgensis delattini* KUDRNA, 1975.

The Principle of Name-Bearing Types states, that every nominal taxon is – actually or potentially – defined by means of its name-bearing type – that is based directly or indirectly on an actual specimen, that constitutes the only objective standard of reference which determines the unequivocal application of the name.

This is one of the most important principles of zoological nomenclature. It implies, that a family-group name is objectively defined by its type-genus, the genus-group name is objectively defined by its type-species and the type-species by its holotype, lectotype or neotype (whichever is applicable). It is important to observe, that the specific name is based on a single specimen, which is the only way to ensure that the objective standard of reference is unambiguous. The fact that in certain circumstances also a complete series of syntypes can serve as a whole as a name-bearing type is not contrary to this principle: the reviser has the right – and indeed the obligation – to select from the series a suitable single specimen and designate it the lectotype of the taxon concerned.

Example: The superfamily Papilionoidea includes the family Papilionidae which in turn includes the subfamily Papilioninae, and further below the tribe Papilionini: they are based on the type-genus *Papilio* LINNAEUS, 1758; this in turn is based on its type-species, *Papilio machaon* LINNAEUS, 1758, and this again on its actual or potential type-specimen.

Formally correct application of the principles and rules of zoological nomenclature ensures that taxonomic publications can be readily understood. The following paragraphs contain explanations of some formal aspects of zoological publications dealing with systematics and taxonomy. Also the following notes are primarily intended for non-taxonomists.

All family-group names, that is the names of superfamilies, families, subfamilies and tribes, are to be written with capital initial letter; they are not to be written in italics. The suffix indicates their taxonomic rank, it being -oidea, -dae, -nae and -ni respectively. Examples: Papilionoidea, Papilionidae, Papilioninae, Papilionini.

All genus-group and species-group names are to be written in italics; the genus-group name begins with a capital initial letter, the species-group name always begins with small initial letter (even if a capital letter would seem to be grammatically justified, such as in case of names based upon names of persons). The species-rank name in trinominal combinations is never to be abbreviated. The generic name may be abbreviated instead of being repeated in the same text by its initial letter, but never by a syllable. Examples: *Hipparchia leighebi* KUDRNA, 1976 (named after G. LEIGHEB); *Parnassius apollo apollo* (LINNAEUS, 1758), never *Parnaissius a. apollo*; *Charaxes* OCHSENHEIMER, 1816, may be abbreviated by *C.*, never by *Ch.* and *Hipparchia* FABRICIUS, 1807, may be abbreviated by *H.*, never by *Hipp.* or otherwise.

The name of author(s) follows immediately after the combination of genus-group with species-group name(s). It is not normally used after family-group names. It is usually quoted after genus-group names only if published uninominally (i.e. never "interpolated" in a combination). The name of author(s) is always to be written in full (i.e. it is not to be abbreviated). The author's name is to be followed by the year of publication of the name, separated from the author's name by a comma: this enables the reader to distinguish between the author of a taxon and a casual reference to a publication. The name of author and the year of publication are to be placed in parenthesis if a species-group taxon was originally established in a different genus from that in the current combination; this rule is important only in purely taxonomic papers and useless in all other publications. The use of brackets implies that the name indicated was published annonymously and is attributed to the author(s) and/or year of publication cited. Examples: *Hipparchia leighebi* KUDRNA, 1976, indicates that the taxon was originally established in the genus *Hipparchia* FABRICIUS, 1807. *Parnassius apollo* (LINNAEUS, 1758) indicates that the taxon was originally established in combination with a generic name other than *Parnassius*, LATREILLE, 1804. *Parnassius apollo* (KUDRNA 1985) indicates that the species is cited in the publication stated. *Papilio alcyone* [DENIS & SCHIFFERMÜLLER, 1775] indicated that the taxon was established in an annonymous publication attributed to the authors and year of publication stated; *Hipparchia alcyone* [(DENIS & SCHIFFERMÜLLER, 1775)] show that the taxon was established annonymously in combination with other generic name than *Hipparchia* FABRICIUS, 1807.

There are no strict rules as to the choice of typeface to be used for the names of author's in taxonomic (and other) publications. Nonetheless, the use of a distinct typeface for all authors' names enables them to be distinguished from the text, like the use of italics for genus-group and species-group names. The use of small capitals is ideal for the purpose (better than capitals) and has become customary in various countries. It would be advantageous if editors of entomological and other journals unanimously adopted this custom.

The type series of a species-group taxon consists of all specimens included by the author in the new nominal taxon, except any specimens which the author expressly excluded from the type series. If the author of a nominal species-group taxon makes no specific designation of the name-bearing type, each specimen of the type series is the syntype of the newly established taxon. If the author of a nominal taxon designates a single specimen as the name-bearing type in the original publication when establishing the name, this specimen is the holotype and the rest of the type series are the paratypes of the taxon (the designation must be published, mere labelling of a specimen in a collection is not adequate for the designation of a holotype). If the taxon is based on a single specimen, this single specimen is automatically the holotype. If the type series contains more than one specimen and a holotype has not been designated, any subsequent author may in a publication designate one of the syntypes as the lectotype; the remaining syntypes become paralectotypes. If in exceptional circumstances specified by the Code it becomes necessary to objectively define a taxon by means of a name-bearing type and the holotype, lectotype or all syntypes of the taxon are beyond reasonable doubt believed lost, any author undertaking revisory work may designate a neotype; it must be the property of a recognized public research or educational institution upon the publication of the designation. Neotypes designated as a matter of curatorial routine, deposited in private collections or which have failed to fulfill other conditions prescribed by the Code have no standing. In certain countries some authors prefer to select one specimen from the type series, the sex of which is the opposite to the holotype, and to "designate" it as the allotype of the taxon; as allotypes are not recognized under the Code, the specimen retains the status of any other paratype. It is strongly recommended to refrain from such useless "designations".

It is customary to indicate in a taxonomic publication all changes of the rank or status of the names proposed and taxa treated by the author. There is a standard system of abbreviations placed after the name of the author(s) of the taxon concerned, printed usually in bold letters, which indicate such changes of taxonomic or nomenclatural status. They are:

| | |
|---|---|
| nom. | nomen, name |
| gen. | genus |
| subgen. | subgenus |
| sp. | species (occasionally spp. as plural) |
| ssp., subsp. | subspecies (occasionally sspp. as plural) |
| stat. | status |
| comb. | combination |
| n., nov. | novus, nova, new |

syn.                    synonym
rev.                    revalidated, reinstated
The meaning of some typical combinations of these abbreviations is as follows:
sp. n., n. sp.          new species
ssp. n., n. ssp.        new subspecies
nom. n., nom. nov       new (replacement) name
comb. n.                species-group name is being placed in a genus with
                        which it has not been associated before
stat. n.                change of rank among taxa of the species-group (sub-
                        species elevated to species and vice versa)
syn. n.                 new synonym

It is to be noted that terms nomen nudum, nomen oblitum and nomen
dubium are not to be abbreviated. The use of possesive pronouns such as
mihi and nobis occasionally used to indicate the authorship of new taxa is
to be avoided, it being unnecessary.

In the past, countless infrasubspecific forms of European butterflies
have been named. Their names are unavailable (excluded) under the
Code. Infrasubspecific names are:

- Names proposed for teratological specimens as such.
- Names proposed for hybrids as such.
- Names for aberrations as such.
- Names for individual, seasonal, sexual and similar forms, which are es-
  sentially applicable only to a part of a local population, even if proposed
  in a trinominal original combination.
- Names proposed in quadrinominal original combinations, for instance of
  races, subraces or varieties.

Also the category "natio", which is rarely used in lepidopterology, implies
the infrasubspecific status.

Names for "forms", "varieties" or "races" proposed in trinominal original combinations have been a cause of concern and instability in zoological
nomenclature for many years. Under the Code, they can be treated either
as subspecific or infrasubspecific according to the circumstances, if they
were originally proposed before 1961. In principle, if they were originally
proposed specifically for a part of a local population, they are to be treated
as infrasubspecific, if they were proposed for the whole local population or
if this is not unequivocally established, they are to be treated as subspecific
names and are therefore available under the Code. Because an infrasubspecific name if elevated to the subspecific rank, takes the author-

ships and date of publication according to the publication containing the act of their elevation, it is often advantageous to treat all "potentially" available "infrasubspecific/subspecific" names proposed before 1961 generously.

If a name originally proposed for a taxon of a species-group later proves to be infrasubspecific (e.g. to be referrable to a hybrid), it remains available.

According to the present Code, the agreement in gender beween the generic and the specific name in a combination must be maintained, exactly as the previous editions prescribed. This most unfortunate rule has been the cause of numerous pointless changes of the ending of many species-group names in the past; it is very often ignored by many taxonomists.

The International Commission on Zoological Nomenclature maintains four indexes containing citations of names and works rejected by the Commission for the purpose of zoological nomenclature. The names contained in these publications are unavailable, unless the Commission by the use of its plenary powers rules otherwise. The full titles of these four indexes are:

– Official Index of Rejected and Invalid Works in Zoological Nomenclature;
– Official Index of Rejected and Invalid Family-Group Names in Zoology;
– Official Index of Rejected and Invalid Generic Names in Zoology;
– Official Index of Rejected and Invalid Specific Names in Zoology.

All four indexes are usually abbreviated: "Official Index".

The Commission also maintains four lists containing citations of available names and works, that have been ruled upon by the Commission; the results of these rulings were published in the Opinions:

– A name entered in the Official List is an available name even if it lacks any officially required qualifications;
– If a name entered in an Official List is thought to be a junior synonym of another available name (whether included in the Official List or not), the Principle of Priority is to apply–unless the Commission rules otherwise or has already done so.

The full titles of the four Official Lists are:

– Official List of Works Approved as Available for Zoological Nomenclature;
– Official List of Family-Group Names in Zoology;
– Official List of Generic Names in Zoology;

– Official List of Specific Names in Zoology.
All four lists are usually abbreviated: "Official List".

The rulings of the Commission are published in the Opinions of the Commission. The Opinions, as well as the applications by zoologists for the use of the plenary powers, are published in the Commission's Bulletin of Zoological Nomenclature (Bull. zool. Nomencl.). The address of the Commission is: International Commission on Zoological Nomenclature, c/o British Museum (Natural History), Cromwell Road, London SW7 5BD, Great Britain.

## 4.3 Taxonomic categories and their pragmatic application

A taxonomic category is a group of real organisms sufficiently distinct to be worthy of recognition as a formal unit at any level in the hierarchic classification (MAYR 1969). As any other theoretic concept also the taxon (i.e. taxonomic category) must be definable. In order to keep the category as objective as possible, the elements of its definition must correspond with the data available on the great majority of taxa potentially referable within the unit of classification concerned.

There are two basic groups of taxonomic categories recognized in zoological taxonomy: the higher taxonomic categories (i.e. the genus and higher) and the lower taxonomic categories (i.e. the species and lower). All taxonomic categories higher than genus are excluded from the discussion here as they are of little significance for the conservation of butterflies and they cannot be proparly studied on European material alone.

The genus

**Definition:** Genus is a taxonomic category containing a single species or a [presumably] monophyletic group of species, which is separated from other related taxa of the same rank (i.e. closely related genera) by a decided gap. (MAYR 1969).

The genus is the lowest category of higher taxonomy and practically the most important taxonomic category after the species. The genus-group name together with the species-group name forms a binomen which is adequate to denote and represent any one nominal animal species. The correct delimitation of a genus is based on the taxonomic examination of all potentially congeneric species, regardless of their distribution. Every such group of species must both exhibit certain features common to all of them and other features separating them from all similar closely related groups by a decisive gap. The identification of such a gap is often difficult and not only because of the number of species that may be involved. The genus should be a well balanced compromise based on an aggregate of characters such as the internal homogenity, size (expressed in the number of subordinate species), the presence of a decisive gap separating it from all other genera and, last but not least, its usefulness to biologists, not only to a narrow circle of specialists (EHRLICH & MURPHY 1982).

There is, unfortunately, no entirely objective way for the taxonomist to make an unequivocal judgement as to the delimitation of a genus. For the non-taxonomist, the intergeneric differences are often of lesser importance than a distinctive generic name and homogenous appearance of the congeneric species. The generic name represents for him a distinct group of species and saves thus both the necessity to memorize their names and to remember that they are all of approximately the same order. The genus *Erebia* in spite of its size contains a group of externally unusually homogenous species and all attempts to split it to subgenera failed although they can be better morphologically defined than morphologically homogenous and externally distinct species-groups of the morphologically extremely homogenous yet externally heterogenous genus *Polyommatus,* which has already been successfully split into several so called genera (e.g. HIGGINS 1976, HIGGINS & RILEY 1970, 1980) which totally lack constant taxonomic characters and cannot be properly defined.

Geographical distribution is of less than secondary significance in the delimitation of a genus: the pierid genera *Colias* and *Gonepteryx* are both closely related and equally well defined yet the former inhabits Europe, Asia, Africa, N. America and reaches S. America while the latter is, except for reaching south-eastern Asia, peculiar to the Palaearctic region. The geological age of congeneric species and their geographic history are the primary factors influencing the range. Useful supplementary characters can often be found in the ecology of the congeneric species that are likely to use similar elementary biotic and abiotic components, although these may well be peculiar to distinct habitat types.

The genus has recently become the subject of splitting into small, occasionally monotypic, units erected according to slight morphological differences (or even no differences at all) normally used to separate morphologically distinct congeneric species, often without any apparent reason. HIGGINS (1978) split a rather weak yet quite useful genus *Euphydryas* into four genera of which two live in Europe: *Eurodryas* and *Hypodryas*; characteristically perhaps, he gave no reason for his action (EHRLICH & MURPHY 1982). Such actions are particularly dangerous in applied taxonomy as the non-specialists using the new "genera" cannot make their own judgement, and are not even expected to do so.

Because of its significance in applied taxonomy stability and a certain amount of healthy conservativism in the generic taxonomy and nomenclature are certainly advantageous for all parties involved (EHRLICH & MURPHY 1982). Only a conservative approach to generic nomenclature can secure nomenclatorial stability. Several corrections at generic level have been made in the checklist of European butterflies forming a part of this chapter, to reestablish well defined genera.

## The subgenus

Subgenus is an optional taxonomic category inserted in parenthesis between the genus-name and the species-name to imply that it is not nomenclatorially obligatory. It is occasionally useful to taxonomists to distinguish groups of supposedly morphologically closely related congeneric species and could be employed in the construction of identification aids, if the decisive constant taxonomic characters are apparent. The usefulness of the subgenus may increase in large genera rich in species, although the use of subgeneric names is never a necessity and may become a burden. For the non-taxonomist the subgenus is of no interest whatsoever. Consequently, all subgeneric names are simply placed in synonymy in the check-list of European butterflies in this work. Taxonomist's views and subjective judgements play a considerably greater role in his recognition of subgenera than in the case of genera.

## The species

**Definition:** Species is a group of actually or potentially interbreeding populations which are reproductively isolated from other such groups (MAYR 1969).

There are two distinct schools of thought relevant to the butterflies which both use the term species (i.e. the biospecies and the morphospecies or phenon) for in principle entirely different but in practice overlapping or even identical entities. The above definition is characteristic of the so called 'biological species concept', i.e. the biospecies. This concept places stress on the reproductive isolation between the distinct species, induced by a genetic programme, a phenomenon particularly well apparent in comparative taxonomic studies of sibling species. Although the biological data are the final proof of the species-rank, it is the availability of the morphological data that is (additionally) required for the recognition of species in the majority of cases. The morphological characters that help to separate *Colias hyale* from *C. alfacariensis* are in most cases adequate for the recognition of set specimens (in spite of some degree of overlap), yet only the biological information shows that the two taxa are two distinct reproductively isolated species. Morphological differences between *C. alfacariensis* and *C. hyale* hardly exceed the infraspecific variation found in other species of the genus *Colias* except for the larvae which are very distinct indeed. There appears to be the same or even greater degree of overlap in the morphological variation of *Maculinea alcon* and *M. rebeli* (KAABER 1964), but it is the biological information that points unmistakeably to the specific status of the two taxa: each species requires peculiar highly specialized and clearly distinct ecological factors and habitat. *M. rebeli* is a xerophil, inhabiting screes and sparse grasslands almost regardles of altitude (i.e. with a span of well over 1,000 m) and its only larval foodplant is *Gentiana cruciata* (monophag); *M. alcon* is a hygrophil, inhabiting wet traditionally managed meadows with plentiful larval foodplant *G. pneumonanthe* (monophag) and is never found at higher altitudes; both species are myrmecophilous but the information available does not allow one to draw a distinct line between the two species from this point of view. Both species are very local, surely primarily owing to the rarity of their respective habitats, hostplants and life histories, and their sympatric (and synchronic) occurrence has never been recorded, and is very unlikely, although it cannot be entirely ruled out. The hypothetical hybrid off-spring of the hypothetical crossing of these two species would presumably be adapted to a broader gradient of habitats than either of the parent species; this would place the hypothetical hybrids at a distinct disadvantage in competition with the parent species for the highly specialized habitats. Such hypothetical hybrids, even if partially fertile and capable of surviving under laboratory conditions, would have negligible chances of survival and reproduction in nature.

The assessment that a taxon is a biospecies depends on the availability of biological information on the taxa compared; this can occasionally be substituted for the evidence that the taxa compared are sympatric and synchronic in at least a part of their ranges, and the knowledge that a biospecies is likely to develop a certain degree of morphological distinctiveness (CAIN 1971). It must not be overlooked that the distinct morphological features comparatively studied by the taxonomist, and usually utilized for the identification of nominal species, are only exceptionally identical with those properties that separate them in nature and prevent their interbreeding. Only WILKINSON (1981) seems to believe that morphological characters evolve first in the process of speciation; unfortunately he (WILKINSON 1981) failed to provide any supporting material for his hypothesis.

The genitalia, particularly of males, are known to provide perhaps the most reliable morphological taxonomic characters in the butterflies (PETERSEN 1904), particularly at the genus and species levels. Yet the distinctive structures of genitalia are very unlikely to serve as a mechanical barrier between closely related (i.e. certainly at least all congeneric) species, so far as the size of male and female apparatus is compatible. Also pairings between the species of two distinct genera have been observed: GEIGER (1977) described a copulation (in nature) of species as distinct as *Aphantopus hyperantus* and *Maniola jurtina,* and OLIVER (1971) reported a copulation between *Lasiommata megera* and *Pararge aegeria,* the latter two genera being taxonomically much closer than the former pair. LOR-KOVIC (1955) removed specifically distinct parts of valvae of males of *P. brassicae, P. rapae, Gonepteryx rhamni, Erebia stirius* and *E. styx,* and subsequently achieved successful artificial copulations with the corresponding females. This most interesting experiment and its rather surprising results point to two different conclusions:

● The individual structures of male genitalia are not of the same functional significance (uncus is probably functionally more important than the often so prominent valvae), and, above all,

● The absence of certain species-specific structures does not prevent a successful copulation (i.e. the variation in shape and/or in size of such structures is unlikely to be functionally specific, that is a successful mating between two species with distinct valvae is mechanically possible).

It is interesting to note that also in case of intergeneric mating reported by GEIGER (1977) and OLIVER (1971) the "substituted" males have similar uncus and overall size of genitalia and very distinct valvae. The significance of phallus or aedoeagus has never been investigated.

It is therefore of utmost importance for a pragmatic taxonomist to try to understand and evaluate the differences between closely related taxa at species-rank (i.e. the potential species) from "their" point of view, i.e. to discover the features used by the species themselves to recognize their own identities. The morphological characters, regardless of how constant they may be, are here only of secondary importance, being entirely overshadowed by the biological factors such as the behaviour (e.g. courtship), chemical factors (e.g. pheromones) and the genetic disposition of the species studied, where the ethological aspects alone are probably adequate to control sexual relationship among sympatric and synchronic species.

Also the existence of sibling species is a proof of the secondary importance of morphology for the recognition of species. Although it is usually possible to find an aggregate of morphological features that enable the identification of distinct sibling species (CAIN 1971), these are usually so "insignificant" to the observer that such species are mostly discovered through the study of their biology and early stages; precisely such studies led to the discoveries by BERGER (1946, 1948) of *Maculinea rebeli* and *Colias alfacariensis*. It may be expected that a systematic and methodical study of the biology and early stages of European butterflies will bring about further similar discoveries.

A useful but elaborate means of assessing the genetic compatibility are electrophoretic studies (e.g. BALLETTO & TOSO 1980) based on purpose collected live or fresh deep-frozen material. Karyological examination, too, presents some appreciable difficulties as well as often interesting results (ROBINSON 1978); bearing in mind that the chromosome numbers are often very similar among closely related or even congeneric species, and that the chromosomes in Lepidoptera are very small and their numbers often rather high, it is frequently very difficult to come to positive conclusions and unequivocal statements. Identical numbers of chromosomes among closely related species are no exception and very similar karyotypes among closely related congeneric species may well contribute to human errors in counting: under the circumstances it is not easy to decide as to whether the two slightly different counts are to be seen as a proof of the specific status of two taxa, or as a human error. Some examples (ROBINSON 1978):

*Brenthis daphne* and *B. ino*: n = 13/14 (both species are morphologically well separated in Europe but appear to be sibling species in Japan);

*Colias alfacariensis, C. erate, C. hyale* and *C. poliographus*: n = 31 (*C. alfacariensis* and *C. hyale* are sibling species, *C. erate* very closely related to them and possibly conspecific with *C. poliographus*);

*Polyommatus albicans, P. hispana* and *P. coridon*: n = 82, 84 and 88 respectively (the differences are small in relation to the possible human error in counting)

*Polyommatus dorylas*: n = 131–148 (results of four various counts by two different authors).

An objective evaluation of morphological characters–including an assessment of their actual or potential significance in the biology of the species concerned–is never an easy task. It is surely safe to assume, that the taxonomic significance of a morphological character grows proportionally with its biological importance for the species. An interesting example is the so called "hidden wing pattern" found in some groups of butterflies.

Butterflies, as many other insects, are able to perceive the so called "black light"–UV light of 365 nm. Some butterfly species look in the visi-

ble light entirely different from in the (to human eyes) invisible light spectrum. It can be assumed, that the hidden wing pattern contributes towards
the mutual recognition by different species, if the differences are clear and
considerable. Small variations of the hidden wing pattern are unlikely to be
registered by butterflies because their eyes, like other insects, can view
shapes rather as a mosaic than sharply and distinctly outlined (MAZOKHIN-
PORSHNYAKOV 1969). The hidden wing pattern is still inadequately known
at present. Taxonomic groups exhibiting distinct, often species specific,
hidden wing pattern include genera *Pieris, Colias, Gonepteryx* and
*Polyommatus* (cf. fig. 31, 32).

Fig. 31. Visible (left) and hidden (right) wing pattern in males: of the genus *Gonepteryx*: (a) *G. cleopatra*, (b) *G. rhamni*, (c) *G. farinosa*. Note: left wings of *G.
cleopatra* show an interesting assymetric malformations of the pattern. (Slightly
reduced).

Fig. 32. Visible (left) and hidden (right) wing pattern in females of the genus *Gonepteryx*: (a) *G. cleopatra*, (b) *G. rhamni*, (c) *G. farinosa*. (Slightly reduced.). Techniques utilized to take this and the previous photograph are briefly mentioned in the text.

Laboratory experiments are often very helpful in furthering our understanding of biological species and speciation in the butterflies and the artificial crossing has often been used with advantage. However, these experiments must remain more or less arbitrary. Experiments with various stocks of *Pieris napi* complex have shown a surprisingly high degree of fertility between some of the paired taxa, occasionally beyond the $F_1$ hybrids, although they do not produce hybrids in nature, surely because of some effective isolation between them. Some hybrid males from laboratory crossings have shown on examination crippled, deformed or deficient androconia which are not found in specimens captured in nature (BOWDEN 1971, WARREN 1971), and which would hardly stand a chance of surviving outside the laboratory. Two closely related allopatric species paired in captivity are known to produce entirely different results under apparently similar conditions: in experimenting with *Pieris brassicae* and *P. cheiranthi* one breeder succeeded in obtaining highly fertile hybrids, two other breeders failed completely (KUDRNA 1973). It seems that the interpretation of breeders results obtained in captivity requires caution.

The minimal biological information necessary to facilitate classification of material according to the biological species concept is not available for more than 50% of European butterfly species, and that even if the standards are set very low. Outside Europe, in the entomologically less well known parts of the world, the proportion of biological data available is much lower, as well as in the less studied taxonomic groups. None the less, taxonomists must identify and classify poorly known samples of material and CAIN (1971) pointed out that more than 75% of animal species are known only from specimens deposited in zoological collections. The taxonomic category appropriate for groups of reasonably uniform samples of specimens which can be separated from the samples of other such units is the morphospecies, which occupies in the taxonomic hierarchy the same level as the biospecies, acting as a substitute for the latter category until the availability of biological data enables a more accurate assessment and reclassification.

Morphological species (i.e. morphospecies, or a phenon of some authors) are the basic units in classification. In the butterflies, morphospecies are more likely to be a morphological aggregate of more than one biospecies than vice versa, although it may well happen that males and females of a biospecies are classified and described at first as two distinct morphospecies, particularly in cases of negligible or insufficient specimen data availability. Without the utilization of the morphospecies, it would hardly be possible to carry out taxonomic revisions, compile catalogues and faunal lists, describe and differentiate genera and other higher taxonomic categories. Also in applied taxonomy the morphospecies continues to have an indispensible role in so far as it cannot be replaced by the biospecies. To appreciate both its advantages and its drawbacks it is necessary to remember one of the most imperative criteria of any classification system:

● Every taxonomic category reflects the data available for the majority of taxa classified,

i.e. it is less confusing to relate a homogenous sample of specimens correctly on its own actual merits then to speculate on its potential biological relationship with one of the morphologically closely related morphospecies (or biospecies), and subsequently give the aggregate the dubious rank of "subspecies" – contradicting thus all basic principles of zoological classification. One example must suffice here: although HIGGINS & RILEY (1980) must have been aware that the biological relationship of two well separated allopatric morphospecies *Gonepteryx cleopatra* and *G. cleobule* is unknown (KUDRNA 1975), they prefered to speculate and considered them conspecific.

It must also be remembered that where there is evolution, there must also be border-line cases of speciation, which are neither "full" species, nor subspecies. Simple use of a trinominal combination to denote them cannot express their status or relationship to closely related taxa; this must be made on their merits, and information available to the taxonomist concerned; the binomen is adequate to distinguish them from all other animal species.

## The superspecies and semispecies

**Definition:** Superspecies is a monophyletic group of closely related and largely or entirely allopatric species. The individual "component" species of the superspecies may be called semispecies (cf. MAYR 1969). Note: the term semispecies is not unequivocal as it is also used to denote various species-like border line cases of speciation characterized by restricted fertility (LORKOVIC 1958).

There is almost indefinite variation of the degree of affinity among the species of a genus, as well as various degrees in the evolution of each of these species. The superspecies and semispecies are the two best known of the so called "modern taxonomic categories" (e.g. BERNARDI 1980, BERNARDI & MELVILLE 1979) which attempt to express graphically by means of a combination of names their order of relationship. The drawback common to all such categories is the general lack of precise data required by the definition of any and each of these units, which make them subjective and not universally applicable.

The perfection and multiplication of lower taxonomic categories could contribute to the advancement of the general understanding of relationships among animal species (and the like)–perhaps at the cost of confusion owing to their subjectivity–only if based on the real improvement of the universal data availability for all (or at least for the decisive majority) of taxa concerned. Unilateral improvements made to the taxonomic categories are nothing more than an academic exercise without much practical application.

For the practical taxonomist these categories are, therefore, of little use, and, to avoid the confusion which they are likely to bring with them, better avoided. They are not necessary to denote a taxon and cannot be substituted for a verbal explanation of its taxonomic affinities and systematic position.

### The subspecies

**Definition:** Subspecies is an aggregate of phenotypically similar populations of a species, inhabiting a geographic subdivision of the species' range, and differing taxonomically from other populations of that species (MAYR 1969). Note: the word species is to be understood as a biospecies and implies at least potential interbreeding between the populations referable to distinct subspecies.

During the second half of the 19th century some lepidopterists became increasingly aware that apart from a degree of individual variation within a population of a species, samples of what they believed to be one species (i.e. morphospecies, or phena, defined by superficial characters in a rather perfunctory and inconsistent mode) which came from different parts of the species range, exhibited certain distinct external features, common to each and every one of the samples (e.g. an aggregate from Greece differed from the one from Italy, and the nominate form described from yet another country). At first each aggregate was usually called varietas and named, towards the end of the last and the beginning of this century, this term was replaced by that of subspecies and became fully established as such around 1910. As each subspecies was believed to be peculiar to a certain definite part of the species range, the aspect of geographical exclusivism became the dominating feature of the category. The degree of understanding and availability of samples of material supported the typological thinking of that period. Nobody found it surprising that samples from various parts of a nominal species range differed from each other and retained some features common to all of them. Many of these taxa have since proved to belong to distinct biospecies and their original lumping into one unit was the result of perfunctory examination. Thus all allopatric morphospecies and sympatric biospecies of the *Hipparchia semele* species-group were treated as subspecies of *H. semele* until their genitalia were examined for the first time (LATTIN 1949). During the early part of the 20th century the numbers of described and named subspecies kept growing at an alarmingly escalating rate. H. FRUHSTORFER (1866–1922) named within less than 15 years (i.e. the period when he was predominantly interested in Palaearctic butterflies) some 400 new subspecies of Papilionoidea from Europe alone, an area on the margin of his interests as a collector and former dealer. R. VERITY (1883–1959) named in all over 1,500 new taxa of Papilionoidea, mostly from Europe and in their majority either directly or by implication of subspecies-rank (KUDRNA 1983). REISS & TREMEWAN (1967) recognized some 120 subspecies of the burnet *Zygaena carniolica* SCOPOLI, 1763, mostly from Europe. It is quite impossible to guess the number of subspecies described and validly named of *Parnassius apollo* and their cataloguing would require a considerable amount of research; subspecies of *P. apollo* have been described from localities where this species never occurred in recent times, just from a few specimens offered by dealers to the more enthusiastic authors. The original descriptions are only very exceptionally adequate to pinpoint the taxon named therein and the examination of the type-material, if still available is the only way to find out the taxon's identity. The past inflation of subspecies-rank names led to such confusion in all popular groups of butterflies that subspecies names can be used only in those rare groups of species where a thorough comprehensive and up-to-date taxonomic revision is available. Over the last 50 years only the following revisions of genera including European species have been published: *Erebia* (WARREN 1936), *Coenonympha* (DAVENPORT 1941), *Melitaea* (HIGGINS 1941, 1955), *Boloria* (WARREN 1944), *Euphydryas* (HIGGINS 1950), *Gonepteryx* (NEKRUTENKO 1968, KUDRNA 1975) and *Hipparchia* (KUDRNA 1977). These genera contain less than 20% of all European species and the revisions are not necessarily up-to-date.

The subspecies is the product of a simple and now obsolete typological way of thinking, perhaps contributed to by the belief that allopatry is synonymous with geographical exclusivism. The concept overlooks the fact that it is not the area but its environment that implies pressures on the animal populations inhabiting them, pressures which under some circumstances may lead towards the populations concerned becoming divergent on aggregate from closely related, and presumably conspecific populations inhabiting territories where they are exposed to different environmental strains, and to survive, must develop a different trend of evolution. There is no particular reason why their internal adaptiveness should be supplemented under all circumstances, i.e. in every complex of similar environmental pressures, additionally by constantly distinct combination of morphological features in every such unit. *Aricia eumedon* inhabits two entirely different types of habitats in central Europe. The majority of populations are confined to wetlands where they live in sheltered sunny places (e.g. along ditches in shallow depressions) in traditionally managed meadows and pastures with a massive occurrence of *Geranium palustre* and *G. pratense*; a (not negligible) minority of populations lives in C. Europe in sheltered places in sparse sunny woodlands, particularly on sandy soils, and their larval foodplant is *G. sylvaticum*. There are no constant morphological features that would facilitate the separation of hygrophilous and xerophilous populations and subsequent recognition of two different sub-species; set specimens cannot be referred to any of the two habitats without ecological data specifically provided. Also *Minois dryas* lives in two extreme habitat types which are geographically isolated, it being both a hygrophil and a xerophil, without having developed constant taxonomic features particular to any habitat type. There are other butterfly species featuring the same or similar properties.

The taxonomic category subspecies is a subject of contradictory concepts. The subspecies is defined through the evaluation of taxonomic characters (i.e. morphological features), for the degree of departure of which there is no objective yardstick. At the same time the subspecies is dependant on biological information (i.e. the genetic compatibility in nature of all subspecies within one biospecies), which is very rarely available, and only exceptionally proved in nature. Although the definition of subspecies given above (MAYR 1969) may appear rather vague, the minimal data necessary to secure correct (and constant) application of this definition are rarely available in butterflies. The subspecies are usually classified simply because the author concerned believed that their biological properties are as implied by the definition. The inclusion of additional data would only have an adverse effect as it would not be readily and universally available for the large majority of taxa classified.

The intended purpose of the subspecies is to enable the biologist (or the taxonomist) to give a precise reference to recognized constant infraspecific units and to show their relationship by means of a trinominal combination consisting of genus, species and subspecies names. Also in the relatively rare cases where the necessary data is available to facilitate judgement based both on the morphological and biological principles, the choice of the correct subspecies-rank names can only be made in the systematic groups for which fully up-to-date taxonomic revisions exist; such groups are few and far between, as already mentioned.

The assignment of aggregates of potentially interbreeding groups of populations to different subspecies presupposes the existence of more or less objective classification, and that their relationship can be expressed by a simple trinomen. If these two premises cannot be fulfilled the classification is useless from the practical point of view. If the morphological criteria for the recognition of subspecies vary considerably from taxonomist to taxonomist, their classification is unappliable by all non-specialists who are unable to make their own judgements, which is clearly not their primary task anyway. And this is the case more often than not. In north Wales (Great Britain) *Hipparchia semele* inhabits two somewhat different habitats: a wind swept Great Orme's Head peninsula is inhabited by a predominantly smaller form named ssp. *thyone,* which is said to be isolated by a narrow gap from the predominantly large *semele,* which is not much (taxonomically) distinct from the nominate form; a taxonomist acquainted with the British populations only is likely to treat the aggregates of both populations as separate subspecies. On the other hand, a taxonomist familiar with *semele* from northern Europe is aware that similar dwarf forms are found in other, but not all, wind swept coastal districts, e.g. in Sweden, where a very similar aggregate has been named ssp. *tristis.* Consequently, the latter taxonomist is unlikely to recognize *thyone* as a distinct subspecies (which may hurt national feelings). Furthermore, if he is aware of the pattern of infraspecific variation over the whole range of the species under consideration, it helps him to judge also the more extreme cases and to achieve as uniform and balanced results as possible in any given group. None the less, author-specific and therefore subjective views (i.e. "lumpers" versus "splitters") can produce entirely different classifications. BRYK (1940) recognized 45 subspecies of *Melitaea didyma* in his revision of the species. One year later and quite independently (i.e. unaware of the earlier revision) HIGGINS (1941) came to the conclusion that only five subspecies of *M. didyma* can be recognized. A taxonomist can make his own judgement after a careful reading of both revisions having first made himself familiar with the work of both authors and the nature of the variation in that species; subsequently, after much work, he is able to make his own opinion, which is likely to be similar to that of HIGGINS (1941), who has got as close to the truth as was possible under the circumstances. A nontaxonomist cannot make such a judgement and it is difficult to imagine how he could make any use of the two revisions.

Widespread species rarely produce distinct geographical forms. They may have some extreme forms but these blend with each other, as the biological nature of the subspecies dictates. The pattern of geographical variation of such species may be described as a mosaic with spots and stretches of varying intensity and size over a uniform background, blending into each other unless separated by barriers. These spots and stretches are extreme forms and clines. *Hipparchia semele* from many localities situated in south-alpine valleys is large and dark and has received numerous subspecies-rank names. Towards the east and west it blends with (taxonomically) distinct populations which (evolve) in long almost transcontinental cline southwards from the north European nominate form. The geological substrata of the locality influences in some areas the additionally distinct groundcolour of the underside of hindwing. In *Hipparchia statilinus* extreme populations differ quite strikingly from each other but they lack individual geographical exclusivism and the character of the variation is perhaps best described as pseudopolytypic (KUDRNA 1977). The segregation of phenotypic and genotypic forms, if they really exist in nature in such pure form, cannot be carried out without long term studies.

The purpose of using subspecific names is to denote apparently geographically denominated groups of populations of a nominal species. None the less, such forms can be described without being named and referred to directly by the name of the area they inhabit (WILSON & BROWN 1953). This system is simple, fulfils the purpose, is also understandable to non-taxonomists, and does not burden zoological nomenclature with further synonyms. *Arethusana arethusa boabdil* (RAMBUR, 1840) and *A. arethusa veleta* (FRUHSTORFER, 1908) are probably synonyms of the same taxon, described from the Sierra Nevada in southern Spain (the identity of *boabdil* is somewhat uncertain and the type-material is lost). Non-taxonomists are unlikely to understand the message coded into these two names, and their questionable identity which can be fixed only by the designation of neotype/s in a taxonomic revision. Contrary to this a simple statement such as '*Arethusana arethusa* from the Sierra Nevada' is easy to understand and, more over, unequivocal; it requires no special taxonomic action.

As one way out a term "major subspecies" has been utilized by various authors (e.g. HIGGINS & RILEY 1980) as if the degree of variation could be measured in real terms and taken as an expression of affinities between two taxa (cf. sibling species). Also BROWN (1977) overlooked that an incipient species (i.e. his own interpretation of the term subspecies) does not necessarily develop a distinct habitus before its biological and genetical properties become stabilized. What more is to be expected from an incipient species than inhabiting distinct ecological niches such as in *Minois dryas*?

The species is the only (natural) unit of zoological classification and a binomen consisting of the genus and species name is adequate to distinguish it from any other similar unit. The biological relationship and evolutionary trends within any given group of populations forming a specific unit are likely to prove more complicated than the most sophisticated linear system of names can express. The simplicity of the zoological system contributes positively towards its understanding and brings about objective universality, which is particularly needed among the non-taxonomists, who are the main and most important users of taxonomists' work. Consequently,

● subspecies is rejected as a taxonomic category not worthy of recognition in (applied) taxonomy,

and morphologically denominated taxonomic aggregates apparently distinct from other such units are treated on their individual merits as morphospecies. This simplification also contributes positively towards greater stability in zoological nomenclature.

Infrasubspecific taxa

Several thousand infrasubspecific forms have been named by collectors of European butterflies. Infrasubspecific names are unavailable according to the International Code of Zoological Nomenclature. Nevertheless, there are all kinds of inventive taxonomic categories used for infrasubspecific names and seriously intended systems and classifications have been presented to validate them usually because of the potential evolutionary significance of such forms (e. g. BERGMANN 1951, POVOLNY 1954, VERITY 1905–11, etc.).

Infrasubspecific names present the taxonomist working on a revision, catalogue or synopsis with an obstacle: he is obliged to make a list of them, study their original description to decide their status, and this again and again as many of these names have been raised to subspecific rank by subsequent authors, often incidentally. The proportion of infrasubspecific names is rather high, particularly concerning taxa described from Europe. Some problems concerning infrasubspecific names are discussed elsewhere in this work (cf. 4.2 and comments thereto), others were dealt with earlier (KUDRNA 1983).

There is no need whatsoever for the erection of infrasubspecific names: teratological and pathological "extreme individual" forms (4.2) are biologically irrelevant, and the same applies to all laboratory produced forms; seasonal forms, recurrent sexual forms can be called according to their properties (e.g. spring form, pale female form, etc.). Naming of individual forms is considered deplorable because they have no useful role in taxonomy.

Hybrids

According to the International Code of Zoological Nomenclature, names specifically proposed for hybrids are unavailable (i.e. they are excluded from the code), but the name remains available if it was later found actually to be a hybrid, as clearly stated in Articles 1; 17(2) and 24(c). In these circumstances it can hardly be expected from a legalistic document to distinguish between recurrent natural hybrids and the hybrid offspring resulting from experiments carried out by means of hand-pairing in captivity. Some aspects of hybridization have already been discussed: as to potential hybrids of ecologically and geographically distinct populations of two morphospecies, considered subspecies by some authors, it has been concluded that their chances of indefinite survival in nature are fairly small, if not negligible.

Quite a different situation may arise between two closely related species inhabiting the same habitat, using similar ecoelements and in some localities sympatric and synchronic. In some localities of east-central Spain (e.g. Prov. Teruel: Moscardon; Prov. Cuenca: Tramacastilla, etc.) *Polyommatus albicans* and *P. caelestissima* fly together and their flight periods overlap significantly. In these localities *Polyommatus caerulescens* is found, apparently a hybrid of the two species. It is recurrent, its abundance seems to vary from year to year and, certainly, from locality to locality (K. G. SCHURIAN pers. comm.). Similarly, in northern Spain (Prov. Burgos: Penahorada, Hontomin) *P. albicans* meets *P. asturiensis* and both species seem to hybridize regularly, though to a much lesser degree than in the case of *P. caerulescens*. It is not known–and has never been determined–if the hybrid *P. caerulescens* is fully or partially fertile, or, indeed, if they are infertile (the latter being least likely). Other similar examples are probably more common among european butterflies than has been anticipated so far. Unfortunately their study has been much neglected.

Recurrent natural hybrids are an important link in the evolution of species: they are potentially or actually "incipient species", very much worthy of both research and conservation. It is to be expected that there are some hybridogenic species among the European butterflies.

## 4.4 Glossary of common taxonomic terms

This alphabetically arranged glossary includes over 200 terms commonly used in the taxonomy of butterflies. Their definitions have been kept as brief as possible. They are based on standard taxonomic works including the Code. The glossary is intended also for the non-taxonomist. Morphological terms are excluded.

**Abbreviation:**–A shortening, usually writing a part of a word for a whole. Names of author(s) of taxa are not to be abbreviated. Generic names may be abbreviated in some circumstances by a single initial letter of the name. Specific names are not to be abbreviated. (cf.: World-List Abbreviation; Acronym).

**Aberration:**–An infrastubspecific taxonomic category; an individual form; names of aberrations are unavailable (excluded) under the Code.

**Acronym:**–A word formed from initial letters of other words, e. g. BMNH for British Museum (Natural History).

**Affinity:**–Relationship, e. g. of two taxa.

**Aggregate:**–(1) A group of species other than a subgenus within a genus.–(2) A group of subspecies within a species.–(3) A group of populations within a species.–An aggregate may be denoted by a species-group name interpolated in parenthesis. (cf.: Collective Name: Superspecies).

**Albinism:**–A substantial reduction or total absence of pigment in an individual. (cf. Melanism).

**Allochronic:**–Of species, populations, which do not occur at the same time. (cf.: Synchronic).

**Allopatric:**–Of species, populations, subspecies occupying mutually exclusive ranges, often adjacent, "replacing" each other in space. (cf. Parapatric; Sympatric).

**Allopatric speciation:**–A formation of a species during its period of isolation as opposed to sympatric speciation. (cf. Speciation; Sympatric speciation).

**Allotype:**–A term not recommended by the Code meaning a specimen, usually a paratype, of the sex opposite to the holotype.

**Anagram:**–A name formed by the rearrangement of the letters of a word or phrase.

**Apomorph:**–A derived or specialized character. (cf.: Plesiomorph).

**Archetype:**–A hypothetical ancestral type arrived at by the elimination of specialized characters.

**Artenkreis:**–(v. Superspecies).

**Availability; Available:**–(1) Of a publication: a work published after 1757 within a meaning of the Code.–(2) Of a name: a scientific name that is not exluded under Article 1(b) and conforms to Articles 10 to 20 of the Code. (cf.: Unavailable; Valid; Invalid).

**Bibliographical reference:**–A published citation referring to a publication.

**Binomen:**–A combination of two names–the first being a generic name and the second a specific name–constituting a scientific name of a species; interpolated names do not form a part of a binomen. (cf.: Interpolated names; Trinomen).

**Binominal nomenclature:**–A system of nomenclature whereby a species– and no other taxon–is denoted by a binomen.

**Biological race:**–Non-interbreeding sympatric populations differing in their biology, but only scarcely (or not at all) in their morphology, supposedly prevented from interbreeding by their ecological specialization.

**Biological species concept; Biospecies:**–A taxonomic concept of the species based on the reproductive isolation; morphological differences are not essential for this concept. (cf. Biomorphospecies; Morphospecies).

**Biomorphospecies:**–A taxonomic species-concept combining both the biospecies and morphospecies properties; scarcely used term. (cf.: Biospecies; Morphospecies).

**Biota:**–The flora and fauna of a region together.

**Brackets:** – A pair of marks [ ] usually called "square brackets". (cf.: Parenthesis).

**Catalogue:** – (1) An annotated checklist of taxa and their bibliography. – (2) An index of taxonomic literature arranged by taxa.

**Category:** – v. Taxonomic Category.

**Character displacement:** – A divergence of equivalent characters in sympatric populations of two or more species resulting from the selective effects of competition.

**Checklist:** – Usually a skeleton classification or a preliminary treatment of a group listed by taxa for quick reference.

**Circular overlap:** – A phenomenon in which a chain of contiguous intergrading populations curves back until the terminal links overlap geographically and behave as two noninterbreeding species.

**Cladism:** – A taxonomic theory arranging all organisms solely according to their recency of common descent, that is on the most recent branching of their phylogeny.

**Clinal:** – Of characters: varying gradually.

**Cline:** – A gradual change of a characters in a series of contiguous populations of a species.

**Collective name:** – A term not regulated by the Code denoting by the oldest specific name a presumable assemblage of at present not adequately recognizeable species. (cf. Complex).

**Colony:** – A population of a species inhabiting a given locality.

**Combination:** – An association of a generic name with a specific name or additionally a subspecific name forming a binomen or a trinomen (interpolated names not counted). (cf.: Original Combination).

**Competitive exclusion:** – The principle that two distinct species with identical ecological requirements cannot coexist in the same locality at the same time.

**Complex:** – Usually of species: a neutral term for a number of apparently closely related taxa difficult to classify. (cf.: Collective Name).

**Conditional:** – A proposal of a name or a type fixation, made with definitely stated reservations; a name proposed conditionally for a taxon after 1960 is unavailable.

**Congeneric:** – A term often applied to two or more species belonging to the same nominal genus. (cf.: Conspecific).

**Conserved name:** – A name previously unavailable or invalid that the Commission has enabled to be used as a valid name by a ruling removing the known obstacles of the use of the name as a valid name.

**Conspecific:** – A term often applied to populations or subspecies belonging to the same nominal species. (cf. Congeneric).

**Continuity:** – An obsolete system of zoological nomenclature by which the continued usage of names was to take precendence over priority of publication.

**Continuous variation:** – The way in which individuals differ from each other in infinitely small characters.

**Convergence:** – Morphological similarity in distantly related taxa. (cf.: Divergence).

**Cotype:** – A term excluded by the Code, formerly used by certain authors for syntypes and/or paratypes.

**Cryptic species:** – v. Sibling species.

**Date of publication:** – The date on which copies of the work became available by purchase or free distribution. (cf. Publication).

**Deem:** – To consider or rule something to be what it may or may not be.

**Definition:** – A statement in words that purports to give characters differentiating a taxon.

**Delimitation:** – In taxonomy a formal statement of the limits of one or more characters of a taxon.

**Deme:** – A community of potentially or actually interbreeding individuals in a given locality; a local population of a species.

**Derived character:** – A taxonomic character differing from the ancestral one; a specialized character. (cf. Apomorph; Plesiomorph).

**Description:** – A comprehensive formal statement of the characters of a taxon without special emphasis on those which can distinguish the taxon from other similar taxa; a statement in words of taxonomic characters of a specimen or a taxon.

**Designation:** – The nomenclatural act fixing by an express statement the name-bearing type of a previously or newly established nominal genus, subgenus, species or subspecies.

**Diacritic mark:** – A mark indicating a changed pronunciation of a letter; diacritic marks must not be used under the Code in zoological names.

**Diagnosis:** – A formal statement pointing out the characters in which a taxon is believed to differ from other taxa.

**Dichotomous:** – Divided or dividing into two parts, usually used of an identification key.

**Dichroism:** – v. Dimorphism.

**Differential diagnosis:** – v. Diagnosis.

**Dimorphism:** – Occurrence of two distinct morphological types in a single population of a species, e.g. seasonal dimorphism, sexual dimorphism.

**Discontinuous variation:** – The way in which individuals of each sample fall into definite groups which do not grade into each other.

**Divergence:** – Morphological distinctness of characters in closely related taxa. (cf.: Convergence).

**Ecological isolation:** – A condition in which interbreeding of two or more sympatric populations is believed to be prevented by their utilization of different ecological niches.

**Ecophenotypic variation:**–A nongenetic modification of a phenotype caused by specific ecological conditions of the environment.

**Ecotype:**–Phenotype ("ecological race") characteristic of a certain environment.

**Emendation:**–Any demonstrably intentional change in the original spelling of an available name, other than a mandatory change; only corrections of an incorrect original spelling constitute a justified emendation.

**Error:**–An incorrect spelling of a name (e.g. typing error, printer's error, copyist's error) other than an author's error. (cf.: Lapsus calami).

**Establish:**–To make available under the provision of the Code.

**Exerge:**–A term introduced by R. Verity to replace the subspecies and later applied by the same author to a "Formenkreis", usually denominated by the geographical area inhabited (e. g. south-western exerge); the Code misinterprets the exerge denoted by a scientific name for a group of subspecies, to be interpolated between the specific and subspecific name in a combination.

**Extant:**–A taxon having living representatives.

**Extinct:**–A taxon having no living representatives.

**Family-group:**–Collective term for the taxonomic categories and names of the superfamily, family, subfamily and tribe or any other category above and exclusive of the genus and below and inclusive of the superfamily.

**Family name:**–A name for a taxon at the rank of a family.

**Faunal work:**–A publication in which taxa are included on the basis of their occurrence in a given area, usually a comprehensive annotated inventory (e.g. faunal monograph).

**First reviser:**–The first author to subsequently cite names, including different original spellings of the same name, or nomenclatural acts published on the same date, and to choose one of them to have precedence over the other.

**Fixation:**–A general term for the determination (designation) of a name-bearing type.

**Form:**–(1) A group of individuals of a species differing in a certain way from other such groups and displaying certain features common to all of them. –(2) In zoological nomenclature a term that if published after 1960 always denotes a taxon of infrasubspecific rank (i.e. unavailable name) and if published before 1961 is deemed to denote a subspecific rank if applied to a population(s) as a whole. –(3) A neutral term for a group of individuals, a phenon or a taxon.

**Formenkreis:**–A neutral collective category of closely related taxa believed to be of subspecific status.

**Generic name:** – (1) A scientific name for a taxon of the rank of genus. – (2) The first name of a binomen or trinomen, always beginning with a capital letter and written in italics.

**Genotype:** – A term used in genetics, formerly used by some authors for a type-species; it is excluded under the Code.

**Genus:** – A taxonomic category including one or more species, presumably of common phylogenetic origin, which is separated from related similar taxonomic units (i.e. other genera) by a decisive gap.

**Genus-group:** – A group of taxonomic categories ranking between species group and family group and including both the genus and the subgenus.

**Genus-group name:** – A scientific name of a taxon of the rank of genus and/ or subgenus.

**Genus name:** – v. Generic name.

**Geographical isolate:** – A population separated by presumably impenetrable geographic barriers from the main body of the species concerned or an isolated species.

**Group:** – A neutral term for a number of related taxa, especially for an assemblage of closely related congeneric species.

**Gynandromorph:** – An individual in which one part of its body is male and the other female, usually divided bilaterally and incapable of reproduction. (cf.: Hermaphrodite).

**Hermaphrodite:** – An individual bearing both male and female sexual organs and often capable of reproduction. (cf.: Gynandromorph).

**Higher taxonomic category:** – A taxonomic category of a higher rank than that of a species-group.

**Holotype:** – A single specimen designated by an author establishing a species group taxon as the name-bearing type of the taxon and published together with the original description (i.e. when the taxon was established), or a single specimen if the taxon was based on a single specimen. It is the objective definition of the taxon.

**Homonym:** – One of two or more identical but independently proposed available names having the same spelling (or deemed to do so) and denoting two or more different nominal taxa within one taxonomic group (e.g. species-group). Of two homonyms the one established first is the senior homonym and the one established later the junior homonym. Primary homonyms were established in combination with the same generic name; secondary homonyms were established in combination with different generic names and subsequently brought together in the same genus.

**Homonymy:** – The relationship between two homonyms.

**Hybrid:** – The progeny of two individuals belonging to two different species (not two different subspecies of the same species). Names proposed specifically for hybrids are unavailable, but if a taxon originally established as a species or a subspecies later proves to be a hybrid, the name remains available.

**Hybrid belt:**–A zone of interbreeding between two usually essentially allopatric species.

**Hybridization:**–Crossing or interbreeding between individuals belonging to two different species.–Allopatric hybridisation: Interbreeding between two esentially allopatric species, usually along a narrow hybrid belt.–Sympatric hybridisation: Occasional interbreeding between individuals of two otherwise distinct sympatric species.

**Hyphen:**–(1) A mark joining a single latin letter to a noun and forming with that noun a species-group name, e.g. *Polygonia c-album.*–(2) A mark joining two or more nouns in a combination forming thus a compound name. This latter use of hyphen is not allowed under the Code and subsequent authors are obliged to treat hyphenated names as a single word, e.g. *Argynnis niobe alpiumsisenna-alpiumlaranda* VERITY, 1936, is to be corrected to *Argynnis niobe alpiumsisennaalpiumlaranda* VERITY, 1936, by the deletion of the hyphen.

**Hypothetical concept:**–A taxonomic concept–excluded under the Code–that when published contained no animal then known to exist in nature, past or present.

**Indication:**–A published information specified by the Code that in the absence of a description allows a name published before 1931, that otherwise satisfies the relevant provisions of the Code, to be available.

**Infraspecific name; infraspecific taxon:**–A general collective term for subspecific and infrasubspecific names and taxa.

**Infrasubspecific name; infrasubspecific taxon:**–(1) Of a rank of a taxon or name: one at the rank lower than that of a subspecies.–(2) A name after a trinomen that is not deemed to be subspecific or interpolated.

**Interpolated name:**–A name placed within parenthesis in a combination, but not constituting a counted element of a binomen or trinomen. Interpolated names may be placed (1) after a generic name to denote a subgenus; (2) after a genus-group name to denote an aggregate of species, such as a superspecies; (3) after a specific name to denote an aggregate of subspecies.

**Invalid name:**–An available name that is not valid under the Code, e.g. a junior synonym. (cf.: Valid name).

**Lapsus calami:**–An author's error, such as a misspelling of a name. (cf.: Error).

**Lectotype:**–A syntype designated as the single name-bearing type specimen subsequently to the establishement of a nominal species or subspecies concerned.

**Lumper:**–A taxonomist who emphasizes the mutual similarities and tends to recognize "larger" taxa. (cf.: Splitter).

**Manuscript name:**–A scientific name of a taxon unpublished under the Code. (cf.: Publication).

**Melanism:**–Substantially increased amount of black pigment in an individual, usually polymorphic or racial.

**Monophiletic:**–A taxon derived from a single immediately ancestral source. (cf.: Polyphiletic).

**Monotypic:**–A nominal taxon containing but one subordinate taxon, e.g. a genus containig only a single species.

**Monotypy:**–A condition of being monotypic.

**Morphological species concept; Morphospecies:**–A taxonomic concept recognizing a species merely on the basis of morphological difference. (cf.: Biological species concept; Biospecies).

**Name-bearing type:**–The type-genus; type-species; holotype; lectotype; complete series of syntypes together; neotype (whichever applicable); name-bearing type provides an objective standard of reference determining the application of the name concerned.

**Neotype:**–The single specimen designated as the name-bearing type of a nominal species or subspecies for which no holotype, lectotype or syntype(s) is believed to exist.

**Nomen conservandum:**–v. Conserved Name.

**Nomen dubium:**–A descriptive term meaning a name of unknown or uncertain application.

**Nomen novum:**–A new name established expressly to replace an already established name.

**Nomen nudum:**–A name that if published before 1931, fails to conform to Article 12 or if published after 1930 additionally fails to satisfy the condition on the Article 13 of the Code. In simple words, nomen nudum is a species-group name published without a definition, description or indication before 1931 and if published after 1930, not accompanied by a statement purporting to differentiate the taxon (an obligatory additional criterion).

**Nomen oblitum:**–A descriptive term meaning a forgotten name (a term not used in the present Code).

**Nominal taxon:**–A nomenclatural taxon denoted by an available name and based upon its name-bearing type (e.g. nominal species as a "real" taxon as compared to a "theoretical concept" of species).

**Nominate:**–A term used formerly in taxonomy and replaced by the term nominotypical in the present Code.

**Nominotypical taxon:**–A subordinate taxon bearing the same name as its immediately superior taxon and serving as its name-bearing type, e.g.

*Parnassius apollo apollo* (LINNAEUS, 1758) is the nominotypical subspecies of *Parnassius apollo* (LINNAEUS, 1758).

**Objective:** – Factual, not a matter of opinion; opposite of subjective.

**Opinion:** – A formal publication by the Commission containing a ruling that applies, interprets or suspends the provisions of the Code in nomenclatural cases specified.

**Original:** – Of a combination or designation: the one used when it was established. Example: Original combination of a taxon known as *Parnassius apollo* (LINNAEUS, 1758) is *Papilio apollo* LINNAEUS, 1758.

**Paralectotype:** – Each specimen of a former syntype-series remaining after the designation of the lectotype.

**Parapatric:** – Of closely related congeneric species which inhabit essentially mutually exclusive ranges and do not interbreed in zones of their overlap.

**Paratype:** – Each specimen from a type-series other than the holotype (if designated).

**Parenthesis:** – A pair of marks ( ) also called "round brackets" as distinct from "square brackets". (cf.: Brackets).

**Phenetic ranking:** – Classifying into categories strictly based on degree of overall similarity.

**Phenon:** – A sample of phenotypically similar specimens, often considered comparable with morphospecies.

**Phenotype:** – The totality of characteristics of the appearance of an individual as a result of interactions between genotype and environment.

**Plenary powers:** – The power of the Commission to suspend the provisions of Articles 1–75 of the Code in particular cases.

**Plesiomorph:** – A primitive or ancestral character. (cf.: Apomorph).

**Polymorphism:** – The simultaneous occurrence of two or more discontinuous phenotypes in a population.

**Polyphiletic:** – A taxon derived from two or more immediately ancestral sources. (cf.: Monophiletic).

**Polytopic:** – A taxon occurring in two or more widely separated localities or areas.

**Polytypic:** – A nominal taxon including two or more immediately subordinate nominal taxa, e.g. a genus including two or more subgenera or a species including two or more subspecies. (cf.: Monotypic).

**Pre-Linnean name:** – A name published before 1st January 1758, the deemed date of publication of 10th edition of Systaema Naturae, the starting point of zoological nomenclature.

**Preoccupied:** – Of a name already used for another taxon and based on a different type.

**Publication:** – A published work or the issuing of a book conforming to Articles 8 and 9 of the Code. (cf.: Date of Publication).

**Rank:** – The level of a taxon in the zootaxonomic hierarchy, e.g. all genera are of the same rank.

**Rassenkreis:** – Another term for a polytypic species.

**Recommendation:** – An advisory statement in an Article of the Code denoted by the number of the Article but distinguished from the mandatory provision by the addition of a capital letter after the number.

**Reject:** – To set aside a work for the purpose of zoological nomenclature.

**Rejected Name:** – A name of a taxon set aside in favour of another name of the taxon.

**Replacement name:** – (1) Any available name, usually a junior synonym, used to replace an older available name. – (2) A new name (nomen novum) established expressly to replace an already established name, assuming that there is not any other existing replacement name.

**Reprint:** – In zoological nomenclature the same as a separate.

**Reproductive isolation:** – A condition in which interbreeding between two or more populations is prevented by intrinsic factors.

**Revision:** – In taxonomy a comprehensive work including new material and/or interpretations integrated together with a comprehensive summary of our present knowledge of the taxonomic group concerned.

**Scientific name:** – A name for a taxon that conforms to Article 11(b) of the Code, as opposed to a vernacular name.

**Secondary homonym:** – Each of two or more homonyms established in a combination with different generic names but subsequently brought in one genus and combined with the same generic name. (cf.: Homonymy; Primary Homonym).

**Semispecies:** – (1) A component species of a superspecies. – (2) An aggregate of populations or a single population which has acquired some, but not yet all, attributes of the rank of a species. – (3) Borderline cases between species and subspecies.

**Separate:** – A copy of a work (contained in a periodical or serial publication or in a book) intended for distribution, usually by the author, independently from the periodical (serial or book) that contains it.

**Sexual dimorphism:** – A phenotypic difference between the two sexes of a species.

**Sibling species:** – Pairs or groups of closely related (congeneric) species which are reproductively isolated from each other, but remain morphologically identical or by and large inseparable.

**Speciation:** – The splitting of a philetic line or the acquiring of reproductive isolation between two or more groups of populations.

**Species:** – (1) A taxon at the rank of a species. – (2) The basic rank in zoological classification.

**Species-group:** – (1) A group of taxonomically closely related congeneric species. – (2) The taxa or names of the rank of species and subspecies together.

**Species-group name:** – A scientific name of a taxow of the rank of a species and/or subspecie.

**Species name; specific name:** – (1) A scientific name of a taxon of the rank of a species. – (2) The second name in a binomen or trinomen (interpolated names not counted).

**Specimen:** – An individual.

**Spelling:** – The choice and arrangements of the letters that form a word.

**Splitter:** – A taxonomist placing stress on the the division of taxa, often based on minimal differences.

**Subfamily:** – (1) A rank of the family-group below the family. – (2) A taxon of the rank of a subfamily.

**Subfamily name:** – A scientific name at the rank of a subfamily.

**Subgeneric name; subgenus name:** – A scientific name of a taxon of a rank of subgenus; if used in a combination, it is to be interpolated in parenthesis immediately after the generic name.

**Subgenus:** – (1) The rank of genus group below a genus. – (2) A taxon of the rank of a subgenus. – (3) An optional taxonomic category containing a group of presumably closely related species within a genus.

**Subjective:** – Depending upon a judgement; a matter of opinion; opposite of objective.

**Subordinate taxon:** – A taxon of a lower rank than the taxon of the same coordinate group it is compared with. (cf.: Superior taxon).

**Subsequent:** – Of an author, nomenclatural act, designation: after the nominal taxon concerned was established.

**Subspecies:** – A taxon of the rank of subspecies, usually defined as one of two or more potentially or actually interbreeding populations of a species, producing fertile offspring, inhabiting a definite subdivision of the species' range and differing taxonomically from other such groups.

**Subspecies name; subspecific name:** – A scientific name of a taxon of the rank of subspecies or a trinomen (interpolated names not counted).

**Substitute name:** – v. Replacement name.

**Superfamily:** – (1) A rank of the family-group above a family. – (2) A taxon of the rank of a superfamily. – (3) The highest rank at which names are regulated by the Code.

**Superfamily name:** – A name of a taxon of the rank of superfamily.

**Superior taxon:** – A taxon of a higher rank than the taxon of the same coordinate group it is compared with. (cf.: Subordinate taxon).

**Superspecies:** – A monophiletic group of essentially allopatric closely related congeneric species; the individual component species of a superspecies are often called semispecies.

**Suppression:** – The use by the Commission of its plenary powers to rule that (1) a work is unavailable for nomenclatural purposes, or (2) that an available name is either never to be used as a valid name or its use as a valid name is subject to specific conditions stated by the Commission, and (3) that a nomenclatural act is invalid.

**Suppressed name:** – A name totally, partially or conditionally suppressed by the Commission. (cf.: Suppression).

**Sympatric hybridization:** – Occasional production of hybrids between individuals of otherwise well distinct sympatric species.

**Sympatric speciation:** – The acquisition of isolating mechanism within a deme. (cf.: Allopatric speciation).

**Synchronic:** – Of species or populations, which occur at the same time (cf. Allochronic).

**Synonym:** – Each of two or more scientific names of the same rank used to denote the same taxon. Senior synonym is the earlier established of two synonyms. Junior synonym is the later established of two synonyms. Objective synonyms are synonyms based on the same name-bearing type. Subjective synonyms are synonyms based on different name-bearing types.

**Synonymy:** – (1) The relationship between two or more synonyms. – (2) A list of synonyms denoting the same nominal taxon.

**Synopsis:** – In taxonomy, a brief summary of current knowledge of a taxonomic group or a taxon.

**Syntype:** – Each specimen of a type-series from which neither a holotype nor a lectotype has been designated. The complete series of syntypes (together) forms a name-bearing type.

**Systematics:** – The science studying and describing the diversity of organisms. (cf.: Taxonomy).

**Tautonymy:** – The use of the same word (i.e. of identical spelling) for a genus and one species or subspecies belonging therein.

**Taxon:** – Any taxonomic unit, whether named (e.g. *Papilio machaon* LINNAEUS, 1758) or not (e.g. a genus or a species). A taxon includes all subordinate taxa belonging therein (e.g. a genus includes all species implied by the generic name concerned, a species all conspecific subspecies). (cf.: Nominal taxon).

**Taxonomic category:** – A scientific concept to which taxa are assigned for the purpose of classification. (cf.: Nominal Taxon).

**Taxonomic character:** – Any feature (or attribute) of a member of a taxon by which it differs from members of a different taxon.

**Taxonomic hierarchy:** – A system of classification based on taxa of decreasing inclusiveness.

**Taxonomic monograph:** – An exhaustive treatment (mostly) of a higher taxon, usually well beyond that of a taxonomic revision. (cf.: Revision).

**Taxonomy:** –The theory and praxis of classifying organisms, often considered the same as classification. (cf.: Systematics).

**Teratological specimen:** –An abnormal specimen or a monstrosity, in lepidopterology often called aberration.

**Termination:** –The ending of a species-group name required by the Latin grammar to conform to the grammatical gender of the generic name concerned.

**Topotype:** –A term not regulated by the Code, often applied to a specimen originating from the type-locality of a species or subspecies, to which it is deemed to belong; it is neither a type nor a member of the type-series concerned. (cf.: Type; Typoid).

**Trinomen:** –A trinominal combination consisting of generic, specific and subspecific names (interpolated names not counted) constituting a name of a subspecies.

**Type:** –(1) A zoological object serving as the base of the name of a taxon. – (2) A term for an element that objectively defines any nominal taxon within the scope and meaning of the Code, potentially a name-bearing type-specimen.

**Type-genus:** –A nominal genus that is the name-bearing type of a nominal family-group taxon.

**Type locality:** –The geographical place of capture of the name-bearing type of a nominal species or subspecies.

**Type-series:** –A series of specimens used by the author for the establishment of a specific or subspecific nominal taxon.

**Type-species:** –The nominal species that is the name-bearing type of a nominal genus or subgenus.

**Typification:** –A designation of a type. (cf.: Fixation).

**Typoid:** –A term not regulated by the Code, used at one time by some German lepidopterologists for some non-name-bearing types and/or specimens believed by the author to be of special taxonomic significance. The term typoid would be a very convenient replacement for the confusing term topotype: topotypoid. (cf.: Topotype).

**Unavailable:** –Of a publication, name or nomenclatural act: the opposite of available. (cf.: Available).

**Uninominal name:** –A name consisting of a single word; such as of a taxon of the family-group or genus-group; uninominally proposed species-group names contravene the Principle of Binominal Nomenclature and are not available under the Code.

**Valid name:** –The correct scientific name of a nominal taxon, usually the oldest available name. (cf.: Available name).

**Variation:** –A deviation from the mean or the type in certain characters.

**Variety:** –A term that if published before 1961 is to be interpreted as either subspecific or infrasubspecific according to the Article 45(g) of the Code, and if published after 1960 always to be treated as infrasubspecific under the Code. (cf.: Form).

**Vernacular name:** – A "common name" as opposed to a scientific name.

**World list abbrevation:** – An abbreviation of the title of a serial or periodical publication, as standardized by the "World List" and utilized by the relevant subsequent publication, recommended for the use in taxonomic publications and required by some editors and publishers.

**Zoological nomenclature:** – The system of scientific names for zoological taxa and the provisions for the formation, treatment and use of these names.

## 4.5 An annotated checklist of European butterflies

A comprehensive annotated checklist of European Papilionoidea is presented here for the first time. The classification (i.e. genus and species concept) follows the principles set out in the preceding discussion. Because this list is not based on a thorough taxonomic revision of all taxa, which is far beyond the scope of this work, it is somewhat preliminary in some respects. This is apparent from the discussion of the status of certain taxa. It is hoped that the names used in this list remain stable until complete taxonomic revisions of European butterflies are available. Recommendations are made to the International Commission on Zoological Nomenclature regarding the conservation of certain long established names that do not conform from a purely formal point of view to the standards and rules set up by the above mentioned body many years after they have become universally accepted. They are: *Pieris adalwinda, P. ergane, Erebia medusa, Aphantopus, Hipparchia, Pseudochazara hippolyte, Melitaea phoebe, Polygonia egea.* Since original combinations of all taxa treated here have not been methodically investigated – this is a task for future taxonomic revisions – two very much disputed rules have been deliberately dispensed with: the use of parenthesis for author's name and year of publication in all non-original combinations (except in the discussion in a few cases to elucidate specific nomenclatural problems) and the agreement in gender between the name and epithet. Opinions are divided as to the practical use of both rules and it is hoped that the new edition of the International Code on Zoological Nomenclature will clarify these matters.

It should be mentioned that some West-Atlantic species, such as *Erebia cyclopius* ERESSMANN, 1844, or *E. ocnus* could be expected to be discovered in the W. Ural Mts.; they are not included in this checklist.

**Order of families:** Papilionidae, Pieridae, Lycaenidae, Riodinidae, Libytheidae, Satyridae, Nymphalidae; they are defined according to WARREN (1947). Numbers in parenthesis following some family names refer to the discussion concerning certain genus-group taxa (where applicable) at the end of the checklist. Genera are arranged alphabetically within each family, species alphabetically within each genus, both for easy orientation of readers not entirely familiar with the taxonomic relationship of taxa listed. Author/s and year of publication of generic names are found in the synonymic list. Arrangement of species' entries: serial number–genus species author/s, year–(reference number to discussion at end of list, if applicable).

It should be mentioned that modern classifications of butterfly families treat Satyridae and Danaidae as subfamilies of Nymphalidae, and Riodinidae as a subfamily of Lycaenidae. Some practical reasons contributed to the choice of the traditional system.

## PAPILIONIDAE

001.  *Archon apollinus* HERBST, 1798
002.  *Iphiclides feisthamelii* DUPONCHEL, 1832 (02)
003.  *Iphiclides podalirius* LINNAEUS, 1758 (02)
004.  *Papilio alexanor* ESPER, 1799
005.  *Papilio hospiton* GENE, 1839
006.  *Papilio machaon* LINNAEUS, 1758
007.  *Parnassius apollo* LINNAEUS, 1758
008.  *Parnassius mnemosyne* LINNAEUS, 1758
009.  *Parnassius phoebus* FABRICIUS, 1793
010.  *Zerynthia cerisyi* GODART, 1822
011.  *Zerynthia cretica* REBEL, 1904 (03)
012.  *Zerynthia polyxena* DENIS & SCHIFFERMÜLLER, 1775
013.  *Zerynthia rumina* LINNAEUS, 1767

## PIERIDAE (82)

014.  *Anthocharis cardamines* LINNAEUS, 1758
015.  *Anthocharis damone* BOISDUVAL, 1836
016.  *Anthocharis euphenoides* STAUDINGER, 1869 (04)
017.  *Anthocharis gruneri* HERRICH-SCHÄFFER, 1851

018.    *Aporia crataegi* LINNAEUS, 1758
019.    *Catopsilia florella* FABRICIUS, 1775
020.    *Colias alfacariensis* BERGER, 1948 (05)
021.    *Colias aurorina* HERRICH-SCHÄFFER, 1850 (06)
022.    *Colias balcanica* REBEL, 1903
023.    *Colias chrysotheme* ESPER, 1780
024.    *Colias crocea* GEOFFROY, 1785
025.    *Colias erate* ESPER, 1905
026.    *Colias hecla* LEFEBVRE, 1836
027.    *Colias hyale* LINNAEUS, 1758
028.    *Colias myrmidone* ESPER, 1780
029.    *Colias nastes* BOISDUVAL, 1832
030.    *Colias palaeno* LINNAEUS, 1758
031.    *Colias phicomone* ESPER, 1780
032.    *Colotis evagore* KLUG, 1829 (07)
033.    *Euchloe ausonia* HÜBNER, 1906 (08)
034.    *Euchloe belemia* ESPER, 1798
035.    *Euchloe charlonia* DONZEL, 1842
036.    *Euchloe crameri* BUTLER, 1869 (08)
037.    *Euchloe insularis* STAUDINGER, 1861 (08)
038.    *Euchloe penia* FREYER, 1852 (08)
039.    *Euchloe simplonia* FREYER, 1829 (08)
040.    *Euchloe tagis* HÜBNER, 1804
041.    *Gonepteryx cleobule* HÜBNER, 1825
042.    *Gonepteryx cleopatra* LINNAEUS, 1767
043.    *Gonepteryx farinosa* ZELLER, 1847
044.    *Gonepteryx maderensis* FELDER, 1862
045.    *Gonepteryx palmae* STAMM, 1963
046.    *Gonepteryx rhamni* LINNAEUS, 1758
047.    *Leptidea duponcheli* STAUDINGER, 1871
048.    *Leptidea morsei* FENTON, 1881
049.    *Leptidea sinapis* LINNAEUS, 1758
050.    *Pieris adalwinda* FRUHSTORFER, 1909 (09)
051.    *Pieris balcana* LORKOVIC, 1970 (10)
052.    *Pieris brassicae* LINNAEUS, 1758
053.    *Pieris bryoniae* HÜBNER, 1806 (14)
054.    *Pieris callidice* ESPER, 1805
055.    *Pieris cheiranthi* HÜBNER, 1808
056.    *Pieris chloridice* OCHSENHEIMER, 1816
057.    *Pieris daplidice* LINNAEUS, 1758
058.    *Pieris ergane* GEYER, 1828 (11)
059.    *Pieris flavescens* MÜLLER, 1933 (12)

060.  *Pieris krueperi* STAUDINGER, 1860
061.  *Pieris mannii* MAYER, 1851
062.  *Pieris maura* WARREN, 1970 (13)
063.  *Pieris napi* LINNAEUS, 1758 (15)
064.  *Pieris rapae* LINNAEUS, 1758
065.  *Zegris eupheme* ESPER, 1805
066.  *Zegris pyrothoe* EVERSMANN, 1832


**LYCAENIDAE** (33, 81, 88)

067.  *Agriades aquilo* BOISDUVAL, 1832
068.  *Agriades dardanus* FREYER, 1832 (16)
069.  *Agriades glandon* PRUNNER, 1798
070.  *Agriades pyrenaicus* BOISDUVAL, 1840
071.  *Agriades zullichi* HEMMING, 1933 (17)
072.  *Albulina orbitulus* PRUNNER, 1798
073.  *Aricia agestis* DENIS & SCHIFFERMÜLLER, 1775
074.  *Aricia allous* GEYER, 1837 (18)
075.  *Aricia artaxerxes* FABRICIUS, 1793 (18, 20)
076.  *Aricia cramera* ESCHSCHOLTZ, 1821
077.  *Aricia eumedon* ESPER, 1780
078.  *Aricia inhonora* JACHONTOV, 1909 (18)
079.  *Aricia morronensis* RIBBE, 1910 (19, 90)
080.  *Aricia nicias* MEIGEN, 1830
081.  *Azanus jesous* GUERIN, 1849
082.  *Callophrys avis* CHAPMAN, 1909
083.  *Callophrys rubi* LINNAEUS, 1758
084.  *Celastrina argiolus* LINNAEUS, 1758
085.  *Chilades galba* LEDERER, 1855
086.  *Chilades trochylus* FREYER, 1844
087.  *Cigaritis acamas* KLUG, 1834
088.  *Cupido alcetas* HOFFMANSEGG, 1804
089.  *Cupido argiades* PALLAS, 1771
090.  *Cupido carswelli* STEMPFFER, 1927 (22)
091.  *Cupido decoloratus* STAUDINGER, 1886
092.  *Cupido lorquinii* HERRICH-SCHÄFFER, 1847
093.  *Cupido minimus* FUESSLY, 1775
094.  *Cupido osiris* MEIGEN, 1829
095.  *Cyaniris antiochena* LEDERER, 1861
096.  *Cyaniris semiargus* ROTTEMBURG, 1775
097.  *Cyclirius webbianus* BRULLE, 1839
098.  *Glaucopsyche alexis* PODA, 1761

099.  *Glaucopsyche melanops* BOISDUVAL, 1828
100.  *Glaucopsyche paphos* CHAPMAN, 1920
101.  *Iolana iolas* OCHSENHEIMER, 1816
102.  *Kretania eurypilus* FREYER, 1852 (23)
103.  *Kretania psylorita* FREYER, 1945
104.  *Laeosopis roboris* ESPER, 1793
105.  *Lampides boeticus* LINNAEUS, 1767
106.  *Lycaeides argyrognomon* BERGSTRÄSSER, 1779
107.  *Lycaeides cleobis* BREMER, 1861 (24)
108.  *Lycaeides corsica* BELLIER, 1862 (25)
109.  *Lycaeides idas* LINNAEUS, 1761 (26)
110.  *Lycaeides nevadensis* OBERTHÜR, 1896 (27)
111.  *Lycaena alciphron* ROTTEMBURG, 1775
112.  *Lycaena candens* HERRICH-SCHÄFFER, 1844 (28)
113.  *Lycaena dispar* HAWORTH, 1803
114.  *Lycaena helle* DENIS & SCHIFFERMÜLLER, 1775
115.  *Lycaena hippothoe* LINNAEUS, 1761 (28)
116.  *Lycaena ochimus* HERRICH- SCHÄFFER, 1851 (72)
117.  *Lycaena ottomanus* LEFEBVRE, 1830
118.  *Lycaena phlaeas* LINNAEUS, 1761
119.  *Lycaena subalpina* SPEYER, 1851 (29)
120.  *Lycaena thersamon* ESPER, 1784 (86)
121.  *Lycaena thetis* KLUG, 1834
122.  *Lycaena tityrus* PODA, 1761
123.  *Lycaena virgaureae* LINNAEUS, 1758
124.  *Maculinea alcon* DENIS & SCHIFFERMÜLLER, 1775 (30)
125.  *Maculinea arion* LINNAEUS, 1758
126.  *Maculinea nausithous* BERGSTRÄSSER, 1779
127.  *Maculinea rebeli* HIRSCHKE, 1904 (30)
128.  *Maculinea teleius* BERGSTRÄSSER, 1779
129.  *Neolycaena rhymnus* EVERSMANN, 1832
130.  *Nordmannia acaciae* FABRICIUS, 1787
131.  *Nordmannia esculi* HÜBNER, 1804
132.  *Nordmannia ilicis* ESPER, 1779
133.  *Nordmannia pruni* LINNAEUS, 1758
134.  *Nordmannia spini* DENIS & SCHIFFERMÜLLER, 1775
135.  *Nordmannia w-album* KNOCH, 1782
136.  *Plebejus argus* LINNAEUS, 1758
137.  *Plebejus hesperica* RAMBUR, 1839
138.  *Plebejus pylaon* FISCHER, 1832
139.  *Plebejus sephirus* FRIVALDSKY, 1835
140.  *Plebejus trappi* VERITY, 1927 (32)

141. *Polyommatus actis* HERRICH-SCHÄFFER, 1851 (71)
142. *Polyommatus admetus* ESPER, 1785
143. *Polyommatus ainsae* FORSTER, 1961
144. *Polyommatus albicans* HERRICH-SCHÄFFER, 1851 (34, 89)
145. *Polyommatus amandus* SCHNEIDER, 1792
146. *Polyommatus aroaniensis* BROWN, 1976
147. *Polyommatus asturiensis* SAGARRA, 1924 (35)
148. *Polyommatus bellargus* ROTTEMBURG, 1775
149. *Polyommatus caelestissima* VERITY, 1921 (35, 89)
150. *Polyommatus coelestinus* EVERSMANN, 1848
151. *Polyommatus coerulescens* TUTT, 1909 (89)
152. *Polyommatus coridon* PODA, 1761
153. *Polyommatus cyane* EVERSMANN, 1837
154. *Polyommatus damon* DENIS & SCHIFFERMÜLLER, 1775
155. *Polyommatus damone* EVERSMANN, 1841
156. *Polyommatus daphnis* DENIS & SCHIFFERMÜLLER, 1775
157. *Polyommatus dolus* HÜBNER, 1823
158. *Polyommatus dorylas* DENIS & SCHIFFERMÜLLER, 1775
159. *Polyommatus eroides* FRIVALDSKY, 1835
160. *Polyommatus eros* OCHSENHEIMER, 1808
161. *Polyommatus escheri* HÜBNER, 1823
162. *Polyommatus exuberans* VERITY, 1926 (92)
163. *Polyommatus fabressei* OBERTHÜR, 1910
164. *Polyommatus galloi* BALLETTO & TOSO, 1979
165. *Polyommatus golgus* HÜBNER, 1813
166. *Polyommatus hispana* HERRICH-SCHÄFFER, 1851
167. *Polyommatus humedasae* TOSO & BALLETTO, 1976
168. *Polyommatus icarus* ROTTEMBURG, 1775
169. *Polyommatus iphigenia* HERRICH-SCHÄFFER, 1847
170. *Polyommatus italaglauca* VERITY, 1939 (37)
171. *Polyommatus menelaos* BROWN, 1976 (38)
172. *Polyommatus nephohiptamenos* BROWN & COUTSIS, 1978
173. *Polyommatus nivescens* KEFERSTEIN, 1851
174. *Polyommatus philippi* BROWN & COUTSIS, 1978 (38)
175. *Polyommatus poseidon* LEDERER, 1852
176. *Polyommatus ripartii* FREYER, 1830
177. *Polyommatus thersites* CANTENER, 1834
178. *Polyommatus violetae* GOMEZ BUSTILLO et al., 1979
179. *Polyommatus virgilius* OBERTHÜR, 1910 (39)
180. *Pseudophilotes abencerragus* PIERRET, 1837
181. *Pseudophilotes barbagiae* PRINS & POORTEN, 1982
182. *Pseudophilotes baton* BERGSTRÄSSER, 1779

183.  *Pseudophilotes bavius* EVERSMANN, 1832
184.  *Pseudophilotes panope* EVERSMANN, 1851 (40)
185.  *Pseudophilotes panoptes* HÜBNER, 1818
186.  *Pseudophilotes schiffermuelleri* HEMMING, 1929 (41)
187.  *Pseudophilotes vicrama* MOORE, 1865 (42)
188.  *Quercusia quercus* LINNAEUS, 1758
189.  *Scolitantides orion* PALLAS, 1771
190.  *Syntarucus pirithous* LINNAEUS, 1767
191.  *Tarucus balcanicus* FREYER, 1845
192.  *Tarucus theophrastus* FABRICIUS, 1793
193.  *Thecla betulae* LINNAEUS, 1758
194.  *Tomares ballus* FABRICIUS, 1787
195.  *Tomares callimachus* EVERSMANN, 1848
196.  *Tomares nogelli* HERRICH-SCHÄFFER, 1852
197.  *Tongeia fischeri* EVERSMANN, 1843
198.  *Turanana panagea* HERRICH-SCHÄFFER, 1852
199.  *Ultraaricia anteros* FREYER, 1839
200.  *Ultraaricia orpheus* NEKRUTENKO, 1980 (87)
201.  *Vacciniina loewi* ZELLER, 1847 (75)
202.  *Vacciniina optilete* KNOCH, 1781
203.  *Zizeeria karsandra* MOORE, 1865
204.  *Zizeeria knysna* TRIMEN, 1862

**RIODINIDAE**

205.  *Hamearis lucina* LINNAEUS, 1758

**LIBYTHEIDAE**

206.  *Libythea celtis* LAICHARTING, 1782

**DANAIDAE**

207.  *Danaus chrysippus* LINNAEUS, 1758
208.  *Danaus plexippus* LINNAEUS, 1758

**SATYRIDAE** (51, 65, 95)

209.  *Aphantopus hyperantus* LINNAEUS, 1758
210.  *Arethusana arethusa* DENIS & SCHIFFERMÜLLER, 1775
211.  *Chazara anthe* HOFFMANSEGG, 1804
212.  *Chazara briseis* LINNAEUS, 1764
213.  *Chazara prieuri* PIERRET, 1837
214.  *Coenonympha amaryllis* STOLL, 1782

215. *Coenonympha arcania* LINNAEUS, 1761
216. *Coenonympha corinna* HÜBNER, 1806 (43)
217. *Coenonympha darwiniana* STAUDINGER, 1871
218. *Coenonympha dorus* ESPER, 1782
219. *Coenonympha elbana* STAUDINGER, 1901 (43)
220. *Coenonympha gardetta* PRUNNER, 1798
221. *Coenonympha glycerion* BORKHAUSEN, 1788
222. *Coenonympha hero* LINNAEUS, 1761
223. *Coenonympha iphioides* STAUDINGER, 1870 (44)
224. *Coenonympha leander* ESPER, 1784
225. *Coenonympha oedippus* FABRICIUS, 1787
226. *Coenonympha pamphilus* LINNAEUS, 1758 (45)
227. *Coenonympha rhodopensis* ELWES, 1900 (46)
228. *Coenonympha thyrsis* FREYER, 1846
229. *Coenonympha tullia* MÜLLER, 1764
230. *Erebia aethiopella* HOFFMANSEGG, 1806
231. *Erebia aethiops* ESPER, 1777
232. *Erebia alberganus* PRUNNER, 1798
233. *Erebia boreomontanum* SEDYKH, 1979 (47)
234. *Erebia calcaria* LORKOVIC, 1953
235. *Erebia cassioides* REINER & HOHENWARTH, 1792 (48)
236. *Erebia christi* RÄTZER, 1890
237. *Erebia claudina* BORKHAUSEN, 1789
238. *Erebia dabanensis* ERSCHOFF, 1871 (73)
239. *Erebia disa* BECKLIN, 1791
240. *Erebia discoidalis* KIRBY, 1837
241. *Erebia edda* MENETRIES, 1854 (74)
242. *Erebia embla* BECKLIN, 1791
243. *Erebia epiphron* KNOCH, 1783
244. *Erebia epistygne* HÜBNER, 1819
245. *Erebia eriphyle* FREYER, 1836
246. *Erebia euryale* ESPER, 1805
247. *Erebia fasciata* BUTLER, 1868
248. *Erebia flavofasciata* HEYNE, 1895
249. *Erebia gorge* ESPER, 1805
250. *Erebia gorgone* BOISDUVAL, 1833
251. *Erebia hispania* BUTLER, 1868
252. *Erebia jeniseiensis* TRYBOM, 1877 (77)
253. *Erebia lefebvrei* BOISDUVAL, 1828
254. *Erebia ligea* LINNAEUS, 1758
255. *Erebia manto* DENIS & SCHIFFERMÜLLER, 1775
256. *Erebia medusa* DENIS & SCHIFFERMÜLLER, 1775 (79)

257.  *Erebia melampus* FUESSLIN, 1775
258.  *Erebia melas* HERBST, 1796
259.  *Erebia meolans* PRUNNER, 1798
260.  *Erebia mnestra* ESPER, 1805
261.  *Erebia montana* PRUNNER, 1798
262.  *Erebia neoridas* BOISDUVAL, 1828
263.  *Erebia nivalis* LORKOVIC & LESSE, 1954
264.  *Erebia oeme* ESPER, 1805
265.  *Erebia orientalis* ELWES, 1900
266.  *Erebia ottomana* HERRICH-SCHÄFFER, 1847
267.  *Erebia palarica* CHAPMAN, 1905
268.  *Erebia pandrose* BORKHAUSEN, 1788
269.  *Erebia pharte* ESPER, 1805
270.  *Erebia pluto* PRUNNER, 1798
271.  *Erebia polaris* STAUDINGER, 1861
272.  *Erebia pronoe* ESPER, 1780
273.  *Erebia rhodopensis* NICHOLL, 1900
274.  *Erebia rossi* CURTIS, 1834
275.  *Erebia scipio* BOISDUVAL, 1832
276.  *Erebia serotina* DESCIMON & LESSE, 1954 (49)
277.  *Erebia sthennyo* GRASLIN, 1850
278.  *Erebia stirius* GODART, 1824
279.  *Erebia styx* FREYER, 1834
280.  *Erebia sudetica* STAUDINGER, 1861 (50)
281.  *Erebia triaria* PRUNNER, 1798
282.  *Erebia tyndarus* ESPER, 1781
283.  *Erebia zapateri* OBERTHÜR, 1875
284.  *Hipparchia aristaeus* BONELLI, 1826 (52)
285.  *Hipparchia autonoe* ESPER, 1783
286.  *Hipparchia azorina* STRECKER, 1899 (83)
287.  *Hipparchia bacchus* HIGGINS, 1967 (83)
288.  *Hipparchia ballettoi* KUDRNA, 1984 (52)
289.  *Hipparchia blachieri* FRUHSTORFER, 1908 (52)
290.  *Hipparchia caldeirense* OEHMIG, 1983 (83)
291.  *Hipparchia christenseni* KUDRNA, 1977
292.  *Hipparchia cretica* REBEL, 1916
293.  *Hipparchia cypriensis* HOLIK, 1949 (83)
294.  *Hipparchia fagi* SCOPOLI, 1763 (53)
295.  *Hipparchia fatua* FREYER, 1945
296.  *Hipparchia fidia* LINNAEUS, 1767
297.  *Hipparchia gomera* HIGGINS, 1967 (83)
298.  *Hipparchia hermione* LINNAEUS, 1764 (53)

299. *Hipparchia leighebi* KUDRNA, 1976 (83)
300. *Hipparchia maderensis* BETHUNE-BAKER, 1891 (52)
301. *Hipparchia malickyi* KUDRNA, 1977 (83)
302. *Hipparchia miguelensis* LE CERF, 1935 (83)
303. *Hipparchia neomyris* GODART, 1823
304. *Hipparchia pellucida* STAUDER, 1923
305. *Hipparchia sbordonii* KUDRNA, 1984
306. *Hipparchia semele* LINNAEUS, 1758
307. *Hipparchia senthes* FRUHSTORFER, 1908 (52)
308. *Hipparchia statilinus* HUFNAGEL, 1766
309. *Hipparchia syriaca* STAUDINGER, 1871
310. *Hipparchia volgensis* MAZOCHIN-PORSHNJAKOV, 1952
311. *Hipparchia wyssii* CHRIST, 1889 (83)
312. *Hyponephele huebneri* KOCAK, 1980 (54)
313. *Hyponephele lupina* COSTA, 1836
314. *Hyponephele lycaon* KÜHN, 1774
315. *Kanetisa circe* FABRICIUS, 1775
316. *Lasiommata achine* LINNAEUS, 1763
317. *Lasiommata climene* ESPER, 1784 (01)
318. *Lasiommata deidamia* EVERSMANN, 1851 (55)
319. *Lasiommata maera* LINNAEUS, 1758
320. *Lasiommata megera* LINNAEUS, 1767
321. *Lasiommata petropolitana* FABRICIUS, 1787
322. *Lasiommata roxelana* CRAMER, 1777
323. *Lasiommata tigelius* BONELLI, 1826
324. *Maniola cypricola* GRAVES, 1928
325. *Maniola jurtina* LINNAEUS, 1758 (57)
326. *Maniola nurag* GHILIANI, 1852
327. *Maniola telmessia* ZELLER, 1847
328. *Melanargia arge* SULZER, 1776
329. *Melanargia galathea* LINNAEUS, 1758
330. *Melanargia ines* HOFFMANSEGG, 1804
331. *Melanargia lachesis* HÜBNER, 1790
332. *Melanargia larissa* ESPER, 1784
333. *Melanargia occitanica* ESPER, 1793
334. *Melanargia pherusa* BOISDUVAL, 1833
335. *Melanargia russiae* ESPER, 1784 (58)
336. *Minois dryas* SCOPOLI, 1763 (59)
337. *Oeneis ammon* ELWES, 1899
338. *Oeneis bore* SCHNEIDER, 1792
339. *Oeneis crambis* FREYER, 1845
340. *Oeneis dembowskyi* SEDYKH, 1974 (60)

341.  *Oeneis dubia* ELWES, 1899
342.  *Oeneis falkovitchi* SEDYKH, 1974 (60)
343.  *Oeneis glacialis* MOLL, 1785
344.  *Oeneis jutta* HÜBNER, 1806
345.  *Oeneis koslowskyi* SEDYKH, 1974 (60)
346.  *Oeneis kusnetzovi* SEDYKH, 1974 (60)
347.  *Oeneis norna* BECKLIN, 1791
348.  *Oeneis pansa* CHRISTOPH, 1893 (84)
349.  *Oeneis saepestriata* SEDYKH, 1974 (60)
350.  *Oeneis semidea* SAY, 1928 (84)
351.  *Oeneis tarpeia* PALLAS, 1771
352.  *Oeneis taygete* GEYER, 1824
353.  *Oeneis tundra* BANG-HAAS, 1912
354.  *Pararge aegeria* LINNAEUS, 1758
355.  *Pararge xiphia* FABRICIUS, 1775
356.  *Pararge xiphioides* STAUDINGER, 1871
357.  *Proterebia afra* FABRICIUS, 1787 (56)
358.  *Pseudochazara amymone* BROWN, 1976 (61)
359.  *Pseudochazara anthelea* LEFEBVRE, 1831
360.  *Pseudochazara cingovskii* GROSS, 1973 (61)
361.  *Pseudochazara euxina* KUSNEZOV, 1909
362.  *Pseudochazara geyeri* HERRICH-SCHÄFFER, 1845
363.  *Pseudochazara graeca* STAUDINGER, 1870
364.  *Pseudochazara hippolyte* ESPER, 1784 (76)
365.  *Pseudochazara orestes* PRINS & POORTEN, 1981 (61)
366.  *Pyronia bathseba* FABRICIUS, 1793
367.  *Pyronia cecilia* VALLANTIN, 1894
368.  *Pyronia tithonus* LINNAEUS, 1771
369.  *Satyrus actaea* ESPER, 1780
370.  *Satyrus ferula* FABRICIUS, 1793
371.  *Triphysa phryne* PALLAS, 1771
372.  *Ypthima asterope* KLUG, 1832


**NYMPHALIDAE** (62)

373.  *Aglais ichnusa* BONELLI, 1826
374.  *Aglais urticae* LINNAEUS, 1758
375.  *Apatura ilia* DENIS & SCHIFFERMÜLLER, 1775
376.  *Apatura iris* LINNAEUS, 1758
377.  *Apatura metis* FREYER, 1829
378.  *Araschnia levana* LINNAEUS, 1758
379.  *Argynnis adippe* LINNAEUS, 1767 (63)

380. *Argynnis aglaja* LINNAEUS, 1758
381. *Argynnis elisa* GODART, 1823
382. *Argynnis niobe* LINNAEUS, 1758 (64)
383. *Argynnis pandora* DENIS & SCHIFFERMÜLLER, 1775 (65)
384. *Argynnis paphia* LINNAEUS, 1758
385. *Argyronome laodice* PALLAS, 1771
386. *Boloria angarensis* ERSCHOFF, 1870
387. *Boloria aquilonaris* STICHEL, 1908
388. *Boloria chariclea* SCHNEIDER, 1794
389. *Boloria dia* LINNAEUS, 1767
390. *Boloria eugenia* EVERSMANN, 1847
391. *Boloria eunomia* ESPER, 1799
392. *Boloria euphrosyne* LINNAEUS, 1758
393. *Boloria freija* BECKLIN, 1791
394. *Boloria frigga* BECKLIN, 1791
395. *Boloria graeca* STAUDINGER, 1870
396. *Boloria improba* BUTLER, 1877
397. *Boloria napaea* HOFFMANSEGG, 1804
398. *Boloria pales* DENIS & SCHIFFERMÜLLER, 1775
399. *Boloria polaris* BOISDUVAL, 1828
400. *Boloria selene* DENIS & SCHIFFERMÜLLER, 1775
401. *Boloria selenis* EVERSMANN, 1837
402. *Boloria thore* HÜBNER, 1806
403. *Boloria titania* ESPER, 1793
404. *Brenthis daphne* BERGSTRÄSSER, 1780
405. *Brenthis hecate* DENIS & SCHIFFERMÜLLER, 1775
406. *Brenthis ino* ROTTEMBURG, 1775
407. *Charaxes jasius* LINNAEUS, 1767
408. *Euphydryas aurinia* ROTTEMBURG, 1775 (66)
409. *Euphydryas beckeri* HERRICH-SCHÄFFER, 1851 (66)
410. *Euphydryas cynthia* DENIS & SCHIFFERMÜLLER, 1775
411. *Euphydryas desfontainii* GODART, 1819
412. *Euphydryas glaciegenita* VERITY, 1928 (66)
413. *Euphydryas iduna* DALMAN, 1816
414. *Euphydryas wolfensbergeri* FREY, 1888 (94)
415. *Euphydryas maturna* LINNAEUS, 1758
416. *Euphydryas orientalis* HERRICH-SCHÄFFER, 1846 (67)
417. *Euphydryas provincialis* BOISDUVAL, 1828 (66)
418. *Inachis io* LINNAEUS, 1758
419. *Issoria lathonia* LINNAEUS, 1758
420. *Limenitis camilla* LINNAEUS, 1764
421. *Limenitis populi* LINNAEUS, 1758

422.  *Limenitis reducta* STAUDINGER, 1901
423.  *Melitaea aetheria* LUCAS, 1848
424.  *Melitaea arduinna* ESPER, 1784
425.  *Melitaea asteria* FREYER, 1828
426.  *Melitaea athalia* ROTTEMBURG, 1775 (68)
427.  *Melitaea aurelia* NICKERL, 1850
428.  *Melitaea britomartis* ASSMAN, 1847
429.  *Melitaea cinxia* LINNAEUS, 1758
430.  *Melitaea deione* DUPONCHEL, 1832
431.  *Melitaea diamina* LANG, 1789
432.  *Melitaea didyma* ESPER, 1779
433.  *Melitaea fascelis* ESPER, 1784 (85)
434.  *Melitaea neglecta* PFAU, 1962 (69)
435.  *Melitaea parthenoides* KEFERSTEIN, 1851
436.  *Melitaea phoebe* GOEZE, 1779 (70)
437.  *Melitaea varia* MEYER-DÜR, 1851
438.  *Neptis rivularis* SCOPOLI, 1763
439.  *Neptis sappho* PALLAS, 1771
440.  *Nymphalis antiopa* LINNAEUS, 1758
441.  *Nymphalis l-album* ESPER, 1780 (80)
442.  *Nymphalis polychloros* LINNAEUS, 1758
443.  *Nymphalis xanthomelas* ESPER, 1781
444.  *Polygonia c-album* LINNAEUS, 1758
445.  *Polygonia egea* CRAMER, 1775 (78)
446.  *Thaleropis ionia* FISCHER & EVERSMANN, 1851 (91)
447.  *Vanessa atalanta* LINNAEUS, 1758
448.  *Vanessa cardui* LINNAEUS, 1758
449.  *Vanessa indica* HERBST, 1794 (73)
450.  *Vanessa virginiensis* DRURY, 1773

## Discussion concerning some taxa of the checklist

(01) – *Lasiommata climene* has been recorded from south-eastern and eastern Europe on several occasions, mostly old records of single specimens from Albania, Bulgaria, Greece, Romania, U.S.S.R. and Yugoslavia (cf. e. g. BRETHERTON 1966, JACHONTOV 1935, KORSHUNOV 1972, WILLEMSE 1977, etc.). A useful brief review of *L. climene* south-eastern European distribution was published by WILLEMSE (1977) who discovered a single specimen of the species in Greece. In 1983 R. F. BRETHERTON (pers. comm.) discovered a rich colony of *L. climene* in northern Greece which is probably

of indefinite character. The Asiatic range of the species is Turkey, Iran, U.S.S.R.: Caucasus and Transcaucasia, Iraq (e. g. ECKWEILER 1980, RÜHL & HEYNE 1892–95, WILTSHIRE 1957, etc.). The habitat has not been adequately described.

(02) – *Iphiclides feisthamelii* differs constantly in certain morphological features from *I. podalirius*. It is, therefore, treated here provisionally as an essentially allopatric morphospecies. It is possible that some very limited degree of interbreeding between the two morphospecies takes place in localities where they meet but the problem has never been investigated.

(03) – *Zerynthia cretica* is a distinct morphospecies closely related to and always allopatric with *Z. cerisyi* and two other Asiatic species *Z. caucasica* LEDERER, 1864 and *Z. deyrollei* OBERTHÜR, 1869. Taxonomic status of *Z. cerisyi* from Cyprus requires investigation.

(04) – *Anthocharis euphenoides* differs from *A. belia* LINNAEUS, 1767 by constant morphological characters found both in adults and the early stages (BACK 1977). Surprisingly the two allopatric morphospecies are still treated as conspecific by some authors (e. g. HIGGINS & RILEY 1980).

(05) – *Colias alfacariensis* BERGER, 1948: nomenclature, authorship and date of publication of all names involved (i. e. *alfacariensis, australis, calida:* cf. synonymic list) are discussed in detail by KUDRNA (1982).

(06) – *Colias aurorina* is an essentially Asiatic species, in Europe confined to some localities in Greece (western limit of its range). The classification of the isolated groups of population of this taxon remains fluid and requires a taxonomic revision. There seems to be no sound reason for the separation of *libanotica* from *aurorina* or for treating the European populations as subspecies *(heldreichi)* of *libanotica*, as proposed by HIGGINS & RILEY (1973, 1980), without any kind of explanation.

(07) – *Colotis evagore* inhabits north-western Africa and its permanent occurrence in Europe is doubtful, in spite of its recent records from southern Spain (MANLEY & ALLCARD 1970).

(08) – *Euchloe ausonia, E. crameri, E. insularis, E. penia* and *E. simplonia* are a group of closely related chiefly allopatric species; their classification, in some cases possibly also their identity, requires a taxonomic revision taking into account both adults and early stages. The present treatment of these taxa is preliminary.

(09) – *Pieris adalwinda* is a monovoltine morphospecies apparently only partly reproductively isolated from the bivoltine *P. napi* of southern Scandinavia. The name *adalwinda* was originally proposed by FRUHSTORFER (1909) uninominally as a race ("Rasse") of *[Pieris] napi*; the generic name was implied indirectly by a reference to and comparison with a taxon *Pieris napi frigida pseudobryoniae* VERITY, 1908, the original combination of which became fully clarified only some three years after its first publication (KUDRNA 1983). Although the original description of *adalwinda* is incomplete and confusing, there has never been confusion as to its identity. The name is well known and well used in literature for this "semispecies". The next alternative is *Pieris arctica* MÜLLER & KAUTZ, 1939; a name originating from the infrasubspecific unavailable name *Pieris napi frigida arctica* VERITY, 1911 and raised to species-group status. The latter name, with its correct authors, has never been accepted in standard literature. I propose that the International Commission on Zoological Nomenclature place *Pieris napi adalwinda* FRUHSTORFER, 1909 on the Official List of Available Names in zoology as it is in the interest of stability of zoological nomenclature.

(10) – *Pieris balcana* was described from Yugoslavia (Macedonia: Skopje: Treska and Bosnia & Herzegovina: Zelenogora: Hrcavka) on account of its genetic incompatibility with *P. napi* in laboratory experiments, shown by an unusually high infertility recorded in $F_1$. Morphological differences are slight, chiefly in the diffused black marking along the veins on the underside of hindwings in the first generation of *balcana*. HIGGINS & RILEY (1973) erroneously sunk *balcana* as a junior synonym of a nomen nudum *Pieris rapae canidioformis* DRENOWSKI, 1910 (KUDRNA 1977) and later the same authors (HIGGINS & RILEY 1980) treated the taxon as a junior synonym of an apparently unavailable infrasubspecific name *Pieris napi canidiaformis* DRENOWSKY, 1925, proposed for a seasonal montane form (summer brood) from Bulgaria: Stara Planina. Morphological differences between *napi* and *canidiaformis* appear to be just the opposite of those between *napi* and *balcana*, regardless of the nomenclatorial status *canidiaformis*. *P. balcana* is probably a sibling species; its ecology, distribution, relationship to *napi* (in nature) and early stages require investigation.

(11) – KOCAK (1981) concluded that the name *ergane* was originally proposed without generic name and replaced it by *Pontia narcaea*, a junior subjective synonym of *ergane*. KOCAK's (1981) action is both logical and consequent but not necessarily unequivocal, based upon his subjective understanding of the "suprageneric" meaning of the taxonomic category "Papiliones II". The mode of utilization of taxonomic categories by classi-

cal authors is often ambiguous and fairly difficult to judge by our standards. The name *Pieris ergane* has been well established for the species in all standard works of reference while *Pieris narcaea* is almost unknown. I suggest that the International Commission on Zoological Nomenclature should place *[Papilio] ergane* Geyer, 1828 on the List of Available Names in zoology to protect the continuity and stability of its long established use.

(12) – MÜLLER (1933) seems to be the first author who raised an unavailable infrasubspecific name *Pieris napi flavescens* WAGNER, 1903, originally proposed for a female aberration, to species-group status. *Pieris napi neobryoniae* SHELJUZHKO, 1913, occasionally used subjectively for the same taxon is also unavailable, it being a replacement for an unavailable infrasubspecific name *Pieris napi bryoniae bryonides* VERITY, 1911, said to be preoccupied by *Pieris napi bryonides* SHELJUZHKO, 1910. The name *P. flavescens* is used here to denote all essentially bivoltine populations replacing *P. bryoniae* at low and moderate altitudes in some areas of the Alps (e. g. Austria: Wien: Mödling – type-locality of *flavescens*) and Carpathians (e. g. Czechoslovakia: Vihorlat Mts.). *P. flavescens* is treated here tentatively as a distinct species on account of its apparent reproductive isolation from the sympatric populations of *P. napi*, and geographic isolation from *P. bryoniae*, in spite of some results of laboratory experiments contradicting this judgement.

(13) – *Pieris napi napi maura* VERITY, 1911 was described as an infrasubspecific "race" (KUDRNA 1983) from Algeria: Blida: Le Tarf. WARREN (1970) established that *maura* is a distinct [morpho]species and raised the name to species-rank taking its authorship (i. e. *Pieris maura* WARREN, 1970, based on the same type-series as the former name). At the same time WARREN (1970) compared the type-series of *maura* with extensive material from Portugal and established that *maura* occurred there, thus recording the species for the first time from Europe. The biological relationship of *P. maura* with the rest of the species of *P. napi* complex remains unknown. I retain *P. maura* tentatively as a morphospecies; it remains to be seen if the Portugese populations are also biologically identical with those of Algeria. More research is much needed in this case.

(14) – *Pieris bryoniae* is treated here as a distinct species, the name being used for the essentially monovoltine high altitude populations of *P. napi*-complex, predominantly reproductively isolated from *P. napi, P. adalwinda,* and at least geographically isolated from *P. flavescens*. It must be mentioned that GEIGER (1978) failed to find any constant difference in the genetic (electrophoretic) pattern between *P. bryoniae* and *P. napi*.

(15) – *Pieris napi* complex consists of "semispecific" units differing partly in their morphology, partly in their biology, from each other, their characters being rarely entirely constant and occasionally contradicting one another, and further complicated by seasonal variation. Reproductive isolation is incomplete and differs probably from population to population. The resulting taxonomic treatment differs accordingly from author to author. This is hardly surprising: the complex offers one of the best examples of the current evolution of species in Europe. Six taxa are recognized and treated tentatively as distinct species: *P. adalwinda, balcana, bryoniae, flavescens, maura* and *napi*. *P. napi* is the widespread essentially polyvoltine and not necessarily homogenous "collective" species: It may consist of additional hitherto unrecognized species.

(16) – *Agriades dardanus* is treated here as a distinct morphospecies closely related to *A. pyrenaicus*.

(17) – *Agriades zullichi* is very closely related to *A. glandon* and its taxonomic status is as yet uncertain; it is an endemic species confined to S. Spain: Sierra Nevada, where it has been found at high altitude only and is believed to be very rare: it has been collected only on a few occasions (MANLEY & ALLCARD 1970).

(18) – *Aricia allous, A. artaxerxes* and *A. inhonora* form a complex of three closely related allopatric morphospecies replacing each other geographically; their biological relationship has not been adequately studied. The alpine populations of *A. allous* do not differ in constant characters from the Iberian populations *(montensis)* of the species.

(19) – *Aricia morronensis* is widespread and yet extremely localized in the mountains of Spain at altitudes ranging from ca. 1000 m in the north to well over 2700 m in the Sierra Nevada in the south; it occurs always in isolated colonies restricted to a small area but usually abundant. Almost every known population has been given a distinct subspecific name in spite of their biological relationship remaining unknown. *A. morronensis* lives in varied open habitats usually near the summit, the most extreme being rocky slopes and small plateaus almost devoid of vegetation next to permanent snow in the Sierra Nevada. The distribution is poorly known and the species is usually difficult to find owing to its low erratic flight, dark colour and small size. Larval hostplant is said to be *Erodium* sp. (MANLEY & ALLCARD 1970), ecology and early stages unknown.

(20) – *Aricia artaxerxes* is restricted here to the British populations (i. e.

northern England and Scotland); the rest of northern Europe is inhabited by *A. inhonora.*

(21) – *Ultraaricia anteros* is an endemic European morphospecies replaced in Asia by *U. dombaiensis* ALBERTI, 1969, and *U. vanderbani* PFEIFFER, 1937.

(22) – *Cupido carswelli* was described from south-eastern Spain (Murcia: Sierra de Espuna: ca. 1100–1200 m) where, as it appears, it has not been found since 1927 and is represented only by a short series of specimens. BRETHERTON (1968) and MANLEY & ALLCARD (1970) reported also a few specimens found at Cieza (Prov. Murcia: ca. 40 km north of Sierra de Espuna) and at Puebla D. Fabrique (Prov. Granada: ca. 80 km west of Sierra de Espuna), in 1922. Quite recently LASSO DE LA VEGA (1978) discovered *carswelli* in southern Spain: Prov. Malaga: Sierra de Tejeda: ca. 1000 m. COOKE (1928) collected *carswelli* only in stony dried-up stream beds. Distribution, ecology, early stages, relationship with *C. minimus* and *C. lorquinii* are unknown or very poorly known. The species is believed to be monovoltine, its flight period being April, in Sierra de Espuna perhaps until early May. Material from the Sierra de Tejeda has not been compared with specimens from Sierra de Espuna; This leaves the identification open to some questions.

(23) – *Kretania eurypilus* is widespread in Turkey and elsewhere in western Asia; it has been reported from southern Greece by BROWN (1977), the record needs confirmation.

(24) – *Lycaeides cleobis* appears to be the senior subjective synonym of *L. sareptensis*, which was described from U.S.S.R.: Lower Volga: Volgograd: Krasnoarmeysk (= Sarepta) (E. BALLETTO pers. comm.) and was not reported from the area for some 50 years (JACHONTOV 1935). The occurrence in Europe of *L. cleobis* is doubtful and requires investigation (Y. P. NEKRUTENKO pers. comm.). The origin of CHAPMAN's material of *sareptensis* is uncertain.

(25) – *Lycaeides corsica* is here classified as an allopatric morphospecies peculiar to Corsica and Sardinia.

(26) – *Lycaeides idas* was originally named *Papilio idas* LINNAEUS, 1761, and the same name was previously given to another species, *Papilio dias* LINNAEUS, 1758, which has never subsequently identified or interpreted. To avoid this case of primary homonymy, the International Commis-

sion on Zoological Nomenclature suppressed the older name, which has never been consistently used, in 1954 (cf. Opinion 269).

(27) – *Lycaeides nevadensis* is separated here from the closely related *L. idas*; it is an allopatric morphospecies described from southern Spain: Sierra Nevada, and recently reported also from Granada: Alfacar (MANLEY & ALLCARD 1970) and east-central Spain: Prov. Teruel: Montes Universales (E. BALLETTO pers. comm.).

(28) – *Lycaena candens* and *L. hippothoe* are two closely related morphospecies, apparently geographicly replacing each other (BEURET 1954). *L. hippothoe* is a collective name for a complex of four morphologically distinct aggregates of uncertain taxonomic status; each of these units inhabits a distinct range: (A) is confined to northern Europe, (B) to central Europe, (C) southern Europe incl. northern Appennines, (D) to southern Italy: Mt. Pollino. *L. hippothoe* complex urgently needs a taxonomic revision.

(29) – *Lycaena subalpina* is a morphospecies closely related to *L. tityrus;* the present treatment is based on DESCIMON's (1980) observations and research, and on comparison of samples of relevant material.

(30) – *Maculinea rebeli* may prove to be identical with *monticola* which is usually treated as subspecies of *M. alcon; monticola* is treated here provisionally as a "synonym" of *rebeli* although it is the older name and would have priority should the two taxa ever prove to be conspecific, unless the International Commission on Zoological Nomenclature takes action to protect *rebeli* as it is the better established name of the two. *M. alcon* and *M. rebeli* although morphologically very similar (overlap in extreme variation) are ecologically isolated and inhabit entirely different extreme biotopes. It is not known whether they are reproductively isolated in captivity, but even if they could occasionally hybridize there, the hybrids would be unlikely to survive in either of their habitats. LORKOVIC (1978) reported from Yugoslavia: Croatia an unidentified *Maculinea* sp. morphologically similar to *M. alcon* and ecologically close to *M. rebeli* and feeding on *Gentiana cruciata*. G. LEIGHEB (pers. comm.) reported from N. Italy: Lago d'Orta vic. a small colony of *M. alcon* (?) inhabiting a site flooded in winter and dry during the summer months.

(32) – *Plebejus trappi* is the valid name for the taxon originally named *Lycaena sephyrus lycidas* TRAPP, 1863, which is not congeneric with *Polyommatus lycidas* MEIGEN, 1830, treated at present as a junior subjec-

tive synonym of *Lycaeides idas* LINNAEUS, 1761, following the International Code of Zoological Nomenclature, Art. 59(b) (i).

(33) – Genus *Polyommatus* comprises all species placed by HIGGINS (1976), HIGGINS & RILEY (1970, 1980) and some other authors in various genera such as *Polyommatus, Agrodiaetus, Lysandra, Plebicula* and *Meleageria*, which lack constant taxonomic characters separating them from each other. This has been adequately shown by the inconsistent treatment of taxa in these genera by the above authors themselves. Consequently, the genus *Polyommatus* is restored here to the status similar to that outlined by FORS-TER (1938) and utilized by SCHWARZ (1949). A taxonomic revision of Polyommatini is long overdue, and until its completion the classification used here must be seen as a preliminary concept, based on the evaluation of male genitalia. Two subgenera are recognized, based upon constant differences in the structure of phallus: *Polyommatus* (type-species *Papilio icarus* ROTTEMBURG, 1775) and *Agrodiaetus* (type-species *Papilio damon* DENIS & SCHIFFERMÜLLER 1775), the latter being the senior subjective synonym of *Lysandra* (type-species *Papilio coridon* PODA, 1761).

(34) – *Polyommatus albicans* is widespread in Spain; its three extreme forms were treated as distinct species by MANLEY & ALLCARD (1970). *P. albicans* is believed to be a monovoltine species with a rather long period of emergence stretching from late June until at least the first half of August (cf. *P. hispana*).

(35) – *Polyommatus asturiensis* and *P. caelestissima* are undoubtedly very closely related allopatric morphospecies, both replacing *P. coridon* in Spain. *P. asturiensis* is believed to hybridize with *P. albicans* occasionally in some localities (e. g. north of Burgos) and the same applies to *P. caelestissima* (e. g. near Moscardon). Ecological requirements of *asturiensis* and *caelestissima* are similar. *P. coridon*, very local and rare in northern Spain, appears to be always isolated from *asturiensis*, which is confined to much lower altitudes.

(36) – *Polyommatus hispana* (STAUDINGER, 1861) is the correct name for the species discovered and (uninominally) named *hispana* HERRICH-SCHÄFFER, 1851; the original combination was *Lycaena corydon hispana*. *P. hispana* is believed to be bivoltine and it is, broadly speaking, indistinguishable from *P. albicans*. It is in certain areas sympatric and its second generation also synchronic with *albicans*. The relationship of both taxa requires investigation which must include their ecology and life histories.

(37) – *Polyommatus italaglauca* is probably a rare natural hybrid between *P. coridon* and *P. bellargus* found occasionally in certain localities of central Italy; at one time it was believed to be an infraspecific form of *P. syriaca*.

(38) – *Polyommatus menelaos* and *P. philippi* are provisionally recognized as two distinct morphospecies in spite of their doubtful taxonomic status; they may prove conspecific with *P. eros* and *P. eroides* respectively.

(39) – *Polyommatus virgilius* is considered to be a distinct morphospecies confined to the mountain areas of central and southern Italy; it is closely related to and allopatric with *P. dolus*.

(40) – *Pseudophilotes panope* was originally described in the genus *Lycaena* and its identity is uncertain; to judge solely from the description and illustration, *panope* seems to be closely related to *P. baton* complex, or to *P. bavius*. It is placed in this genus tentatively. It was reported from the steppes of southern Ural Mts., but there are no records since the beginning of this century. The taxonomic status of *panope* is at present uncertain (R. H. T. MATTONI pers. comm.) and its occurrence in Europe rather doubtful (Y. P. NEKRUTENKO pers. comm.).

(41) – *Pseudophilotes schiffermuelleri* is considered distinct from the morphologically closely allied *P. vicrama:* the latter species is a high altitude hygrophil inhabiting wet alpine grassland usually next to stream beds, in Tibet (cf. *P. vicrama*). *P. schiffermuelleri* is always allopatric in relation to *P. baton*, this being the only reason for conspecific treatment of the two by some authors (e. g. HIGGINS & RILEY 1980).

(42) – *Philotes vicrama* is said to have been found in Greece by J. G. COUTSIS (E. BALLETTO pers. comm.); it is therefore placed provisionally in this checklist, awaiting further information (cf. *P. schiffermuelleri*).

(43) – *Coenonympha corinna* and *C. elbana* are treated here as two very closely related allopatric morphospecies following HIGGINS (1976); their status requires further confirmation.

(44) – *Coenonympha iphioides* is occasionally considered conspecific with *C. glycerion* by some authors (e. g. HIGGINS & RILEY 1980). Both species are undoubtedly closely related but they differ constantly except for a few populations (north-eastern limit of the Spanish cline of *iphioides*) which are believed to produce some transitional forms or individuals thought to be hybrids. The relationship of the two species has never been seriously investigated.

(45) – *Coenonympha pamphilus* is morphologically so heterogenous that at least its extreme forms may prove to be genetically incompatible; as their relationship has never been studied *pamphilus* is at present just a convenient collective name for the aggregate.

(46) – *Coenonympha rhodopensis* differs constantly from the closely allied *C. tullia* and is not a hygrophil (as the latter species).

(47) – *Erebia boreomontanum* was so inadequately described that its identity is a puzzle to everyone except, perhaps, its author. Only an examination of the type-material can elucidate its identity.

(48) – *Erebia cassioides* was erroneously treated as nomen nudum by WARREN (1981) on account of the confusion surrounding its identity. The taxon is retained here and treated provisionally as a senior subjective synonym of *neleus* pending designation of neotype/s as may be necessary. Also *E. aquitania* (sensu WARREN 1981) is considered conspecific with *cassioides*. *E. nivalis* is recognized as a distinct species in spite of WARREN's (1981) opinion, who considered the two "round-winged" forms *cassioides* and *nivalis* conspecific and distinct from the "pointed-winged" form *neleus*. The present treatment of all taxa concerned is motivated purely by convenience; it must not be understood as a rejection of WARREN's (1959) paper. Further morphological and above all biological data are required to solve this taxonomically difficult puzzle.

(49) – *Erebia serotina* is a very rare natural hybrid between *E. epiphron* and *E. manto* (BOURGOGNE 1964, WARREN 1981); it is included in this check-list chiefly because it is still treated as a distinct species by some authors apparently unaware of its status (e. g. HIGGINS 1976, HIGGINS & RILEY 1980).

(50) – *Erebia sudetica* inhabits in its true form five isolated areas: Czechoslovakia: Praded Mt. (= Altvater); France: Massif Central; Poland: Bialski Mts.: Ladek Zdroj; Romania: Retezat Mts.; and Switzerland: Grindelwald; the morphologically distinct *E. sudetica* from Austria (W. ARNSCHEID pers. comm.) is only provisionally treated as conspecific with the above taxon. Further research required.

(51) – According to KOCAK (1982) the correct generic name for *Hipparchia* is *Eumenis* HÜBNER, 1819 (type-species *Papilio autonoe* ESPER, 1783) while the name *Hipparchia* FABRICIUS, 1807 (type-species *Papilio hyperantus* LINNAEUS, 1758) should replace *Aphantopus*. This most drastic change in the

nomenclature and meaning of two long established generic names is based upon the discovery made by KOCAK (1982) of a formal error in the original designation of *Papilio fagi* SCOPOLI, 1763 (as the type-species of *Hipparchia*) at the time believed identical with *Papilio hermione* LINNAEUS, 1764, listed among the species named in the original description of *Hipparchia*. The case is discussed at some length by KUDRNA (1983) and a recommendation is made to the International Commission on Zoological Nomenclature to use its plenary powers to protect the stability of *Hipparchia* and *Aphantopus* in their traditional meanings.

(52) – *Hipparchia aristaeus* complex is represented in Europe by the following allopatric morphospecies: *H. aristaeus, H. ballettoi, H. blachieri, H. maderensis* and *H. senthes*; the last named taxon is a collective name for a morphologically heterogeneous aggregate of possibly two or three allopatric morphospecies. Biological relationship of the above taxa is unknown. The subjective availability of the name *aristaeus* is discussed by KUDRNA (1983).

(53) – *Hipparchia fagi* and *H. hermione:* the identity and synonymy of these taxa is discussed by KUDRNA (1983) and requires a ruling by the International Commission on Zoological Nomenclature.

(54) – *Hyponephele huebneri* was apparently last reported from the European part of the U.S.S.R. by JACHONTOV (1935) and its occurrence is uncertain (Y. P. NEKRUTENKO pers. comm.).

(55) – *Lasiommata deidamia* has been recorded on a few occasions in the European part of the U.S.S.R. (KORSHUNOV 1972) and it may live in the southern part of the Ural Mts.; confirmation required (Y. P. NEKRUTENKO pers. comm.).

(56)–Preliminary hitherto unpublished results of original research strongly indicate that *P. afra* and *P. dalmata* are two distinct allopatric morphospecies; at present (including this work) the latter is usually treated as a synonym or subspecies of the former taxon. The genus *Proterebia* is recognized only tentatively; it may prove to be only a subgenus or a synonym of the genus *Callerebia*. Complete research results will be published separately in due course.

(57) – *Maniola jurtina* is used here as a collective name for a complex of closely related taxa of which at least *hispulla* may prove better placed as a distinct species than a subjective junior synonym of *jurtina*. It appears that there is only a narrow belt of apparently interbreeding populations between

the central-eastern *jurtina* and south-western *hispulla*. Opinions as to where to find the apparently interbreeding populations differ (e. g. LATTIN 1968, THOMSON 1973). Contradicting morphological evidence and lack of biological data make unequivocal conclusions impossible at present, this in spite of a taxonomic revision being available (THOMSON 1973).

(58) – *Melanargia russiae* forms in Europe at least three taxonomically distinct groups of populations, which inhabit (1) Portugal, Spain, southern France and north-western Italy *(cleanthe);* (2) southern Italy *(japygia);* (3) south-western Russia *(russiae).* Specimens reported from the Balkan Peninsula appear to be very similar to those from southern Italy and those from Hungary, where the species was discovered and became extinct at the beginning of this century were very close to or identical with those from southern Russia.

(59) – *Minois dryas* may prove to be a complex of two (or more) ecologically isolated sibling species lacking constant morphological features separating them from each other. *Minois dryas* lives in the following habitats:
– Open extremely xerothermophilous rocky slopes covered with sparse grassland (e. g. N. Italy: Südtirol);
– Open grass covered spaces in subnemoral xerothermophilous habitats (e. g. forest-steppe) (e. g. in most of south-eastern Europe);
– Dry open grassland in sparsely wooded annually flooded river valleys in central Europe (e. g. Czechoslovakia: Vltava river valley south of C. Budejovice and Germany: Inntal; similar habitats in N. Italy);
– Watermeadows and fens in Bayern (Germany).

*M. dryas* thus appears to be both an extreme hygrophil and xerothermophil. It is unlikely that potential hybrids would be ecologically viable in either of the extreme habitats.

(60) – *Oeneis dembowskyi, O. falkovitchi, O. koslowskyi, O. kusnetzovi* and *O. saepestriata* are species recently described from Polar Ural Mts. (U.S.S.R.) by either SEDYKH alone or SEDYKH et al. (1974). Their descriptions are inadequate to recognize them, figures very poor indeed, showing only the wing surface. Type-material is not available for comparison at present. Unfortunately their names are available. Until more information, including type-material, becomes available these "nomina dubia" are best ingnored by all zoologists.

(61) – *Pseudochazara amymone, P. cingovskii* and *P. orestes* are all closely related geographically and have been discovered in recent years. Together with

a similar species *P. graeca* they form a group of apparently closely related allopatric species (there are more members of the group in Asia). *Pseudochazara* taxa lack most of clear cut morphological features (e. g. male genitalia) characteristic of some other satyrid genera (e. g. *Hipparchia*) and their classification must remain rather fluid until biological information becomes available. A traditional taxonomic revision is unlikely to solve all the problems outstanding.

(62) – Subfamily Argynninae (or tribe Argynnini according to some authors) has suffered from considerable instability in its generic classification over the past decades. The European species, in all 29, have been in the extreme grouped in about ten genera (e. g. HIGGINS & RILEY 1980) or in just two genera (e. g. BLAB & KUDRNA 1982), (HOWARTH 1973). Morphological criteria for all these classifications have been laid down by WARREN (1944, 1955) who precisely defined ten European genera: *Boloria, Proclossiana, Clossiana, Argyronome, Issoria, Brenthis, Mesoacidalia, Fabriciana, Argynnis* and *Damora*. They are based on the examination of male genitalia (female genitalia have not been taken into consideration) and differ somewhat from the results of the studies carried out at the same time by PASSOS & GREY (1945). Some of the genera recognized by WARREN (1944, 1955) are not separated by a decisive gap from the next closely related genus: for instance monotypic genus *Proclossiana* appears to be too closely related to both *Boloria* and *Clossiana* to be worthy of recognition. The complex structural modifications in male genitalia make the classification very much subject to individual interpretations and tastes. It will be necessary to study also female genitalia on the same scale as WARREN's (1955) examination of males as well as including the rest of the African and American species before a final generic classification can be produced; this is not likely to be in the foreseeable future. A brief preliminary examination of female genitalia of some European species suggests that there are probably two distinct groups within the tribe. For the purpose of this work five distinct genera have been recognized, based upon taxonomic characters known to WARREN (1944) and using the same terminology:

– *Boloria:* proximal end of aedoeagus closed; uncus simple terminating bifid. European subgenera recognized: *Boloria, Proclossiana, Clossiana.*
– *Argyronome:* proximal end of aedoeagus closed; uncus specialised terminating in a single prong; monotypic in Europe.
– *Issoria:* proximal end of aedoeagus open, uncus simple terminating in a single prong; monotypic in Europe.
– *Brenthis:* proximal end of aedoeagus open; uncus simple terminating trifid; no subgenera recognized.

– *Argynnis:* proximal end of aedoeagus open; uncus specialised terminating in a single prong (subgeneric modifications); European subgenera recognized: *Argynnis, Damora, Fabriciana, Mesoacidalia.*

It should be noted that *Pandoriana* WARREN, 1942 recognized by HIGGINS (1976) and HIGGINS & RILEY (1980) was erected erroneously for *Papilio maja* CRAMER, 1775, and subsequently sunk as a junior subjective synonym of *Damora* NORDMANN 1851 by WARREN (1955).

(63) – *Argynnis adippe* differs in Spain and Portugal in constant morphological features *(Chlorodippe)* from the rest of European populations, except in some Catalonian colonies (MANLEY & ALLCARD 1970) where the Iberian form is not exclusive and its characters are less marked. *A. adippe* is at present no more than a convenient collective name for the whole complex which requires full investigation taking into account also biological aspects.

(64) – *Argynnis niobe* from Spain *(altonevadensis)* and possibly also from southern Italy *(rubida)* are so distinct from the rest of the European populations that they may prove to be specifically distinct.

(65) – Genera *Arethusana, Chazara, Hipparchia, Kanetisa, Minois, Pseudochazara* and *Satyrus* form a relatively homogenous complex; their recognition here follows LESSE (1952). It may prove convenient to "lump" them in one genus after clarification of the validity of the name *Hipparchia.*

(66) – *Euphydryas aurinia, E. beckeri, E. glaciegenita* and *E. provincialis* are treated here as four distinct essentially allopatric morphospecies; each of them lives in a different specialized biotope. Nomenclature of *E. glaciegenita* is discussed by KUDRNA (1983).

(67) – *Euphydryas orientalis* is considered specifically distinct (HIGGINS 1950, KORSHUNOV 1972); it resembles *E. desfontainii* so closely that examination of male genitalia is necessary for their correct identification, apart from widely separated ranges (i. e. vicariant species). The species is ecologically similar to *E. beckeri* and *E. provincialis* and, therefore, distinct from the hygrophilous *E. aurinia.*

(68) – *Melitaea athalia* is a collective name for a complex of forms believed to be conspecific although some of them (e. g. *nevadensis*) differ morphologically to such a degree that they may prove to be specifically distinct.

(69) – *Melitaea neglecta* is tentatively treated as a distinct species; it was originally described from the German Democratic Republic and subsequently reported also from Czechoslovakia: Sumava (= Böhmerwald) Mts. (WEISS 1967); it is a tyrphophil confined to peat bogs. Taxonomic status, distribution, ecology and early stages of *M. neglecta* require investigation.

(70) – KOCAK (1982) replaced nomen nudum *Papilio phoebe* DENIS & SCHIFFERMÜLLER 1775 by *Papilio corythallia* ESPER, 1780. The former name was rejected earlier by PACLT (1949) and replaced by *Papilio paedotrophos* BERGSTRÄSSER, 1780, which was treated later by KOCAK (1982) as junior subjective synonym of *P. corythallia*. Later KOCAK (1983) established that the correct name for the species is *Papilio phoebe* GOEZE, 1779. Although *Papilio phoebe* DENIS & SCHIFFERMÜLLER, 1775, is a nomen nudum – the fact was unfortunately overlooked by HIGGINS (1941) and HIGGINS & RILEY (1970, 1980) – the identity of the species has never been questioned. The International Commission on Zoological Nomenclature would be advised to take any action necessary to protect the name *Papilio phoebe,* currently treated in the genus *Melitaea* FABRICIUS, 1807, perhaps by placing it on the list of available specific names in zoology. Should the authorship of DENIS & SCHIFFERMÜLLER, 1775, be prefered to that of GOEZE, 1797, the non-existent original description can be replaced by the one given by HIGGINS (1941).

(71) – The occurrence in Europe of *Polyommatus actis* is doubtful (Y. P. NEKRUTENKO pers. comm.), based on an old record or misidentification (KORSHUNOV 1972).

(72) – *Lycaena ochimus* was reported by REBEL (1913) from Macedonia: Bitola: Monastir: 1 ♂. LORKOVIC & JAKSIC (1979) consider that its occurrence in Yugoslavia is possible. This appears to be the only record of the species from anywhere in Europe.

(73) – *Erebia dabanensis* is an Asiatic species rather difficult to identify; it was reported from the Polar Ural Mts. on one occasion some 60 years ago and subsequently said to have been found also by K. F. SEDYKH (pers. comm.). Confirmation required.

(74) – *Erebia edda* was reported once from the Polar Ural Mts. (1 ♂) some 60 years ago and its occurrence has subsequently never been confirmed (K. F. SEDYKH pers. comm.).

(75) – *Vacciniina loewi:* transfer of *loewi* from *Plebejus* to *Vacciniina* follows recommendation made by E. BALLETTO (pers. comm.); the occurrence of the species in Europe (Greece: Rhodos) requires confirmation.

(76) KOCAK (1982) pointed out that *Papilio hippolyte* ESPER, 1784, is a junior primary homonym of *Papilio hyppolyte* DRURY, 1782, and replaced the invalid name by an almost unused junior subjective synonym *Satyrus mercurius* STAUDINGER, 1887 (the two taxa are not necessarily conspecific). Unless the redrawn principle of homonymy in the third edition of the International Code of Zoological Nomenclature (Art. 52, 53, 57–60) prevents the substitution, the International Commission on Zoological Nomenclature should take action under its plenary powers to protect the continued long established use of *Pseudochazara hippolyte* (ESPER, 1784); secondary homonymy does not exist between the two names concerned.

(77) – *Erebia jeniseiensis* is an Asiatic species closely resembling European *E. euryale*; it was apparently recently recorded in U.S.S.R.: Komi: Vorkuta by K. F. SEDYKH (pers. comm.). Confirmation required.

(78) – KOCAK (1980) drew attention to the homonymy between *Papilio egea* FABRICIUS, 1775, and *Papilio egea* CRAMER, 1775, and subsequently replaced the junior homonym by *Papilio i-album* ESPER, 1793. Later KOCAK (1981) established that *Papilio i-album* is a junior synonym of *Papilio vau-album* ESPER, 1780 because the latter name is not a junior primary homonym of nomen nudum *Papilio vau-album* DENIS & SCHIFFERMÜLLER, 1775. *Polygonia egea* (CRAMER, 1775) is a well established name and the International Commission on Zoological Nomenclature should use its plenary powers to protect its continued use unchanged.

(79) – PACLT (1952) drew attention to the fact that *Papilio medusa* DENIS & SCHIFFERMÜLLER, 1775, is a nomen nudum and requested its protection as it is a well established name the identity of which has never been disputed. The International Commission on Zoological Nomenclature has taken no action, being apparently unaware of this request (R. V. MELVILLE pers. comm.). KOCAK (1982) replaced *Papilio medusa* by *Papilio psodea* HÜBNER, 1806, a name probably never used for the species in any standard work (the taxa are doubtless conspecific). I propose that the International Commission on Zoological Nomenclature takes an urgent action to protect the unchanged continued use of *Erebia medusa* (DENIS & SCHIFFERMÜLLER 1775) as defined by WARREN (1936). It must be pointed out that the definition WARREN (1936) presumed to constitute the original description of *Papilio medusa* is not applicable (i. e. not crossreferenced) to that species.

(80) – KOCAK (1981) pointed out that *Papilio vau-album* DENIS & SCHIFFER-MÜLLER, 1775 was published without description, definition or indication and is, therefore, a nomen nudum. KOCAK (1981) replaced it by *Papilio l-album* ESPER, 1780, which was used for the species almost exclusively until it was replaced by the above mentioned nomen nudum by HIGGINS & RILEY (1970).

(81) – Genus *Lycaena* is accepted here as defined by KLOTS (1936). Two distinct subgenera appear to be worthy of recognition: *Lycaena* with type-species *Papilio phlaeas* LINNAEUS, 1761, and *Palaechrysophanus* with type-species *Papilio hippothoe* LINNAEUS, 1761; (cf. 3.4: synonymic list).

(82) – Genus *Pieris* was defined by KLOTS (1933); three European subgenera are recognized: *Artogeia* (type-species *Papilio napi* LINNAEUS, 1758), *Pieris* (type-species *Papilio brassicae* LINNAEUS, 1758) and *Pontia* (type-species *Papilio daplidice* LINNAEUS, 1758).

(83) – *Hipparchia bacchus, H. gomera* and *H. wyssii* are three allopatric geographically isolated morphospecies. The present treatment of *Hipparchia azorina, H. caldeirense* and *H. miguelensis* follows OEHMIG (1983). Reclassification of *Hipparchia cypriensis, H. leighebi* and *H. malickyi* resulted from the consequent applications of taxonomic principles and categories outlined earlier in this chapter.

(84) – *Oeneis pansa* and *O. semidea* are very closely allied and may prove conspecific.

(85) – *Melitaea fascelis* was used by PACLT (1949) to replace nomen nudum *Papilio trivia* DENIS & SCHIFFERMÜLLER, 1775; unfortunately this escaped the attention of HIGGINS (1976) and HIGGINS & RILEY (1970, 1980) who continued to use the nomen nudum, probably following HIGGINS (1941) who must have failed to check its availability. There are no special reasons calling for the protection of this nomen nudum and KOCAK (1981) already used the correct name for the species.

(86) – KOCAK (1983) concluded that *Papilio thersamon* ESPER, 1784 is a junior subjective synonym of *Papilio hyllus* CRAMER, 1775, and sunk the former name. KOCAK's (1983) conclusion is based on the fact that both taxa have similar external features, and that the type-locality of *hyllus* is "Smirne", which he believes is to be interpreted as the name of a city in Turkey. HOWE's (1975) figure of *Lycaena hyllus* shows that the species is similar to *L. thersamon*; the inadequacy of the original descriptions and illustra-

tions of both taxa is not surprising. KOCAK (1983) probably overlooked that apart from the Turkish Smyrna (or Smirna, correctly Izmir) there are at least two towns called Smyrna in the U.S.A., the type-locality of *hyllus*. The name *Lycaena thersamon*, and its identity, has never been questioned. To protect its long established use I suggest that the International Commission should use its plenary powers to place *Papilio thersamon* ESPER, 1784 on the official list of available names in zoology.

(87) – *Ultraaricia orpheus* is considered to be an individual form of *U. anteros* and subsequently synonymized by KOCAK (1983).

(88) – *Nordmannia* is applied here as a collective generic name to all European species usually placed in two or more genera (cf. synonymic list); the genus (s. l.) requires a full taxonomic revision.

(89) – *Polyommatus coerulescens* appears to be a natural hybrid between *P. albicans* and *P. caelestissima* (MANLEY & ALLCARD 1970, K. G. SCHURIAN pers. comm.), although it has been found also in localities where apparently only one parent species occurs (KUDRNA 1974). It is possible that *P. coerulescens* is partially fertile and represents thus an incipient species; the taxon has never been adequately studied in the field.

(90) – *Lycaena morronensis* RIBBE, 1910, is a junior subjective synonym of *Lycaena idas* RAMBUR, 1842. The latter name was rejected and replaced by *Lycaena ramburi* VERITY, 1913, on account of its being a secondary junior homonym of *Papilio idas* LINNAEUS, 1761; the taxa are not considered congeneric at present. According to the Article 59(b) (i) of the International Code of Zoological Nomenclature, the secondary junior homonym is rejected permanently because the action was taken before 1961.

(91) – *Thaleropis ionia* is reported for the first time from Europe. J. G. COUTSIS (pers. comm.) found and identified 1 ♂ of this species in the Lepidoptera collection of the Goulandris Museum (Greece: Kifisia). Locality: Island of Kastelorizon (a small off-shore island south of the Turkish town of Kas, some 140 km east of Rhodos.

(92) – *Polyommatus exuberans* was originally considered conspecific with either *P. admetus* or *P. ripartii* and treated as a "race" (i. e. in this case subspecies by implication). Recent research (E. BALLETTO pers. comm.) has shown, that *exuberans* is better placed as a distinct morphospecies. Biological affinity of *exuberans* to its close allies is unknown and as the species is now apparently extinct, it cannot be clarified.

(93) – *Hipparchia occidentalis* SOUSA, 1982, is the valid name of the species called *Hipparchia caldeirense* OEHMIG, 1983, throughout this work. Whereas the latter name was published in a well known lepidopterological journal, the former name appeared in a supplement containing a congress report, which is rarely found in major European entomological libraries and was unavailable at the time of writing the work. I am indebted to A.B. de SOUSA for sending me a copy of the supplement concerned as well as a reprint of the publication containing the original description of *H. occidentalis*. I propose to sink the following synonymy (retaining for that purpose the original combinations):

*Hipparchia azorina occidentalis* SOUSA, 1982
*Hipparchia caldeirense* OEHMIG, 1983, **syn. n.**

because both names denote the same taxon. I further propose to elevate the valid name of this taxon to the species-rank:

*Hipparchia occidentalis* SOUSA, 1982, **stat. n.**

as it is an allopatric morphospecies of *H. azorina* complex.


(94) – *Euphydryas wolfensbergeri* is considered specifically distinct from *E. intermedia* of eastern Asia; both species differ morphologically and have widely separated ranges.


(95) – Asiatic species *Erebia cyclopius* EVERSMANN, 1844 and *E. ocnus* EVERSMANN, 1843, are not included in this checklist. As they reach westwards the Ural Mts., their occurrence in Europe is possible.


## 4.6 A provisional synonymic check-list of generic and specific names of European butterflies

The following check-list includes about 1000 genus-group and species-group names of European butterflies and gives all common synonyms to enable the reader to use and understand all widespread books and works published after about 1900. The arrangement and selection of names included are governed by purely pragmatic reasons, with the simplicity of use in mind. For this reason, apart from bona fide synonyms of available names, also names of misidentified taxa and certain as available name commonly misinterpreted unavailable names, are listed, without change of author's name following the misidentification. Where a further confusion could possibly arise, such names are marked with an asterisk. This is particularly important to observe in case of all extra-European polytypic species whose nominate forms have been reported in the past from Europe in connection with a subspecies-rank name, treated here as a species-rank name (i. e. some allopatric morphospecies). Where it was thought necessary for taxonomic or any other reasons, also some "genuine" infraspecific names are listed among the synonyms. All names are arranged in alphabetic order. Pattern of arrangement of individual entries:

- Genus-group names:
  Valid: genus-group name author, year–(synonyms, if applicable)–(abbreviated family name).
  Junior synonyms: genus-group name author, year–reference to valid generic name.

- Species-group names:
  Valid: species-group name author/s, year–(synonyms, if applicable)–valid generic name–(abbreviated family name)–serial number in the annotated checklist.
  Junior synonyms: species group name author, year–reference to valid specific name.

Family names are abbreviated as follows: Danaidae: (DA); Libytheidae: (LI); Lycaenidae: (LY); Nymphalidae: (NY); Papilionidae: (PA); Pieridae: (PI); Riodinidae: (RI); Satyridae: (SA). Colon is used to indicate that a reference follows or continues. Subjectively recognized subgeneric names are not distinguished from synonyms.

*abencerragus* PIERRET, 1837 *(amelia)*: *Pseudophilotes* (LY): 180
*acaciae* FABRICIUS, 1787: *Nordmannia* (LY): 130
*acamas* KLUG, 1834: *Cigaritis* (LY): 087
*aceris* LEPECHIN, 1774: *sappho*
*achine* SCOPOLI, 1763 *(dejanira)*: *Lasiommata* (SA): 316
*acis* DENIS & SCHIFFERMÜLLER, 1775: *semiargus*
*actaea* ESPER, 1780: *Satyrus* (SA): 369
*actis* HERRICH-SCHÄFFER, 1851: *Polyommatus* (LY): 141
*adalwinda* FRUHSTORFER, 1909 *(arctica)*: *Pieris* (PI): 050
*adippe* LINNAEUS, 1767 *(chlorodippe, cydippe, phryca)*: *Argynnis* (NY): 379
*admetus* ESPER, 1785: *Polyommatus* (LY): 142
*adonis* DENIS & SCHIFFERMÜLLER, 1775: *bellargus*
*adrasta* ILLIGER, 1807: *maera*
*adyte* HÜBNER, 1822: *euryale*
*aegeria* LINNAEUS, 1758 *(aegerides, tircis, vulgaris)*: *Pararge* (SA): 354
*aegidion* MEISNER, 1818: *argus*
*aegon* DENIS & SCHIFFERMÜLLER, 1775: *argus*

*aegus* CHAPMAN, 1917: *argyrognomon*
*aelia* HOFFMANSEGG, 1804: *hermione*
*aello* HÜBNER, 1804: *glacialis*
*aetheria* ESPER, 1805: *epiphron*
*aetheria* LUCAS, 1848 *(aetherie)*: *Melitaea* (NY): 423
*aetherie* HÜBNER, 1826: *aetheria*
*aethiopella* HOFFMANSEGG, 1806 *(gorgophone)*: *Erebia* (SA): 230
*aethiops* ESPER, 1777 *(medea)*: *Erebia* (SA): 231
*afer* ESPER, 1783: *afra*
*afra* FABRICIUS, 1787 *(afer, dalmata, phegea)*: *Proterebia* (SA): 357
*Agapetes* BILLBERG, 1820: *Melanargia*
*agathon* GODART, 1819: *amandus*
*agenjoi* FORSTER, 1965: *fabressei*
*agestis* DENIS & SCHIFFERMÜLLER, 1775 *(astrarche, medon)*: *Aricia* (LY):
    073
*agestor* GODART, 1824: *escheri*
*Aglais* DALMAN, 1816: (NY)
*aglaja* LINNAEUS, 1758 *(charlotta)*: *Argynnis* (NY): 380
*Agriades* HÜBNER, 1819: (LY)
*Agrodiaetus* HÜBNER, 1822: *Polyommatus*
*ainsae* FORSTER, 1961: *Polyommatus* (LY): 143
*alberganus* PRUNNER, 1798 *(ceto, phorcys)*: *Erebia* (SA): 232
*albicans* HERRICH-SCHÄFFER, 1851 *(arragonensis, bolivari, caerulescens)*:
    *Polyommatus* (LY): 144
*Albulina* TUTT, 1909: (LY)
*alcestis* \* ZERNY, 1932: *aroaniensis*
*alcetas* HOFFMANSEGG, 1804 *(coretas)*: *Cupido* (LY): 088
*alciphron* ROTTEMBURG, 1775 *(gordius, hipponoe, melibaeus)*: *Lycaena*
    (LY): 111
*alcon* DENIS & SCHIFFERMÜLLER, 1775: *Maculinea* (LY): 124
*alcyone* DENIS & SCHIFFERMÜLLER, 1775: *hermione*
*alecto* HÜBNER, 1806: *manto*
*alecto* GODART, 1823: *lefebvrei*
*alecto* BOISDUVAL, 1832: *pluto*
*alethea* HEMMING, 1934: *aquilonaris*
*alexanor* ESPER, 1799 *(polychaon)*: *Papilio* (PA): 004
*alexis* PODA, 1761 *(cyllarus)*: *Glaucopsyche* (LY): 098
*alexius* FREYER, 1858: *thersites*
*alfacariensis* BERGER, 1948 *(alfacariensis, australis, calida)*: *Colias* (PI): 020
*alfacariensis* \* RIBBE, 1905: *alfacariensis*
*algirica* \* OBERTHÜR, 1876: *aristaeus*
*Allancastria* BRYK, 1934: *Zerynthia*

*allionia* FABRICIUS, 1781: *statilinus*
*allionii* HÜBNER, 1824: *fatua*
*allous* GEYER, 1837 *(montana, montensis, nevadensis)*: *Aricia* (LY): 074
*alpicola* GALVAGNI, 1918: *cynthia*
*alsus* DENIS & SCHIFFERMÜLLER, 1775: *minimus*
*altonevadensis* REISSER, 1927: *niobe*
*amalthea* FRIVALDSKY, 1845: *anthelea*
*amandus* SCHNEIDER, 1792 *(agathon, icarius)*: *Polyommatus* (LY): 145
*amaryllis* STOLL, 1782: *Coenonympha* (SA): 214
*amathusia* ESPER, 1784: *titania*
*amelia* HEMMING, 1927: *abencerragus*
*ammon* ELWES, 1899: *Oeneis* (SA): 337
*ammonia* HERRICH-SCHÄFFER, 1951: *ionia*
*amphidamas* ESPER, 1780: *helle*
*amymone* BROWN, 1976: *Pseudochazara* (SA): 338
*amynta* DENIS & SCHIFFERMÜLLER, 1775: *argiades*
*amyntas* PODA, 1761: *glycerion*
*andera* FRUHSTORFER, 1911: *epistygne*
*angarensis* ERSCHOFF, 1870: *Boloria* (NY): 386
*anonyma* LEWIS, 1872: *reducta*
*anteros* FREYER, 1839: *Ultraaricia* (LY): 199
*anthe* HOFFMANSEGG, 1804: *Chazara* (SA): 211
*anthelea* LEFEBVRE, 1831 *(amalthea)*: *Pseudochazara* (SA): 359
*Anthocaris* HEMMING, 1934: *Anthocharis*
*Anthocharis* BOISDUVAL, 1833 *(Anthocaris)*: (PI)
*antiochena* LEDERER, 1861 *(helena)*: *Cyaniris* (LY): 095
*antiopa* LINNAEUS, 1758: *Nymphalis* (NY): 440
*Apatura* FABRICIUS, 1807: (NY)
*Apelles* HEMMING, 1931: *Glaucopsyche*
*Aphantopus* WALLENGREN, 1853: (SA)
*Apharitis* RILEY, 1925: *Cigaritis*
*aphirape* HÜBNER, 1806: *eunomia*
*aphrodite* HEMMING, 1934: *cecilia*
*apollinus* HERBST, 1798: *Archon* (PA): 001
*apollo* LINNAEUS, 1758: *Parnassius* (PA): 007
*Aporia* HÜBNER, 1819: (PI)
*aquilo* BOISDUVAL, 1832: *Agriades* (LY): 067
*aquilonaris* STICHEL, 1908 *(alethea, arsilache, sifanica)*: *Boloria* (NY): 387
*aquilonia* HIGGINS, 1969: *dorus*
*aquitania* FRUHSTORFER, 1909: *cassioides*
*arachne* ESPER, 1793: *statilinus*

*arachne* DENIS & SCHIFFERMÜLLER, 1775: *pronoe*
*Araschnia* HÜBNER, 1819: (NY)
*arcania* LINNAEUS, 1761: *Coenonympha* (SA): 215
*arcas* ROTTEMBURG, 1775: *nausithous*
*archippus* FABRICIUS, 1793: *plexippus*
*Archon* HÜBNER, 1822 *(Doritis)*: (PA)
*arcilacis* RILEY, 1927: *carswelli*
*arctica* \* VERITY, 1911: *adalwinda*
*arctica* MÜLLER & KAUTZ, 1939: *adalwinda*
*arduinna* ESPER, 1784 *(rhodopensis)*: *Melitaea* (NY): 424
*arete* FABRICIUS, 1787: *claudina*
*arethusa* DENIS & SCHIFFERMÜLLER, 1775 *(boabdil, dentata, erythia)*:
    *Arethusana* (SA): 210
*Arethusana* LESSE, 1951: (SA)
*Arge* \* HÜBNER, 1819: *Melanargia*
*arge* SULZER, 1776: *Melanargia* (SA): 328
*Argeformia* VERITY, 1953: *Melanargia*
*argester* BERGSTRÄSSER, 1779: *dorylas*
*argiades* PALLAS, 1771 *(amynta, tiresias)*: *Cupido* (LY): 089
*argiolus* LINNAEUS, 1758: *Celastrina* (LY): 084
*argus* LINNAEUS, 1758 *(aegidion, aegon, corsicus, hypochiona, sylvius)*:
    *Plebejus* (LY): 136
*Argynnis* FABRICIUS, 1807 *(Damora, Dryas, Fabriciana, Mesoacidalia,*
    *Mesodryas, Pandoriana)*: (NY)
*argyrognomon* BERGSTRÄSSER, 1779 *(aegon, ismenias, lycidas)*: *Lycaeides*
    (LY): 106
*Aricia* R. L., 1817 *(Eumedonia, Pseudaricia)*: (LY)
*arion* LINNAEUS, 1758 *(ligurica, obscura)*: *Maculinea* (LY): 125
*aristaeus* BONELLI, 1826 *(algirica, sardoa)*: *Hipparchia* (SA): 284
*aristolochiae* SCHNEIDER, 1787: *polyxena*
*aroaniensis* BROWN, 1976 *(alcestis)*: *Polyommatus* (LY): 146
*arragonensis* GERHARD, 1851: *albicans*
*arsilache* HÜBNER, 1786: *aquilonaris*
*artaxerxes* FABRICIUS, 1793: *Aricia* (LY): 075
*artemis* DENIS & SCHIFFERMÜLLER, 1775: *aurinia*
*Artogeia* VERITY, 1947: *Pieris*
*arvernensis* OBERTHÜR, 1908: *cassioides*
*asteria* FREYER, 1828: *Melitaea* (NY): 425
*asterope* KLUG, 1832: *Ypthima* (SA): 372
*astrarche* BERGSTRÄSSER, 1779: *agestis*
*astur* OBERTHÜR, 1884: *lefebvrei*
*asturiensis* OBERTHÜR, 1910: *pyrenaicus*

*asturiensis* SAGARRA, 1924 *(manleyi)*: *Polyommatus* (LY): 147
*atalanta* LINNAEUS, 1758: *Vanessa* (NY): 447
*athalia* ROTTEMBURG, 1775 *(biedermanni, boris, celadussa, helvetica, nevadensis, norvegica, pseudathalia)*: *Melitaea* (NY): 426
*Athaliaeformia* VERITY, 1950: *Melitaea*
*athene* BORKHAUSEN, 1788: *dryas*
*aurelia* NICKERL, 1850 *(parthenie)*: *Melitaea* (NY): 427
*aurinia* ROTTEMBURG, 1775 *(artemis)*: *Euphydryas* (NY): 408
*aurorina* HERRICH-SCHÄFFER, 1850 *(heldreichi, libanotica)*: *Colias* (PI): 021
*ausonia* HÜBNER, 1804: *Euchloe* (PI): 033
*australis* * VERITY, 1911: *alfacariensis*
*autonoe* ESPER, 1784: *Hipparchia* (SA): 285
*avis* CHAPMAN, 1909: *Callophrys* (LY): 082
*Azanus* MOORE, 1881: (LY)
*azorina* STRECKER, 1899 *(picoensis)*: *Hipparchia* (SA): 286


*bacchus* HIGGINS, 1967: *Hipparchia* (SA): 287
*bachmatjewi* DRENOWSKI, 1923: *rhodopensis*
*baetica* RAMBUR, 1858: *desfontainii*
*balcana* LORKOVIC, 1970 *(canidiaformis)*: *Pieris* (PI): 051
*balcanica* REBEL, 1903: *graeca*
*balcanica* REBEL, 1903: *Colias* (PI): 022
*balcanica* REBEL, 1903: *ottomana*
*balcanicus* FREYER, 1845: *Tarucus* (LY): 191
*ballettoi* KUDRNA, 1984: *Hipparchia* (SA): 288
*ballus* FABRICIUS, 1787: *Tomares* (LY): 194
*barbagiae* PRINS & POORTEN, 1982: *Pseudophilotes* (LY): 181
*barcina* VERITY, 1927: *ilia*
*batava* OBERTHÜR, 1920: *dispar*
*bathseba* FABRICIUS, 1793 *(pasiphae)*: *Pyronia* (SA): 366
*baton* BERGSTRÄSSER, 1779 *(hylas)*: *Pseudophilotes* (LY): 182
*battus* DENIS & SCHIFFERMÜLLER, 1775: *orion*
*bavius* EVERSMANN, 1832 *(hungaricus)*: *Pseudophilotes* (LY): 183
*beckeri* HERRICH-SCHÄFFER, 1851 *(iberica)*: *Euphydryas* (NY): 409
*bejarensis* CHAPMAN, 1902: *meolans*
*belemia* ESPER, 1798 *(hesperidum)*: *Euchloe* (PI): 034
*belia* * LINNAEUS, 1767: *euphenoides*
*bellargus* ROTTEMBURG, 1775 *(adonis, thetis)*: *Polyommatus* (LY): 148
*bellidice* BRAHM, 1805: *daplidice*
*bellieri* OBERTHÜR, 1910: *corsica*
*bellinus* PRUNNER, 1798: *eumedon*
*belzebub* COSTA, 1839: *pluto*

*berisalii* Rühl, 1891: *deione*
*betulae* Linnaeus, 1758: *Thecla* (LY): 193
*biedermanni* Querci, 1932: *athalia*
*bieli* Staudinger, 1901: *dorus*
*Bithys* Hübner, 1818: *Quercusia*
*biton* Sulzer, 1776: *damon*
*blachieri* Fruhstorfer, 1908 *(siciliana)*: *Hipparchia* (SA): 289
*bleusei* Oberthür, 1884: *tityrus*
*boabdil* Rambur, 1842: *arethusa*
*boeticus* Linnaeus, 1767: *Lampides* (LY): 105
*bolivari* Romei, 1927: *albicans*
*Boloria* Moore, 1900 *(Clossiana, Proclossiana)*: (NY)
*bore* Esper, 1790: *Oeneis* (SA): 338
*borealis* Staudinger, 1861: *thore*
*boreomontanum* Sedykh, 1979: *Erebia* (SA): 233
*boris* Fruhstorfer, 1917: *athalia*
*brassicae* Linnaeus, 1758 *(wollastoni)*: *Pieris* (PI): 052
*Brenthis* Hübner, 1819: (NY)
*Brintesia* Fruhstorfer, 1911: *Kanetisa*
*briseis* Linnaeus, 1764 *(pirata)*: *Chazara* (SA): 212
*britomartis* Assman, 1847 *(melathalia, veronicae)*: *Melitaea* (NY): 428
*bryce* Hübner, 1806: *ferula*
*Bryna* Evans, 1912: *Polyommatus*
*bryoniae* Hübner, 1806: *Pieris* (PI): 053
*bulgarica* Drenowsky, 1932: *ottomana*
*bureschi* Warren, 1936: *ottomana*

*cadmus* Fruhstorfer, 1908: *semele*
*caelestissima* Verity, 1921: *Polyommatus* (LY): 149
*caerulescens* Tutt, 1909: *albicans*
*calaritas* Fruhstorfer, 1918: *meolans*
*c-album* Linnaeus, 1758: *Polygonia* (NY): 444
*calcaria* Lorkovic, 1949: *Erebia* (SA): 234
*caldeirense* Oehmig, 1983 *(occidentalis)*: *Hipparchia* (SA): 290
*calida* Verity, 1916: *alfacariensis*
*calleuphenia* Butler, 1869: *euphenoides*
*callidice* Hübner, 1800: *Pieris* (PI): 054
*callimachus* Eversmann, 1848: *Tomares* (LY): 195
*calliopis* Boisduval, 1832: *idas*
*calliroe* Hübner, 1808: *indica*
*Callophrys* Billberg, 1820: (LY)
*camilla* Linnaeus, 1764 *(sibilla)*: *Limenitis* (NY): 420

*camilla* DENIS & SCHIFFERMÜLLER, 1775: *reducta*
*canariensis* BLACHIER, 1821: *cramera*
*candens* HERRICH-SCHÄFFER, 1844 *(leonhardi)*: *Lycaena* (LY): 112
*canidiaformis* \* DRENOWSKI, 1925: *balcana*
*canidiaformis* DRENOWSKI, 1925: *napi*
*cardamines* LINNAEUS, 1758: *Anthocharis* (PI): 014
*cardui* LINNAEUS, 1758: *Vanessa* (NY): 448
*carswelli* STEMPFFER, 1927 *(arcilacis)*: *Cupido* (LY): 090
*cassioides* REINER & HOHENWARTH, 1792 *(aquitania, arvernensis, neleus)*:
   *Erebia* (SA): 235
*cassiope* FABRICIUS, 1787: *epiphron*
*Catopsilia* HÜBNER, 1819: (PI)
*cecilia* VALLANTIN, 1894 *(aphrodite, ida)*: *Pyronia* (SA): 367
*cecilia* ESPER, 1805: *oeme*
*celadussa* FRUHSTORFER, 1910: *athalia*
*Celastrina* TUTT, 1906 *(Lycaenopsis)*: (LY)
*celtis* LAICHARTING, 1782: *Libythea* (LI): 206
*cerisyi* GODART, 1822 *(ferdinandi)*: *Zerynthia* (PA): 010
*ceto* HÜBNER, 1806: *alberganus*
*Charaxes* OCHSENHEIMER, 1816: (NY)
*chariclea* SCHNEIDER, 1794: *Boloria* (NY): 388
*charlonia* DONZEL, 1842: *Euchloe* (PI): 035
*charlotta* HOWARTH, 1802: *aglaja*
*Chattendenia* TUTT, 1908: *Nordmannia*
*Chazara* MOORE, 1893: (SA)
*cheiranthi* HÜBNER, 1808: *Pieris* (PI): 055
*Chilades* MOORE, 1881 *(Freyeria)*: (LY)
*Chionabas* BOISDUVAL, 1833: *Oeneis*
*chiron* ROTTEMBURG, 1775: *eumedon*
*chloridice* OCHSENHEIMER, 1816: *Pieris* (PI): 056
*chlorodippe* HERRICH-SCHÄFFER, 1851: *adippe*
*Chortobius* DUNNING & PICARD, 1858: *Coenonympha*
*christenseni* KUDRNA, 1977: *Hipparchia* (SA): 291
*christi* RÄTZER, 1890: *Erebia* (SA): 236
*chryseis* DENIS & SCHIFFERMÜLLER, 1775: *hippothoe*
*chrysippus* LINNAEUS, 1758: *Danaus* (DA): 207
*Chrysophanus* \* HÜBNER, 1818: *Lycaena*
*chrysotheme* ESPER, 1780: *Colias* (PI): 023
*Cigaritis* DONZEL, 1847 *(Apharitis)*: (LY)
*Cinclidia* HÜBNER, 1819: *Melitaea*
*cingovskii* GROSS, 1973: *Pseudochazara* (SA): 360
*cinxia* LINNAEUS, 1758 *(pilosellae)*: *Melitaea* (NY): 429

*circe* \* DENIS & SCHIFFERMÜLLER, 1775: *tityrus*
*circe* FABRICIUS, 1775 *(proserpina)*: *Kanetisa* (SA): 315
*claudina* BORKHAUSEN, 1789 *(arete)*: *Erebia* (SA): 237
*cleo* HÜBNER, 1806: *tyndarus*
*cleobis* BREMER, 1861 *(sareptensis)*: *Lycaeides* (LY): 107
*cleobule* HÜBNER, 1825 *(eversi)*: *Gonepteryx* (PI): 041
*cleodoxa* ESPER, 1788: *niobe*
*cleopatra* LINNAEUS, 1767: *Gonepteryx* (PI): 042
*climene* ESPER, 1784: *Lasiommata* (SA): 317
*Clossiana* REUSS, 1920: *Boloria*
*clotho* HÜBNER, 1800: *russiae*
*coelestinus* EVERSMANN, 1848: *Polyommatus* (LY): 150
*coenobita* GOEZE, 1779: *rivularis*
*Coenonympha* HÜBNER, 1819 *(Chortobius, Lyela, Sicca)*: (SA)
*coerulescens* TUTT, 1909: *Polyommatus* (LY): 151
*Colias* FABRICIUS, 1807: (PI)
*Colotis* HÜBNER, 1819: (PI)
*constans* EIFFINGER, 1908: *manto*
*cordula* FABRICIUS, 1793: *ferula*
*coretas* OCHSENHEIMER, 1808: *alcetas*
*coridon* PODA, 1761: *Polyommatus* (LY): 152
*corinna* HÜBNER, 1806 *(norax)*: *Coenonympha* (SA): 216
*corsica* BELLIER, 1862 *(bellieri)*: *Lycaeides* (LY): 108
*corsicus* BELLIER, 1862: *argus*
*corythallia* ESPER, 1780: *phoebe*
*Cosmolyce* TOXOPEUS, 1927: *Lampides*
*cotys* JACHONTOV, 1935: *pellucida*
*crambis* FREYER, 1845 *(oeno, polycena)*: *Oeneis* (SA): 339
*cramera* ESCHSCHOLTZ, 1821 *(canariensis)*: *Aricia* (LY): 076
*crameri* BUTLER, 1869: *Euchloe* (PI): 036
*crataegi* LINNAEUS, 1758: *Aporia* (PI): 018
*cretica* REBEL, 1904: *Zerynthia* (PA): 011
*cretica* REBEL, 1916: *Hipparchia* (SA): 292
*crocea* GEOFFROY, 1785 *(edusa, electo)*: *Colias* (PI): 024
*Cupido* SCHRANK, 1801 *(Everes, Tiora, Zizera)*: (LY)
*cyane* EVERSMANN, 1837: *Polyommatus* (LY): 153
*Cyaniris* DALMAN, 1816: (LY)
*Cyclirius* BUTLER, 1897: (LY)
*cydippe* LINNAEUS, 1761: *adippe*
*cyllarus* ROTTEMBURG, 1775: *alexis*
*Cynthia* FABRICIUS, 1807: *Vanessa*
*cynthia* DENIS & SCHIFFERMÜLLER, 1775 *(alpicola, trivia)*: *Euphydryas*

(NY): 410
*cyparissus* HÜBNER, 1808: *optilete*
*cypriaca* STAUDINGER, 1879: *syriaca*
*cypricola* GRAVES, 1928: *Maniola* (SA): 324
*cypriensis* HOLIK, 1949 *(pellucida)*: *Hipparchia* (SA): 293
*cypris* MEIGEN, 1828: *titania*
*cyrene* HÜBNER, 1824: *elisa*


*dabanensis* ERSCHOFF, 1871 *(tundra)*: *Erebia* (SA): 238
*daira* KLUG, 1829: *evagore*
*dalmata* GODART, 1824: *afra*
*damon* DENIS & SCHIFFERMÜLLER, 1775 *(biton)*: *Polyommatus* (LY): 154
*damone* EVERSMANN, 1841: *Polyommatus* (LY): 155
*damone* BOISDUVAL, 1836: *Anthocharis* (PI): 015
*Damora* NORDMANN, 1851: *Argynnis*
*Danais* LATREILLE, 1807: *Danaus*
*Danaus* KLUK, 1802 *(Danais)*: (DA)
*daphne* BERGSTRÄSSER, 1780: *Brenthis* (NY): 404
*daphnis* DENIS & SCHIFFERMÜLLER, 1775 *(meleager)*: *Polyommatus* (LY): 156
*daplidice* LINNAEUS, 1758 *(bellidice, raphani)*: *Pieris* (PI): 057
*dardanus* FREYER, 1844: *Agriades* (LY): 068
*darwiniana* STAUDINGER, 1871: *Coenonympha* (SA): 217
*davus* FABRICIUS, 1777: *tullia*
*debilis* * OBERTHÜR, 1909: *glaciegenita*
*decolorata* FRUHSTORFER, 1909: *tithonus*
*decoloratus* STAUDINGER, 1886 *(sebrus)*: *Cupido* (LY): 091
*deidamia* EVERSMANN, 1851: *Lasiommata* (SA): 315
*deione* DUPONCHEL, 1832 *(berisalii, rosinae)*: *Melitaea* (NY): 430
*dejanira* LINNAEUS, 1764: *achine*
*delattini* KUDRNA, 1975: *volgensis*
*delius* ESPER, 1800: *phoebus*
*dembowskyi* SEDYKH, 1974: *Oeneis* (SA): 340
*demophile* FREYER, 1844: *tullia*
*dentata* STAUDINGER, 1871: *arethusa*
*desfontainii* GODART, 1819 *(baetica)*: *Euphydryas* (NY): 411
*dia* LINNAEUS, 1767: *Boloria* (NY): 389
*diamina* LANG, 1789 *(dictynna, vernetensis, wheeleri)*: *Melitaea* (NY): 431
*dictynna* ESPER, 1779: *diamina*
*didyma* ESPER, 1779 *(meridionalis, occidentalis)*: *Melitaea* (NY): 429
*Didymaeformia* VERITY, 1950: *Melitaea*
*Dira* * HÜBNER, 1819: *Lasiommata*

*disa* BECKLIN, 1791 *(stheno)*: *Erebia* (SA): 239
*dispar* HAWORTH, 1803 *(batava, rutila)*: *Lycaena* (LY): 113
*discoidalis* KIRBY, 1837: *Erebia* (SA): 240
*dobrogensis* CARADJA, 1895: *nogelli*
*dolus* HÜBNER, 1823 *(vittatus)*: *Polyommatus* (LY): 157
*donzeli* BOISDUVAL, 1832: *nicias*
*dorilis* HUFNAGEL, 1766: *tityrus*
*Doritis* * FABRICIUS, 1807: *Archon*
*dorus* ESPER, 1782 *(aquilonia, bieli, mathewi)*: *Coenonympha* (SA): 218
*dorylas* DENIS & SCHIFFERMÜLLER, 1775 *(argester, hylas)*: *Polyommatus*
    (LY): 158
*dovrensis* STRAND, 1902: *ligea*
*dromus* FABRICIUS, 1793: *tyndarus*
*dryas* SCOPOLI, 1763 *(athene, phaedra)*: *Minois* (SA): 336
*Dryas* * HÜBNER, 1806: *Argynnis*
*dubia* ELWES, 1899: *Oeneis* (SA): 381
*dubiosa* * RÖBER, 1907: *napi*
*duponcheli* STAUDINGER, 1871 *(lathyri)*: *Leptidea* (PI): 047

*edda* MENETRIES, 1854: *Erebia* (SA): 241
*edusa* FABRICIUS, 1787: *crocea*
*Edwardsia* * TUTT, 1907: *Nordmannia*
*egea* CRAMER, 1775 *(vau-album)*: *Polygonia* (NY): 445
*egerides* STAUDINGER, 1871: *aegeria*
*elbana* STAUDINGER, 1901: *Coenonympha* (SA): 219
*electo* * LINNAEUS, 1763: *crocea*
*elisa* GODART, 1823 *(cyrene)*: *Argynnis* (NY): 381
*Elphinstonia* KLOTS, 1930: *Euchloe*
*embla* BECKLIN, 1791: *Erebia* (SA): 242
*Epinephele* HÜBNER, 1819: *Maniola*
*Epinephele* * HÜBNER, 1819: *Hyponephele, Pyronia*
*epiphron* KNOCH, 1783 *(aetheria, cassiope, mnemon, pyrenaica, scotica)*:
    *Erebia* (SA): 243
*epistygne* HÜBNER, 1819 *(andera, viriathus)*: *Erebia* (SA): 244
*erate* ESPER, 1805: *Colias* (PI): 025
*Erebia* DALMAN, 1816 *(Marica, Medusia, Phorcis, Simplicia, Syngea,*
    *Triariia, Truncaefalcia)*: (SA)
*ergane* GEYER, 1828 *(narcaea)*: *Pieris* (PI): 058
*eriphyle* FREYER, 1836 *(tristis)*: *Erebia* (SA): 245
*eris* MEIGEN, 1829: *niobe*
*eroides* FRIVALDSKY, 1835: *Polyommatus* (LY): 159
*eros* OCHSENHEIMER, 1808: *Polyommatus* (LY): 160

*erynis* ESPER, 1805: *gorge*
*erythia* HÜBNER, 1805: *arethusa*
*escheri* HÜBNER, 1823 *(agestor, olympena, splendens)*: Polyommatus (LY): 161
*esculi* HÜBNER, 1804 *(ilicioides)*: Nordmannia (LY): 131
*Euchloe* HÜBNER, 1819: (PI)
*eugenia* EVERSMANN, 1847: *Boloria* (NY): 390
*Eugonia* HÜBNER, 1819: *Polygonia*
*eumedon* ESPER, 1780 *(bellinus, chiron)*: Aricia (LY): 077
*Eumenis* HÜBNER, 1819: *Hipparchia*
*eunomia* ESPER, 1799 *(aphirape, ossianus)*: Boloria (NY): 391
*eupheme* ESPER, 1805 *(meridionalis)*: Zegris (PI): 065
*euphemus* HÜBNER, 1800: *teleius*
*eupheno* * LINNAEUS, 1767: *euphenoides*
*euphenoides* STAUDINGER, 1869 *(belia, calleuphenia, eupheno)*: Anthocharis (PI): 016
*euphrasia* LEWIN, 1795: *selene*
*euphrosyne* LINNAEUS, 1758: *Boloria* (NY): 392
*Euphydryas* SCUDDER, 1872 *(Eurodryas, Hypodryas)*: (NY)
*eupompa* FRUHSTORFER, 1918: *pharte*
*euridice* ROTTEMBURG, 1775: *hippothoe*
*Eurodryas* HIGGINS, 1978: *Euphydryas*
*europome* ESPER, 1779: *palaeno*
*europomene* OCHSENHEIMER, 1816: *palaeno*
*euryale* ESPER, 1805 *(adyte, isarica, ocellaris)*: Erebia (SA): 246
*eurybia* OCHSENHEIMER, 1808: *hippothoe*
*eurydame* HOFFMANSEGG, 1806: *hippothoe*
*eurypilus* FREYER, 1852: *Kretania* (LY): 102
*Euvanessa* SCUDDER, 1889: *Nymphalis*
*euxina* KUSNEZOV, 1909: *Pseudochazara* (SA): 361
*evagore* KLUG, 1829 *(daira)*: Colotis (PI): 032
*Everes* HÜBNER, 1819: *Cupido*
*eversi* REHNELT, 1974: *cleobule*
*evias* GODART, 1823: *triaria*
*exuberans* VERITY, 1926: *Polyommatus* (LY): 162

*fabressei* OBERTHÜR, 1910 *(agenjoi)*: Polyommatus (LY): 163
*Fabriciana* REUSS, 1920: *Argynnis*
*fagi* SCOPOLI, 1763 *(hermione*)*: Hipparchia (SA): 294
*falkovitchi* SEDYKH, 1974: *Oeneis* (SA): 341
*farinosa* ZELLER, 1847: *Gonepteryx* (PI): 043
*fascelis* ESPER, 1784 *(ignasiti, iphigenia, trivia)*: Melitaea (NY): 433

*fasciata* BUTLER, 1868: *Erebia* (SA): 247
*fasciata* SPULER, 1901: *pharte*
*fatua* FREYER, 1844 *(allionii, sichaea)*: *Hipparchia* (SA): 295
*fauna* SULZER, 1776: *statilinus*
*feisthamelii* DUPONCHEL, 1832: *Iphiclides* (PA): 002
*Felderia\** TUTT, 1907: *Nordmannia*
*ferdinandi* STICHEL, 1907: *cerisyi*
*ferula* FABRICIUS, 1793 *(bryce, cordula)*: *Satyrus* (SA): 370
*fidia* LINNAEUS, 1767: *Hipparchia* (SA): 296
*fischeri* EVERSMANN, 1843: *Tonegia* (LY): 197
*Fixsenia* TUTT, 1907: *Nordmannia*
*flavescens\** WAGNER, 1903: *flavescens*
*flavescens* MÜLLER, 1933 *(flavescens\*, neobryoniae, vihorlatensis)*: *Pieris* (PI): 059
*flavofasciata* HEYNE, 1895: *Erebia* (SA): 248
*florella* FABRICIUS, 1775: *Catopsilia* (PI): 019
*freija* BECKLIN, 1791: *Boloria* (NY): 393
*Freyeria* COURVOISIER, 1920: *Chilades*
*frigga* BECKLIN, 1791: *Boloria* (NY): 394


*galathea* LINNAEUS, 1758 *(leucomelas, procida)*: *Melanargia* (SA): 329
*galba* LEDERER, 1855: *Chilades* (LY): 085
*galloi* BALLETTO & TOSO, 1979: *Polyommatus* (LY): 164
*Ganoris* DALMAN, 1816: *Pieris*
*gardetta* PRUNNER, 1798 *(neoclides, philea, satyrion)*: *Coenonympha* (SA): 220
*gavarniensis* WARREN, 1913: *manto*
*geyeri* HERRICH-SCHÄFFER, 1845: *Pseudochazara* (SA): 361
*ghigii* TURATI, 1929: *syriaca*
*glacialis* MOLL, 1785 *(aello)*: *Oeneis* (SA): 343
*glacialis* ESPER, 1804: *pluto*
*glaciegenita* VERITY, 1928 *(debilis, merope)*: *Euphydryas* (NY): 412
*glandon* PRUNNER, 1798 *(orbitulus)*: *Agriades* (LY): 690
*Glaucopsyche* SCUDDER, 1872: (LY)
*glottis* FRUHSTORFER, 1920: *pronoe*
*glycerion* BORKHAUSEN, 1788 *(amyntas, iphis)*: *Coenonympha* (SA): 221
*goante* ESPER, 1805: *montana*
*golgus* HÜBNER, 1813: *Polyommatus* (LY): 165
*gomera* HIGGINS, 1967: *Hipparchia* (SA): 297
*Gonepteryx* LEACH, 1815 *(Gonoptera, Rhodocera)*: (PI)
*Gonoptera* BILLBERG, 1820: *Gonepteryx*
*gordius* SULZER, 1776: *alciphron*

*gorge* ESPER, 1805 *(erynis, gorgone, ramondi, triopes)*: *Erebia* (SA): 249
*gorge* GODART, 1823: *scipio*
*gorgone* BOISDUVAL, 1833: *Erebia* (SA): 250
*gorgone* HERRICH-SCHÄFFER, 1846: *gorge*
*gorgophone* BELLIER, 1863: *aethiopella*
*graeca* STAUDINGER, 1870 *(balcanica)*: *Boloria* (NY): 395
*graeca* STAUDINGER, 1870 *(mamurra)*: *Pseudochazara* (SA): 363
*Graphium* * SCOPOLI, 1777: *Iphiclides*
*Grapta* KIRBY, 1837: *Polygonia*
*gruneri* HERRICH-SCHÄFFER, 1851: *Anthocharis* (PI): 017


*Hamearis* HÜBNER, 1819 *(Nemeobius)*: (RI)
*hecate* DENIS & SCHIFFERMÜLLER, 1775: *Brenthis* (NY): 405
*hecla* LEFEBVRE, 1836 *(sulitelma)*: *Colias* (PI): 026
*heldreichi* STAUDINGER, 1862: *aurorina*
*helena* STAUDINGER, 1862: *antiochena*
*helle* DENIS & SCHIFFERMÜLLER, 1775 *(amphidamas)*: *Lycaena* (LY): 114
*Helleia* VERITY, 1943: *Lycaena*
*helvetica* RÜHL, 1888: *athalia*
*Heodes* DALMAN, 1816: *Lycaena*
*hermione* LINNAEUS, 1764 *(aelia, alcyone)*: *Hipparchia* (SA): 298
*hermione* * LINNAEUS, 1764: *fagi*
*hero* LINNAEUS, 1761: *Coenonympha* (SA): 222
*herse* BORKHAUSEN, 1788: *tyndarus*
*herta* GEYER, 1828: *larissa*
*hesperica* RAMBUR, 1839: *Plebejus* (LY): 137
*hesperidum* ROTHSCHILD, 1913: *belemia*
*hiera* FABRICIUS, 1777: *maera*
*hiera* HÜBNER, 1799: *petropolitana*
*hiera* * FABRICIUS, 1777: *petropolitana*
*Hipparchia* FABRICIUS, 1807 *(Eumenis, Neohipparchia, Nytha, Parahippar-
     chia, Pseudotergumia)*: (SA)
*hippolyte* ESPER, 1784 *(mercurius)*: *Pseudochazara* (SA): 364
*hippomedusa* OCHSENHEIMER, 1820: *medusa*
*hipponoe* BERGSTRÄSSER, 1779: *alciphron*
*hippothoe* LINNAEUS, 1761 *(chryseis, euridice, eurybia, eurydame, stiberi)*:
     *Lycaena* (LY): 115
*Hirsutina* TUTT, 1909: *Polyommatus*
*hispana* HERRICH-SCHÄFFER, 1852 *(rezniceki)*: *Polyommatus* (LY): 166
*hispania* BUTLER, 1868 *(rondoui)*: *Erebia* (SA): 251
*hispanica* HEYNE, 1895: *triaria*
*hispulla* ESPER, 1804: *jurtina*

*hoffmanseggi* ZELLER, 1850: *pirithous*
*homole* FRUHSTORFER, 1918: *montana*
*hospiton* GENE, 1839: *Papilio* (PA): 005
*huebneri* KOCAK, 1980 *(narica)*: *Hyponephele* (SA): 312
*humedasae* TOSO & BALLETTO, 1976: *Polyommatus* (LY): 167
*hungarica* REBEL, 1900: *oedippus*
*hungaricus* DIOSZEGHY, 1913: *bavius*
*huntera* FABRICIUS, 1775: *virginensis*
*hyale* LINNAEUS, 1758: *Colias* (PI): 027
*hylas* LINNAEUS, 1758: *sappho*
*hylas* DENIS & SCHIFFERMÜLLER, 1775: *schiffermuelleri*
*hylas* * DENIS & SCHIFFERMÜLLER, 1775: *baton*
*hylas* ESPER, 1777: *dorylas*
*hyperantus* LINNAEUS, 1758: *Aphantopus* (SA): 209
*hypermnestra* SCOPOLI, 1763: *polycena*
*hypochiona* RAMBUR, 1858: *argus*
*Hypodryas* HIGGINS, 1978: *Euphydryas*
*Hyponephele* MUSCHAMP, 1915 *(Epinephele)*: (SA)
*hypsipyle* FABRICIUS, 1777: *polyxena*

*iberica* OBERTHÜR, 1909: *beckeri*
*icarius* ESPER, 1790: *amandus*
*icarus* ROTTEMBURG, 1775 *(polyphemus)*: *Polyommatus* (LY): 168
*ichnea* BOISDUVAL, 1833; *iduna*
*ichnea** BOISDUVAL, 1833: *wolfensbergeri*
*ichnusa* HÜBNER, 1824: *Aglais* (NY): 373
*ida* ESPER, 1785: *cecilia*
*idas* LINNAEUS, 1761 *(calliopis)*: *Lycaeides* (LY): 109
*idas* RAMBUR, 1842: *morronensis*
*Idata* LESSE, 1952: *Pyronia*
*iduna* DALMAN, 1816: *Euphydryas* (NY): 413
*ignasiti* SAGARRA, 1926: *fascelis*
*ilia* DENIS & SCHIFFERMÜLLER, 1776 *(barcina)*: *Apatura* (NY): 375
*ilicioides* GERHARD, 1850: *esculi*
*ilicis* ESPER, 1779: *Nordmannia* (LY): 132
*immaculata* BELLIER, 1862: *paphia*
*improba* BUTLER, 1877 *(improbula)*: *Boloria* (NY): 396
*improbula* BRYK, 1920: *improba*
*Inachis* HÜBNER, 1819: (NY)
*indica* HERBST, 1794 *(calliroe, occidentalis, vulcanica)*: *Vanessa* (NY): 449
*ines* HOFFMANSEGG, 1804: *Melanargia* (SA): 330
*infernalis* VARGA, 1971: *orientalis*

*inhonora* JACHONTOV, 1909: *Aricia* (LY): 078
*innominata* LEWIS, 1872: *rivularis*
*ino* ROTTEMBURG, 1775: *Brenthis* (NY): 406
*insularis* STAUDINGER, 1861: *Euchloe* (PI): 037
*intermedia\** MENETRIES, 1859: *wolfensbergeri*
*io* LINNAEUS, 1758: *Inachis* (NY): 418
*iola* CRAMER, 1775: *virginensis*
*Iolana* BETHUNE-BAKER, 1914: (LY)
*iolas* OCHSENHEIMER, 1816: *Iolana* (LY): 101
*ionia* FISCHER & EVERSMANN, 1851: *Thaleropis* (NY): 446
*Iphiclides* HÜBNER, 1819 *(Graphium)*: (PA)
*iphigenia* ESPER, 1782: *fascelis*
*iphigenia* HERRICH-SCHÄFFER, 1847 *(nonacriensis)*: *Polyommatus* (LY): 169
*iphioides* STAUDINGER, 1870 *(pearsoni)*: *Coenonympha* (SA): 223
*iphis* DENIS & SCHIFFERMÜLLER, 1775: *glycerion*
*irene* HPBNER, 1806: *meolans*
*iris* LINNAEUS, 1758: *Apatura* (NY): 376
*isarica* HEYNE, 1895: *euryale*
*isis* HÜBNER, 1799: *napaea*
*ismenias* MEIGEN, 1829: *argyrognomon*
*Issoria* HÜBNER, 1819: (NY)
*italaglauca* VERITY, 1939 *(syriaca)*: *Polyommatus* (LY): 170
*italica* VERITY, 1913: *rhodopensis*

*janira* LINNAEUS, 1758: *jurtina*
*japygia* CIRILLO, 1787: *russiae*
*jasius* LINNAEUS, 1767 *(jason)*: *Charaxes* (NY): 407
*jason* LINNAEUS, 1764: *jasius*
*jeniseiensis* TRYBOM, 1877: *Erebia* (SA): 252
*jesous* GUERIN, 1849: *Azanus* (LY): 081
*jolaus* BONELLI, 1826: *neomiris*
*jurtina* LINNAEUS, 1758 *(hispulla, jurtina)*: *Maniola* (SA): 325
*jutta* HÜBNER, 1806: *Oeneis* (SA): 344

*Kanetisa* MOORE, 1893 *(Brintesia)*: (NY)
*karsandra* MOORE, 1865: *Zizeeria* (LY): 203
*katarae* COUTSIS, 1972: *leander*
*kefersteini* GERHARD, 1850: *ochimus*
*Kirinia* MOORE, 1893: *Lasiommata*
*Klugia\** TUTT, 1907: *Nordmannia*
*knysna* TRIMEN, 1862 *(lysimon)*: *Zizeeria* (LY): 204
*koslowskyi* SEDYKH, 1974: *Oeneis* (SA): 345

*Kretania* BEURET, 1959: (LY)
*krueperi* STAUDINGER, 1860: *Pieris* (PI): 060
*kusnetzovi* SEDYKH, 1974: *Oeneis* (SA): 346

*lachesis* HÜBNER, 1790: *Melanargia* (SA): 331
*Ladoga* MOORE, 1898: *Limenitis*
*Laeosopis* RAMBUR, 1858: (LY)
*l-album* ESPER, 1780 *(vau-album)*: *Nymphalis* (NY): 441
*Lampides* HÜBNER, 1819: (LY)
*Langia* TUTT, 1906: *Syntarucus*
*laodice* PALLAS, 1771: *Argyronome* (NY): 385
*lappona* THUNBERG, 1791: *pandrose*
*lariana* FRUHSTORFER, 1910: *orion*
*larissa* BOISDUVAL, 1828 *(herta)*: *Melanargia* (NY): 332
*Lasiommata* WESTWOOD, 1841 *(Kirinia, Lopinga)*: (SA)
*lathonia* LINNAEUS, 1758: *Issoria* (NY): 419
*lathyri* DUPONCHEL, 1832: *duponcheli*
*Latiorina* TUTT, 1909: *Agriades*
*leander* ESPER, 1784 *(katarae, orientalis, skypetarum)*: *Coenonympha* (SA): 224
*Leechia* * TUTT, 1907: *Nordmannia*
*lefebvrei* BOISDUVAL, 1828 *(alecto, astur, pyrenaea)*: *Erebia* (SA): 253
*leighebi* KUDRNA, 1976: *Hipparchia* (SA): 299
*leonhardi* FRUHSTORFER, 1917: *candens*
*leonhardi* FURHSTORFER, 1918: *melas*
*Leptidea* BILLBERG, 1820 *(Leptosia, Leucophasia)*: (PI)
*Leptosia* * HÜBNER, 1818: *Leptidea*
*Leucochloe* RÖBER, 1907: *Pieris*
*leucomelas* ESPER, 1782: *galathea*
*Leucophasia* STEPHEN, 1827: *Leptidea*
*levana* LINNAEUS, 1758 *(porima, prorsa)*: *Ataschnia* (NY): 358
*libanotica* LEDERER, 1858: *aurorina*
*Libythea* FABRICIUS, 1807: (LI)
*ligea* LINNAEUS, 1758 *(dovrensis)*: *Erebia* (SA): 254
*ligurica* WAGNER, 1904: *arion*
*ligurica* OBERTHÜR, 1910: *argyrognomon*
*Limenitis* FABRICIUS, 1807 *(Ladoga)*: (NY)
*loewi* ZELLER, 1847: *Vacciniina* (LY): 201
*Lopinga* MOORE, 1893: *Lasiommata*
*lorkovici* SIJARIC & CARNELUTTI, 1976: *tullia*
*lorquinii* HERRICH-SCHÄFFER, 1847: *Cupido* (LY): 092
*Loweia* TUTT, 1906: *Lycaena*

*lucilla* ESPER, 1779: *reducta*
*lucilla* DENIS & SCHIFFERMÜLLER, 1775: *rivularis*
*lucilla* SCHRANK, 1801: *sappho*
*lucina* LINNAEUS, 1758: *Hamearis* (RI): 205
*lugens* STAUDINGER, 1901: *oeme*
*lupina* COSTA, 1836 *(rhamnusia)*: *Hyponephele* (SA): 313
*Lycaeides* HÜBNER, 1819: (LY)
*Lycaena* FABRICIUS, 1807 *(Chrysophanus, Helleia, Heodes, Loweia, Palaeochrysophanus, Palaeoloweia, Rumicia, Thersamonia)*: (LY)
*Lycaenopsis* FELDER & FELDER, 1865: *Celastrina*
*lycaon* KÜHN, 1774: *Hyponephele* (SA): 314
*lycidas* TRAPP, 1863: *trappi*
*lycidas* MEIGEN, 1830: *argyrognomon*
*Lyela* SWINHOE, 1892: *Coenonympha*
*lyllus* ESPER, 1805: *pamphilus*
*lynceus* FABRICIUS, 1787: *ilicis*
*lynceus* ESPER, 1777: *spini*
*Lysandra* HEMMING, 1933: *Polyommatus*
*lysimon* HÜBNER, 1803: *knysna*

*machaon* LINNAEUS, 1758 *(sphyrus)*: *Papilio* (PA): 006
*Maculinea* ECKE, 1915: (LY)
*maderensis* FELDER, 1862: *Gonepteryx* (PI): 044
*maderensis* BETHUNE-BAKER, 1891: *Hipparchia* (SA): 300
*maera* LINNAEUS, 1758 *(adrasta, hiera, monotonia)*: *Lasiommata* (SA): 319
*maja* CRAMER, 1775: *pandora*
*major*\* GRUND, 1905: *morsei*
*malickyi* KUDRNA, 1977: *Hipparchia* (SA): 301
*mamurra*\* HERRICH-SCHÄFFER, 1852: *graeca*
*Mancipium* HÜBNER, 1806: *Pieris*
*Maniola* SCHRANK, 1801 *(Epinephele)*: (SA)
*manleyi* LESSE, 1962: *asturiensis*
*mannii* MAYER, 1851: *Pieris* (PI): 061
*manto* DENIS & SCHIFFERMÜLLER, 1775 *(alecto, constans, gavarniensis, pyrrhula, vogesiaca)*: *Erebia* (SA): 255
*mantoides* BUTLER, 1868: *pandrose*
*margarita* OBERTHÜR, 1896: *neoridas*
*Marica* HÜBNER, 1819: *Erebia*
*marmorae* HÜBNER, 1826: *neomiris*
*mathewi* TUTT, 1904: *dorus*
*maturna* LINNAEUS, 1758: *Euphydryas* (NY): 415
*maura*\* VERITY, 1911: *maura*

*maura* WARREN, 1970 *(maura): Pieris* (PI): 062
*medea* DENIS & SCHIFFERMÜLLER, 1775: *aethiops*
*medesicaste* HOFFMANSEGG, 1803: *rumina*
*medon* HUFNAGEL, 1766: *agestis*
*medusa* DENIS & SCHIFFERMÜLLER, 1775 *(hippomedusa, psodea): Erebia* (SA): 256
*Medusia* VERITY, 1953: *Erebia*
*megera* LINNAEUS, 1767: *Lasiommata* (SA): 320
*melampus* FUESSLIN, 1775: *Erebia* (SA): 257
*Melanargia* MEIGEN, 1828 *(Agapetes, Arge, Argeformia):* (SA)
*melanops* BOISDUVAL, 1828: *Glaucopsyche* (LY): 099
*melas* HERST, 1796 *(leonhardi): Erebia* (SA): 258
*melathalia* ROCCI, 1930: *britomartis*
*meleager* ESPER, 1777: *daphnis*
*Meleageria* SAGARRA, 1925: *Polyommatus*
*melibaeus* STAUDINGER, 1879: *alciphron*
*melissa* * FABRICIUS, 1775: *semidea*
*Melitaea* FABRICIUS, 1807 *(Athaliaeformia, Cinclidia, Didymaeformia, Mellicta):* (NY)
*Mellicta* BILLBERG, 1820: *Melitaea*
*menalcas* PODA, 1761: *pamphilus*
*menelaos* BROWN, 1976: *Polyommatus* (LY): 171
*meolans* PRUNNER, 1798 *(bejarensis, calaritas, irene, pirene, pyrene, stygne, valesiaca): Erebia* (SA): 259
*mercurius* STAUDINGER, 1887: *hippolyte*
*meridionalis* LEDERER, 1852: *eupheme*
*meridionalis* HEYNE, 1895: *napi*
*meridionalis* STAUDINGER, 1870: *didyma*
*merope* PRUNNER, 1798: *glaciegenita*
*mersina* * STAUDINGER, 1871: *malickyi*
*Mesoacidalia* REUSS, 1926: *Argynnis*
*Mesodryas* REUSS, 1927: *Argynnis*
*metis* FREYER, 1829: *Apatura* (NY): 377
*Microzegris* ALPHERAKY, 1913: *Zegris*
*miegi* VOGEL, 1857: *virgaureae*
*miguelensis* LE CERF, 1935: *Hipparchia* (SA): 302
*minimus* FUESSLIN, 1775 *(alsus, trinacriae): Cupido* (LY): 093
*Minois* HÜBNER, 1819: (SA)
*mnemon* HAWORTH, 1812: *epiphron*
*mnemosyne* LINNAEUS, 1758: *Parnassius* (PA): 008
*mnestra* ESPER, 1805: *Erebia* (SA): 260
*monotonia* SCHILDE, 1885: *maera*

*montana* PRUNNER, 1798 *(goante, homole)*: *Erebia* (SA): 261
*montana* \* HEYNE, 1895: *allous*
*montanus* MEYER-DÜR, 1851: *virgaureae*
*montensis* VERITY, 1928: *allous*
*monticola* STAUDINGER, 1901: *rebeli*
*morronensis* RIBBE, 1910 *(idas, ramburi)*: *Aricia* (LY): 079
*morsei* FENTON, 1881 *(major)*: *Leptidea* (PI): 048
*morula* SPEYER, 1865: *styria*
*muelleri* KUDRNA, 1975: *volgensis*
*myrmidone* ESPER, 1780: *Colias* (PI): 028


*napaea* HOFFMANSEGG, 1804 *(isis)*: *Boloria* (NY): 397
*napaeae* ESPER, 1804: *napi*
*napi* LINNAEUS, 1758 *(canidiaformis, dubiosa, meridionalis, napaeae)*:
  *Pieris* (PI): 063
*narcaea* FREYER, 1828: *ergane*
*narica* HÜBNER, 1813: *huebneri*
*nastes* BOISDUVAL, 1832 *(werdandi)*: *Colias* (PI): 029
*nausithous* BERGSTRÄSSER, 1779 *(arcas)*: *Maculinea* (LY): 126
*neglecta* PFAU, 1962: *Melitaea* (NY): 434
*neleus* FREYER, 1833: *cassioides*
*Nemeobius* STEPHENS, 1827: *Hamearis*
*neobryoniae* \* SHELJUZHKO, 1913: *flavescens*
*neoclides* HÜBNER, 1805: *gardetta*
*Neohipparchia* LESSE, 1952: *Hipparchia*
*Neolycaena* NICEVILLE, 1890: (LY)
*Neolysandra* KOCAK, 1977: *Polyommatus*
*neomyris* GODART, 1823 *(jolaus, marmorae)*: *Hipparchia* (SA): 303
*neoridas* BOISDUVAL, 1828 *(margarita, sibyllina)*: 262
*nephele* HUFNAGEL, 1766: *pamphilus*
*nephohiptamenos* BROWN & COUTSIS, 1978: *Polyommatus* (LY): 172
*Neptis* FABRICIUS, 1807: (NY)
*nerine* FREYER, 1831: *styrius*
*nevadensis* OBERTHÜR, 1896: *Lycaeides* (LY): 110
*nevadensis* OBERTHÜR, 1910: *allous*
*nevadensis* OBERTHÜR, 1904: *athalia*
*nevadensis* ZULLICH, 1928: *zullichi*
*nicholli* OBERTHÜR, 1896: *pluto*
*nicias* MEIGEN, 1830 *(donzeli, scandica)*: *Aricia* (LY): 080
*niobe* LINNAEUS, 1758 *(altonevadensis, cleodoxa, eris, rubida)*: *Argynnis*
  (NY): 382
*nivalis* LORKOVIC & LESSE, 1954: *Erebia* (SA): 263

*nivescens* KEFERSTEIN, 1851: *Polyommatus* (LY): 173
*nogelli* FREYER, 1862 *(dobrogensis)*: *Tomares* (LY): 196
*nonacriensis* BROWN, 1976: *iphigenia*
*norax* BONELLI, 1826: *corinna*
*Nordmannia* TUTT, 1907 *(Chattendenia, Edwardsia, Felderia, Fixsenia, Klugia, Leechia, Satyrium, Strymon, Strymonidia, Thecliola, Tuttiola)*: (LY)
*norna* BECKLIN, 1791: *Oeneis* (SA): 347
*norvegica* AURIVILLIUS, 1888: *athalia*
*nurag* GHILIANI, 1852: *Maniola* (SA): 326
*Nymphalis* KLUK, 1802 *(Euvanessa)*: (NY)
*Nytha* BILLBERG, 1820: *Hipparchia*
*Nytha** BILLBERG, 1820: *Arethusana*

*occidentalis* SOUSA, 1982: *caldeirense*
*obscura* CHRIST, 1878: *arion*
*occidentalis* STAUDINGER, 1861: *didyma*
*occidentalis* FELDER, 1862: *indica*
*occitanica* ESPER, 1793 *(psyche, syllius)*: *Melanargia* (SA): 333
*occitanica* STAUDINGER, 1871: *phoebe*
*occupata* REBEL, 1903: *rhodopensis*
*ocellaris* STAUDINGER, 1861: *euryale*
*ochimus* HERRICH-SCHÄFFER, 1851 *(kefersteini)*: *Lycaena* (LY): 116
*oedippus* FABRICIUS, 1787 *(hungarica)*: *Coenonympha* (SA): 225
*oeme* ESPER, 1805 *(cecilia, lugens, spodia)*: *Erebia* (SA): 264
*Oeneis* HÜBNER, 1819 *(Chionabas)*: (SA)
*oeno** BOISDUVAL, 1832: *crambis*
*olympena* VERITY, 1936: *escheri*
*ominata* KRULIKOWSKI, 1903: *petropolitana*
*optilete* KNOCH, 1781 *(cyparissus)*: *Vacciniina* (LY): 202
*orbitulus* PRUNNER, 1798 *(phéretes)*: *Albulina* (LY): 072
*orbitulus* ESPER, 1800: *glandon*
*oreas* WARREN, 1933: *pluto*
*orestes* PRINS & POORTEN, 1981: *Pseudochazara* (SA): 365
*orientalis* HERRICH-SCHÄFFER, 1846: *Euphydryas* (NY): 416
*orientalis* ELWES, 1900 *(infernalis)*: *Erebia* (SA): 263
*orientalis* GOLTZ, 1930: *pandrose*
*orientalis* REBEL, 1913: *leander*
*orion* PALLAS, 1771 *(battus, lariana)*: *Scolitantides* (LY): 189
*orpheus* NEKRUTENKO, 1980: *Ultraaricia* (LY): 200
*osiris* MEIGEN, 1829 *(sebrus)*: *Cupido* (LY): 094
*ossianus* HERBST, 1800: *eunomia*

*ottomana* HERRICH-SCHÄFFER, 1847 *(balcanica, bulgarica, bureschi, tardenota)*: *Erebia* (SA): 266
*ottomanus* LEFEBVRE, 1830: *Lycaena* (LY): 117

*paedotrophos* BERGSTRÄSSER, 1780: *phoebe*
*palaeno* LINNAEUS, 1761 *(europome, europomene, philomene)*: *Colias* (PI): 030
*Palaeochrysophanus* VERITY, 1943: *Lycaena*
*Palaeoloweia* VERITY, 1934: *Lycaena*
*palarica* CHAPMAN, 1905: *Erebia* (SA): 267
*pales* DENIS & SCHIFFERMÜLLER, 1775 *(palustris, pyrenemiscens)*: *Boloria* (NY): 398
*palmae* STAMM, 1963: *Gonepteryx* (PI): 045
*palustris* FRUHSTORFER, 1909: *pales*
*pamphila* HÜBNER, 1803: *pamphilus*
*pamphilus* LINNAEUS, 1758 *(lyllus, menalcas, nephele, pamphila)*: *Coenonympha* (SA): 226
*panagea* HERRICH-SCHÄFFER, 1852 *(taygetica)*: *Turanana* (LY): 198
*pandora* DENIS & SCHIFFERMÜLLER, 1775 *(maja)*: *Argynnis* (NY): 383
*pandrose* BORKHAUSEN, 1788 *(lappona, mantoides, orientalis, pyrrha)*: *Erebia* (SA): 268
*panope* EVERSMANN, 1851: *Pseudophilotes* (LY): 184
*panoptes* HÜBNER, 1813: *Pseudophilotes* (LY): 185
*pansa* CHRISTOPH, 1893: *Oeneis* (SA): 348
*paphia* LINNAEUS, 1758 *(immaculata)*: *Argynnis* (NY): 384
*paphos* CHAPMAN, 1920: *Glaucopsyche* (LY): 100
*Papilio* LINNAEUS, 1758 *(Pterourus)*: (PA)
*Parahipparchia* KUDRNA, 1977: *Hipparchia*
*paramegaera* * HÜBNER, 1824: *tigelius*
*Parapieris* NICEVILLE, 1897: *Pieris*
*Pararge* HÜBNER, 1819: (SA)
*Parnalius* RAFINESQUE, 1815: *Zerynthia*
*parnassia* STAUDINGER, 1870: *semiargus*
*Parnassius* LATREILLE, 1804: (PA)
*parthenie* BORKHAUSEN, 1788: *aurelia*
*parthenie* GODART, 1819: *parthenoides*
*parthenoides* KEFERSTEIN, 1851 *(parthenie)*: *Melitaea* (NY): 435
*pasiphae* ESPER, 1781: *bathseba*
*Pasiphana* LESSE, 1952: *Pyronia*
*pearsoni* ROMEI, 1927: *iphioides*
*pellucida* * STAUDER, 1923: *cypriensis*
*pellucida* STAUDER, 1923 *(cotys)*: *Hipparchia* (SA): 304

*pelopi* BROWN, 1976: *ripartii*
*penia* FREYER, 1852: *Euchloe* (PI): 038
*petropolitana* FABRICIUS, 1787 *(hiera, ominata)*: *Lasiommata* (SA): 321
*phaedra* LINNAEUS, 1764: *dryas*
*pharte* ESPER, 1805 *(eupompa, fasciata, phartina)*: *Erebia* (SA): 269
*phegea* BORKHAUSEN, 1788: *afra*
*pheretes* HOFFMANSEGG, 1804: *orbitulus*
*pherusa* BOISDUVAL, 1833: *Melanargia* (SA): 334
*phicomone* ESPER, 1780: *Colias* (PI): 031
*philea* HÜBNER, 1800: *gardetta*
*philippi* BROWN & COUTSIS, 1978: *Polyommatus* (LY): 174
*philomene* HÜBNER, 1805: *palaeno*
*Philotes** SCHUDDER, 1876: *Pseudophilotes*
*philoxenus* ESPER, 1780: *tullia*
*phlaeas* LINNAEUS, 1761 *(phlaeoides, polaris)*: *Lycaena* (LY): 118
*phlaeoides* STAUDINGER, 1901: *phlaeas*
*phoebe** DENIS & SCHIFFERMÜLLER, 1775: *phoebe*
*phoebe* GOEZE, 1779 *(corythallia, occitanica, paedotrophos, phoebe)*:
    *Melitaea* (NY): 436
*phoebe* KNOCH, 1783: *phoebe*
*phoebus* FABRICIUS, 1793 *(delius, sacerdos)*: *Parnassius* (PA): 009
*Phorcis* HÜBNER, 1819: *Erebia*
*phorcys* FREYER, 1836: *alberganus*
*phryne* PALLAS, 1771 *(phryneus, tircis)*: *Triphysa* (SA): 371
*phryxa* BERGSTRÄSSER, 1780: *adippe*
*picoensis* LE CERF, 1935: *azorina*
*Pieris* SCHRANK, 1801 *(Artogeia, Ganoris, Leucochloe, Mancipium,*
    *Parapieris, Pontia, Pontioeuchloia, Synchloe)*: (PI)
*pilosellae* ROTTEMBURG, 1775: *cinxia*
*pirata* ESPER, 1793: *briseis*
*pirene* HÜBNER, 1799: *meolans*
*pirithous* LINNAEUS, 1767 *(hoffmanseggi, telicanus)*: *Syntarucus* (LY): 190
*pitho* HÜBNER, 1806: *pronoe*
*Plebejus* KLUK, 1802: (LY)
*Plebicula* HIGGINS, 1969: *Polyommatus*
*plexippus* LINNAEUS, 1758 *(archippus)*: *Danaus* (DA): 208
*pluto* PRUNNER, 1798 *(alecto, belzebub, glacialis, nicholli, oreas)*: *Erebia*
    (SA): 270
*podalirius* LINNAEUS, 1758 *(sinon)*: *Iphiclides* (PA): 103
*polaris* STAUDINGER, 1861: *Erebia* (SA): 271
*polaris* BOISDUVAL, 1828: *Boloria* (NY): 399
*polaris* COURVOISIER, 1911: *phlaeas*

*polychaon* LOCHE, 1801: *alexanor*
*polychloros* LINNAEUS, 1758: *Nymphalis* (NY): 442
*Polygonia* HÜBNER, 1819 *(Eugonia)*: (NY)
*Polyommatus* LATREILLE, 1804 *(Agrodiaetus, Hirsutina, Lysandra, Meleageria, Neolysandra, Plebicula, Uranops)*: (LY)
*polyphemus* ESPER, 1777: *icarus*
*polyxena* DENIS & SCHIFFERMÜLLER, 1775 *(aristolochiae, hypermnestra, hypsipyle)*: *Zerynthia* (PA): 012
*polyxena* * FABRICIUS, 1775: *crambis*
*Pontia* FABRICIUS, 1807: *Pieris*
*Pontioeuchloia* VERITY, 1929: *Pieris*
*populi* LINNAEUS, 1758 *(tremulae)*: *Limenitis* (NY): 421
*porima* OCHSENHEIMER, 1807: *levana*
*poseidon* LEDERER, 1852: *Polyommatus* (LY): 175
*prieuri* PIERRET, 1837: *Chazara* (SA): 213
*procida* HERBST, 1796: *galathea*
*Proclossiana* REUSS, 1926: *Boloria*
*pronoe* ESPER, 1780 *(arachne, glottis, pitho, vergy)*: *Erebia* (SA): 272
*proserpina* DENIS & SCHIFFERMÜLLER, 1775: *circe*
*Proterebia* ROOS & ARNSCHEID, 1980: (SA)
*provincialis* BOISDUVAL, 1828: *Euphydryas* (NY): 417
*pruni* LINNAEUS, 1758: *Nordmannia* (LY): 133
*pseudathalia* REVERDIN, 1921: *athalia*
*Pseudoaricia* BEURET, 1959: *Aricia*
*Pseudochazara* LESSE, 1952: (SA)
*Pseudophilotes* BEURET, 1958 *(Philotes)*: (LY)
*Pseudotergumia* AGENJO, 1947: *Hipparchia*
*psodea* HÜBNER, 1806: *medusa*
*psyche* HÜBNER, 1793: *occitanica*
*psylorita* FREYER, 1845: *Kretania* (LY): 103
*Pterourus* * SCOPOLI, 1777: *Papilio*
*pylaon* FISCHER, 1832: *Plebejus* (LY): 138
*Pyrameis* HÜBNER, 1819: *Vanessa*
*pyrenaea* OBERTHÜR, 1884: *lefebvrei*
*pyrenaica* * HERRICH-SCHÄFFER, 1851: *epiphron*
*pyrenaica* STAUDINGER, 1871: *triaria*
*pyrenaicus* BOISDUVAL, 1840 *(asturiensis)*: *Agriades* (LY): 070
*pyrene* ESPER, 1804: *meolans*
*pyrenemiscens* VERITY, 1932: *pales*
*Pyronia* HÜBNER, 1819 *(Epinephele, Idata, Pasiphana, Tisiphone)*: (SA)
*pyrothoe* EVERSMANN, 1793: *Zegris* (PI): 066
*pyrrha* * DENIS & SCHIFFERMÜLLER, 1775: *pandrose*

*pyrrhula* FREY, 1880: *manto*

*quercus* LINNAEUS, 1758: *Quercusia* (LY): 188
*Quercusia* VERITY, 1943 *(Bithys, Zephyrus)*: (LY)

*ramburi* VERITY, 1929: *morronensis*
*ramondi* OBERTHÜR, 1909: *gorge*
*rapae* LINNAEUS, 1758: *Pieris* (PI): 064
*raphani* ESPER, 1783: *daplidice*
*rebeli* HIRSCHKE, 1904 *(monticola, xerophila)*: *Maculinea* (LY): 127
*reducta* STAUDINGER, 1901 *(anonyma, camilla, lucilla, revularis, schiffer-muelleri)*: *Limenitis* (NY): 422
*reichlini* HERRICH-SCHÄFFER, 1860: *styx*
*rezniceki* BARTEL, 1905: *hispana*
*rhamni* LINNAEUS, 1758: *Gonepteryx* (PI): 046
*rhamnusia* FREYER, 1845: *lupina*
*Rhodocera* BOISDUVAL & LECONTE, 1830: *Gonepteryx*
*rhodopensis* FREYER, 1836: *arduinna*
*rhodopensis* ELWES, 1900 *(italica, occupata, tiphonides)*: *Coenonympha* (SA): 227
*rhodopensis* NICHOLL, 1900 *(bachmatjewi)*: *Erebia* (SA): 273
*rhymnus* EVERSMANN, 1832: *Neolycaena* (LY): 129
*ripartii* FREYER, 1830 *(exuberans, pelopi, rippertii)*: *Polyommatus* (LY): 176
*rippertii* BOISDUVAL, 1832: *ripartii*
*rivularis* STICHEL, 1907: *reducta*
*rivularis* SCOPOLI, 1763 *(innominata, lucilla, coenobita)*: *Neptis* (NY): 438
*roboris* ESPER, 1793: *Laeosopis* (LY): 104
*rondoui* OBERTHÜR, 1908: *hispania*
*rosinae* REBEL, 1911: *deione*
*rossi* CURTIS, 1834: *Erebia* (SA): 274
*rothliebii* HERRICH-SCHÄFFER, 1851: *tullia*
*roxelana* CRAMER, 1777: *Lasiommata* (SA): 322
*rubi* LINNAEUS, 1758: *Callophrys* (LY): 083
*Rumicia* TUTT, 1906: *Lycaena*
*rumina* LINNAEUS, 1758 *(medesicaste)*: *Zerynthia* (PA): 013
*russiae* ESPER, 1784 *(clotho, japygia, suwarovius)*: *Melanargia* (SA): 335
*rutila* WERNEBURG, 1864: *dispar*
*Ryawardia* TUTT, 1908: *Syntarucus*

*sacerdos* STICHEL, 1906: *phoebus*
*saepestriata* SEDYKH, 1974: *Oeneis* (SA): 349
*sappho* PALLAS, 1771 *(aceris, hylas, lucilla)*: *Neptis* (NY): 439

*sardoa* SPULER, 1902: *aristaeus*
*sareptensis* CHAPMAN, 1917: *cleobis*
*satyrion* ESPER, 1804: *gardetta*
*Satyrium* \* SCUDDER, 1876: *Nordmannia*
*Satyrus* LATREILLE, 1810: (SA)
*sbordonii* KUDRNA, 1984: *Hipparchia* (SA): 305
*scandica* WAHLGREN, 1930: *nicias*
*schiffermuelleri* HEMMING, 1929 *(hylas)*: *Pseudophilotes* (LY): 186
*schiffermuelleri* HIGGINS, 1932: *reducta*
*scipio* BOISDUVAL, 1832 *(gorge)*: *Erebia* (SA): 275
*Scolitantides* HÜBNER, 1819: (LY)
*scotica* STAUDINGER, 1901: *tullia*
*scotica* COOKE, 1943: *epiphron*
*sebrus* BOISDUVAL, 1832: *osiris*
*sebrus* HÜBNER, 1824: *decoloratus*
*sedykhi* CROSSON DU CORMIER, 1977: *napaea*
*selene* DENIS & SCHIFFERMÜLLER, 1775 *(euphrasia)*: *Boloria* (NY): 400
*selenis* EVERSMANN, 1837: *Boloria* (NY): 401
*semele* LINNAEUS, 1758 *(cadmus, wilkinsoni)*: *Hipparchia* (SA): 306
*semiargus* ROTTEMBURG, 1775 *(acis, parnassia)*: *Cyaniris* (LY): 096
*semidea* SAY, 1828: *Oeneis* (SA): 350
*senthes* FRUHSTORFER, 1908: *Hipparchia* (SA): 304
*sephirus* FRIVALDSKY, 1835: *Plebejus* (LY): 139
*serotina* DESCIMON & LESSE, 1954: *Erebia* (SA): 276
*sibylla* HUFNAGEL, 1766: *camilla*
*sibyllina* VERITY, 1913: *neoridas*
*Sicca* VERITY, 1953: *Coenonympha*
*sichaea* LEDERER, 1857: *fatua*
*siciliana* OBERTHÜR, 1914: *blachieri*
*sifanica* \* GRUM-GRSHIMAILO, 1891: *aquilonaris*
*Simplicia* VERITY, 1953: *Erebia*
*simplonia* FREYER, 1829: *Euchloe* (PI): 039
*sinapis* LINNAEUS, 1758: *Leptidea* (PI): 049
*sinon* PODA, 1761: *podalirius*
*skypetarum* REBEL & ZERNY, 1931: *leander*
*sphyrus* HÜBNER, 1823: **machaon**
*spini* FABRICIUS, 1787 *(lynceus)*: *Nordmannia* (LY): 134
*splendens* STEFANELLI, 1904: *escheri*
*spodia* STAUDINGER, 1871: *oeme*
*statilinus* HUFNAGEL, 1766 *(allionia, arachne, fauna, sylvicola)*: *Hipparchia*
    (SA): 308
*sthennyo* GRASLIN, 1850: *Erebia* (SA): 277

*stheno* HÜBNER, 1804: *disa*
*stiberi* GERHARD, 1853: *hippothoe*
*stirius* GODART, 1824 *(morula, nerine)*: *Erebia* (SA): 278
*Strymon* \* HÜBNER, 1818: *Nordmannia*
*Strymonidia* TUTT, 1908: *Nordmannia*
*stygne* OCHSENHEIMER, 1807: *meolans*
*styx* FREYER, 1834 *(reichlini, trentae, triglites)*: *Erebia* (SA): 279
*subalpina* SPREYER, 1851: *Lycaena* (LY): 119
*sudetica* STAUDINGER, 1861: *Erebia* (SA): 280
*suecica* HEMMING, 1936: *tullia*
*sulitelma* AURIVILLIUS, 1890: *hecla*
*suwarovius* HERBST, 1796: *russiae*
*syllius* HERBST, 1796: *occitanica*
*sylvicola* \* AUSTAUT, 1879: *statilinus*
*sylvius* PODA, 1761: *argus*
*Syngea* HÜBNER, 1819: *Erebia*
*Synchloe* HÜBNER, 1818: *Pieris*
*Syntarucus* BUTLER, 1901: (LY)
*syriaca* STAUDINGER, 1871 *(cypriaca, ghigii)*: *Hipparchia* (SA): 309
*syriaca* \* TUTT, 1910: *italaglauca*

*tagis* HÜBNER, 1804: *Euchloe* (PI): 040
*tardenota* PRAVIEL, 1941: *ottomana*
*tarpeia* PALLAS, 1771: *Oeneis* (SA): 351
*Tarucus* MOORE, 1881: (LY)
*taygete* GEYER, 1824: *Oeneis* (SA): 352
*taygetica* REBEL, 1902: *panagea*
*teleius* BERGSTRÄSSER, 1779 *(euphemus, teloganus)*: *Maculinea* (LY): 128
*telicanus* LANG, 1789: *pirithous*
*telmessia* ZELLER, 1847: *Maniola* (SA): 327
*teloganus* BERGSTRÄSSER, 1779: *teleius*
*Thais* FABRICIUS, 1807: *Zerynthia*
*Thaleropis* STAUDINGER, 1871: (NY)
*Thecla* FABRICIUS, 1807 *(Zephyrus)*: (LY)
*Thecliola* STRAND, 1910: *Nordmannia*
*theophrastus* FABRICIUS, 1793: *Tarucus* (LY): 192
*thersamon* ESPER, 1784: *Lycaena* (LY): 120
*Thersamonia* VERITY, 1919: *Lycaena*
*thersites* CANTENER, 1834 *(alexius)*: *Polyommatus* (LY): 177
*Thestor* HÜBNER, 1819: *Tomares*
*thetis* KLUG, 1834: *Lycaena* (LY): 121
*thetis* ROTTEMBURG, 1775: *bellargus*

*thore* HÜBNER, 1806 *(borealis)*: *Boloria* (NY): 402
*thyrsis* FREYER, 1846: *Coenonympha* (SA): 228
*tigelius* BONELLI, 1826 *(paramegaera)*: *Lasiommata* (SA): 323
*Tiora* EVANS, 1912: *Cupido*
*tiphon* ROTTEMBURG, 1775: *tullia*
*tiphonides* STAUDINGER, 1901: *rhodopensis*
*tircis* STOLL, 1782: *phryne*
*tircis* BUTLER, 1867: *aegeria*
*Tisiphone* MUSCHAMP, 1915: *Pyronia*
*tiresias* ROTTEMBURG, 1775: *argiades*
*titania* ESPER, 1793 *(amathusia, cypris)*: *Boloria* (NY): 403
*tithonus* LINNAEUS, 1771 *(decolorata)*: *Pyronia* (SA): 368
*tityrus* PODA, 1761 *(bleusei, circe, dorilis)*: *Lycaena* (LY): 122
*Tomares* RAMBUR, 1840 *(Thestor)*: (LY)
*Tongeia* TUTT, 1908: (LY)
*trappi* VERITY, 1927 *(lycidas)*: (LY): 140
*tremulae* ESPER, 1800: *populi*
*trentae* LORKOVIC, 1952: *styx*
*triaria* PRUNNER, 1798 *(evias, hispanica, pyrenaica)*: *Erebia* (SA): 281
*Triariia* VERITY, 1953: *Erebia*
*triglites* FRUHSTORFER, 1918: *styx*
*trinacriae* VERITY, 1919: *minimus*
*triopes* SPEYER, 1865: *gorge*
*Triphysa* ZELLER, 1850: (SA)
*tristis* HERRICH-SCHÄFFER, 1848: *eriphyle*
*trivia*\* DENIS & SCHIFFERMÜLLER, 1775: *fascelis*
*trivia* ESPER, 1780: *cynthia*
*trochylus* FREYER, 1844: *Chilades* (LY): 086
*Truncaefalcia* VERITY, 1953: *Erebia*
*tullia* MÜLLER, 1864 *(davus, demophile, lorkovici, philoxenus, rothliebii, scotica, suecica, tiphon)*: *Coenonympha* (SA): 229
*tundra* STAUDINGER, 1887: *dabanensis*
*tundra* BANG-HAAS, 1912: *Oeneis* (SA): 353
*Turanana* BETHUNE-BAKER, 1916: (LY)
*Turania*\* BETHUNE-BAKER, 1914: *Pseudophilotes*
*Tuttiola* STRAND, 1910: *Nordmannia*
*tyndarus* ESPER, 1781 *(cleo, dromus, herse)*: *Erebia* (SA): 282

*Ultraaricia* BEURET, 1959: (LY)
*Uranops* HEMMING, 1929: *Polyommatus*
*urticae* LINNAEUS, 1758: *Aglais* (NY): 374

*Vacciniina* Tutt, 1909: (LY)
*v-album* Hofmann, 1887: *w-album*
*valesiaca* Elwes, 1898: *meolans*
*Vanessa* Fabricius, 1807 *(Cynthia, Pyrameis)*: (NY)
*varia* Meyer-Dür, 1851: *Melitaea* (NY): 437
*vau-album* Esper, 1780: *egea*
*vau-album* \* Denis & Schiffermüller, 1775: *l-album*
*vergy* Warren, 1807: *pronoe*
*vernetensis* Rondou, 1902: *diamina*
*veronicae* Dorfmeister, 1853: *britomartis*
*vicrama* Moore, 1865: *Pseudophilotes* (LY): 187
*vicrama* \* Moore, 1865: *schiffermuelleri*
*vihorlatensis* Moucha, 1956; *flavescens*
*violetae* Gomez Bustillo, Exposito Hermosa & Martinez Borrego,
    1979: *Polyommatus* (LY): 178
*virgaureae* Linnaeus, 1758 *(miegi, montanus)*: *Lycaena* (LY): 123
*virgilius* Oberthür, 1910: *Polyommatus* (LY): 179
*virginensis* Drury, 1773 *(huntera, iola)*: *Vanessa* (NY): 450
*viriathus* Sheldon, 1913: *epistygne*
*vittatus* Oberthür, 1892: *dolus*
*vogesiaca* Christ, 1882: *manto*
*volgensis* Mazochin-Porshnjakov, 1952 *(delattini, muelleri)*: *Hipparchia*
    (SA): 310
*vulcanica* Godart, 1819: *indica*
*vulgaris* Zeller, 1847: *aegeria*


*w-album* Knoch, 1782 *(v-album)*: *Nordmannia* (LY): 135
*webbianus* Brulle, 1839: *Cyclirius* (LY): 097
*werdandi* Zetterstedt, 1840: *nastes*
*wheeleri* Chapman, 1910: *diamina*
*wilkinsoni* Kudrna, 1977: *semele*
*williamsi* Romei, 1927: *hippolyte*
*wolfensbergeri* Frey, 1880 *(intermedia, ichnea)*: *Euphydryas* (NY): 414
*wollastoni* Butler, 1886; *brassicae*
*wyssii* Christ, 1889: *Hipparchia* (SA): 311


*xanthomelas* Esper, 1781: *Nymphalis* (NY): 443
*xerophila* Berger, 1946: *rebeli*
*xiphia* Fabricius, 1775: *Pararge* (SA): 355
*xiphioides* Staudinger, 1871: *Pararge* (SA): 356

*Ypthima* HÜBNER, 1818: (SA)

*zapateri* OBERTHÜR, 1875: *Erebia* (SA): 283
*Zegris* BOISDUVAL, 1836 *(Microzegris)*: (PI)
*Zephyrus* DALMAN, 1816: *Thecla*
*Zephyrus* * DALMAN, 1816: *Quercusia*
*Zerynthia* OCHSENHEIMER, 1816 *(Allancastria, Parnalius, Thais)*: (PA)
*Zizeeria* CHAPMAN, 1910: (LY)
*Zizera* * MOORE, 1881: *Cupido*
*zullichi* HEMMING, 1933 *(nevadensis)*: *Agriades* (LY): 071

# 4.7  Priority tasks in taxonomic research

A full taxonomic revision of European butterflies, including a comprehensive identification aid (or key) down to species, suitable for both the adults and early stages, is the most important long term task of lepidopterological taxonomy in Europe. The significance of this task is so great because only a taxonomic revision can objectively and definitely settle both the nomenclature and classification of all taxa. Such a project must form a part of a monograph and is likely to take some 10–20 years to complete, a time which may prove critical for the survival of many European butterfly species. It is, therefore, necessary to define certain short term priorities according to both their urgency and significance for the conservation of European butterfly fauna. These tasks can be divided into two distinct groups according to their aims:

● Maintaining of stability of zoological names until they can be definitely stabilized and objectively defined in a taxonomic revision, and confirmed (i. e. conserved) by the International Commission on Zoological Nomenclature. This task must specifically include the following aspects:

– Voluntary curbs on all avoidable (unnecessary) changes of zoological names motivated by formal and selfinterested reasons outside taxonomic revisions;

– Voluntary curbs on further splitting of established genera outside full taxonomic revisions treating all potentially congeneric taxa (regardless of the territory they inhabit), observing the principles discussed elsewhere;

– Voluntary curbs on further description of subspecies (and the like) outside taxonomic revisions or, better still, unconditionally;

−Unconditional ban on the naming of infrasubspecific taxa and utilization of their names.

The ultimate success of these measures depends, apart from the taxonomists themselves, on the active cooperation of editors of lepidopterological and other relevant journals; also the International Commission on Zoological Nomenclature and its individual members could play an active part in the realization of these tasks.

● Intensification of research to close the existing gaps in our knowledge of European butterflies, concentrating particularly on the following specific tasks:

−Construction of practical identification aids based on reliable morphological features, concerning early stages and taxonomically difficult groups of species;

−Studies of material from critical zones of species not satisfactorily defined at present, utilizing modern biological methods and concepts (e. g. relationship of *Maculinea alcon* and *M. rebeli*) which are apparent from the discussion concerning the taxonomic status of certain taxa mentioned earlier in this chapter, with particular concern for rare endemic species and endangered species, perhaps also vulnerable species;

−Studies of critical species, both so far as their presence in Europe and/or taxonomic status is/are concerned;

−Compilatory work concerning synonymic lists, catalogues and lists of type-material (regardless of whether according to author, depository or taxonomic group concerned.

Reading of taxonomic notes forming a part of this chapter indicates objectively the principal deficiencies which are to be answered by taxonomists.

Propositions and suggestions concerning the work of the International Commission on Zoological Nomenclature also form a part of this consideration. The principal necessities−the simplification of the International Code of Zoological Nomenclature and effective ways towards conservation of well established zoological names have been discussed elsewhere.

# 5 Applied biogeography of European butterflies

Biogeography – as defined below – utilizes the relevant results of taxonomic research and combines them with data concerning both the ecological and geographical aspects of the contemporary ranges of nominal species. Methodical application of the results of biogeographical research enables an evaluation (i. e. classification) of the biogeographical status of nominal species and their ranges, classified against the background of their contemporary natural disposition and anthropogenically influenced condition. Additionally, biogeography facilitates an evaluation of all individual components of a nominal species' range (i. e. colonies) for the long term survival of that species.

## 5.1 Biogeography as an applied science

Opinions differ slightly from author to author, and perhaps also from country to country, as to what biogeography is. A fairly neutral and adequately broad definition is preferred here (e. g. Cox, HEALEY & MOORE 1973, HOLMES 1979, LATTIN 1967, etc.):

● Biogeography is the scientific study of the patterns of distribution of organisms in space and time.

To avoid any possible confusion: zoogeography is therefore according to the above definition animal biogeography (cf. phytogeography), while

● Faunistics is the inventory of the animals, or their selected taxonomic groups, of a given territory (cf. floristics).

Nonetheless, mere comparison or cumulative summarising of distribution patterns is no longer satisfactory as a branch of biological science: biogeography must take into account the causes of these patterns as well as their dynamics. Biogeography is, therefore, to be understood primarily as "ecology in space and time".

The primary task of biogeography is to discover and describe the factors that determine the distribution patterns, their evolution, origin and relationship, whether natural or of anthropogenic character. Applied biogeography must, therefore, include the scientific study of the remedies necessary for the prevention of adverse anthropogenic effects, and where these adverse effects cannot be eliminated by effective preventive measures, applied biogeography must show how to "live with them", i. e. how to minimize their destructive repercussions upon our natural environment. To do this, biogeography depends on a whole spectrum of other scientific disciplines, such as geology, geography, climatology, taxonomy, faunistics, paleontology, plant and animal ecology, and others.

In this respect, the tasks of applied biogeography range from the study of the causes determining the occurrence of any given nominal species, whether in general terms or within a given territory, to the study of the history of the fauna (or flora, or both) of a continent. It seems that the more "simple" of these tasks – which are the necessary basic units of classified information decisive for the formation of all those "higher" prestigious theories – are more often neglected or even totally overlooked than not: there is not one butterfly species in Europe of which the complex reasons for its occurrence are adequately known.

Only one form of application of biogeography is discussed here, the one that produces a decisive feedback for this scientific discipline:

the conservation of nature and environment, taking the butterflies as a selected representative animal group.

Applied biogeography is for this purpose seen as a compound scientific discipline encompassing the faunistics and ecology of butterflies. In this respect, the ultimate task of applied biogeography (with all its subordinate disciplines) is to provide a comprehensive directly applicable scientific basis for the conservation of butterflies (or other animal groups) in Europe (or any other area). Contemporary applied biogeography is still very far from achieving this aim. Therefore, how to utilize our present knowledge of the biogeography of European butterflies for their conservation in Europe is shown in this chapter.

## 5.2 Survey of the colonies of European butterflies

Within the range of any nominal species, the individual colonies are not of equal long term viability and, therefore, not of the same value for the existence (i. e. long term survival) of the species; this applies regardless of the anthropogenic influences and pressures but is still further enhanced by them. Isolated populations located towards the biogeographical limits of any nominal species are less stable, both in relative and absolute terms, than those populations situated within the species' "headquarters" (i. e. natural centre/s of its distribution). The value of an isolated colony diminishes with its distance and the degree of its isolation from the continuous range of the species, as well as with its "extreme" ecological character. This statement can be well illustratet by the example of *Hipparchia statilinus:* this Mediterranean species (of expansive type) has a near-continuous distribution in southern Europe and some isolated colonies in central Europe, where it has been recorded as far north as the Netherlands, German Democratic Republic and Poland. These colonies represent a negligible proportion of the total stock of the species and, because they are distant from the natural biogeographical limit of the species, which in Europe is situated very approximately south of the Alps, the loss of any one (or more) colonies does not represent a threat to the species as a whole. Long term successful survival of any such colony is quite irrelevant to the survival of the species. Nonetheless, such colonies are often of immense regional or local interest and under certain circumstances they may become nuclei of incipient biological units, the future allopatric species. Being outside the dispersal potential of the stronger colonies from the "headquarters" of the same species, their localities cannot be recolonized at present or in the foreseeable future. Artificial reintroduction with stock of southern European origin is unlikely to be successful in the very specific ecological conditions of the extreme habitats. These extreme colonies became established during the expansive phase of the species, and–at least those successfully surviving–became so far adapted to their unique environmental conditions, that they were able to survive in those by and large unfavourable, for the majority of the species' stock perhaps even hostile, ecological surroundings.

Classified solely according to their individual value for the long term (i. e. indefinite) survival of any nominal species, two basic types of colonies can be recognized:

● **Principal colonies** are strong, well established "permanent" colonies situated chiefly within the nominal species' "headquarters", i. e. near the centre of the relatively continuous distribution; such colonies are decisive for the long term survival of the species as a whole. In general, such colonies are not exposed to extreme environmental conditions, in addition to the anthropogenic pressures.

● **Complementary colonies** are usually situated towards the biogeographical limits of the species, they are vulnerable to both the extreme environmental factors and to the anthropogenic pressures, and their vulnerability to both is high; this makes them on the whole quite instable. Long term survival of such colonies is not essential for the species.

These considerations allow one to come to the following logical conclusion with regard to the conservation of (European butterfly) species:

● Long term (i. e. indefinite) survival of any one nominal species depends on securing the existence of its principal colonies.

Consequently, one of the priority tasks of any species conservation programme must be the securing of the primary colonies, particularly if they are already (in part or in their majority) suffering from some anthropogenic pressures.

An **analysis of the ranges of all European butterfly species,** based upon the examination of published data and, above all, my own experience, shows that five different modes of recorded occurrence can be recognized. They are expressed in the following tables by five symbols, each showing the presence of the nominal species (listed in horizontal line) in the country (listed in vertical column):

● principal colonies present
● principal colonies anticipated
⊙ complementary colonies present
○ recorded (possibly/probably present)
? uncertain (doubtful, possible)

Regular migrants capable of establishing temporary colonies in a given country are classified as "recorded"; migrations of adults not followed by breeding are not noted. Species of uncertain taxonomic status are classified as "recorded" in the countries with their type-localities. Question mark (i. e. "uncertain") is used in some cases to indicate possible occurrence. Needless to mention that the accuracy of this classification depends on the availability of the relevant information, which is not always adequate and rarely fully satisfactory; this cannot be surprising: this method of evelation is entirely new, used here for the first time. The pragmatic application of the term "principal colony" in the tables is, of course, relative: the decisive factor must always be the value of the colony for the survival of the species in Europe. Whereas it is possible to differentiate in the case of the majority of species, in some extreme cases all colonies are considered to be of principal value. This is always so in cases of rare endemic species confined to extremely restricted areas (e. g. *Cupido carswelli* and *Polyommatus humedasae*) and endangered species which have become extinct in significant parts of their European "headquarters" (e. g. *Coenonympha oedippus*). It is believed that every established colony represents in such cases an indispensible proportion of the total (European) stock.

All European countries are listed in vertical columns, arranged in alphabetical order; the abbreviations used are the national automobile registration letters:

| | |
|---|---|
| A | Austria |
| AL | Albania |
| | Andorra v. Spain (E) |
| B | Belgium |
| BG | Bulgaria |
| | Channel Islands v. Great Britain (GB) |
| CH | Switzerland (incl. Liechtenstein) |
| CS | Czechoslovakia |
| CY | Cyprus |
| D | Germany (Federal Republic) |
| DDR | Germany (Eastern "Democratic Republic") |
| DK | Denmark |
| E | Spain (incl. Andorra, Gibraltar) |
| F | France (incl. Monaco) |
| | Gibraltar v. Spain (E) |
| GB | Great Britain (incl. Channel Islands) |
| GR | Greece |
| H | Hungary |
| | Iceland (excluded: no native butterflies except migrants) |
| I | Italy (incl. San Marino and Vatican) |
| IRL | Ireland (Republic) |
| | Liechtenstein v. Switzerland (CH) |
| L | Luxembourg |
| M | Malta |
| | Monaco v. France (F) |
| N | Norway |
| NL | Netherlands |
| P | Portugal |
| PL | Poland |
| R | Romania |
| | San Marino v. Italy (I) |
| S | Sweden |
| SF | Finland |
| SU | Soviet Union (U.S.S.R.) |
| TR | Turkey (European only) |
| | Vatican v. Italy (I) |
| YU | Yugoslavia |

All major islands forming politically and/or geographically a part of Europe but not constituting separate sovereign states are not individually recognized or listed here. The nominal species are given according to the country they are united with, e. g.

Azores, Madeira v. Portugal (P);
Canary Islands v. Spain (E);
Corsica v. France (F);
Crete, Rhodos, etc. v. Greece (GR);
Elba, Sardinia, Sicily v. Italy (I).

This treatment is motivated by purely practical reasons: (1) sovereign states carry primary responsibility for the conservation of nature within their boundaries and (2) recognition of smaller natural units within any one country is considered to be beyond the scope of this work. Where necessary (e. g. rare endemic species, threatened species, etc.) a further reference to the distribution of some island isolates is given elsewhere.

Species columns (PAPILIONIDAE then PIERIDAE):

1. *Archon apollinus*
2. *Iphiclides feisthamelii*
3. *Iphiclides podalirius*
4. *Papilio alexanor*
5. *Papilio hospiton*
6. *Papilio machaon*
7. *Parnassius apollo*
8. *Parnassius mnemosyne*
9. *Parnassius phoebus*
10. *Zerynthia cerisyi*
11. *Zerynthia cretica*
12. *Zerynthia polyxena*
13. *Zerynthia rumina*
14. *Anthocharis cardamines*
15. *Anthocharis damone*
16. *Anthocharis euphenoides*
17. *Anthocharis gruneri*
18. *Aporia crataegi*
19. *Catopsilia florella*

| Country | 1 | 2 | 3 | 4 | 5 | 6 | 7 | 8 | 9 | 10 | 11 | 12 | 13 | 14 | 15 | 16 | 17 | 18 | 19 |
|---|---|---|---|---|---|---|---|---|---|---|---|---|---|---|---|---|---|---|---|
| YU |  | ● | ● |  | ● | ● | ● |  | ● |  | ● |  |  | ● | ● |  | ● | ● |  |
| TR | ● |  | ● | ? |  | ● |  |  |  |  | ◉ |  |  | ● |  |  |  | ● |  |
| SU |  |  | ● |  |  | ● | ● | ● |  |  | ● |  |  | ● |  |  |  | ● |  |
| SF |  |  |  |  |  | ● | ◉ | ● |  |  |  |  |  | ◉ |  |  |  | ● |  |
| S |  |  |  |  |  | ● | ● | ● |  |  |  |  |  | ◉ |  |  |  | ● |  |
| R |  |  | ● |  |  | ● | ● | ● |  |  | ● |  |  | ● |  |  |  | ● |  |
| PL |  |  | ◉ |  |  | ● | ◉ | ● |  |  |  |  |  | ● |  |  |  | ● |  |
| P | ● |  |  |  |  | ● |  |  |  |  |  | ● |  | ◉ |  | ● |  | ● |  |
| NL |  |  | ◉ |  |  |  |  |  |  |  |  |  |  | ● |  |  |  | ◉ |  |
| N |  |  | ◉ |  |  | ◉ | ◉ | ○ |  |  |  |  |  | ◉ |  |  |  | ◉ |  |
| M |  |  | ◉ |  |  |  |  |  |  |  |  |  |  |  |  |  |  |  |  |
| L |  |  | ◉ |  |  | ◉ |  |  |  |  |  |  |  | ◉ |  |  |  |  |  |
| IRL |  |  |  |  |  |  |  |  |  |  |  |  |  | ● |  |  |  |  |  |
| I |  |  | ● | ● | ● | ● | ● | ● | ● |  | ● |  |  | ● | ● | ● |  | ● |  |
| H |  |  | ● |  |  | ● | ? | ● |  |  | ● |  |  | ● |  |  |  | ● |  |
| GR | ● |  | ● | ● |  | ● | ● |  | ● | ● | ● |  |  | ● | ● |  | ● | ● |  |
| GB |  |  |  |  |  | ◉ |  |  |  |  |  |  |  | ● |  |  |  |  |  |
| F |  | ◉ | ● | ● | ● | ● | ● | ● | ● |  |  | ● |  | ● |  | ● |  | ● |  |
| E | ● | ◉ |  |  |  | ● | ● | ◉ |  |  |  | ● |  | ● |  | ● |  | ● | ● |
| DK |  |  | ◉ |  |  | ● |  |  |  |  |  |  |  | ● |  |  |  | ◉ |  |
| DDR |  |  | ◉ |  |  | ● |  | ◉ |  |  |  |  |  | ● |  |  |  | ● |  |
| D |  |  | ● |  |  | ● | ● | ◉ | ◉ |  |  |  |  | ● |  |  |  | ● |  |
| CY |  |  | ● |  |  | ● |  |  |  | ● |  |  |  | ◉ |  |  |  |  |  |
| CS |  |  | ● |  |  | ● | ● | ● |  |  | ● |  |  | ● |  |  |  | ● |  |
| CH |  |  | ● |  |  | ● | ● | ● | ● |  | ? |  |  | ● |  |  |  | ● |  |
| BG |  |  | ● |  |  | ● | ◉ | ● |  | ● | ● |  |  | ● |  |  |  | ● |  |
| B |  | ◉ |  |  |  | ● |  |  |  |  |  |  |  | ● |  |  |  | ◉ |  |
| AL |  |  | ● | ◑ |  | ● | ● | ● |  | ○ |  | ○ |  | ● |  |  | ○ | ● |  |
| A |  |  | ● |  |  | ● | ● | ● | ● |  | ● |  |  | ● |  |  |  | ● |  |

| Country | C. alfacariensis | C. aurorina | C. balcanica | C. chrysotheme | C. crocea | C. erate | C. hecla | C. hyale | C. myrmidone | C. nastes | C. palaeno | C. phicomone | Colotis evagore | E. ausonia | E. belemia | E. charlonia | E. crameri | E. insularis | E. penia | E. simplonia | E. tagis | Gonepteryx cleobule |
|---|---|---|---|---|---|---|---|---|---|---|---|---|---|---|---|---|---|---|---|---|---|---|
| YU | ● | ? | ● |   | ● | ◉ |   | ● | ● |   |   |   |   | ● |   |   |   |   |   | ● | ● |   |
| TR |   | ? |   | ◉ | ● | ◉ |   |   |   |   |   |   |   | ● |   |   |   |   |   | ● |   |   |
| SU |   | ? |   | ● | ● | ● | ● | ● | ● | ● | ● |   |   | ◐ |   |   |   |   |   |   |   |   |
| SF |   |   |   |   |   | ● | ○ |   |   | ● | ● |   |   |   |   |   |   |   |   |   |   |   |
| S |   |   |   |   |   | ● | ○ |   |   | ● | ● |   |   |   |   |   |   |   |   |   |   |   |
| R | ○ |   |   | ○ | ○ | ● |   | ● | ◉ |   | ? |   |   | ○ |   |   |   |   |   | ? | ● |   |
| PL | ◉ |   |   |   | ○ |   |   | ● | ● |   | ● |   |   |   |   |   |   |   |   |   |   |   |
| P | ● |   |   | ● |   |   |   |   |   |   |   |   | ● |   |   |   |   |   |   | ● | ● |   |
| NL |   |   |   |   | ○ |   |   | ◉ |   |   |   |   |   |   |   |   |   |   |   |   |   |   |
| N |   |   |   |   |   | ● |   |   |   | ● | ● |   |   |   |   |   |   |   |   |   |   |   |
| M |   |   |   | ● |   |   |   |   |   |   |   |   |   |   |   |   | ○ |   |   |   | ○ |   |
| L | ◉ |   |   |   | ○ |   |   | ● |   |   |   |   |   |   |   |   |   |   |   |   |   |   |
| IRL |   |   |   |   |   |   |   |   |   |   |   |   |   |   |   |   |   |   |   |   |   |   |
| I | ● |   |   | ● |   |   |   | ● |   | ● | ● |   | ● |   |   |   |   | ● |   | ● | ● |   |
| H | ● |   | ● |   | ○ |   |   |   | ● |   |   |   | ● |   |   |   |   |   |   |   |   |   |
| GR | ● | ● | ? |   | ● | ◉ |   | ? |   |   |   |   |   |   |   |   | ◐ |   | ● | ● |   |   |
| GB | ○ |   |   |   | ○ |   |   | ○ |   |   |   |   |   |   |   |   |   |   |   |   |   |   |
| F | ● |   |   |   | ● |   |   | ● |   |   | ◉ | ● | ● |   |   | ● | ● |   | ● | ● |   |   |
| E | ● |   |   |   | ● |   |   | ◉ |   |   | ● | ? |   | ● | ● |   |   |   | ● | ● | ● |   |
| DK | ? |   |   |   | ? |   |   |   |   |   |   |   |   |   |   |   |   |   |   |   |   |   |
| DDR | ◉ |   |   |   | ○ |   |   | ● |   |   | ◉ |   |   |   |   |   |   |   |   |   |   |   |
| D | ● |   |   |   | ○ |   |   | ● | ● |   | ● | ◉ |   |   |   |   |   |   |   |   |   |   |
| CY |   |   |   |   | ● |   |   |   |   |   |   |   |   |   |   | ● |   |   |   |   |   |   |
| CS | ● |   |   | ○ | ○ |   |   | ● | ● |   | ● |   |   |   |   |   |   |   |   |   |   |   |
| CH | ● |   |   |   | ○ |   |   | ● |   |   | ● | ● | ● |   |   |   |   |   |   | ● |   |   |
| BG | ● |   | ? | ○ | ○ | ● |   | ● |   |   |   |   |   |   |   |   | ? |   | ? | ● |   |   |
| B | ○ |   |   |   | ○ |   |   | ● |   |   | ◉ |   |   |   |   |   |   |   |   |   |   |   |
| AL | ? |   |   |   | ● |   |   | ? |   |   |   |   | ◐ |   |   |   |   |   |   | ● |   |   |
| A | ● |   |   | ● | ○ |   |   | ● | ● |   | ● | ● |   |   |   |   |   |   |   |   |   |   |

| | G. cleopatra | G. farinosa | G. maderensis | G. palmae | G. rhamni | L. duponcheli | L. morsei | L. sinapis | P. adalwinda | P. balcana | P. brassicae | P. bryoniae | P. callidice | P. cheiranthi | P. chloridice | P. daplidice | P. ergane | P. flavescens | P. krueperi | P. mannii | P. maura | P. napi |
|---|---|---|---|---|---|---|---|---|---|---|---|---|---|---|---|---|---|---|---|---|---|---|
| YU | ● | ● | | | ● | ● | ● | ● | | ● | ● | ● | ● | | ● | ● | ● | ● | ● | ● | | ● |
| TR | ? | ? | | | ● | ◉ | | ● | | | ● | | | | | ◉ | | | | | | ● |
| SU | | | | | ● | | ? | ● | ● | | ● | ● | ○ | | ◐ | ● | ? | ? | ? | ◐ | | ● |
| SF | | | | | ● | | | ● | ● | | ● | | | | ? | | | | | | | ● |
| S | | | | | ● | | | ● | ● | | ● | | | | ◉ | | | | | | | ● |
| R | | | | | ● | | ● | ● | | | ● | ● | | | ● | ● | ? | | ○ | | | ● |
| PL | | | | | ● | | | ● | | | ● | ● | | | | ● | | | | | | ● |
| P | ● | | ● | | ● | | | ● | | | ● | | | | ● | | | | | ? | | ● |
| NL | | | | | ● | | | ◉ | | | ● | | | | ○ | | | | | | | ● |
| N | | | | | ● | | | ● | ● | | ● | | | | | | | | | | | ● |
| M | | ◉ | | | | | | | | | ● | | | | ● | | | | | | | |
| L | | | | | ● | | | ◉ | | | ● | | | | ● | | | | | | | ● |
| IRL | | | | | ● | | | ● | | | ● | | | | | | | | | | | ● |
| I | ● | | | | ● | ? | | ● | | | ● | ● | ● | | ● | ● | | | ● | | | ● |
| H | | | | | ● | | ● | ● | | | ● | | | | ◉ | ◉ | ● | | ◉ | | | ● |
| GR | ● | ● | | | ● | ● | ● | ? | | ● | | | | ● | ● | ● | | ● | ● | | | ● |
| GB | | | | | ● | | | ◉ | | | ● | | | | ○ | | | | | | | ● |
| F | ● | | | | ● | ● | | ● | | | ● | ● | ● | | ● | ● | ? | | ● | | | ● |
| E | ● | | | ● | ● | | | ● | | | ● | ◉ | ● | | ● | ● | | | ● | | | ● |
| DK | | | | | ● | | | | | | ● | | | | ? | | | | | | | ● |
| DDR | | | | | ● | | | ● | | | ● | | | | ◉ | | | | | | | ● |
| D | | | | | ● | | | ● | | | ● | ◉ | | | ◉ | | | | | | | ● |
| CY | ● | | | | | | | | | | ● | | | ◐ | ● | | | | | | | |
| CS | | | | | ● | | ● | ● | | | ● | ● | | | ◉ | | ● | | ◉ | | | ● |
| CH | | | | | ● | | | ● | | | ● | ● | ● | | ◉ | ○ | | ● | | | | ● |
| BG | | | | | ● | ● | ● | ● | | | ● | | | | ? | ● | ● | | ● | ● | | ● |
| B | | | | | ● | | | ◉ | | | ● | | | | ◉ | | | | | | | ● |
| AL | ● | ● | | | ● | ○ | ? | ● | | | ● | | | | ○ | ● | ● | | ○ | ● | | ◐ |
| A | | | | | ● | | ● | ● | | | ● | ● | ● | | ◉ | ◉ | ● | | ◉ | | | ● |

| Country | Pieris rapae | Zegris eupheme | Zegris pyrothoe | LYCAENIDAE | Agriades aquilo | Agriades dardanus | Agriades glandon | Agriades pyrenaicus | Agriades zullichi | Albulina orbitulus | Aricia agestis | Aricia allous | Aricia artaxerxes | Aricia cramera | Aricia eumedon | Aricia inhonora | Aricia morronensis | Aricia nicias | Azanus jesous | Callophrys avis | Callophrys rubi | Celastrina argiolus |
|---|---|---|---|---|---|---|---|---|---|---|---|---|---|---|---|---|---|---|---|---|---|---|
| YU | ● | | | | | | ● | ○ | | | ● | ● | ● | | ◉ | | | | | | ● | ● |
| TR | ● | | | | | | | ○ | | | ● | | | | | | | | | | ● | ● |
| SU | ● | ● | ● | | | | ◐ | ◐ | | | ● | | | | ● | ● | | ○ | | | ● | ● |
| SF | ● | | | | | | ● | | | | ● | | | | ● | ● | ● | | | | ● | ● |
| S | ● | | | | | | ● | | | ● | ◉ | | | | ● | ● | ● | | | | ● | ● |
| R | ● | | | | | | | | | | ● | ● | | | ● | | | | | | ● | ● |
| PL | ● | | | | | | | | | | ● | | | | ● | ● | | | | | ● | ● |
| P | ● | | | | | | | | | | | | | ● | | | | ? | | ● | ● | ● |
| NL | ● | | | | | | | | | | ● | | | | | | | | | | ● | ● |
| N | ● | | | | | | ● | | | | ● | | | | ● | ● | | | | | ● | ● |
| M | ● | | | | | | | | | | ● | | | | | | | | | | | ● |
| L | ● | | | | | | | | | | ◉ | | | | | | | | | | ● | ● |
| IRL | ● | | | | | | | | | | | | ◉ | | | | | | | | | ● |
| I | ● | | | | | | | ● | | | ● | ● | ● | | ● | ● | | ● | | | ● | ● |
| H | ● | | | | | | | | | | ● | ◉ | | | ◉ | | | | | | ● | ● |
| GR | ● | | | | | | | | | | ● | ● | | | ◉ | | | | | | ● | ● |
| GB | ● | | | | | | | | | | ● | | ● | | | | | | | | ● | ● |
| F | ● | | | | | | ● | ● | | | ● | ● | ● | | ● | | ● | | | ● | ● | ● |
| E | ● | ● | | | | | ◉ | ● | ● | | | | | ● | ● | | ● | ◉ | | ● | ● | ● |
| DK | ● | | | | | | | | | | ● | | | | | | | | | | ● | ● |
| DDR | ● | | | | | | | | | | ● | | | | ◉ | | | | | | ● | ● |
| D | ● | | | | | | ● | | | | ● | ● | ◉ | | ● | | | | | | ● | ● |
| CY | ● | | | | | | | | | | ● | | | | | | | ● | | | | ● |
| CS | ● | | | | | | | | | | ● | ? | | | ● | | | | | | ● | ● |
| CH | ● | | | | | | ● | | | | ● | ● | ● | | ● | | ● | | | | ● | ● |
| BG | ● | | | | | | ◐ | | | | ● | ? | | | ● | | | | | | ● | ● |
| B | ● | | | | | | | | | | | | | | | | | | | | ● | ● |
| AL | ● | | | | | | | | | | ● | | | | ● | | | | | | ● | ● |
| A | ● | | | | | | ● | | | | ● | ● | ◉ | | ● | | | | | | ● | ● |

| | *Chilades galba* | *Chilades trochylus* | *Cigaritis acamas* | *Cupido alcetas* | *Cupido argiades* | *Cupido carswelli* | *Cupido decoloratus* | *Cupido lorquinii* | *Cupido minimus* | *Cupido osiris* | *Cyaniris antiochena* | *Cyaniris semiargus* | *Cyclirius webbianus* | *Glaucopsyche alexis* | *Glaucopsyche melanops* | *Glaucopsyche paphos* | *Iolana iolas* | *Kretania eurypilus* | *Kretania psylorita* | *Laeosopis roboris* | *Lampides boeticus* | *Lycaeides argyrognomon* |
|---|---|---|---|---|---|---|---|---|---|---|---|---|---|---|---|---|---|---|---|---|---|---|
| YU | | | | ● | ● | | ● | | ● | ● | | ● | | ● | | | ● | | | | ● | ● |
| TR | | ● | | | | | | | ? | ? | | ◐ | | | | | ? | | | | ◐ | |
| SU | | | | ◐ | ● | | ◐ | | ● | ◐ | | ◐ | | ● | | | ? | | | | ◐ | ◐ |
| SF | | | | | | | | | ● | | | ● | | ◉ | | | | | | | | |
| S | | | | | | | | | ● | | | ● | | ◉ | | | | | | | | ○ |
| R | | | | ● | ● | | ● | | ● | ○ | | ● | | ● | | | ● | | | | ◉ | ● |
| PL | | | | ? | ● | | ? | | ◉ | | | ● | | ◉ | | | | | | | | ◉ |
| P | | | | | ? | | | ● | ◉ | ○ | | ◉ | | ○ | ● | | ? | | | ● | ● | |
| NL | | | | | | | | | ◉ | | | ● | | | | | | | | | | |
| N | | | | | | | | | ● | | | ● | | ◉ | | | | | | | | ○ |
| M | | | | | | | | | | | | | | | | | | | | | ● | |
| L | | | | | | | | | ● | | | ● | | ◉ | | | | | | | | |
| IRL | | | | | | | | | ◉ | | | | | | | | | | | | | |
| I | | | | ● | ● | | | | ● | ● | | ● | | ● | ● | | ● | | | | ● | ● |
| H | | | | ◉ | ● | | ● | | ● | ○ | | ● | | ● | | | ● | | | | | ● |
| GR | ● | | | ◉ | ● | | | | ● | ◐ | ● | ● | | ● | | | ● | ● | ● | | ● | ◐ |
| GB | | | | | ◉ | | | | ◉ | | | | | | | | | | | | | |
| F | | | | ● | ● | | | ● | ● | ● | | ● | | ● | ● | | ● | | | ● | ● | ● |
| E | | | | ◉ | ◉ | ● | | ● | ● | ● | | ● | ● | ● | ● | | ● | | | ● | ● | |
| DK | | | | | | | | | ● | | | | | | | | | | | | | |
| DDR | | | | | ● | | | | ● | | | ● | | ◉ | | | | | | | | ? |
| D | | | | | ● | | | | ● | | | ● | | ● | | | | | | | | ◉ |
| CY | ● | ● | ● | | | | | | | | | | | ? | | ● | ● | | | | ● | |
| CS | | | | ◉ | ● | | ◉ | | ● | ○ | | ● | | ◉ | | | ? | | | | | ● |
| CH | | | | ? | ● | | | | ● | ● | | ● | | ● | | | ● | | | | | ● |
| BG | | | | ◉ | ● | | ● | | ● | ○ | | ● | | ● | | | ● | | | | ◉ | ◐ |
| B | | | | | | | | | ● | | | ● | | ◉ | | | | | | | | ○ |
| AL | | | | ? | ● | | ● | | ● | ○ | | ● | | ● | | | ● | | | | ● | ● |
| A | | | | ● | ● | | ● | | ● | ● | | ● | | ● | | | ● | | | | | ● |

| Country | cleobis | corsica | idas | nevadensis | alciphron | candens | dispar | helle | hippothoe | ochimus | ottomanus | phlaeas | subalpina | thersamon | thetis | tityrus | virgaureae | alcon | arion | nausithous | rebeli | teleius |
|---|---|---|---|---|---|---|---|---|---|---|---|---|---|---|---|---|---|---|---|---|---|---|
| YU |  | ● |  | ● | ● | ● |  |  | ● | ? | ● | ● |  | ● |  | ● | ● | ? | ● | ◐ | ● | ◐ |
| TR |  |  |  |  | ? | ? | ○ |  |  | ? | ● | ● |  | ? | ? | ◐ |  |  | ◐ |  |  |  |
| SU | ? |  | ◐ |  | ● |  | ◐ | ● | ● |  |  | ● |  |  |  | ● | ● | ◐ | ● | ◐ | ? | ◐ |
| SF |  |  | ● |  |  |  |  | ● | ● |  |  | ● |  |  |  |  | ● |  | ◉ |  |  |  |
| S |  |  | ● |  |  |  |  | ● | ● |  |  | ● |  |  |  | ● | ● | ◉ |  | ◉ |  |  |
| R |  |  | ● |  | ● | ○ | ● |  |  |  |  | ● |  | ● |  | ● | ● |  | ● |  |  |  |
| PL |  |  | ● |  | ● |  | ● | ● | ● |  |  | ● |  |  |  | ● | ● | ◉ | ● | ● |  | ● |
| P |  |  | ○ |  | ◉ |  |  |  |  |  | ○ | ● |  |  |  | ○ | ◉ |  | ○ |  |  |  |
| NL |  |  | ◉ |  |  |  | ● |  | ? |  |  | ● |  |  |  | ● |  | ● |  | ? | ● | ? |
| N |  |  | ● |  |  |  |  | ● | ● |  |  | ● |  |  |  | ● |  |  |  |  |  |  |
| M |  |  |  |  |  |  |  |  |  |  |  | ◉ |  |  |  |  |  |  |  |  |  |  |
| L |  |  |  |  | ● | ● | ● |  |  |  |  | ● |  |  |  | ◉ | ● |  | ● |  |  |  |
| IRL |  |  |  |  |  |  |  |  |  |  |  | ● |  |  |  |  |  |  |  |  |  |  |
| I | ● | ● |  | ● |  | ● | ? | ● |  |  | ● | ● | ● | ● |  | ● | ● | ? | ● |  | ● | ● |
| H |  | ◉ |  | ◉ |  | ● |  | ● |  |  | ● | ● |  | ● |  | ● | ● | ● | ● | ◉ | ● | ● |
| GR |  | ◐ |  | ◐ | ● | ? |  |  | ? | ● | ● | ● |  | ● | ● | ● | ◉ | ? | ● |  | ? |  |
| GB |  |  |  |  |  | ◉ |  |  |  |  |  | ● |  |  |  |  |  | ? |  |  |  |  |
| F | ● | ● |  | ● |  | ● | ● | ● |  |  | ● | ● | ● |  | ● | ● | ● | ● | ● | ● | ● | ● |
| E |  | ● | ● | ● |  |  |  |  | ◉ |  |  | ● | ? |  |  | ● | ? | ◉ | ○ | ? | ? |  |
| DK |  |  |  |  |  |  |  |  |  |  |  |  |  |  | ◉ |  | ◉ |  | ◉ |  |  |  |
| D DDR |  | ● |  | ● |  | ● | ● | ● |  |  |  | ● |  |  |  | ● | ● | ◉ | ◉ | ◉ | ? | ◉ |
| D |  | ● |  | ● |  | ● | ● | ● |  |  |  | ● |  |  |  | ● | ● | ● | ● | ● | ● | ● |
| CY |  |  |  |  |  |  |  |  |  |  |  | ● |  | ● |  |  |  |  |  |  |  |  |
| CS |  | ● |  | ● |  | ● |  | ● |  |  |  | ● |  | ● |  | ● | ● | ● | ● | ● | ◐ |  |
| CH |  | ● |  | ● |  |  | ● | ● |  |  |  | ● | ● |  |  | ● | ● | ? | ● | ● | ● |  |
| BG |  | ● |  | ● | ● | ● |  |  | ● | ● |  | ● |  | ● | ? | ● | ● |  | ● | ? | ◐ |  |
| B |  | ◉ |  |  |  | ● | ● | ● |  |  |  | ● |  |  |  | ● | ● | ◉ | ◉ |  | ● | ○ |
| AL |  |  |  | ● | ● | ◐ |  | ? |  |  | ● | ● | ◐ |  |  | ● | ◐ | ○ | ● |  | ? |  |
| A |  | ● |  | ● |  | ● | ○ | ● |  |  |  | ● | ● | ● |  | ● | ● | ● | ● | ● | ● | ● |

Lycaeides cleobis, Lycaeides corsica, Lycaeides idas, Lycaeides nevadensis, Lycaena alciphron, Lycaena candens, Lycaena dispar, Lycaena helle, Lycaena hippothoe, Lycaena ochimus, Lycaena ottomanus, Lycaena phlaeas, Lycaena subalpina, Lycaena thersamon, Lycaena thetis, Lycaena tityrus, Lycaena virgaureae, Maculinea alcon, Maculinea arion, Maculinea nausithous, Maculinea rebeli, Maculinea teleius

| | Neolycaena rhymnus | Nordmannia acaciae | Nordmannia esculi | Nordmannia ilicis | Nordmannia pruni | Nordmannia spini | Nordmannia w-album | Plebejus argus | Plebejus hesperica | Plebejus pylaon | Plebejus sephirus | Plebejus trappi | Polyommatus actis | Polyommatus admetus | Polyommatus ainsae | Polyommatus albicans | Polyommatus amandus | Polyommatus aroaniensis | Polyommatus asturiensis | Polyommatus bellargus | Polyommatus caelestissima | Polyommatus coelestinus | Polyommatus coerulescens | |
|---|---|---|---|---|---|---|---|---|---|---|---|---|---|---|---|---|---|---|---|---|---|---|---|---|
| YU | ● | | ● | ◐ | ● | ● | ● | | | ◐ | | | | ● | | | ● | | | ● | | | | YU |
| TR | ◐ | | ◐ | | ● | ● | | | | | | | | | | | | | | ● | | | | TR |
| SU | ● | | ● | ● | ● | ● | ● | | ● | | | | ? | ◐ | | | ● | | | ● | | ● | ＼ | SU |
| SF | | | | ● | | | ● | | | | | | | | | | ● | | | | | | | SF |
| S | | | ◉ | ◉ | | ● | ● | | | | | | | | | | ● | | | | | | | S |
| R | ● | | ● | ◉ | ● | ◉ | ● | | ● | | | | | ○ | | | ○ | | | ● | | | | R |
| PL | ◉ | | ● | ● | ◉ | ● | ● | | | | | | | | | | ● | | | ● | | | | PL |
| P | ◉ | ● | ◉ | | ● | | ● | | | | | | | | | | ? | | | ● | | | | P |
| NL | | | ● | ○ | | ◉ | ● | | | | | | | | | | | | | | | | | NL |
| N | | | ○ | | | ○ | ● | | | | | | | | | | ◉ | | | | | | | N |
| M | | | | | | | | | | | | | | | | | | | | | | | | M |
| L | ○ | | ◉ | ◉ | ? | ◉ | ◉ | | | | | | | | | | ◉ | | | | | | | L |
| IRL | | | | | | | | | | | | | | | | | | | | | | | | IRL |
| I | ● | ● | ● | ● | ● | ● | ● | | | | | | ● | | | | ● | | | ● | | | | I |
| H | ● | | ● | ● | ● | ● | ● | | | | | | | ◉ | | ● | ◉ | | | ● | | | | H |
| GR | ● | | ● | | ● | ◉ | ● | | | | | | | ● | | | ● | | ● | ● | | ● | | GR |
| GB | | | | ◉ | | ● | ● | | | | | | | | | | | | | ● | | | | GB |
| F | ● | ● | ● | ● | ● | ● | ● | | | | | | | | | | ● | | | ● | | | | F |
| E | ● | ● | ● | ○ | ● | ◉ | ● | ● | | | | | | | | ● | ● | ◉ | | ● | ● | ● | ● | E |
| DK | | | ◉ | | | ● | ● | | | | | | | | | | ● | | | | | | | DK |
| DDR | ◉ | | ◉ | ◉ | ◉ | ● | ● | | | | | | | | | | ● | | | ● | | | | DDR |
| D | ◉ | | ● | ● | ● | ● | ● | | | | | | | | | | ● | | | ● | | | | D |
| CY | | | ? | | | | | | | | | | | | | | | | | | | | | CY |
| CS | ◉ | | ● | ● | ● | ● | ● | | | | | | | | | | ● | | | ● | | | | CS |
| CH | ● | | ● | ● | ● | ● | ● | | | | | ● | | | | | ● | | | ● | | | | CH |
| BG | ● | | ○ | ● | ● | ● | ● | | ● | | | | ● | | | | ● | | | ● | | | | BG |
| B | ○ | | ● | ◉ | | ◉ | ● | | | | | | | | | | | | | ◉ | | | | B |
| AL | ● | | ● | | ● | ○ | ● | | ○ | | | | ○ | | | | ● | | | ● | | | | AL |
| A | ◉ | | ● | ● | ● | ● | ● | | | | | | | | | | ● | | | ● | | | | A |

| | coridon | cyane | damon | damone | daphnis | dolus | dorylas | eroides | eros | escheri | ezuberans | fabressei | galloi | golgus | hispana | humedasae | icarus | iphigenia | italaglauca | menelaos | nephohiptamenos | nivescens | philippi | poseidon |
|---|---|---|---|---|---|---|---|---|---|---|---|---|---|---|---|---|---|---|---|---|---|---|---|---|
| YU | ● | | ● | | ● | | ● | ● | ● | ● | | | | | | | ● | | | | | | | |
| TR | | | | | | | | | | | | | | | | | ● | | | | | | | |
| SU | ● | ● | ◐ | ● | ● | | ● | ◐ | | ◐ | | ○ | | | | | ● | | | | | | | ● |
| SF | | | | | | | | | | | | | | | | | ● | | | | | | | |
| S | | | | | | | ◉ | | | | | | | | | | ● | | | | | | | |
| R | ● | ? | ● | | | | ● | | | | | | | | | | ● | | | | | | | |
| PL | ● | ◉ | ◉ | | | | ● | ● | | | | | | | | | ● | | | | | | | |
| P | | | | | | | ? | | ○ | | | | | | | | ● | | | | | | | |
| NL | ○ | | | | | | | | | | | | | | | | ● | | | | | | | |
| N | | | | | | | | | | | | | | | | | ● | | | | | | | |
| M | | | | | | | | | | | | | | | | | ● | | | | | | | |
| L | ◉ | | | | | | | | | | | | | | | | ● | | | | | | | |
| IRL | | | | | | | | | | | | | | | | | ● | | | | | | | |
| I | ● | | ● | | ● | ● | ● | | ● | ● | ? | | ● | | ● | ● | ● | | ○ | | | | | |
| H | ● | | ◉ | | ● | | ● | | | | | | | | | | ● | | | | | | | |
| GR | ● | | ◐ | | ● | | ● | ◐ | ● | ● | | | | | | | ● | ● | | ● | ● | | ● | |
| GB | ● | | | | | | | | | | | | | | | | ● | | | | | | | |
| F | ● | | ● | | ● | ● | ● | | ● | ● | | | | ● | | | ● | | | | | | | |
| E | ○ | | ● | | ◉ | ● | ● | | ◉ | ● | | ● | | ● | ● | | ● | | | | | ● | | |
| DK | ● | | ◉ | ? | | | ◉ | | | | | | | | | | ● | | | | | | | |
| DDR/D | ● | | ◉ | ◉ | | | ◉ | | ◉ | | | | | | | | ● | | | | | | | |
| CY | | | | | | | | | | | | | | | | | ● | | | | | | | |
| CS | ● | | ● | | ● | | ● | ○ | | | | | | | | | ● | | | | | | | |
| CH | ● | | ● | | ● | | ● | | ● | ● | | | | | | | ● | | | | | | | |
| BG | ● | | ○ | ◐ | ● | | ● | ● | ○ | ○ | | | | | | | ● | | | | ? | | ? | |
| B | ◉ | | | | | | ◉ | | | | | | | | | | ● | | | | | | | |
| AL | ● | | ● | | ● | | ○ | ◐ | | | | | | | | | ● | | | | | | | |
| A | ● | | | | ● | | ● | | ● | | | | | | | | ● | | | | | | | |

| | Polyommatus ripartii | Polyommatus thersites | Polyommatus violetae | Polyommatus virgilius | Pseudophilotes abencerragus | Pseudophilotes barbagiae | Pseudophilotes baton | Pseudophilotes bavius | Pseudophilotes panope | Pseudophilotes panoptes | Pseudophilotes schiffermuelleri | Pseudophilotes vicrama | Quercusia quercus | Scolitantides orion | Syntarucus pirithous | Tarucus balcanicus | Tarucus theophrastus | Thecla betulae | Tomares ballus | Tomares callimachus | Tomares nogelli | Tongeia fischeri |
|---|---|---|---|---|---|---|---|---|---|---|---|---|---|---|---|---|---|---|---|---|---|---|
| YU | ● | ● | | | | | | | ● | | ● | | ◉ | ● | ● | ● | | ◉ | | | | |
| TR | | | | | | | | ? | | | ● | | | ● | ● | | | | | | | |
| SU | ○ | ◐ | | | | | | ◐ | ? | | ● | | ● | ● | ● | | | ● | | ● | ● | ● |
| SF | | | | | | | | | | ◉ | | | ○ | ● | | | | ● | | | | |
| S | | | | | | | | | | ◉ | | | ◉ | ● | | | | ● | | | | |
| R | | ● | | | | | | | ○ | | ● | | ● | ● | | | | ● | | ● | | |
| PL | ○ | ◉ | | | | | ○ | | | | ◉ | | ● | ◉ | | | | ● | | | | |
| P | | ◉ | | | ● | | ◉ | | | | ● | | | ● | | | ● | | | | | |
| NL | | | | | | | | | | | ● | | | | | | | ● | | | | |
| N | | | | | | | | | | | ◉ | ◉ | | | | | | ◉ | | | | |
| M | | | | | | | | | | | | ● | | | | | | | | | | |
| L | | | | | | | ○ | | | | ◉ | | | | | | | ◉ | | | | |
| IRL | | | | | | | | | | | ◉ | | | | | | | ◉ | | | | |
| I | ● | ● | | ● | | ● | ● | | ● | | ● | ● | ● | | ? | | ● | | | | | |
| H | | ● | | | | | ? | | ● | | ● | ● | ● | | | | ● | | | | | |
| GR | ● | ● | | | | ● | | | ● | ? | ● | ● | ● | ● | | | ○ | | | | | |
| GB | | | | | | | | | | | ◉ | | | | | | | ● | | | | |
| F | ● | ● | | | ● | | | | | | ● | ● | ● | | | | ● | ● | | | | |
| E | ● | ● | ● | ● | | ● | | | ● | | ● | ◉ | ● | | ● | | ◉ | ● | | | | |
| DK | | | | | | | | | | | ● | | | | | | | ● | | | | |
| DDR | | ◉ | | | | ◉ | | | ◉ | | ● | ◉ | | | | | | ● | | | | |
| D | | ● | | | | ● | | | | | ● | ● | | | | | | ● | | | | |
| CY | | | | | | | ● | | ◉ | | | ● | ● | | | | | | | | | |
| CS | | ● | | | | | | | ● | | ● | ● | | | | | | ● | | | | |
| CH | ◐ | ● | | | ● | | | | ○ | | ● | ● | | | | | | ● | | | | |
| BG | ○ | ● | | | | | | | ● | | ● | ● | ● | ● | | | | ● | | | | |
| B | | ◉ | | | | ◉ | | | ● | | | ● | | | | | | ● | | | | |
| AL | ? | ◐ | | | | | | | ● | | ○ | ● | ● | ● | | | ○ | | | | | |
| A | | ● | | | ● | | | | ● | | ● | ● | | | | | | ● | | | | |

| Country | Turana panagea | Ultraaricia anteros | Ultraaricia orpheus | Vacciniina loewi | Vacciniina optilete | Zizeeria karsandra | Zizeeria knysna | **RIODINIDAE** Hamearis lucina | **LIBYTHEIDAE** Libythea celtis | **DANAIDAE** Danaus chrysippus | Danaus plexippus | **SATYRIDAE** Aphantopus hyperantus | Arethusana arethusa | Chazara anthe |
|---|---|---|---|---|---|---|---|---|---|---|---|---|---|---|
| YU | ● | | | | ● | | | ● | ● | | | ● | ● | |
| TR | ● | | | | | ● | | ● | | | | | ? | |
| SU | ○ | | | | ● | | | ● | ● | | | ● | ● | ● |
| SF | | | | | ● | | | | | | | ● | | |
| S | | | | | ● | | | ◉ | | | | ● | | |
| R | | ○ | | | | | | ● | | | | ● | ● | |
| PL | | | | | ● | | | ● | | | | ● | | |
| P | | | | | | | ● | ◉ | ◉ | | | | ◉ | |
| NL | | | | | ● | | | | | | | ● | | |
| N | | | | | ● | | | | | | | ● | | |
| M | | | | | | | | | | | | | | |
| L | | | | | | | | ◉ | | | | ● | | |
| IRL | | | | | | | | | | | | ● | | |
| I | | | | | ● | ? | | ● | ● | ○ | | ● | ● | |
| H | | | | | | | | ● | ● | | | ● | ● | |
| GR | ● | ◑ | ● | | ● | | | ◉ | ● | | | ◉ | ● | |
| GB | | | | | | | | ◉ | | | | ● | | |
| F | | | ◉ | | | | | ● | ● | | | ● | ● | |
| E | | | | | | | ● | ● | ● | ● | ● | ● | ● | |
| DK | | | ◉ | | | | | | | | | ● | | |
| DDR | | | ● | | | | | ● | | | | ● | | |
| D | | | ● | | | | | ● | | | | ● | ? | |
| CY | | | | ● | | | ● | | | ◉ | | | | ? |
| CS | | | ● | | | | | ● | | | | ● | ● | |
| CH | | | ● | | | | | ● | ● | | | ● | | |
| BG | | ● | ● | | | | | ● | ● | | | ● | ● | |
| B | | | | | | | | ◉ | | | | ● | ○ | |
| AL | | ● | | | | | | ● | ● | | | ● | ● | |
| A | | | ● | | | | | ● | ◉ | | | ● | ● | |

| | Chazara briseis | Chazara prieuri | Coenonympha amaryllis | Coenonympha arcania | Coenonympha corinna | Coenonympha darwiniana | Coenonympha dorus | Coenonympha elbana | Coenonympha gardetta | Coenonympha glycerion | Coenonympha hero | Coenonympha iphioides | Coenonympha leander | Coenonympha oedippus | Coenonympha pamphilus | Coenonympha rhodopensis | Coenonympha thyrsis | Coenonympha tullia | Erebia aethiopella | Erebia aethiops | Erebia alberganus | Erebia boreomontanum |
|---|---|---|---|---|---|---|---|---|---|---|---|---|---|---|---|---|---|---|---|---|---|---|
| YU | ● | | | ● | | | | | ● | ● | | | ● | ● | ● | ● | | ● | | ● | | |
| TR | ? | | | ● | | | | | | | | | | | ● | | | | | | | |
| SU | ● | | ● | ● | | | | | ● | ◑ | | | ● | ● | ● | | | ● | | ● | | ○ |
| SF | | | | | | | | | ● | ● | | | | | ● | | | ● | | | | |
| S | | | | ● | | | | | | ● | | | | | ● | | | ● | | | | |
| R | ● | | | ● | | | | | | ● | | | ● | | ● | ● | | ◉ | | ● | | |
| PL | ◉ | | | ● | | | | | ● | ◉ | | | ● | | ● | | | ● | | ● | | |
| P | | | | ○ | | | ● | | | | | | | | ● | | | | | | | |
| NL | | | | ● | | | | | | ◉ | | | | | ● | | | ● | | | | |
| N | | | | ○ | | | | | | ◉ | | | | | ● | | | ◉ | | | | |
| M | | | | | | | | | | | | | | | ● | | | | | | | |
| L | | | | ◉ | | | | | | ◉ | | | | | ● | | | | | ? | | |
| IRL | | | | ◉ | | | | | | | | | | | ● | | | ◉ | | | | |
| I | ● | | | ● | ● | ● | ● | ● | ● | ● | | | ● | ● | ● | | | ● | ● | ● | ● | |
| H | ● | | | ● | | | | | ● | ● | ? | | ● | | ● | | | ◉ | | ◉ | | |
| GR | | | | ● | | | | | | ◉ | | | ● | | ● | ● | ● | | | | | |
| GB | | | | ◉ | | | | | | | | | | | ● | | | ● | | ● | | |
| F | ● | | | ● | ● | ● | ● | | ◉ | ● | ● | | ● | | ● | | | ● | ● | ● | ● | |
| E | ● | ● | | ● | | | ● | | | | | ● | | | ● | | | ● | | | | ○ |
| DK | | | | | | | | | | ◉ | | | | | ● | | | ● | | | | |
| DDR | ● | | | ● | | | | | ● | ◉ | | | | | ● | | | ● | | ● | | |
| D | ● | | | ● | | | | | ◉ | ● | ● | | | | ● | | | ● | | ● | | |
| CY | ● | | | | | | | | | | | | | | ? | | | | | | | |
| CS | ● | | | ● | | | | | ● | ○ | | | | | ● | | | ● | | ● | | |
| CH | ● | | | ● | | ● | | | ● | ● | | | ○ | ● | ● | | | ◉ | | ● | ● | |
| BG | ● | | | ● | | | | | ● | | | | ? | ● | ● | ● | | | | ● | ● | |
| B | | | | ● | | | | | ○ | ● | | | | | ● | | | ● | | ◉ | | |
| AL | ● | | | ● | | | ○ | | | | ○ | | ● | ○ | ● | | | ● | | | | |
| A | ● | | | ● | | ● | | | ● | ● | ? | | ● | | ● | | | ● | | ● | ● | |

| | *E. calcaria* | *E. cassioides* | *E. christi* | *E. claudina* | *E. dabanensis* | *E. disa* | *E. discoidalis* | *E. edda* | *E. embla* | *E. epiphron* | *E. epistygne* | *E. eriphyle* | *E. euryale* | *E. fasciata* | *E. flavofasciata* | *E. gorge* | *E. gorgone* | *E. hispania* | *E. jeniseiensis* | *E. lefeburei* | *E. ligea* | *E. manto* |
|---|---|---|---|---|---|---|---|---|---|---|---|---|---|---|---|---|---|---|---|---|---|---|
| YU | ● | ● | | | | | | | | ● | | | ● | | | ● | | | | | ● | ● |
| TR | | | ? | ● | ● | ? | ● | | | | | | ● | ● | | | | | | ? | ● | ● |
| SU | | | ? | ● | ● | ? | ● | | | | | | ● | ● | | | | | | ? | ● | ● |
| SF | | | | ● | | | ● | | | | | | | | | | | | | | ● | |
| S | | | | ● | | | ● | | | | | | | | | | | | | | ● | |
| R | | ● | | | | | | | | ● | | | ● | | | ● | | | | | ● | ● |
| PL | | | | | | | | | | ● | | | ● | | | ◉ | | | | | ● | ◉ |
| P | | | | | | | | | | | | | | | | | | | | | | |
| NL | | | | | | | | | | | | | | | | | | | | | | |
| N | | | | | | ◉ | | ◉ | | | | | | | | | | | | | ● | |
| M | | | | | | | | | | | | | | | | | | | | | | |
| L | | | | | | | | | | | | | | | | | | | | | | |
| IRL | | | | | | | | | | | | | | | | | | | | | | |
| I | ● | ● | ● | | | | | | ? | ● | | ◉ | ● | | | ● | ● | | | | ● | ● |
| H | | | | | | | | | | | | | | | | | | | | | ● | |
| GR | | | | | | | | | | ○ | | | | | | | | | | | | |
| GB | | | | | | | | | | ● | | | | | | | | | | | | |
| F | | ● | | | | | | | | ● | ● | ● | ● | | | ● | ● | ● | | ● | ● | ● |
| E | | ● | | | | | | | | ● | ● | | ● | | | ● | ● | ● | | ● | | ● |
| DK | | | | | | | | | | ? | | | | | | | | | | | ● | |
| DDR | | | | | | | | | | ● | | ● | ● | | | ◉ | | | | | ● | ● |
| D | | | | | | | | | | ● | | ● | ● | | | ◉ | | | | | ● | ● |
| CY | | | | | | | | | | | | | | | | | | | | | | |
| CS | | | | | | | | | | ● | | ● | ● | | | ◉ | | | | | ● | ● |
| CH | | ● | ● | | | | | | | ● | | ● | ● | ● | | ● | | | | | ● | ● |
| BG | | ● | | | | | | | | | | | ● | | | ○ | | | | | ● | |
| B | | | | | | | | | | | | | | | | | | | | | ○ | |
| AL | ◐ | ◐ | | | | | | | | ● | | | ● | | | ● | | | | | ● | ● |
| A | | ● | ● | | | | | | | ● | | | ● | ● | | ● | | | | | ● | ● |

| | medusa | melampus | melas | meolans | mnestra | montana | neoridas | nivalis | oeme | orientalis | ottomana | palarica | pandrose | pharte | pluto | polaris | pronoe | rhodopensis | rossi | scipio | serotina | sthennyo |
|---|---|---|---|---|---|---|---|---|---|---|---|---|---|---|---|---|---|---|---|---|---|---|
| YU | ● | | ● | | | | | | ● | | ● | | ● | ○ | ● | | ● | ● | | | | |
| TR | | | | | | | | | | | | | | | | | | | | | | |
| SU | ◐ | | | | | | | | | | | | ● | | ◐ | ● | | | ● | | | |
| SF | | | | | | | | | | | | | ● | | ● | | | | | | | |
| S | | | | | | | | | | | | | ● | | ● | | | | | | | |
| R | ● | | ● | | | | | | | | | | ● | ○ | | | ● | | | | | |
| PL | ● | | | | | | | | | | | | ● | ● | | | ⊙ | | | | | |
| P | | | | | | | | | | | | | | | | | | | | | | |
| NL | ○ | | | | | | | | | | | | | | | | | | | | | |
| N | | | | | | | | | | | | | ● | | ● | | | | | | | |
| M | | | | | | | | | | | | | | | | | | | | | | |
| L | ● | | | | | | | | | | | | | | | | | | | | | |
| IRL | | | | | | | | | | | | | | | | | | | | | | |
| I | ● | ● | | ● | ● | ● | ● | ○ | ● | | ● | | ● | ● | ● | | ● | | ● | | | |
| H | ⊙ | | | | | | | | | | | | | | | | | | | | | |
| GR | ● | | ● | | | | | | ● | | ● | | | | | | | | | | | |
| GB | | | | | | | | | | | | | | | | | | | | | | |
| F | ● | ● | | ● | ● | ● | ● | | ● | ● | | | ● | ⊙ | ● | | ● | | | ● | ○ | ● |
| E | | ● | | ⊙ | ⊙ | | | | | | | ● | ⊙ | | | | | | | ? | | ● |
| DK | ● | | | ⊙ | | | | | | | | | | | | | | | | | | |
| DDR | ● | | | | | | | | | | | | | | | | | | | | | |
| D | ● | ● | | ● | | | | | ● | | | | ● | ● | ⊙ | | ⊙ | | | | | |
| CY | | | | | | | | | | | | | | | | | | | | | | |
| CS | ● | | | | | | | | | | | | ● | ● | | | ● | | | | | |
| CH | ● | ● | | ● | ● | ● | | | ● | | | | ● | ● | ● | | ● | | | | | |
| BG | ● | ○ | | | | | | | ● | ● | ● | | ● | | | | ● | ● | | | | |
| B | ● | | | | | | | | | | | | | | | | | | | | | |
| AL | ● | | ● | | | | | | ● | ◐ | | | ● | | | | ● | ? | | | | |
| A | ● | ● | | ● | ● | ● | | | ● | ● | | | ● | ● | ● | | ● | | | | | |

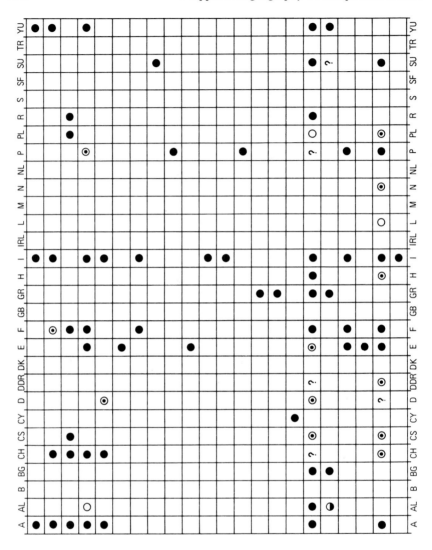

| Country | Hipparchia maderensis | Hipparchia malickyi | Hipparchia miguelensis | Hipparchia neomiris | Hipparchia pellucida | Hipparchia sbordonii | Hipparchia semele | Hipparchia senthes | Hipparchia statilinus | Hipparchia syriaca | Hipparchia volgensis | Hipparchia wyssii | Hyponephele huebneri | Hyponcphele lupina | Hyponephele lycaon | Kanetisa circe | Lasiommata achine | Lasiommata climene | Lasiommata deidamia | Lasiommata maera | Lasiommata megera | Lasiommata petropolitana | Lasiommata roxelana |
|---|---|---|---|---|---|---|---|---|---|---|---|---|---|---|---|---|---|---|---|---|---|---|---|
| YU |  |  |  |  |  |  | ● | ● | ● | ● | ● |  |  | ● | ● | ● | ● | ● |  | ● | ● | ● | ● |
| TR |  |  |  |  |  |  | ? | ● | ● | ● |  |  |  | ● | ? | ● |  |  |  | ● | ● |  | ● |
| SU |  |  |  |  | ● |  | ● |  | ● |  | ● |  | ? | ● | ● | ● | ◐ | ● | ? | ● | ● | ● | ? |
| SF |  |  |  |  |  |  | ● |  |  |  |  |  | ? |  |  | ● |  |  |  | ● | ○ | ● |  |
| S |  |  |  |  |  |  | ● |  |  |  |  |  |  |  |  | ◉ |  |  |  | ● | ● | ● |  |
| R |  |  |  |  |  |  | ● |  | ● | ● |  |  |  | ● | ● | ○ | ○ |  |  | ● | ● | ○ | ● |
| PL |  |  |  |  |  |  | ● |  |  |  |  |  |  | ◉ | ◉ | ● |  |  |  | ● | ● | ● |  |
| P | ● |  | ● |  |  |  | ● |  | ● |  |  |  |  | ◉ | ◉ | ● |  |  |  | ● | ● |  |  |
| NL |  |  |  |  |  |  | ● |  | ● |  |  |  |  |  |  |  |  |  |  | ● | ● |  |  |
| N |  |  |  |  |  |  | ● |  |  |  |  |  |  |  |  |  |  |  |  | ● | ◉ | ● |  |
| M |  |  |  |  |  |  | ● |  |  |  |  |  |  |  |  |  |  |  |  | ● |  |  |  |
| L |  |  |  |  |  |  | ○ |  |  |  |  |  |  |  |  | ? |  |  |  | ◉ | ● |  |  |
| IRL |  |  |  |  |  |  | ◉ |  |  |  |  |  |  |  |  |  |  |  |  | ● |  |  |  |
| I |  |  |  | ● |  | ● | ● |  | ● |  |  |  |  | ● | ● | ● | ● |  |  | ● | ● | ● |  |
| H |  |  |  |  |  |  | ● |  | ● |  |  |  | ○ | ● | ● | ● |  |  |  | ● | ● | ◉ |  |
| GR |  | ● |  | ● |  |  | ● | ● | ● | ● |  |  |  | ● | ● | ● |  | ● |  | ● | ● | ● | ● |
| GB |  |  |  |  |  |  | ● |  |  |  |  |  |  |  |  |  |  |  |  | ● |  |  |  |
| F |  |  |  | ● |  |  | ● |  | ● |  |  |  |  | ● | ● | ● | ● |  |  | ● | ● | ● |  |
| E |  |  |  |  |  |  | ● |  | ● |  |  | ● |  | ● | ● | ● | ◉ |  |  | ● | ● |  |  |
| DK |  |  |  |  |  |  | ● |  |  |  |  |  |  |  |  |  |  |  |  | ● |  |  |  |
| DDR |  |  |  |  |  |  | ● |  | ◉ |  |  |  |  | ◉ | ? | ◉ |  |  |  | ● | ● |  |  |
| D |  |  |  |  |  |  | ● |  | ? |  |  |  |  | ◉ | ● | ● |  |  |  | ● | ● | ● |  |
| CY |  |  |  |  |  |  |  |  |  | ● |  |  |  | ● |  |  |  |  |  | ◉ | ● |  | ● |
| CS |  |  |  |  |  |  | ● |  | ◉ |  |  |  |  | ● | ● | ● |  |  |  | ● | ● | ● |  |
| CH |  |  |  |  |  |  | ● |  | ● |  |  |  |  | ● | ● | ◉ |  |  |  | ● | ● | ● |  |
| BG |  |  |  |  |  |  | ● | ● | ● | ● | ● |  |  | ● | ● | ? | ? |  |  | ● | ● | ● | ● |
| B |  |  |  |  |  |  | ◉ |  |  |  |  |  |  |  |  |  |  |  |  | ◉ | ● |  |  |
| AL |  |  |  |  |  |  | ? | ● | ● | ● |  |  |  | ○ | ● | ● |  | ○ |  | ● | ● | ○ | ● |
| A |  |  |  |  |  |  | ● |  | ● |  |  |  |  | ● | ● | ● |  |  |  | ● | ● | ● |  |

| Country | Lasiommata tigelius | Maniola cypricola | Maniola jurtina | Maniola nurag | Maniola telmessia | Melanargia arge | Melanargia galathea | Melanargia ines | Melanargia lachesis | Melanargia larissa | Melanargia occitanica | Melanargia pherusa | Melanargia russiae | Minois dryas | Oeneis ammon | Oeneis bore | Oeneis crambis | Oeneis dembowskyi | Oeneis dubia | Oeneis falkovitchi | Oeneis glacialis | Oeneis jutta |
|---|---|---|---|---|---|---|---|---|---|---|---|---|---|---|---|---|---|---|---|---|---|---|
| YU | | | ● | | | | ● | | | ● | | | ◐ | ● | | | | | | | | |
| TR | | | ● | | | | ● | | | ● | | | | | | | | | | | | |
| SU | | | ● | | | | ● | | | | | | ● | ○ | ? | ● | ○ | ○ | ? | ○ | | ● |
| SF | | | ● | | | | | | | | | | | | | ● | | | | | | ● |
| S | | | ● | | | | | | | | | | | | | ● | | | | | | ● |
| R | | | ● | | | | ● | | | | | | ● | | | | | | | | | |
| PL | | | ● | | | | ● | | | | | | ● | | | | | | | | | ● |
| P | | | ● | | | | | ● | ● | | ◉ | | ◐ | | | | | | | | | |
| NL | | | ● | | | | ◉ | | | | | | | | | | | | | | | |
| N | | | ● | | | | | | | | | | | | | ● | | | | | | ● |
| M | | | ● | | | | | | | | | | | | | | | | | | | |
| L | | | ● | | | | ● | | | | | | | | | | | | | | | |
| IRL | | | ● | | | | | | | | | | | | | | | | | | | |
| I | ● | | ● | ● | | ● | ● | | | | | ● | ● | ● | | | | | | | ● | |
| H | | | ● | | | | ● | | | | | | | ● | | | | | | | | |
| GR | | | ● | | ● | | ● | | | ● | | | | ● | | | | | | | | |
| GB | | | ● | | | | ● | | | | | | | | | | | | | | | |
| F | ● | | ● | | | | ● | ● | | | ● | ● | ● | | | | | | | | ● | |
| E | | | ● | | | | ◉ | ● | ● | | ● | | ● | ○ | | | | | | | | |
| DK | | | ● | | | | | | | | | | | | | | | | | | | |
| DDR | | | ● | | | | ● | | | | | | ● | | | | | | | | | |
| D | | | ● | | | | ● | | | | | | ● | | | | | | | | ◉ | |
| CY | | ● | | | | | | | | | | | | | | | | | | | | |
| CS | | | ● | | | | ● | | | | | | ● | | | | | | | | | |
| CH | | | ● | | | | ● | | | | | | ● | | | | | | | | ● | |
| BG | | | ● | | | | ● | | | ● | | | ● | | | | | | | | | |
| B | | | ● | | | | ◉ | | | | | | | | | | | | | | | |
| AL | | | ● | | | | ● | | | ● | | | | | ○ | ○ | | | | | | |
| A | | | ● | | | | ● | | | | | | ● | | | | | | | | ● | |

| Species | A | AL | B | BG | CH | CS | CY | D | DDR | DK | E | F | GB | GR | H | I | IRL | L | M | N | NL | P | PL | R | S | SF | SU | TR | YU |
|---|---|---|---|---|---|---|---|---|---|---|---|---|---|---|---|---|---|---|---|---|---|---|---|---|---|---|---|---|---|
| *Oeneis koslowskyi* |  |  |  |  |  |  |  |  |  |  |  |  |  |  |  |  |  |  |  |  |  |  |  |  |  |  | ○ |  |  |
| *Oeneis kusnetzovi* |  |  |  |  |  |  |  |  |  |  |  |  |  |  |  |  |  |  |  |  |  |  |  |  |  |  | ○ |  |  |
| *Oeneis norma* |  |  |  |  |  |  |  |  |  |  |  |  |  |  |  |  |  |  |  | ● |  |  |  |  | ● | ● | ● |  |  |
| *Oeneis pansa* |  |  |  |  |  |  |  |  |  |  |  |  |  |  |  |  |  |  |  |  |  |  |  |  |  |  | ○ |  |  |
| *Oeneis saepestriata* |  |  |  |  |  |  |  |  |  |  |  |  |  |  |  |  |  |  |  |  |  |  |  |  |  |  | ○ |  |  |
| *Oeneis semidea* |  |  |  |  |  |  |  |  |  |  |  |  |  |  |  |  |  |  |  |  |  |  |  |  |  |  | ? |  |  |
| *Oeneis tarpeia* |  |  |  |  |  |  |  |  |  |  |  |  |  |  |  |  |  |  |  |  |  |  |  |  |  |  | ● |  |  |
| *Oeneis taygete* |  |  |  |  |  |  |  |  |  |  |  |  |  |  |  |  |  |  |  |  |  |  |  |  |  |  | ? |  |  |
| *Oeneis tundra* |  |  |  |  |  |  |  |  |  |  |  |  |  |  |  |  |  |  |  |  |  |  |  |  |  |  | ? |  |  |
| *Pararge aegeria* | ● | ● | ● | ● | ● | ● | ● | ● | ● | ● | ● | ● | ● | ● | ● | ● | ● | ● | ⊙ | ● | ● | ● | ● | ● | ● | ● | ● | ? | ● |
| *Pararge xiphia* |  |  |  |  |  |  |  |  |  |  |  |  |  |  |  |  |  |  |  |  |  | ● |  |  |  |  |  |  |  |
| *Pararge xiphioides* |  |  |  |  |  |  |  |  |  |  | ● |  |  |  |  |  |  |  |  |  |  |  |  |  |  |  |  |  |  |
| *Proterebia afra* |  |  |  |  |  |  |  |  |  |  |  |  |  | ● |  |  |  |  |  |  |  |  |  |  |  |  |  |  |  |
| *Pseudochazara amymone* |  |  |  |  |  |  |  |  |  |  |  |  |  | ● |  |  |  |  |  |  |  |  |  |  |  |  |  |  | ● |
| *Pseudochazara anthelea* |  |  |  |  |  |  |  |  |  |  |  |  |  | ● |  |  |  |  |  |  |  |  |  |  |  |  | ● |  |  |
| *Pseudochazara cingovskii* |  | ○ |  |  |  |  |  |  |  |  |  |  |  |  |  |  |  |  |  |  |  |  |  |  |  |  |  |  | ● |
| *Pseudochazara euxina* |  |  |  |  | ● | ● |  |  |  |  |  |  |  |  |  |  |  |  |  |  |  |  |  |  |  |  | ● |  | ● |
| *Pseudochazara geyeri* | ● |  |  |  |  |  |  |  |  |  |  |  |  |  |  |  |  |  |  |  |  |  |  |  |  |  | ● |  | ● |
| *Pseudochazara graeca* |  |  |  |  |  |  |  |  |  |  |  |  |  | ● |  |  |  |  |  |  |  |  |  |  |  |  |  |  |  |
| *Pseudochazara hippolyte* |  |  |  |  |  |  |  |  |  |  | ● |  |  |  |  |  |  |  |  |  |  |  |  |  |  |  | ● |  |  |
| *Pseudochazara orestes* |  |  |  |  |  |  |  |  |  |  |  |  |  | ● |  |  |  |  |  |  |  |  |  |  |  |  |  |  |  |
| *Pyronia bathseba* |  |  |  |  |  |  |  |  |  |  | ● | ● |  |  |  |  |  |  |  |  |  | ● |  |  |  |  |  |  |  |

# 5 Applied biogeography of European butterflies

Country codes (columns, left to right as labelled on both margins):

YU · TR · SU · SF · S · R · PL · P · NL · N · M · L · IRL · I · H · GR · GB · F · E · DK · DDR · D · CY · CS · BG · CH · B · AL · A

Species (rows):

- *Pyronia cecilia*
- *Pyronia tithonus*
- *Satyrus actaea*
- *Satyrus ferula*
- *Triphysa phryne*
- *Ypthima asterope*

**NYMPHALIDAE**

- *Aglais ichnusa*
- *Aglais urticae*
- *Apatura ilia*
- *Apatura iris*
- *Apatura metis*
- *Araschnia levana*
- *Argynnis adippe*
- *Argynnis aglaja*
- *Argynnis elisa*
- *Argynnis niobe*
- *Argynnis pandora*
- *Argynnis paphia*
- *Argyronome laodice*
- *Boloria angarensis*

| | B. aquilonaris | B. chariclea | B. dia | B. eugenia | B. eunomia | B. euphrosyne | B. freija | B. frigga | B. graeca | B. improba | B. napaea | B. pales | B. polaris | B. selene | B. selenis | B. thore | B. titania | Br. daphne | Br. hecate | Br. ino | Ch. jasius | E. aurinia |
|---|---|---|---|---|---|---|---|---|---|---|---|---|---|---|---|---|---|---|---|---|---|---|
| YU | | ● | | | ● | | | ● | | | ● | | ● | | ● | ● | ● | ● | ● | ● | ● | ● |
| TR | | ● | | | | | | | | | | | | | | | ● | ● | | | ? | |
| SU | ● | ● | ● | ● | ● | ● | ● | ● | | | ● | ? | ? | ● | ● | ● | ● | ● | ◐ | ◐ | ● | | ● |
| SF | ● | ● | | | ● | ● | ● | ● | | ● | ● | | ● | ● | | ● | ● | | | ● | | ● |
| S | ● | ● | | | ● | ● | ● | ● | | ● | ● | | ● | ● | | ● | | | | ● | | ● |
| R | | ● | | | ● | | | | | | | | ◉ | ● | | | ○ | ● | ● | ○ | | ○ | | ○ |
| PL | ● | ◉ | | | ● | ● | | | | | | | ◉ | ● | | | ◉ | ◉ | ● | | | ● |
| P | | | | | | ◉ | | | | | | | ◉ | | | | | | | ● | |
| NL | ● | ? | | | | | | | | | | | | ● | | | ◉ | | | | | ○ |
| N | ● | ● | | | ● | ● | ● | ● | | ● | ● | | ● | ● | | ● | | | | ● | |
| M | | | | | | | | | | | | | | | | | | | | | | |
| L | | ◉ | | | ◉ | ◉ | | | | | | | | ◉ | | | | | | ◉ | | ◉ |
| IRL | | | | | | ◉ | | | | | | | | | | | | | | ◉ | | ◉ |
| I | | ● | | | ● | ● | | | ● | | ● | ● | | ● | | ● | ● | ● | ● | ● | ● | ● |
| H | | ● | | | | ● | | | | | | | | ● | | | ◉ | ● | ● | ◉ | | ◉ |
| GR | | ◉ | | | | ◐ | | | ● | | | | | ● | | | | ● | ◉ | | ● | |
| GB | | | | | | ● | | | | | | | | ● | | | | | | | | ● |
| F | ● | | ● | ◉ | ● | ● | | | ● | | ● | ● | | ● | | | ● | ● | ● | ● | ● | ◉ |
| E | | ◉ | | | ◉ | ◉ | | | | | | ● | | ● | | | ● | ● | ● | ● | | |
| DK | ● | | | | ● | | | | | | | | | ● | | | | | | | | ◉ |
| DDR | ● | ● | | | ● | ● | | | | | | | | ● | | | | ◉ | | ● | | ● |
| D | ● | ● | | | ● | ● | | | | ◉ | ◉ | | | ● | | ● | ● | | | ● | | ● |
| CY | | | | | | | | | | | | | | | | | | | | | ◉ | |
| CS | ● | ● | | | ◉ | ● | | | | | ◉ | | | ● | | | ● | ◉ | ● | | | ◉ |
| CH | ● | ● | | ? | ● | | | | | | ● | ● | | ● | | ● | ● | ● | | ● | | ● |
| BG | | ◉ | | ○ | ◉ | | | ○ | | | | | ● | ● | | | ● | ● | ● | | ○ | |
| B | ● | ● | | | ● | ◉ | | | | | | | | ● | | | | | | ● | | ◉ |
| AL | | ● | | | ● | | | | ● | | | ● | | | | | ○ | ○ | ○ | ○ | ○ | ? |
| A | ● | ● | | | ● | ● | | | | | ● | ◉ | ◉ | ● | | ● | ● | ● | ● | ○ | | ● |

| | Euphydryas beckeri | Euphydryas cynthia | Euphydryas desfontainii | Euphydryas glaciegenita | Euphydryas iduna | Euphydryas wolfensbergeri | Euphydryas maturna | Euphydryas orientalis | Euphydryas provincialis | Inachis io | Issoria lathonia | Limenitis camilla | Limenitis populi | Limenitis reducta | Melitaea aetheria | Melitaea arduinna | Melitaea asteria | Melitaea athalia | Melitaea aurelia | Melitaea britomartis | Melitaea cinxia | Melitaea deione |
|---|---|---|---|---|---|---|---|---|---|---|---|---|---|---|---|---|---|---|---|---|---|---|
| YU | | | | | | ● | ● | | | ● | ● | ● | ◐ | ● | ● | | ● | ● | ● | ● | ◐ | ● |
| TR | | | | | | | | | | | ? | ● | ◉ | ? | | | | | ◉ | | ● | |
| SU | | | | ● | ● | ● | | | | ● | ● | ● | ● | ● | | ○ | | ● | ● | ○ | | ● |
| SF | | | | ● | | ● | | | | ● | ● | | ● | | | | | ● | | | | ● |
| S | | | | ● | | ● | | | | ● | ● | | ● | | | | | ● | | ◉ | | ● |
| R | | | | ● | | | | | | ● | ● | ● | ● | ◉ | | ○ | | ● | ● | ● | ○ | ● |
| PL | | | | ● | | | | | | ● | ● | ● | ● | | ● | | | ● | ◉ | ◉ | | ● |
| P | ● | ◉ | | | | | | | | ● | ● | | ● | | | ● | | ◉ | | | ○ | ● |
| NL | | | | | | | | | | ● | ● | ● | ○ | | | | | ● | | | ◉ | |
| M | | | | ● | | | | | | ● | ● | | ○ | | | | | ● | | | ◉ | |
| L | | | | | | ○ | | | | ● | ◉ | ◉ | ◉ | | | | | ◉ | ◉ | | ◉ | |
| IRL | | | | | | | | | | ● | | | | | | | | | | | | |
| I | | ● | | ● | | ● | | | | ● | ● | ● | ● | ● | ● | ● | ● | ● | ● | ● | ● | ● |
| H | | | | | | ● | | | | ● | ● | ● | ◉ | ◉ | ◉ | | | ● | ● | ● | ● | |
| GR | | | | | | ◉ | | | | ● | ● | | | ◉ | ◉ | | ● | ● | | | ● | |
| GB | | | | | | | | | | ● | ◉ | ● | | | | | | ◉ | | | ◉ | |
| F | ◉ | ● | ◉ | ● | | ● | | | | ● | ● | ● | ● | ● | ● | | | ● | ● | | ● | ● |
| E | ● | | ● | ? | | | | | | ● | ● | ● | ◉ | | ● | ● | | ● | | | ◉ | ● |
| DK | | | | ◉ | | | | | | ● | ◉ | ◉ | | | | | | ◉ | | | ● | |
| DDR | | | | ◉ | | | | | | ● | ● | ● | ◉ | | | | | ● | ◉ | ◉ | ● | |
| D | ◉ | | ◉ | ● | | | | | | ● | ● | ● | ● | ◉ | | | | ● | ● | ● | ● | |
| CY | | | | | | | | | | | | | | ◉ | | | | | | | | |
| CS | | | | ● | | | | | | ● | ● | ● | ● | ◉ | | | | ● | ● | ● | ● | |
| CH | ● | | ● | ● | ◉ | | | | | ● | ● | ● | ◉ | ○ | | | ● | ● | ● | ? | | ◉ |
| BG | ● | | | ● | | | | | | ● | ● | ○ | ◉ | ◉ | | ● | | ● | ● | ● | ● | |
| B | | | | ○ | | | | | | ● | ◉ | ● | ● | | | | | ◉ | ◉ | | ● | |
| AL | | | | ◐ | | ◐ | | | | ● | ● | | | | ○ | ● | | | | | ● | |
| A | ● | | ● | | ● | ● | | | | ● | ● | ● | ● | ● | | | ● | ● | ● | ● | ● | |

| | Melitaea diamina | Melitaea didyma | Melitaea fascelis | Melitaea neglecta | Melitaea parthenoides | Melitaea phoebe | Melitaea varia | Neptis rivularis | Neptis sappho | Nymphalis antiopa | Nymphalis l-album | Nymphalis polychloros | Nymphalis xanthomelas | Polygonia c-album | Polygonia egea | Thaleropis ionia | Vanessa atalanta | Vanessa cardui | Vanessa indica | Vanessa virginiensis |
|---|---|---|---|---|---|---|---|---|---|---|---|---|---|---|---|---|---|---|---|---|
| YU | ● | ● | ● | | | ● | | ● | ● | ● | ◉ | ● | ◉ | ● | ● | | ● | ● | | |
| TR | | ● | | | | | | | | ● | | | | ● | ● | | ? | ● | | |
| SU | ◑ | ● | ○ | | | ◑ | | ● | ● | ● | ● | ● | ● | ● | ○ | | ● | ● | | |
| SF | ● | | | | | | | | | ● | ○ | ◉ | ● | ● | | | ◉ | ○ | | |
| S | ● | | | | | | | | | ● | ○ | ● | ? | ● | | | ◉ | ○ | | |
| R | ● | ● | ● | | | ● | | ● | ● | ● | ● | ● | ● | ● | ◉ | | ● | ◉ | | |
| PL | ◉ | ◉ | | | | ◉ | | ◉ | ◉ | ● | ○ | ● | ◉ | ● | | | ● | ○ | | |
| P | | ● | ● | | ◉ | ● | | | | ◉ | | ● | | ● | | | ● | ● | | |
| NL | ◉ | | | | | | | | | ◉ | | ○ | | ● | | | ◉ | ◉ | | |
| N | ◉ | | | | | | | | | ◉ | | ◉ | | ● | | | ○ | ○ | | |
| M | | | | | | | | | | | | | | | | | ● | ● | | |
| L | ◉ | | | | | | | | | ◉ | | ◉ | | ◉ | | | ◉ | ◉ | | |
| IRL | | | | | | | | | | | | | | | | | ◉ | ○ | | |
| I | ● | ● | ● | | ● | ● | ● | ● | ● | ● | | ● | | ● | ● | | ● | ● | | |
| H | ● | ● | ● | | | ● | | ● | ● | ● | ○ | ● | ● | ● | | | ◉ | ◉ | | |
| GR | | ● | ● | | | ● | | | | ● | | ● | | ● | ● | ? | ● | ● | | |
| GB | | | | | | ● | | | | ○ | | ◉ | | ● | | | ◉ | ○ | | |
| F | ● | ● | | | ● | ● | ◉ | | | ● | | ● | | ● | ● | | ● | ● | | |
| E | ◉ | ● | ● | | ● | ● | | | | ◉ | | ● | | ● | | | ● | ● | ● | ● |
| DK | | | | | | | | | | ◉ | | | | | | | | ○ | | |
| D DDR | ● | ◉ | | ● | | ◉ | ? | | | ● | | ● | ? | ● | | | ● | ◉ | | |
| D | ● | ● | | | ◉ | ◉ | | | | ● | | ◉ | | ● | | | ● | ◉ | | |
| CY | | | | | | ? | | | | | ? | | | ? | | | ● | ● | | |
| CS | ● | ● | ◉ | ○ | | ● | | ● | ◉ | ● | ○ | ● | ● | ● | | | ● | ◉ | | |
| CH | ● | ● | | | ● | ◉ | ● | ◉ | | ● | | ◉ | | ● | | | ● | ◉ | | |
| BG | ◉ | ● | ● | | | ● | | ● | ○ | ● | ○ | ● | ● | ● | ◉ | | ● | ● | | |
| B | ● | ◉ | | | | ◉ | | | | ◉ | | ● | | ● | | | ◉ | ◉ | | |
| AL | | ● | ● | | | ● | | | | ○ | | ● | ○ | ● | ● | | ● | ● | | |
| A | ● | ● | ◉ | | | ● | ● | ● | ○ | ● | ○ | ● | ◉ | ● | | | ● | ◉ | | |

## 5.3 Biogeographic evaluation of nominal species

Biogeographic value of any one nominal species consists of two independant elements: biogeographic disposition expressed in the numerical value of the chorological index and biogeographic condition expressed numerically as the vulnerability index. Together they indicate the natural potential of the species and its anthropogenically influenced contemporary situation.

### 5.3.1 Biogeographic disposition

Biogeographic disposition of a nominal species is a new term indicating the species' potential maximum viability in contemporary terms, regardless of the present anthropogenic pressures. It is defined by three relatively well descriptive dimensions:

- size of the nominal species' range;
- continuity of colonies of the nominal species' range;
- affinity of the nominal species' range.

The first two elements are reliable indicators of the long term success of the species' strategy: species that are able to extend – and maintain – their continuous ranges have proved to be successful. Good examples of such species are some widespread mesophils, above all perhaps *Polyommatus icarus*, *Coenonympha pamphilus* and *Maniola jurtina*, and, of course, all ubiquists, such as the migrants *Pieris rapae*, *Aglais urticae* or *Inachis io*. DOWDESWELL (1981) studied and described some of the characteristic strategies and properties of one of them: *Maniola jurtina*. It is interesting to compare here some of the decisive ecological properties of the most successful European butterfly species:

- only a few of them are particularly strong fliers (e. g. *Aglais urticae*, *Inachis io*);
- some of them have monophagous larvae (e. g. *Aglais urticae*, primarily also *Inachis io*);
- some of them are monovoltine (e. g. *Maniola jurtina*);
- some of them are multivoltine (e. g. *Pieris rapae*, *Polyommatus icarus*, *Coenonympha pamphilus*).

All of them have the following properties in common: they utilize biotic and abiotic elements widespread and common "everywhere" in the countryside (e. g. the larval hostplant of the monophagous *Aglais urticae* is *Ur-*

*tica dioica* growing in the open country) and they can either live at least temporarily in habitats of negligible size (e. g. *Polyommatus icarus, Coenonympha pamphilus*) or their adult biotope can be widely separated from their larval biotope (e. g. *Aglais urticae, Inachis io*); all of them are also very tolerant of various climatic conditions and latitude.

Although even the most successful butterfly species is bound to suffer some losses in its range continuity, and subsequently also in the total territory inhabited and in its total stocks, as the result of the most adverse human activities, its biogeographic disposition makes it more resistant to harmful anthropogenic factors and therefore less vulnerable to the prevailing anthropogenically influenced conditions, as they are found in most of present day Europe.

Optimal density of the individual colonies related to the species' dispersal potential (range composition) enables natural replacement of any accidentally lost population – an important aspect of the species' natural resistance.

The third indicator – the nominal species' range affinity – is defined by the total range of the species in relation to its European distribution. That is the significance of the species' European colonies as a proportion of the total stocks.

All these three aspects can be numerically expressed objectively for the overwhelming majority of European butterfly species, so they are fully comparable. Only in case of species with a very restricted range a compensation must be made for the small total of the stocks, which are in such an extreme situation no longer reflected satisfactorily by the composition of the range. For example *Polyommatus caelestissima* and *Erebia zapateri* have all their colonies relatively densely distributed over a small area of east-central Spain and in spite of their apparent abundance in some localities and incomplete isolation of some colonies, their total stocks are low and, therefore, vulnerable. The same applies to all species represented by a single (known) colony, regardless of its abundance in that colony. The reasons why such species are apparently unable to spread outside their localities, despite their local abundance year after year, are not known.

A cumulative value of the three dimensions discussed above is called the chorological index. It is an approximate numerical expression of the biogeographic disposition (or natural potential) of any species.

In the tables following this section (p. 256) the biogeographic disposition of European butterfly species is classified and expressed in numeric values (points) according to the principles defined below. Values marked by asterisk (i. e.*) are preliminary; a few species remain unclassified: they are the species of most uncertain taxonomic status (i. e. unidentifiable "nomina dubiosa") or of uncertain occurrence in Europe. The abbreviations used in the tables are shown in parenthesis after each aspect classified.

## Range size (RS) (Fig. 33–37)

The vulnerability of any nominal species increases with the decrease in the size of its range; species confined to particularly small areas are more vulnerable to both environmental and anthropogenic pressures for this reason alone.

1 Species widespread over the whole (or nearly all of) Europe, including migrants capable of establishing only semipermanent colonies over a part of the territory; examples: *Pieris rapae, Aglais urticae, Vanessa cardui.*

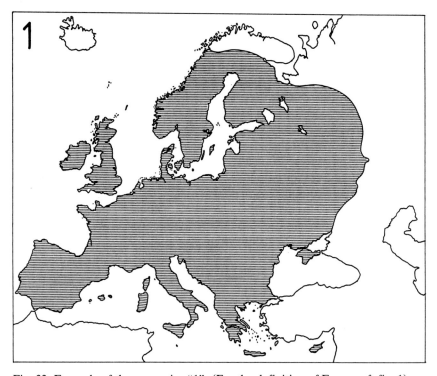

Fig. 33. Example of the range-size "1". (For the definition of Europe cf. fig. 1).

2 Species widespread over large parts of Europe; examples: *Iphiclides podalirius, Melanargia galathea*.

3 Species distributed over one or more smaller parts of Europe, (i. e. a "medium sized" distribution); examples: *Melanargia russiae, Zerynthia polyxena*.

4 Species restricted to one or more territories smaller than the above; examples: *Iphiclides feisthamelii, Melanargia lachesis, Euphydryas glaciegenita*.

5 Species confined to a small area, such as an island, a mountain range, or a single (known) site; examples: *Cupido carswelli, Maniola nurag, Melanargia arge, Polyommatus humedasae*.

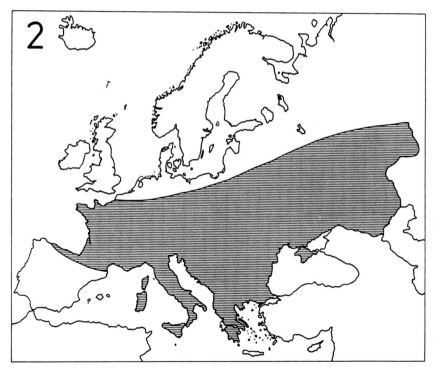

Fig. 34. Example of the range-size "2". (For the definition of Europe cf. fig. 1).

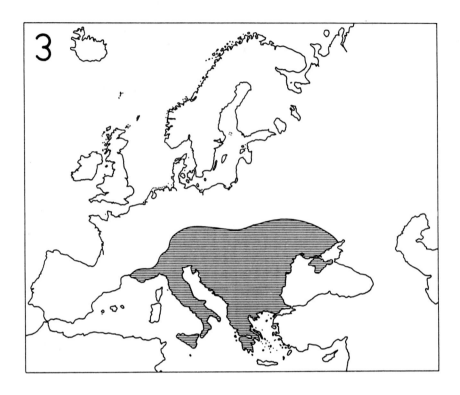

Fig. 35. Example of the range-size "3". (For the definition of Europe cf. fig. 1).

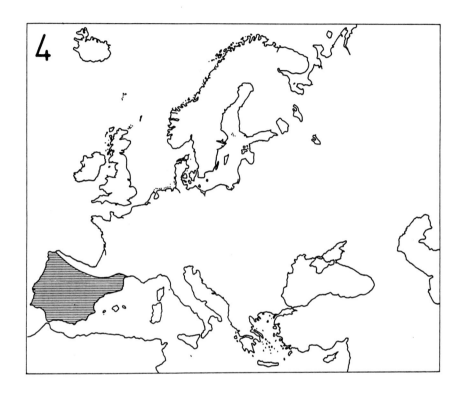

Fig. 36. Example of the range-size "4". (For the definition of Europe cf. fig. 1).

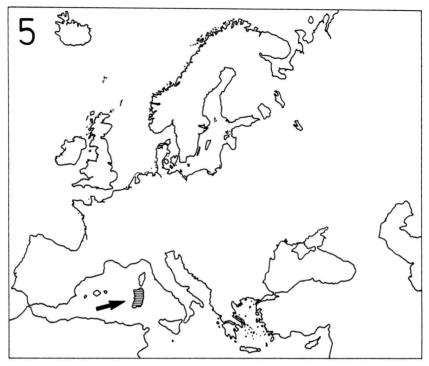

Fig. 37. Example of the range-size "5". (For the definition of Europe cf. fig. 1).

## Range composition (RC) (Fig. 38)

Continuity of distribution, that is in the extreme the ability of individuals of one colony to reach the individuals of the other, is a valuable aspect of the species' resistance to both natural and, particularly, to anthropogenic pressures as it allows natural reinvasion by the species of lost sites so far as they remain inhabitable; isolated colonies are in the case of any local extinction lost for ever. Since a very small range–always coupled with low stocks, regardless of the relative abundance–makes every nominal species more vulnerable, allowance is made particularly in the last category for extreme cases. In general, the vulnerability of any one nominal species increases with the isolation of its colonies.

1 Continuous, or nearly continuous, distribution over nearly the whole European range of the species; examples: *Gonepteryx rhamni, Pieris rapae, Maniola jurtina.*

2 Predominantly continuous distribution over most of the European range, with a small proportion of relatively isolated colonies in some areas; examples: *Papilio machaon, Melanargia galathea.*

3 Predominantly isolated colonies, with a good proportion of more continuous distribution ("headquarters") in significant central parts of the species' range; examples: *Colias palaeno, Polyommatus coridon.*

4 Discontinuos distribution over nearly the whole European range of the species, consisting by and large of isolated colonies, or compensated by relatively continuous distribution over a small territory, with low stocks; examples: *Archon apollinus, Coenonympha hero.*

5 Widely separated isolated single colonies or small groups of populations, or compensated extremely low stocks and very restricted range; examples: *Cupido carswelli, Coenonympha oedippus.*

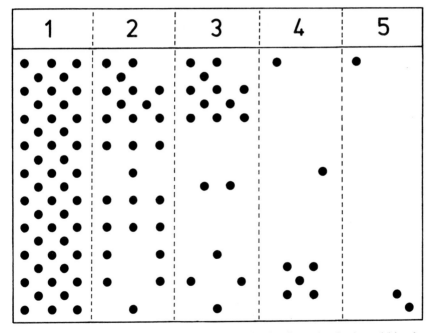

Fig. 38. Range composition: Model of the distribution of colonies within the species' range as expressed by values 1–5.

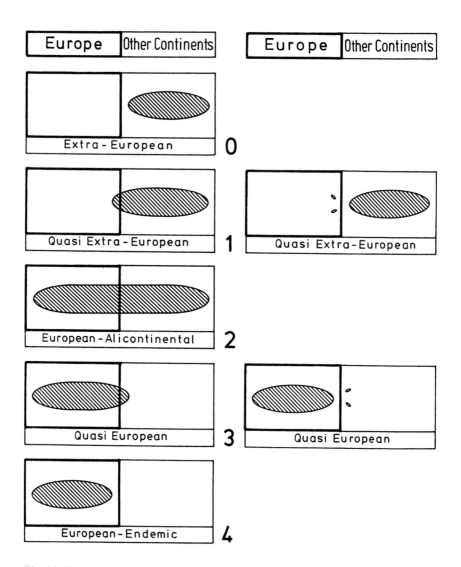

Fig. 39. Types of range affinity, expressed by values 1–4.

## Range affinity (RA) (Fig. 39)

The relationship between the species' European distribution and its world range is a supplementary indicator of the relative significance of the species' European colonies for its overall survival. At the same time this relationship indicates in all extreme cases the natural vulnerability (and relative insignificance) of European colonies of the extra-European species just reaching their natural boundaries in Europe, perhaps having established only semipermanent colonies or being often reported as (vagrant) individuals (i. e. records of single specimens, whether reported repeatedly or not). The other extreme is represented by all endemic species peculiar to Europe only.

1 Extra-European species (as characterized above); examples: *Archon apollinus, Zegris pyrothoe, Catopsilia florella.*
2 "Neutral" species with distribution "headquarters" both within and outside Europe, regardless of the respective range proportions; examples: *Papilio machaon, Gonepteryx rhamni, Aglais urticae.*
3 Species with their "headquarters" in Europe but known also from Asia, Africa or America (the European colonies are particularly significant for the survival of these species); examples: *Chazara prieuri, Colias alfacariensis.*
4 Endemic species peculiar to Europe; examples: *Cupido carswelli, Maniola nurag, Melanargia arge, Fabriciana elisa.*

## Chorological index (CI)

The biogeographic disposition of every species classified is shown numerically by its chorological index, it being the cumulative total of the numerical values showing the nominal species'

● Range size + Range composition + Range affinity = Chorological index,

that is in case of for example *Iphiclides podalirius* $2+2+2 = 6$. The value of the chorological index increases with the reduction of the biogeographic disposition (i. e. the natural resistance potential) of the species. The lowest value possible is 4, it being an indicator of the most successful species; the highest value possible amounts to 14 and indicates an endemic (European) species restricted to a very small territory. Some typical examples:

CI =   4: *Aglais urticae* (Nymphalidae); (1+1+2 = 4)
CI =   5: *Papilio machaon* (Papilionidae); (1+2+2 = 5)
CI =   6: *Iphiclides podalirius* (Papilionidae); (2+2+2 = 6)
CI =   7: *Aricia agestis* (Lycaenidae); (2+3+2 = 7)
CI =   8: *Parnassius apollo* (Papilionidae); (3+3+2 = 7)
CI =   9: *Albulina orbitulus* (Lycaenidae); (4+3+2 = 9)
CI = 10: *Parnassius phoebus* (Papilionidae); (4+4+2 = 10)
CI = 11: *Polyommatus hispana* (Lycaenidae); (4+3+4 = 11)
CI = 12: *Cupido lorquinii* (Lycaenidae); (5+4+3 = 12)
CI = 13: *Hipparchia neomiris* (Satyridae); (5+4+4 = 13)
CI = 14: *Cupido carswelli* (Lycaenidae); (5+5+4 = 14).

### 5.3.2 Biogeographic condition

Whereas the biogeographic disposition expresses the natural (maximum) viability of the species, the biogeographic condition shows the anthropogenic threats indicated in numerical values in points. As only cases of severe threats are considered here, subject to the data available at present for the decisive majority of European nominal species, only two grades are recognized at present: 1 point shows severe threat, 2 points show very severe threat to the species, its habitat or indicates its recent decline. The classification is tentative and incomplete owing to the lack of accurate reliable data, many species are left unclassified at present, which certainly must not be taken as a statement showing that anthropogenic threats do not exist. The biogeographic condition is expressed by the Vulnerability index value and based on the examination of three aspects of threat. Abbreviations used in the tables (p. 256 to 267) are given here in parenthesis.

Decline recorded (DR)

Only cases of very serious decline concerning at least a large part of the species' European range are considered here; one point indicates approximately vulnerable species, two points endangered species (i. e. acute threat of extinction). Examples: *Parnassius apollo* (1 point) and *Coenonympha oedippus* (2 points).

Habitat vulnerability (HV)

Habitat destruction (whatever its form may be) is responsible for the decline of the overwhelming majority of the butterfly species threatened in

Europe. Indirect threats, such as air pollution, and all natural changes, such as landslides or climatic changes, are not considered here.

## Species vulnerability (SV)

Only a relatively small number of European butterfly species are seriously threatened by collectors (overcollecting): they are commercially attractive panoramic species and rare endemic species.

## Vulnerability index (VI)

The biogeographic condition of every species classified here is shown numerically by its vulnerability index, it being the cumulative total of the numerical values expressing

● Decline recorded + Habitat vulnerability + Species vulnerability = Vulnerability index,

that is in case of for example *Coenonympha oedippus* $2+2+1 = 5$. The value of the vulnerability index increases with the increase of anthropogenic threat to the nominal species under consideration ranging from the minimum expressed by 1 point to the maximum shown by 6 points.

Although combined values of chorological index and vulnerability index are strictly speaking not directly comparable at present owing to the different nature of available data, any combination of high chorological index and high vulnerability index for the same nominal species indicates the generally low resistance of that species to any and all anthropogenic pressures.

This can be exemplified by *Coenonympha oedippus:* $CI\ 12 + VI\ 5 = 17$; the species has declined tremendously over the last five or more decades and is doubtless the most seriously threatened non-endemic species in Europe. The habitat of *C. oedippus* is essentially lowland open flat fens (at altitudes ranging from sea level to about 500 m) which must stay free of cultivation and which apparently must never be cut for hay (BISCHOF 1968).

There is no species with a vulnerability index value amounting to the full six points. Species with a vulnerability index 4 and 5 are very seriously threatened, their extinction being a real possibility if no steps are taken to protect them. Species with vulnerability index 3 are seriously threatened, but not in acute danger of becoming extinct in Europe.

### 5.3.3 Biogeographic disposition and condition of European butterflies [1]

Explanation of abbreviations used in the following table (pp. 256–267):

Disposition = Biogeographic disposition (BD), cf. p. 244
RS    = Range size (p. 246)
RC    = Range composition (p. 250)
RA    = Range affinity (p. 253)
CI    = Chorological index (p. 253)

Condition = Biogeographic condition (BC) cf. p. 254
DR    = Decline recorded (p. 254)
HV    = Habitat vulnerability (p. 254)
SV    = Species vulnerability (p. 255)
VI    = Vulnerability index (p. 255)

| SPECIES | DISPOSITION | | | | CONDITION | | | |
|---|---|---|---|---|---|---|---|---|
|  | RS | RC | RA | CI | DR | HV | SV | VI |
| **Papilionidae** | | | | | | | | |
| *Archon apollinus* | 5 | 4 | 1 | 10 | – | – | 1 | 1 |
| *Iphiclides feisthamelii* | 4 | 2 | 2 | 8 | – | – | – | – |
| *Iphiclides podalirius* | 2 | 2 | 2 | 6 | – | – | – | – |
| *Papilio alexanor* | 4 | 4 | 2 | 10 | – | 1 | 1 | 2 |
| *Papilio hospiton* | 5 | 4 | 4 | 13 | – | – | 2 | 2 |
| *Papilio machaon* | 1 | 2 | 2 | 5 | – | – | – | – |
| *Parnassius apollo* | 3 | 3 | 2 | 8 | 1 | 1 | 1 | 3 |
| *Parnassius mnemosyne* | 3 | 3 | 2 | 8 | 1 | 2 | 1 | 4 |
| *Parnassius phoebus* | 4 | 4 | 2 | 10 | – | – | 1 | 1 |
| *Zerynthia cerisyi* | 4 | 3 | 2 | 9 | – | – | 1 | 1 |
| *Zerynthia cretica* | 5 | 4 | 4 | 13 | – | – | 1 | 1 |
| *Zerynthia polyxena* | 3 | 3 | 2 | 8 | – | 1 | 1 | 2 |
| *Zerynthia rumina* | 4 | 2 | 2 | 8 | – | 1 | 1 | 2 |
| **Pieridae** | | | | | | | | |
| *Anthocharis cardamines* | 1 | 2 | 2 | 5 | – | – | – | – |
| *Anthocharis damone* | 4 | 5 | 2 | 11 | – | – | – | – |
| *Anthocharis euphenoides* | 3 | 3 | 4 | 10 | – | – | – | – |
| *Anthocharis gruneri* | 4 | 4 | 2 | 10 | – | – | – | – |
| *Aporia crataegi* | 1 | 2 | 2 | 5 | – | – | – | – |

---

[1] Explanation of calculation see p. 253–255.
   Numbers marked by asterisk indicate preliminary values

| SPECIES | DISPOSITION | | | | CONDITION | | | |
|---|---|---|---|---|---|---|---|---|
| | RS | RC | RA | CI | DR | HV | SV | VI |
| *Catopsilia florella* | 5 | 5 | 1 | 11 | – | – | – | – |
| *Colias alfacariensis* | 2 | 2 | *3 | 7 | – | – | – | – |
| *Colias aurorina* | 5 | 4 | 2 | 11 | – | – | 1 | 1 |
| *Colias balcanica* | 5 | 5 | 4 | 14 | – | 1 | 2 | 3 |
| *Colias chrysotheme* | 4 | 3 | 2 | 9 | – | – | – | – |
| *Colias crocea* | 3 | 1 | 2 | 6 | – | – | – | – |
| *Colias erate* | 3 | 3 | 2 | 8 | – | – | – | – |
| *Colias hecla* | 5 | 3 | 2 | 10 | – | – | – | – |
| *Colias hyale* | 2 | 2 | 2 | 6 | – | – | – | – |
| *Colias myrmidone* | 4 | 3 | 2 | 9 | – | – | – | – |
| *Colias nastes* | 5 | 3 | 2 | 10 | – | – | – | – |
| *Colias palaeno* | 3 | 3 | 2 | 8 | 2 | 2 | – | 4 |
| *Colias phicomone* | 4 | 2 | 4 | 10 | – | – | – | – |
| *Colotis evagore* | 5 | 5 | 1 | 11 | – | – | – | – |
| *Euchloe ausonia* | 4 | 2 | 4 | 10 | – | – | – | – |
| *Euchloe belemia* | 4 | 3 | 3 | 10 | – | – | – | – |
| *Euchloe charlonia* | 5 | 5 | 2 | 12 | – | – | – | – |
| *Euchloe crameri* | 4 | 4 | *4 | 12 | – | – | – | – |
| *Euchloe insularis* | 5 | 2 | 4 | 11 | – | – | – | – |
| *Euchloe penia* | *5 | 5 | 2 | 12 | – | – | – | – |
| *Euchloe simplonia* | 3 | 2 | 3 | 8 | – | – | – | – |
| *Euchloe tagis* | 4 | 3 | 2 | 9 | – | – | – | – |
| *Gonepteryx cleobule* | 5 | 3 | 4 | 12 | 1 | 2 | 1 | 4 |
| *Gonepteryx cleopatra* | 3 | 2 | 2 | 7 | – | – | – | – |
| *Gonepteryx farinosa* | 4 | 3 | 2 | 9 | – | – | – | – |
| *Gonepteryx maderensis* | 5 | 5 | 4 | 14 | 1 | 1 | 1 | 3 |
| *Gonepteryx palmae* | 5 | 3 | 4 | 12 | – | – | – | – |
| *Gonepteryx rhamni* | 1 | 1 | 2 | 4 | – | – | – | – |
| *Leptidae duponcheli* | 3 | 4 | 2 | 9 | – | – | – | – |
| *Leptidea morsei* | 3 | 3 | 2 | 8 | – | – | – | – |
| *Leptidea sinapis* | 1 | 2 | 2 | 5 | – | – | – | – |
| *Pieris adalwinda* | 5 | 2 | *4 | 11 | – | – | – | – |
| *Pieris balcana* | 5 | *4 | 4 | 13 | – | – | 1 | 1 |
| *Pieris brassicae* | 1 | 1 | 2 | 4 | – | – | – | – |
| *Pieris bryoniae* | 4 | 3 | 4 | 11 | – | – | – | – |
| *Pieris callidice* | 4 | 4 | 2 | 10 | – | – | – | – |
| *Pieris cheiranthi* | 5 | 4 | 4 | 13 | – | – | – | – |
| *Pieris chloridice* | 4 | 4 | 2 | 10 | – | – | – | – |
| *Pieris daplidice* | 2 | 1 | 2 | 5 | – | – | – | – |
| *Pieris ergane* | 3 | 3 | 2 | 8 | – | – | – | – |
| *Pieris flavescens* | 4 | 3 | 4 | 11 | – | – | – | – |

| SPECIES | DISPOSITION | | | | CONDITION | | | |
|---|---|---|---|---|---|---|---|---|
| | RS | RC | RA | CI | DR | HV | SV | VI |
| *Pieris krueperi* | 4 | 3 | 2 | 9 | – | – | – | – |
| *Pieris mannii* | 3 | 4 | 2 | 10 | – | – | – | – |
| *Pieris maura* | – | – | – | – | – | – | – | – |
| *Pieris napi* | 1 | 1 | 2 | 4 | – | – | – | – |
| *Pieris rapae* | 1 | 1 | 2 | 4 | – | – | – | – |
| *Zegris eupheme* | 4 | 3 | 3 | 10 | – | – | – | – |
| *Zegris pyrothoe* | 5 | *3 | 1 | 9 | – | – | – | – |
| **Lycaenidae** | | | | | | | | |
| *Agriades aquilo* | 5 | 4 | 2 | 11 | – | – | – | – |
| *Agriades dardanus* | 5 | 4 | 4 | 13 | – | – | – | – |
| *Agriades glandon* | 4 | 3 | 4 | 11 | – | – | – | – |
| *Agriades pyrenaicus* | 5 | 4 | 4 | 13 | – | – | – | – |
| *Agriades zullichi* | 5 | 5 | 4 | 14 | – | – | 2 | 2 |
| *Albulina orbitulus* | 4 | 3 | 2 | 9 | – | – | – | – |
| *Aricia agestis* | 2 | 3 | 2 | 7 | – | – | – | – |
| *Aricia allous* | 3 | 3 | 2 | 8 | – | – | – | – |
| *Aricia artaxerxes* | 5 | 5 | 4 | 14 | – | – | 1 | 1 |
| *Aricia cramera* | 3 | 3 | 3 | 9 | – | – | – | – |
| *Aricia eumedon* | 2 | 3 | 2 | 7 | – | – | – | – |
| *Aricia inhonora* | 3 | 3 | 4 | 10 | – | – | – | – |
| *Aricia morronensis* | 4 | 5 | 4 | 13 | – | – | – | – |
| *Aricia nicias* | 4 | 3 | 4 | 11 | – | – | – | – |
| *Azanus jesous* | 5 | 4 | 1 | 10 | – | – | – | – |
| *Callophrys avis* | 4 | 4 | 3 | 11 | – | – | – | – |
| *Callophrys rubi* | 1 | 1 | 2 | 4 | – | – | – | – |
| *Celastrina argiolus* | 1 | 1 | 2 | 4 | – | – | – | – |
| *Chilades galba* | 5 | 2 | 1 | 8 | – | – | – | – |
| *Chilades trochylus* | 4 | 3 | 2 | 9 | – | – | – | – |
| *Cigaritis acamas* | 5 | 4 | 1 | 10 | – | – | – | – |
| *Cupido alcetas* | 3 | 3 | 4 | 10 | – | – | – | – |
| *Cupido argiades* | 2 | 2 | 2 | 6 | – | – | – | – |
| *Cupido carswelli* | 5 | 5 | 4 | 14 | – | 2 | 1 | 3 |
| *Cupido decoloratus* | 3 | 3 | 4 | 10 | – | – | – | – |
| *Cupido lorquinii* | 5 | 4 | 3 | 12 | – | – | – | – |
| *Cupido minimus* | 2 | 2 | 2 | 6 | – | – | – | – |
| *Cupido osiris* | 3 | 3 | 3 | 9 | – | – | – | – |
| *Cyaniris antiochena* | 5 | 4 | 2 | 12 | – | – | – | – |
| *Cyaniris semiargus* | 1 | 2 | 2 | 5 | – | – | – | – |
| *Cyclirius webbianus* | 5 | 2 | 4 | 11 | – | – | – | – |
| *Glaucopsyche alexis* | 2 | 3 | 2 | 7 | – | – | – | – |
| *Glaucopsyche melanops* | 4 | 3 | 3 | 10 | – | – | – | – |

| SPECIES | DISPOSITION | | | | CONDITION | | | |
| --- | --- | --- | --- | --- | --- | --- | --- | --- |
|  | RS | RC | RA | CI | DR | HV | SV | VI |
| *Glaucopsyche paphos* | 5 | 4 | 4 | 13 | – | – | – | – |
| *Iolana iolas* | 3 | 4 | 3 | 10 | 1 | 1 | 1 | 3 |
| *Kretania eurypilus* | *5 | *5 | 1 | 11 | – | – | – | – |
| *Kretania psylorita* | 5 | 5 | 4 | 14 | – | – | – | – |
| *Laeosopis roboris* | 4 | 2 | 3 | 9 | – | – | – | – |
| *Lampides boeticus* | 3 | 1 | 2 | 6 | – | – | – | – |
| *Lycaeides argyrognomon* | 2 | 3 | 2 | 7 | – | – | – | – |
| *Lycaeides cleobis* | – | – | – | – | – | – | – | – |
| *Lycaeides corsica* | 5 | 5 | 4 | 14 | – | – | – | – |
| *Lycaeides idas* | 1 | 2 | 2 | 5 | – | – | – | – |
| *Lycaeides nevadensis* | 5 | 5 | 4 | 14 | – | – | – | – |
| *Lycaena alciphron* | 2 | 3 | 2 | 7 | – | – | – | – |
| *Lycaena candens* | 4 | 3 | 2 | 9 | – | – | – | – |
| *Lycaena dispar* | 3 | 5 | 2 | 10 | 2 | 2 | 2 | 6 |
| *Lycaena helle* | 4 | 4 | 2 | 10 | 2 | 2 | – | 4 |
| *Lycaena hippothoe* | 2 | 3 | 2 | 7 | – | – | – | – |
| *Lycaena ochimus* | – | – | – | – | – | – | – | – |
| *Lycaena ottomanus* | 4 | 4 | 3 | 11 | – | – | – | – |
| *Lycaena phlaeas* | 1 | 1 | 2 | 4 | – | – | – | – |
| *Lycaena subalpina* | 4 | 2 | 4 | 10 | – | – | – | – |
| *Lycaena thersamon* | 3 | 4 | 2 | 9 | – | – | – | – |
| *Lycaena thetis* | 5 | 4 | 2 | 11 | – | – | – | – |
| *Lycaena tityrus* | 2 | 2 | 2 | 6 | – | – | – | – |
| *Lycaena virgaureae* | 2 | 3 | 2 | 7 | – | – | – | – |
| *Maculinea alcon* | 3 | 4 | 2 | 9 | 2 | 2 | – | 4 |
| *Maculinea arion* | 2 | 3 | 2 | 7 | 1 | – | – | 1 |
| *Maculinea nausithous* | 3 | 3 | 4 | 10 | 1 | 2 | – | 3 |
| *Maculinea rebeli* | 3 | 4 | 4 | 11 | – | – | – | – |
| *Maculinea teleius* | 3 | 3 | 2 | 8 | 1 | 2 | – | 3 |
| *Neolycaena rhymnus* | 4 | 3 | 2 | 9 | – | – | – | – |
| *Nordmannia acaciae* | 2 | 2 | 3 | 7 | – | – | – | – |
| *Nordmannia esculi* | 4 | 2 | 3 | 9 | – | – | – | – |
| *Nordmannia ilicis* | 2 | 2 | 2 | 6 | – | – | – | – |
| *Nordmannia pruni* | 2 | 2 | 2 | 6 | – | – | – | – |
| *Nordmannia spini* | 2 | 2 | 2 | 6 | – | – | – | – |
| *Nordmannia w-album* | 2 | 3 | 2 | 7 | – | – | – | – |
| *Plebejus argus* | 1 | 2 | 2 | 5 | – | – | – | – |
| *Plebejus hesperica* | 5 | 4 | 4 | 13 | – | – | 1 | 1 |
| *Plebejus pylaon* | 4 | 3 | 2 | 9 | – | – | – | – |
| *Plebejus sephirus* | 4 | 4 | 4 | 12 | – | – | – | – |
| *Plebejus trappi* | 5 | 4 | 4 | 13 | – | – | 1 | 1 |

| SPECIES | DISPOSITION | | | | CONDITION | | | |
|---|---|---|---|---|---|---|---|---|
|  | RS | RC | RA | CI | DR | HV | SV | VI |
| *Polyommatus actis* | – | – | – | – | – | – | – | – |
| *Polyommatus admetus* | 4 | 3 | 3 | 10 | – | – | – | – |
| *Polyommatus ainsae* | 5 | 5 | 4 | 14 | – | – | 1 | 1 |
| *Polyommatus albicans* | 4 | 3 | 4 | 11 | – | – | – | – |
| *Polyommatus amandus* | 2 | 2 | 3 | 7 | – | – | 1 | 1 |
| *Polyommatus aroaniensis* | 5 | 5 | 4 | 14 | – | – | – | – |
| *Polyommatus asturiensis* | 5 | 4 | 4 | 13 | – | – | – | – |
| *Polyommatus bellargus* | 2 | 2 | 2 | 6 | – | – | – | – |
| *Polyommatus caelestissima* | 5 | 4 | 4 | 13 | – | – | – | – |
| *Poloymmatus coelestinus* | 5 | 4 | 2 | 11 | – | – | – | – |
| *Polyommatus coerulescens* | 5 | 4 | 4 | 13 | – | – | – | – |
| *Polyommatus coridon* | 2 | 3 | 4 | 9 | – | – | – | – |
| *Polyommatus cyane* | 5 | 5 | 1 | 11 | – | – | – | – |
| *Polyommatus damon* | 3 | 3 | 2 | 8 | – | – | – | – |
| *Polyommatus damone* | 4 | 3 | 2 | 9 | – | – | – | – |
| *Polyommatus daphnis* | 3 | 3 | 3 | 9 | – | – | – | – |
| *Polyommatus dolus* | 5 | 5 | 4 | 14 | – | – | 1 | 1 |
| *Polyommatus dorylas* | 3 | 3 | 3 | 9 | – | – | – | – |
| *Polyommatus eroides* | 4 | 4 | 3 | 11 | – | – | – | – |
| *Polyommatus eros* | 4 | 3 | 3 | 10 | – | – | – | – |
| *Polyommatus escheri* | 3 | 3 | 3 | 9 | – | – | – | – |
| *Polyommatus exuberans* | 5 | 5 | 4 | 14 | apparently extinct | | | |
| *Polyommatus fabressei* | 5 | 5 | 4 | 14 | – | – | 1 | 1 |
| *Polyommatus galloi* | 5 | 5 | 4 | 14 | – | – | 1 | 1 |
| *Polyommatus golgus* | 5 | 5 | 4 | 14 | – | 1 | 1 | 2 |
| *Polyommatus hispana* | 4 | 3 | 4 | 11 | – | – | – | – |
| *Polyommatus humedasae* | 5 | 5 | 4 | 14 | – | – | 1 | 1 |
| *Polyommatus icarus* | 1 | 1 | 2 | 4 | – | – | – | – |
| *Polyommatus iphigenia* | 5 | 5 | 1 | 11 | – | – | – | – |
| *Polyommatus italaglauca* | – | – | – | – | – | – | – | – |
| *Polyommatus menelaos* | 5 | 5 | 4 | 14 | – | – | 1 | 1 |
| *Polyommatus nephihoptamenos* | 5 | 5 | 4 | 14 | – | – | 1 | 1 |
| *Polyommatus nivescens* | 4 | 4 | 4 | 12 | – | – | – | – |
| *Polyommatus philippi* | 5 | 5 | 4 | 14 | – | – | 1 | 1 |
| *Polyommatus poseidon* | 4 | 3 | 2 | 9 | – | – | – | – |
| *Polyommatus ripartii* | 4 | 4 | 3 | 11 | – | – | – | – |
| *Polyommatus thersites* | 3 | 3 | 2 | 8 | – | – | – | – |
| *Polyommatus violetae* | 5 | 5 | 4 | 14 | – | – | 1 | 1 |
| *Polyommatus virgilius* | 5 | 5 | 4 | 14 | – | – | 1 | 1 |
| *Pseudophilotes abencerragus* | 5 | 4 | 3 | 12 | – | – | – | – |
| *Pseudophilotes barbagiae* | 5 | 5 | 4 | 14 | – | – | 1 | 1 |

| SPECIES | DISPOSITION | | | | CONDITION | | | |
|---|---|---|---|---|---|---|---|---|
| | RS | RC | RA | CI | DR | HV | SV | VI |
| *Pseudophilotes baton* | 3 | 3 | 4 | 10 | – | – | – | – |
| *Pseudophilotes bavius* | 4 | 4 | 2 | 10 | – | – | – | – |
| *Pseudophilotes panope* | – | – | – | – | – | – | – | – |
| *Pseudophilotes panoptes* | 5 | 5 | 4 | 14 | – | – | – | – |
| *Pseudophilotes schiffermuelleri* | 3 | 3 | 2 | 8 | – | – | – | – |
| *Pseudophilotes vicrama* | – | – | – | – | – | – | – | – |
| *Quercusia quercus* | 1 | 2 | 2 | 5 | – | – | – | – |
| *Scolitantides orion* | 3 | 3 | 2 | 8 | – | – | – | – |
| *Syntarucus pirithous* | 3 | 1 | 2 | 6 | – | – | – | – |
| *Tarucus balcanicus* | 3 | 3 | 2 | 8 | – | – | – | – |
| *Tarucus theophrastus* | 4 | 3 | 2 | 9 | – | – | – | – |
| *Thecla betulae* | 2 | 2 | 2 | 6 | – | – | – | – |
| *Tomares ballus* | 4 | 3 | 3 | 10 | – | – | – | – |
| *Tomares callimachus* | 4 | 4 | 3 | 11 | – | – | – | – |
| *Tomares nogelli* | 4 | 4 | 3 | 11 | – | – | – | – |
| *Tongeia fischeri* | 5 | 3 | 1 | 9 | – | – | – | – |
| *Turanana panagea* | 5 | 4 | 2 | 11 | – | – | – | – |
| *Ultraaricia anteros* | 4 | 4 | 4 | 12 | – | – | – | – |
| *Ultraaricia orpheus* | 5 | 4 | 4 | 13 | – | – | – | – |
| *Vacciniina loewi* | 5 | *4 | 1 | 10 | – | – | – | – |
| *Vacciniina optilete* | 3 | 3 | 2 | 8 | 1 | 2 | – | 3 |
| *Zizeeria karsandra* | 5 | 4 | 1 | 10 | – | – | – | – |
| *Zizeeria knysna* | 4 | 4 | 2 | 10 | – | – | – | – |
| **Riodinidae** | | | | | | | | |
| *Hamearis lucina* | 2 | 2 | 2 | 6 | – | – | – | – |
| **Libytheidae** | | | | | | | | |
| *Libythea celtis* | 3 | 3 | 2 | 8 | – | – | – | – |
| **Danaidae** | | | | | | | | |
| *Danaus chrysippus* | 5 | *3 | 1 | 9 | – | – | – | – |
| *Danaus plexippus* | 5 | *3 | 1 | 9 | – | – | – | – |
| **Satyridae** | | | | | | | | |
| *Aphantopus hyperantus* | 2 | 2 | 2 | 6 | – | – | – | – |
| *Arethusana arethusa* | 3 | 3 | 2 | 8 | – | – | – | – |
| *Chazara anthe* | 5 | 4 | 2 | 11 | – | – | – | – |
| *Chazara briseis* | 3 | 3 | 2 | 8 | – | – | – | – |
| *Chazara prieuri* | 5 | 4 | 3 | 12 | 1 | 1 | 1 | 3´ |
| *Coenonympha amaryllis* | 5 | 5 | 1 | 11 | – | – | – | – |
| *Coenonympha arcania* | 2 | 2 | 2 | 6 | – | – | – | – |
| *Coenonympha corinna* | 5 | 3 | 4 | 12 | – | – | – | – |

| SPECIES | DISPOSITION | | | | CONDITION | | | |
|---|---|---|---|---|---|---|---|---|
| | RS | RC | RA | CI | DR | HV | SV | VI |
| Coenonympha darwiniana | 4 | 4 | 4 | 12 | – | – | – | – |
| Coenonympha dorus | 4 | 2 | 3 | 9 | – | – | – | – |
| Coenonympha elbana | 5 | 4 | 4 | 13 | – | – | – | – |
| Coenonympha gardetta | 4 | 3 | 4 | 11 | – | – | – | – |
| Coenonympha glycerion | 3 | 2 | 2 | 7 | – | – | – | – |
| Coenonympha hero | 4 | 4 | 2 | 10 | 2 | 2 | 1 | 5 |
| Coenonympha iphioides | 4 | 2 | 4 | 10 | – | – | – | – |
| Coenonympha leander | 4 | 4 | 2 | 10 | – | – | – | – |
| Coenonympha oedippus | 5 | 5 | 2 | 12 | 2 | 2 | 1 | 5 |
| Coenonympha pamphilus | 1 | 1 | 2 | 4 | – | – | – | – |
| Coenonympha rhodopensis | 4 | 4 | 4 | 12 | – | – | – | – |
| Coenonympha thyrsis | 5 | 4 | 4 | 13 | – | – | – | – |
| Coenonympha tullia | 3 | 4 | 2 | 9 | 1 | 2 | – | 3 |
| Erebia aethiopella | 5 | 4 | 4 | 13 | – | – | – | – |
| Erebia aethiops | 3 | 2 | 2 | 7 | – | – | – | – |
| Erebia alberganus | 4 | 3 | 4 | 11 | – | – | – | – |
| Erebia boreomontanum | – | – | – | – | – | – | – | – |
| Erebia calcaria | 5 | 4 | 4 | 13 | – | – | – | – |
| Erebia cassioides | 3 | 3 | 4 | 10 | – | – | – | – |
| Erebia christi | 5 | 5 | 4 | 14 | 1 | – | 1 | 2 |
| Erebia claudina | 5 | 4 | 4 | 13 | – | – | – | – |
| Erebia dabanensis | – | – | – | – | – | – | – | – |
| Erebia disa | 5 | 3 | 2 | 10 | – | – | – | – |
| Erebia discoidalis | 4 | 2 | 2 | 8 | – | – | – | – |
| Erebia edda | – | – | – | – | – | – | – | – |
| Erebia embla | 5 | 3 | 2 | 10 | – | – | – | – |
| Erebia epiphron | 4 | 4 | 4 | 12 | – | – | – | – |
| Erebia epistygne | 5 | 4 | 4 | 13 | – | – | – | – |
| Erebia eriphyle | 5 | 4 | 4 | 13 | – | – | – | – |
| Erebia euryale | 3 | 3 | 2 | 8 | – | – | – | – |
| Erebia fasciata | 5 | 4 | 1 | 10 | – | – | – | – |
| Erebia flavofasciata | 5 | 5 | 4 | 14 | – | – | 1 | 1 |
| Erebia gorge | 4 | 3 | 4 | 11 | – | – | – | – |
| Erebia gorgone | 5 | 4 | 4 | 13 | – | – | – | – |
| Erebia hispania | 5 | 4 | 4 | 13 | – | – | – | – |
| Erebia jeniseiensis | – | – | – | – | – | – | – | – |
| Erebia lefebvrei | 5 | 3 | 4 | 12 | – | – | – | – |
| Erebia ligea | 2 | 2 | 2 | 6 | – | – | – | – |
| Erebia manto | 4 | 3 | 4 | 11 | – | – | – | – |
| Erebia medusa | 2 | 2 | 2 | 6 | – | – | – | – |
| Erebia melampus | 4 | 4 | 4 | 12 | – | – | – | – |

| SPECIES | DISPOSITION | | | | CONDITION | | | |
|---|---|---|---|---|---|---|---|---|
| | RS | RC | RA | CI | DR | HV | SV | VI |
| *Erebia melas* | 5 | 4 | 4 | 13 | – | – | – | – |
| *Erebia meolans* | 3 | 3 | 4 | 10 | – | – | – | – |
| *Erebia mnestra* | 4 | 4 | 4 | 12 | – | – | – | – |
| *Erebia montana* | 4 | 4 | 4 | 12 | – | – | – | – |
| *Erebia neoridas* | 4 | 4 | 4 | 12 | – | – | – | – |
| *Erebia nivalis* | 5 | 4 | 4 | 13 | – | – | – | – |
| *Erebia oeme* | 3 | 3 | 4 | 10 | – | – | – | – |
| *Erebia orientalis* | 5 | 4 | 4 | 13 | – | – | – | – |
| *Erebia ottomana* | 4 | 5 | 2 | 11 | – | – | – | – |
| *Erebia palarica* | 5 | 4 | 4 | 13 | – | – | – | – |
| *Erebia pandrose* | 3 | 3 | 2 | 8 | – | – | – | – |
| *Erebia pharte* | 4 | 3 | 4 | 11 | – | – | – | – |
| *Erebia pluto* | 4 | 3 | 4 | 11 | – | – | – | – |
| *Erebia polaris* | 5 | 3 | 2 | 10 | – | – | – | – |
| *Erebia pronoe* | 4 | 2 | 4 | 10 | – | – | – | – |
| *Erebia rhodopensis* | 5 | 4 | 4 | 13 | – | – | – | – |
| *Erebia rossi* | *4 | *4 | 2 | 10 | – | – | – | – |
| *Erebia scipio* | 5 | 5 | 4 | 14 | – | – | 1 | 1 |
| *Erebia serotina* | – | – | – | – | – | – | – | – |
| *Erebia sthennyo* | 5 | 4 | 4 | 13 | – | – | – | – |
| *Erebia stirius* | 4 | 4 | 4 | 12 | – | – | – | – |
| *Erebia styx* | 4 | 4 | 4 | 12 | – | – | – | – |
| *Erebia sudetica* | 4 | 4 | 4 | 12 | – | – | – | – |
| *Erebia triaria* | 4 | 3 | 4 | 11 | – | – | – | – |
| *Erebia tyndarus* | 5 | 3 | 4 | 12 | – | – | – | – |
| *Erebia zapateri* | 5 | 5 | 4 | 14 | – | – | 1 | 1 |
| *Hipparchia aristaeus* | 5 | 4 | 4 | 12 | – | – | – | – |
| *Hipparchia autonoe* | 4 | 3 | 2 | 9 | – | – | – | – |
| *Hipparchia azorina* | 5 | 4 | 4 | 13 | – | – | – | – |
| *Hipparchia bacchus* | 5 | 5 | 4 | 14 | – | – | – | – |
| *Hipparchia ballettoi* | 5 | 5 | 4 | 14 | – | 1 | 1 | 2 |
| *Hipparchia blachieri* | 5 | 2 | 4 | 11 | – | – | – | – |
| *Hipparchia caldeirense* | 5 | 4 | 4 | 13 | – | – | – | – |
| *Hipparchia christenseni* | 5 | 5 | 4 | 14 | – | – | – | – |
| *Hipparchia cretica* | 5 | 4 | 4 | 13 | – | – | – | – |
| *Hipparchia cypriensis* | 5 | 4 | 4 | 13 | – | – | – | – |
| *Hipparchia fagi* | 3 | 3 | 4 | 10 | – | – | – | – |
| *Hipparchia fatua* | 4 | 3 | 2 | 9 | – | – | – | – |
| *Hipparchia fidia* | 4 | 2 | 3 | 9 | – | – | – | – |
| *Hipparchia gomera* | 5 | 5 | 4 | 14 | – | – | – | – |
| *Hipparchia hermione* | 3 | 2 | 3 | 8 | – | – | – | – |

| SPECIES | DISPOSITION | | | | CONDITION | | | |
|---|---|---|---|---|---|---|---|---|
| | RS | RC | RA | CI | DR | HV | SV | VI |
| *Hipparchia leighebi* | 5 | 4 | 4 | 13 | – | – | 1 | 1 |
| *Hipparchia maderensis* | 5 | 4 | 4 | 13 | – | – | 1 | 1 |
| *Hipparchia malickyi* | 5 | 5 | 4 | 14 | – | – | – | – |
| *Hipparchia miguelensis* | 5 | 4 | 4 | 13 | – | – | – | – |
| *Hipparchia neomiris* | 5 | 4 | 4 | 13 | – | – | – | – |
| *Hipparchia pellucida* | 5 | 5 | 2 | 12 | – | – | – | – |
| *Hipparchia sbordonii* | 5 | 4 | 4 | 13 | – | – | – | – |
| *Hipparchia semele* | 3 | 2 | 4 | 9 | – | – | – | – |
| *Hipparchia senthes* | 4 | 3 | 2 | 9 | – | – | – | – |
| *Hipparchia statilinus* | 3 | 2 | 3 | 8 | – | – | – | – |
| *Hipparchia syriaca* | 4 | 3 | 2 | 9 | – | – | – | – |
| *Hipparchia volgensis* | 4 | 4 | 4 | 12 | – | – | – | – |
| *Hipparchia wyssii* | 5 | 4 | 4 | 13 | – | – | – | – |
| *Hyponephele huebneri* | – | – | – | – | – | – | – | – |
| *Hyponephele lupina* | 3 | 4 | 2 | 9 | – | – | – | – |
| *Hyponephele lycaon* | 2 | 3 | 2 | 7 | – | – | – | – |
| *Kanetisa circe* | 3 | 3 | 3 | 9 | – | – | – | – |
| *Lasiommata achine* | 2 | 4 | 2 | 8 | – | – | – | – |
| *Lasiommata climene* | *5 | *5 | 2 | 12 | – | – | – | – |
| *Lasiommata deidamia* | – | – | – | – | – | – | – | – |
| *Lasiommata maera* | 1 | 2 | 2 | 5 | – | – | – | – |
| *Lasiommata megera* | 1 | 1 | 2 | 4 | – | – | – | – |
| *Lasiommata petropolitana* | 3 | 4 | 2 | 9 | – | – | – | – |
| *Lasiommata roxelana* | 4 | 3 | 2 | 9 | – | – | – | – |
| *Lasiommata tigelius* | 5 | 3 | 4 | 12 | – | – | – | – |
| *Maniola cypricola* | 5 | 3 | 4 | 12 | – | – | – | – |
| *Maniola jurtina* | 1 | 1 | 2 | 4 | – | – | – | – |
| *Maniola nurag* | 5 | 4 | 4 | 13 | – | – | – | – |
| *Maniola telmessia* | 5 | 3 | 3 | 11 | – | – | – | – |
| *Melanargia arge* | 5 | 4 | 4 | 13 | 1 | 1 | 1 | 3 |
| *Melanargia galathea* | 2 | 2 | 3 | 7 | – | – | – | – |
| *Melanargia ines* | 4 | 3 | 3 | 10 | – | – | – | – |
| *Melanargia lachesis* | 4 | 2 | 4 | 10 | – | – | – | – |
| *Melanargia larissa* | 4 | 3 | 3 | 10 | – | – | – | – |
| *Melanargia occitanica* | 4 | 3 | 4 | 10 | – | – | – | – |
| *Melanargia pherusa* | 5 | 5 | 4 | 14 | 1 | 1 | 1 | 3 |
| *Melanargia russiae* | 3 | 3 | 3 | 9 | – | – | – | – |
| *Minois dryas* | 3 | 3 | 2 | 8 | 1 | – | – | 1 |
| *Oeneis ammon* | – | – | – | – | – | – | – | – |
| *Oeneis bore* | 5 | 4 | 2 | 11 | – | – | – | – |
| *Oeneis crambis* | *5 | *4 | 1 | 10 | – | – | – | – |

| SPECIES | DISPOSITION | | | | CONDITION | | | |
|---|---|---|---|---|---|---|---|---|
| | RS | RC | RA | CI | DR | HV | SV | VI |
| *Oeneis dembowskyi* | – | – | – | – | – | – | – | – |
| *Oeneis dubia* | – | – | – | – | – | – | – | – |
| *Oeneis falkovitchi* | – | – | – | – | – | – | – | – |
| *Oeneis glacialis* | 5 | 5 | 4 | 14 | – | – | 1 | 1 |
| *Oeneis jutta* | 4 | 4 | 2 | 10 | – | – | – | – |
| *Oeneis koslowskyi* | – | – | – | – | – | – | – | – |
| *Oeneis kusnetzovi* | – | – | – | – | – | – | – | – |
| *Oeneis norna* | 5 | 4 | 2 | 11 | – | – | – | – |
| *Oeneis pansa* | *5 | *3 | 1 | 9 | – | – | – | – |
| *Oeneis saepestriata* | – | – | – | – | – | – | – | – |
| *Oeneis semidea* | – | – | – | – | – | – | – | – |
| *Oeneis tarpeia* | 4 | 3 | 2 | 9 | – | – | – | – |
| *Oeneis taygete* | – | – | – | – | – | – | – | – |
| *Oeneis tundra* | – | – | – | – | – | – | – | – |
| *Pararge aegeria* | 1 | 1 | 2 | 4 | – | – | – | – |
| *Pararge xiphia* | 5 | 4 | 4 | 13 | – | – | – | – |
| *Pararge xiphioides* | 5 | 4 | 4 | 13 | – | – | – | – |
| *Proterebia afra* | 4 | 4 | 2 | 10 | – | 1 | 1 | 2 |
| *Pseudochazara amymone* | 5 | 5 | 4 | 14 | – | – | 1 | 1 |
| *Pseudochazara anthelea* | 4 | 4 | 2 | 10 | – | – | – | – |
| *Pseudochazara cingovskii* | 5 | 5 | 4 | 14 | – | 1 | 1 | 2 |
| *Pseudochazara euxina* | 5 | 5 | 4 | 14 | – | – | – | – |
| *Pseudochazara geyeri* | 5 | 3 | 2 | 10 | – | – | – | – |
| *Pseudochazara graeca* | 5 | 4 | 4 | 13 | – | – | – | – |
| *Pseudochazara hippolyte* | 4 | 4 | 2 | 10 | – | – | – | – |
| *Pseudochazara orestes* | 5 | 5 | 4 | 14 | – | – | – | – |
| *Pyronia bathseba* | 4 | 2 | 3 | 9 | – | – | – | – |
| *Pyronia cecilia* | 3 | 3 | 3 | 9 | – | – | – | – |
| *Pyronia tithonus* | 2 | 3 | 2 | 7 | – | – | – | – |
| *Satyrus actaea* | 3 | 3 | 2 | 8 | – | – | – | – |
| *Satyrus ferula* | 3 | 3 | 2 | 8 | – | – | – | – |
| *Triphysa phryne* | 4 | 3 | 2 | 9 | – | – | – | – |
| *Ypthima asterope* | 5 | *3 | 1 | 9 | – | – | – | – |
| **Nymphalidae** | | | | | | | | |
| *Aglais ichnusa* | 5 | 5 | 4 | 14 | – | – | 1 | 1 |
| *Aglais urticae* | 1 | 1 | 2 | 4 | – | – | – | – |
| *Apatura ilia* | 2 | 2 | 2 | 6 | – | – | 1 | 1 |
| *Apatura iris* | 2 | 2 | 2 | 6 | – | – | 1 | 1 |
| *Apatura metis* | 5 | 5 | *4 | 14 | – | 1 | 1 | 2 |
| *Araschnia levana* | 3 | 2 | 2 | 7 | – | – | – | – |

| SPECIES | DISPOSITION | | | | CONDITION | | | |
|---|---|---|---|---|---|---|---|---|
| | RS | RC | RA | CI | DR | HV | SV | VI |
| Argynnis adippe | 1 | 2 | 2 | 5 | – | – | – | – |
| Argynnis aglaja | 1 | 2 | 2 | 5 | – | – | – | – |
| Argynnis elisa | 5 | 4 | 4 | 13 | – | – | 1 | 1 |
| Argynnis niobe | 1 | 2 | 2 | 5 | – | – | – | – |
| Argynnis pandora | 3 | 3 | 2 | 8 | – | – | 1 | 1 |
| Argynnis paphia | 1 | 2 | 2 | 5 | – | – | – | – |
| Argyronome laodice | 4 | 3 | 2 | 9 | – | – | 1 | 1 |
| Boloria angarensis | 4 | 2 | 2 | 8 | – | – | – | – |
| Boloria aquilonaris | 4 | 4 | 2 | 10 | 1 | 2 | – | 3 |
| Boloria chariclea | 5 | 4 | 2 | 11 | – | – | – | – |
| Boloria dia | 2 | 2 | 2 | 6 | – | – | – | – |
| Boloria eugenia | 5 | 4 | 2 | 11 | – | – | – | – |
| Boloria eunomia | 4 | 4 | 2 | 10 | 1 | 2 | – | 3 |
| Boloria euphrosyne | 1 | 2 | 2 | 5 | – | – | – | – |
| Boloria freija | 5 | 4 | 2 | 11 | – | – | – | – |
| Boloria frigga | 5 | 4 | 2 | 11 | – | – | – | – |
| Boloria graeca | 4 | 5 | 4 | 13 | – | – | – | – |
| Boloria improba | 5 | 5 | 2 | 12 | – | – | – | – |
| Boloria napaea | 4 | 4 | 2 | 10 | – | – | – | – |
| Boloria pales | 4 | 4 | 2 | 10 | – | – | – | – |
| Boloria polaris | 5 | 5 | 2 | 12 | – | – | – | – |
| Boloria selene | 1 | 2 | 2 | 5 | – | – | – | – |
| Boloria selenis | 5 | 4 | 2 | 11 | – | – | – | – |
| Boloria thore | 4 | 4 | 2 | 10 | – | – | – | – |
| Boloria titania | 4 | 4 | 2 | 10 | – | – | – | – |
| Brenthis daphne | 3 | 3 | 2 | 8 | – | – | – | – |
| Brenthis hecate | 3 | 3 | 2 | 8 | – | – | – | – |
| Brenthis ino | 2 | 3 | 2 | 7 | – | – | – | – |
| Charaxes jasius | 4 | 3 | 2 | 9 | 1 | 1 | 1 | 3 |
| Euphydryas aurinia | 3 | 3 | 2 | 8 | 1 | 1 | – | 2 |
| Euphydryas beckeri | 4 | 3 | 4 | 11 | – | – | – | – |
| Euphydryas cynthia | 4 | 3 | 4 | 11 | – | – | – | – |
| Euphydryas desfontainii | 4 | 3 | 3 | 10 | – | – | – | – |
| Euphydryas glaciegenita | 4 | 3 | 4 | 11 | – | – | – | – |
| Euphydryas iduna | 5 | 4 | 2 | 11 | – | – | – | – |
| Euphydryas maturna | 3 | 4 | 2 | 9 | 1 | 1 | – | 2 |
| Euphydryas orientalis | 4 | 3 | 2 | 9 | – | – | – | – |
| Euphydryas provincialis | 4 | 4 | 5 | 13 | – | – | – | – |
| Euphydryas wolfensbergeri | 5 | 5 | 4 | 14 | – | – | – | – |
| Inachis io | 1 | 1 | 2 | 4 | – | – | – | – |
| Issoria lathonia | 1 | 1 | 2 | 4 | – | – | – | – |

| SPECIES | DISPOSITION | | | | CONDITION | | | |
|---|---|---|---|---|---|---|---|---|
| | RS | RC | RA | CI | DR | HV | SV | VI |
| *Limenitis camilla* | 2 | 3 | 2 | 7 | – | – | – | – |
| *Limenitis populi* | 2 | 3 | 2 | 7 | – | – | 1 | 1 |
| *Limenitis reducta* | 3 | 3 | 2 | 8 | – | – | – | – |
| *Melitaea aetheria* | 5 | *5 | 2 | 12 | – | – | – | – |
| *Melitaea arduinna* | 4 | 4 | 2 | 10 | – | – | – | – |
| *Melitaea asteria* | 5 | 5 | 4 | 14 | – | – | 1 | 1 |
| *Melitaea athalia* | 1 | 2 | 2 | 5 | – | – | – | – |
| *Melitaea aurelia* | 3 | 4 | 2 | 9 | – | – | – | – |
| *Melitaea britomartis* | 3 | 4 | 2 | 9 | – | – | – | – |
| *Melitaea cinxia* | 1 | 2 | 2 | 5 | – | – | – | – |
| *Melitaea deione* | 4 | 3 | 3 | 10 | – | – | – | – |
| *Melitaea diamina* | 2 | 3 | 2 | 7 | 1 | 1 | – | 2 |
| *Melitaea didyma* | 2 | 3 | 2 | 7 | – | – | – | – |
| *Melitaea fascelis* | 3 | 3 | 2 | 8 | – | – | – | – |
| *Melitaea neglecta* | *5 | *5 | 4 | 14 | – | 1 | – | 1 |
| *Melitaea parthenoides* | 3 | 3 | 4 | 10 | – | – | – | – |
| *Melitaea phoebe* | 2 | 3 | 2 | 7 | – | – | – | – |
| *Melitaea varia* | 5 | 4 | 4 | 13 | – | – | – | – |
| *Neptis rivularis* | 3 | 4 | 2 | 9 | 1 | 1 | – | 2 |
| *Neptis sappho* | 4 | 4 | 2 | 10 | – | – | – | – |
| *Nymphalis antiopa* | 2 | 2 | 2 | 6 | – | – | – | – |
| *Nymphalis l-album* | 4 | 4 | 2 | 10 | – | – | – | – |
| *Nymphalis polychloros* | 2 | 2 | 2 | 6 | – | – | – | – |
| *Nymphalis xanthomelas* | 4 | 3 | 2 | 9 | – | – | – | – |
| *Polygonia c-album* | 1 | 2 | 2 | 5 | – | – | – | – |
| *Polygonia egea* | 3 | 3 | 3 | 9 | – | – | – | – |
| *Thaleropis ionia* | *5 | *5 | 1 | 11 | – | – | – | – |
| *Vanessa atalanta* | 1 | 1 | 2 | 4 | – | – | – | – |
| *Vanessa cardui* | 1 | 1 | 2 | 4 | – | – | – | – |
| *Vanessa indica* | 5 | 2 | 1 | 8 | – | – | – | – |
| *Vanessa virginensis* | 5 | 2 | 1 | 8 | – | – | – | – |

### 5.3.4 Application of the Chorological index (CI) values

The chorological index values of nearly all nominal species of European butterflies are definitive. Only the values including preliminary estimates of one or more parameters (i. e. the values marked with asterisk) and the taxonomically "instable" taxa (i. e. collective species, some of the morphospecies of uncertain status and the like) may change in the course of the next few years, subject to the advancement of our knowledge. In general, the "critical" species are usually pairs or small groups of taxonomically very closely related taxa. Further research should also clarify the European status of species left unclassified at present since their occurrence in Europe has not been established beyond doubt. The chorological index allows, therefore

● evaluation of the biogeographic disposition of (nearly) all European butterfly species from the nature conservation point of view, and
● evaluation and comparison of habitats (localities) based solely upon the composition of their butterfly fauna.

Whereas the first application is quite self-explanatory, the second one needs a few words of explanation.

The **absolute value** of the butterfly fauna of a given defined habitat (locality) is the cumulative total of all chorological index values of all species established there; the **relative value** is the absolute value divided by the number of species. The resulting average species chorological index is important for highly specialized stenotopic habitats inhabited by a small number of "rare" species, each with a high chorological index (e. g. raised peat bogs and similar habitats).

This form of standard objective habitat evaluation is intended as a guide for decision makers and officials of nature conservation active in species and habitat protection. This method makes the present conventional utilization in some countries of "red lists" for this purpose outdated, subjective and inaccurate. The present method also facilitates the direct comparison of two or more sites of similar character. This may come in particularly useful when considering purchases of new sites as potential nature reserves, applications for building permissions, and similar cases.

A faunistic survey of a large (ca. 1 km$^2$) ecologically diverse montane site (KUDRNA 1968) could serve as a convenient example showing a (species-rich) fauna of a relatively undisturbed habitat. Location of the site: Czechoslovakia: Sumava (Böhmerwald) Mts.: Vimperk vic.: 800 m.

| | | | |
|---|---|---|---|
| *Papilio machaon* | 5 | *Hipparchia semele* | 9 |
| *Anthocharis cardamines* | 5 | *Lasiommata maera* | 5 |
| *Colias hyale* | 6 | *Lasiommata megera* | 5 |
| *Gonepteryx rhamni* | 4 | *Maniola jurtina* | 4 |
| *Leptidea sinapis* | 5 | *Melenargia galathea* | 7 |
| *Pieris brassicae* | 4 | *Pararge aegeria* | 5 |
| *Pieris napi* | 4 | *Aglais urticae* | 4 |
| *Pieris rapae* | 4 | *Apatura ilia* | 6 |
| *Callophrys rubi* | 4 | *Apatura iris* | 6 |
| *Celastrina argiolus* | 4 | *Araschnia levana* | 6 |
| *Cupido argiades* | 6 | *Argynnis adippe* | 5 |
| *Cyaniris semiargus* | 5 | *Argynnis aglaja* | 5 |
| *Lycaena alciphron* | 7 | *Argynnis niobe* | 5 |
| *Lycaena hippothoe* | 7 | *Argynnis paphia* | 5 |
| *Lycaena phlaeas* | 4 | *Boloria dia* | 6 |
| *Lycaena tityrus* | 6 | *Boloria euphrosyne* | 5 |
| *Lycaena virgaureae* | 7 | *Boloria selene* | 5 |
| *Maculinea nausithous* | 10 | *Brenthis ino* | 7 |
| *Plebejus argus* | 5 | *Inachis io* | 4 |
| *Polyommatus icarus* | 4 | *Issoria lathonia* | 4 |
| *Thecla betulae* | 6 | *Melitaea athalia* | 5 |
| *Aphantopus hyperantus* | 6 | *Melitaea diamina* | 7 |
| *Coenonympha arcania* | 6 | *Nymphalis antiopa* | 6 |
| *Coenonympha glycerion* | 7 | *Nymphalis polychloros* | 6 |
| *Coenonympha pamphilus* | 4 | *Polygonia c-album* | 5 |
| *Erebia medusa* | 6 | *Vanessa atalanta* | 4 |
| *Erebia euryale* | 8 | *Vanessa cardui* | 4 |

Total of species recorded: 54; total cumulative chorological index value: 294; average species chorological index: 294 : 54 = 5,44. (Note: nomenclature of the species originally listed has been brought up-to-date; figures following the names of species are chorological index values).

### 5.3.5 Application of the Vulnerability index (VI) values

The application for the conservation purposes of the Vulnerability index is at present only complementary to the chorological index and rather subjective. Its importance will become fully comparative only when (and if) the values become well established and accepted for the decisive majority of species. Only then it will be possible to appreciate its advantages over the at present usual red lists of threatened species. The reason for this is the lack of accurate data based upon adequate representative samples. It is impossible to express the degree of habitat vulnerability when the habitat is not adequately known – and it is the habitat destruction that is responsible for the extinction of threatened species in most cases. The decline can only be recorded accurately where there is the basic information collected over the years. In the case of many rare endemic species there are no records for several decades (e. g. *Cupido carswelli* in its type-locality), although precisely such species are the most critical in this respect. It must be remembered that red lists also suffer from the lack of adequate data and that many of so called "professional judgements" (HEATH 1981) are no more than blind guessing.

The provision and regular revision of information concerning the trend of stocks development of European butterflies is a long term task of the conservation orientated lepidopterology. Nonetheless, a decisive step forward in the application of the Vulnerability index will become possible after the completion of (1) faunistic surveys of the butterflies of (nearly) all European countries, and (2) compilation of reports on the threatened species in Europe, as well as (3) completion of the reports concerning the conservation and decline of butterflies in all European countries.

## 5.4 Preliminary considerations concerning the ecology of European butterflies

A comprehensive (or concise) study of the ecology of European butterflies does not exist. BLAB & KUDRNA (1982) published a critical conservation biased survey of the ecology of German butterflies and E. BALLETTO, A. LATTES & G. G. Toso (pers. comm.) prepared "An ecological study of the Italian Rhopalocera" and the senior author was kind enough to make their (at the time of writing this work hitherto) unpublished results available to me. The tasks of ecology in the conservation of butterflies are manifold and remain at present mostly unfulfilled. The purpose of this chapter is to critically discuss certain aspects and tasks of butterfly ecology so far as they are significant for their conservation.

Purely ecological studies, and studies using butterflies as tools and models to answer certain theoretical questions (e. g. WIKLUND 1973, 1974, 1975, 1977, etc.) are rarely directly applicable in the conservation practice, the exception being if the species selected are threatened and questions answered may help in their protection, but they are often useful from the methodical point of view. Most valuable are autecological studies of selected threatened and/or rare endemic species showing their ecological requirements, reasons for their decline or extinction (and remedies), development of directly applicable methods and techniques (such as how to estimate size and monitor trend of butterfly colonies and species): e. g. DOUWES 1977, POLLARD 1977, THOMAS 1980, THOMAS & SIMCOX 1982. Principal tasks of applied ecology are:

1. ecological classification of European butterflies;
2. proposals concerning habitat management;
3. definition of ecological requirements of (endangered and rare endemic) nominal species;
4. compilation of lists of larval and adult hostplants.

It is the purpose of this chapter to discuss some principles of the ecological classification of butterflies and to provide brief comments regarding some of the other tasks.

A definitive, entirely objective ecological classification of European butterflies would have to be based on quantitative evaluation of qualitatively defined ecological requirements of each and every nominal species, taking into consideration also the geographical variations of these factors.

Information necessary to faciliate such classification is not available at present, and unlikely to become available in the forseeable future. Attempts have been made to relate butterflies to phytosociological units (e. g. BATA 1930, BERGMANN 1951, 1952): they are more of a subjective description of their habitats than an ecological classification as such.

BLAB & KUDRNA (1982) devised a simple ecological classification for the purposes of natural conservation, based upon typified dominant ecofactors common to all nominal species aggregated in one ecological formation, divided further into units according to the terrestrial habitat-type utilized. In all five butterfly formations can be recognized:

● **Ubiquists** (dominant ecofactor: none): Eurychoric eurytopic species with great dispersal potential, usually migratory, capable of inhabiting at least temporarily almost any of the terrestrial habitats suitable to butterflies, and characteristic of none. The species utilize trivial ecoelements (e. g. *Urtica dioica* is the larval hostplant of four from the total of six ubiquists living permanently in central Europe) and the larval breeding site can be widely separated from the adults' haunts. Examples: *Aglais urticae, Inachis io, Pieris brassicae.*

● **Mesophils** (dominant ecofactor: broad spectrum of essentially medium values): Mostly eurychoric species characteristic of a combination of moderate temperature and humidity values and usually relatively toler-

Fig. 40. Meadows and pastures rich in flowers and inhabited by divers communities of butterflies, particularly if they are exposed to the south and well sheltered from the north (i. e. somewhat xerotherm), if situated in central or northern Europe. Here a locality in Germany: Bavaria: Unterfranken: Rhön: vic. Weisbach. (Photo O. KUDRNA, 1984).

ant either way; their biotopes are widespread in a well balanced environment. The formation is subdivided into three subformations according to the three main habitat types (Fig. 40):

– Grassland species inhabit open mesophilic permanent grassland, such as traditionally managed meadows and pastures. Examples: *Coenonympha pamphilus*, *Maniola jurtina*, *Melanargia galathea*, *Polyommatus icarus*, *Lasiommata megera*, *Pieris napi*.

– Seminemoral species inhabit mesophilic scrubland and the transitional zone between grassland and woodland, such as woodland edges and some clearings, old-fashioned orchards, etc. Examples: *Araschnia levana*, *Argynnis aglaja*, *Celastrina argiolus*, *Coenonympha arcania*, *Everes argiades*.

– Nemoral species inhabit mesophilic sparse woodlands, rides, the canopy, and similar biotopes. Examples: *Apatura ilia*, *Argynnis paphia*, *Erebia aethiops*, *Limenitis populi*, *Lasiommata maera*.

| CI | SPECIES (FAMILY) | MODE OF DISPERSAL | | | |
|---|---|---|---|---|---|
| | | (1) | (2) | (3) | (4) |
| 4 | *Aglais urticae* (NY) | + | | | |
| 4 | *Anthocharis cardamines* (PI) | | + | + | |
| 5 | *Boloria selene* (NY) | | + | + | |
| 4 | *Callophrys rubi* (LY) | | + | + | |
| 4 | *Celastrina argiolus* (LY) | | + | + | |
| 4 | *Coenonympha pamphilus* (SA) | | + | + | |
| 5 | *Cyaniris semiargus* (LY) | | + | + | |
| 4 | *Gonepteryx rhamni* (PI) | | + | | |
| 4 | *Inachis io* (NY) | + | | | |
| 4 | *Issoria lathonia* (NY) | + | + | | |
| 5 | *Lasiommata maera* (SA) | | + | | |
| 4 | *Lasiommata megera* (SA) | | + | | |
| 5 | *Leptidea sinapis* (PI) | | + | | |
| 4 | *Lycaena phlaeas* (LY) | | + | | |
| 4 | *Maniola jurtina* (SA) | | + | + | |
| 5 | *Papilio machaon* (PA) | | + | + | |
| 4 | *Pararge aegeria* (SA) | | + | | |
| 4 | *Pieris brassicae* (PI) | + | | | + |
| 4 | *Pieris napi* (PI) | | + | + | |
| 4 | *Pieris rapae* (PI) | + | | | + |
| 5 | *Plebejus argus* (LY) | | + | | |
| 5 | *Polygonia c-album* (NY) | | + | | |
| 4 | *Polyommatus icarus* (LY) | | + | + | |
| 4 | *Vanessa atalanta* (NY) | + | | | |
| 4 | *Vanessa cardui* (NY) | + | | | |
| CI | SPECIES (FAMILY) | (1) | (2) | (3) | (4) |

**Explanation: CI** = chorological index; Modes of dispersal: **1** = migrant; **2** = utilizes seral stages of vegetation succession; **3** ‹ inhabits traditionally managed meadows and similar secondary habitats related to certain specific forms of agriculture; **4** = pest of certain crops (in some conditions and regions).

Fig. 41: Mode of dispersal of the most successful European butterfly species, with their affinities to agriculture shown.

Fig. 42. Numerous species of European satyrids frequent dried-up river beds and only rarely visit flowers; their larvae feed on grasses growing in vicinity. Here shown habitat of *Chazara prieuri* in east-central Spain: Prov. Teruel: Albarracin district; other species inhabiting the locality include *Chazara briseis, Hipparchia statilinus, H. fidia* and others. (Photo O. KUDRNA, 1976).

● **Xerothermophils** (dominant ecofactor: warm and dry biotopes): Mostly species with their European centre of distribution in the Mediterranean region, and reaching their northern biogeographical limit in central Europe, but including some pure xerophils tolerant of cold winters, and south-eastern European species (often referred to the ponto-mediterranean and pannonic faunal elements) reaching their western biogeographical limit in central Europe, tolerant of cold winters and demanding long, dry summers (e. g. as in the steppe). Three subformations are recognized (Fig. 42–44):

  –Grassland species inhabiting open country ranging from screes to open herbaceous habitats (often on calcareous soils). Examples: *Arethusana arethusa, Aricia agestis, Colias chrysotheme, Hipparchia statilinus, Maculinea rebeli, Parnassius apollo, Polyommatus daphnis.*

  –Seminemoral species inhabiting scrub and transitional zone between grassland and woodland. Examples: *Iphiclides podalirius, Melitaea britomartis, Nordmannia spini.*

  –Nemoral species inhabiting sparse xerothermophilic woodland. Examples: *Argynnis pandora, Hipparchia hermione, Zerynthia polyxena.*

Fig. 43. In Germany *Parnassius apollo* inhabitats some unusual extreme habitats, such as abandoned vineyards in the Moseltal west of Koblenz. (Photo O. KUDRNA, 1981).

Fig. 44. A. habitat of a calciphilous satyrid *Proterebia afra* in Yugoslavia: Dalmatia: Sibenik district. (Photo G. C. BOZZANO, 1985).

- **Hygrophils** (dominant ecofactor: high ground water level): Species inhabiting sites with high ground water tables which are generally at least periodically annually flooded, such as wetlands ranging from wet traditionally managed meadows to acid peat bogs, feeding as larvae on hygrophilic or semiaquatic herbaceous plants. Although the extreme ends of the scale are well recognizable, the continuous transition makes it impossible to define subformations, except perhaps the (regional) tyrphophils which inhabit only peat bogs in lowland and at moderate altitudes but are found in open grassland at high altitudes. Examples: *Boloria aquilonaris, Brenthis ino, Coenonympha oedippus, Colias palaeno, Lycaena dispar, Vacciniina optilete.*

- **Alpicols** (dominant ecofactor: altitude): Species confined to mountains (in central Europe). This is a formation of convenience, dominated geographically rather than ecologically, as it includes both high altitude xerophils and hygrophils, justified because the species are exposed to similar, relatively low, anthropogenic pressures. Some alpicols inhabit much lower altitudes in northern Europe. Two subformations are recognized (Fig. 45, 46):

    – Montane species inhabit chiefly woodland dominated biotopes. Examples: *Boloria titania, Erebia euryale, Lasiommata petropolitana, Pieris bryoniae.*

    – Alpine species inhabit mainly open grassland above the upper tree line. Examples: *Agriades glandon, Boloria pales, Colias phicomone, Erebia epiphron, Oeneis glacialis, Parnassius phoebus.*

An ecological classification fulfils a useful purpose in the conservation of nature because it groups together species characterized by similar biotope requirements, inhabiting similar sites, and exposed to similar anthropogenic pressures. However, the classification must remain (at least at present) strongly regionally biased and the distinct ecological formations, and particularly their subformations, must not be taken too rigidly. For instance, transitions exist not only between the various "grades" of mesophils inhabiting traditionally managed meadows, but also between them and some moderate hygrophils (e. g. *Coenonympha glycerion, Maculinea nausithous, M. teleius* and *Aricia eumedon*) on the one hand, as well as some moderate xerophils and xerothermophils (e. g. *Aricia agestis, Polyommatus bellargus*): cf. fig. 47. Additionally, some stenotopic species inhabit a different ecological niche in different habitat types: e. g. the above mentioned moderate hygrophil inhabits in central Europe wet meadows with a transition to mesophilic meadows and (rarely) dry sunny clearings in sparse mesophilic woodlands (cf. fig. 47). In Italy *A. eumedon*

Fig. 45. In some of its localities, *Parnassius apollo* inhabits open grassland and pastures, withstanding grazing by flocks of sheep. Here a well known locality Monasterio de Rodilla (N. Spain: Prov. Burgos) at ca. 1000 m. (Photo O. KUDRNA, 1974).

Fig. 46. Open alpine pastures, usually at around 2000 m and above, are inhabited by *Colias phicomone, Pieris callidice, Agriades glandon, Albulina orbitulus, Euphydryas glaciegenita* and many other butterfly species. Here a typical habitat in N. Italy: Südtirol: Schnalstal: ca. 1900 m. (Photo O. KUDRNA, 1980).

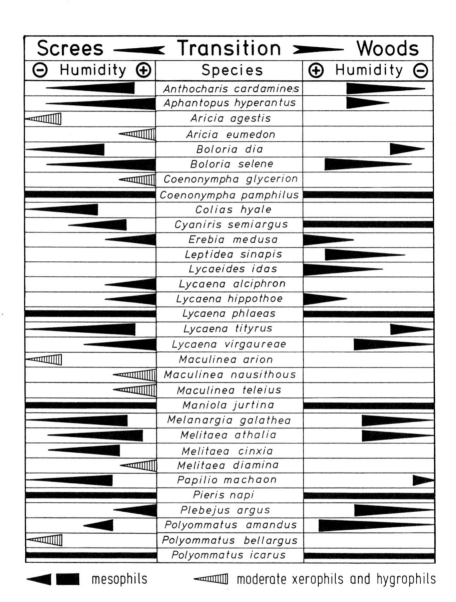

Fig. 47: Ecological preferences of relatively widespread butterfly species inhabiting meadows in central Europe.

is absent from meadows and confined to seminemoral mesophilic habitats of the upper montane zone (E. BALLETTO pers. comm.). Nevertheless, a speculative explanation may be possible in case of *A. eumedon:* the whole species' life cycle is centered on and in the immediate vicinity of its hostplants (used by both larvae and adults): *Geranium palustre, G. pratense, G. sylvaticum,* so far as it grows in profusion and is sheltered from wind; such conditions are fulfilled in small shallow depressions and along ditches where the humidity requirements of the species are satisfied also in moderately wet (i. e. essentially mesophilic) meadows. Nonetheless, no satisfactory explanation can be offered with regard to the colonies living in woodlands on *G. sylvaticum,* unless they represent a distinct genetical (and evolutionary) unit.

The regional bias of any conventional ecological classification is caused by the species distinct biotope preferences in different parts of its range; this is also evidenced by the comparison with the ecological classification of Italian butterflies (E. BALLETTO pers. comm.). The following examples are instructive:

*Melanargia galathea* inhabits xerothermophilic grassland on calcareous soils in England, mesophilic grassland (e. g. meadows) in central Europe, and mesophilic seminemoral habitats in Italy.

*Hipparchia semele* inhabits mesophilic beech woods in Sicily, seminemoral (sparse pine woods and clearings) mainly at altitudes between 1000 and 1700 m in Spain, open to seminemoral habitats in central Europe, xerothermophilic sites at sea level in northern Europe.

*Zerynthia polyxena* inhabits xerothermophilic seminemoral habitats in southern parts of central Europe and natural clearings in mesophilic woodlands in Italy.

The differences in the ecological preferences of a nominal species inhabiting larger geographical areas are expected: the species' adaptivness must have surely been one of the preconditions of its successful expansion. Nevertheless, the inhabiting of different habitats over an appreciable geographical range by the same nominal species could also be due to the presence in similar quality and quantity of the same ecoelements (cf. *Aricia eumedon,* above).

BALLETTO & KUDRNA (1985) analyzed ecological preferences of Italian butterfly species and arrived at the following conclusions.

Italian butterfly species, generally speaking, can be divided into two major ecological groups:
– species inhabiting alpine and subalpine ecological zones;
– species living at lower altitudes.

The species belonging to the first category are mostly linked to biotopes in their climax stage, the only exception are a few endemic species living on the screes. On the contrary, species living in the mediterranean and montane ecological zones are scarcely, if ever, inhabiting biotopes in their climax stage. Only very few species, in fact, appear to be primarily inhabitants of the woods. Woodlands, of course, are practically the only climax stage–though differentiated depending on local ecological factors–of the lower montane vegetational levels. It is interesting to note here, that apart from *Maniola nurag* (a rare endemic species confined to Sardinia, where it is linked to climax *Quercus ilex* woodlands) all other nemoral species living in Italy are fairly widespread in Europe. These butterflies are either common in central and northern Europe (e.g. *Apatura ilia, A. iris, Limenitis populi*) or in southern Europe (e.g. *Argynnis pandora*), or in eastern Europe (e.g. *Neptis rivularis, N. sappho*), or practically everywhere (e.g. *Argynnis paphia, Pararge aegeria, Celastrina argiolus, Thecla betulae,* etc.). The most characteristic feature common to nearly all nemoral species is that they spend much of their adult lives in the tree canopy (e.g. *Argynnis paphia, A. pandora, Apatura iris, A. ilia, Limenitis populi, L. camilla, L. reducta, Thecla betulae,* etc.), and normally come down to the ground level only to feed on some particularly attractive flowers and for oviposition, particularly if their larvae feed on herbaceous foodplants in the undergrowth. Only a few nemoral species live mostly at ground level (e.g. *Erebia aethiops, E. ligea, Pararge aegeria*).

All other species of the mediterranean and montane zones are linked to various seral stages. Subnemoral species form a large group of them even though, they show from species to species different levels of association with the woodland. These species were originally primarily inhabitants of natural woodland clearings, before the growing human populations devastated large areas of woodlands and utilized them for primitive farming and live stock grazing. It must be remembered that even in the absence of man, natural clearings were certainly rather widespread in the woods because of the combined action of the physical factors (e.g. lightenings, forest fires) and grazing of strong herds of large wild herbivores. Like the nemoral species, also the subnemoral butterflies are mostly widespread in Europe, with the exception of a few essentially insular isolates, mostly endemic (e.g. *Hipparchia blachieri, H. aristaeus, H. leighebi*). Hygrophilous species, too, form a particularly specialized group of species linked to certain seral stages; those living in Italy are all of central European origin, confined mainly to the north of the country. Another extreme ecological group consists of butterflies inhabiting screes, either at the alpine ecological zone, or lower down at the mediterranean vegetational zone. Owing to the well known selective factors deriving from the very extreme ecological con-

Fig. 48. A. habitat of European endemic species *Oeneis glacialis* in northern Italy: Südtirol: Schnalstal: ca. 2100 m. (Photo O. KUDRNA, 1980).

ditions afforded by the screes, this type of biotope was colonized by many species with restricted range, particularly endemic (butterflies, but also plants, etc.) which were thus allowed to escape overwhelming competition with more recent and more successful species. The following Italian butterflies are typical inhabitants of screes:

– *Erebia pluto, Oeneis glacialis:* alpine screes; (Fig. 48)
– *Erebia gorge:* alpine/subalpine screes;
– *Erebia scipio:* subalpine screes;
– *Erebia styx, E. montana:* subalpine/montane screes;
– *Parnassius apollo, Erebia meolans:* upper montane screes;
– *Erebia styrius:* lower montane screes;
– *Hipparchia neomiris:* mediterranean screes;
– *Euchloe tagis:* azonal screes.

The following four species are good examples to show the association between the butterfly, its larval hostplant, and a certain stage of succession of the vegetation of its biotope:

– *Anthocharis damone*–montane landslips (lava): mesophilous woodland–*Isatis tinctoria;*

Fig. 49. Adults of *Zerynthia polyxena* prefer in Italy open sunny places in vicinity of their larval biotope (cf. fig. 50). Here a locality in N. Italy: Piedmont: Novara: vic. Greggio. (Photo O. KUDRNA, 1985).

Fig. 50. Larval biotope of *Zerynthia polyxena*: natural succession in "abandoned" forests contributes to the spread of this on *Aristolochia* spp. feeding butterfly in many Italian localities (cf. fig. 49). Locality: N. Italy: Piedmont: Novara: vic. Greggio. (Photo O. KUDRNA, 1985).

Fig. 51. At high altitudes in the Alps, *Vaccinium* spp. and *Rhododendron* spp. offer a welcome shelter to many butterfly species and are often frequented by *Erebia epiphron, E. melampus, E. pandrose* and others. The habitat shown is in N. Italy: Südtirol: Schnalstal: ca. 2000 m. (Photo O. KUDRNA, 1980).

– *Iolana iolas*–montane landslips: mesophilous woodland–*Colutea arborescens;*
– *Zerynthia polyxena*–abandoned meadows: mesophilous woodland–*Aristolochia* spp.; (Fig. 49, 50);
– *Coenonympha corinna*–grazed maquis: ungrazed maquis–*Brachypodium ramosum* (?).

Less than 10% of Italian butterflies are strictly stenotopic species closely linked to a specific vegetational formation, as shown below:

– Rhododendro-Vaccinion: *Colias palaeno, Aricia nicias, Vacciniina optilete, Erebia aethiopella, E. euryale;* (Fig. 51);
– Laserpitio-Festucetum alpestris: *Erebia ottomana;*
– Nardo-Callunetea: *Erebia calcaria;*
– Carlino-Seslerium: *Erebia calcaria;*
– Festucetalia valesiacae (assoc. undef.): *Polyommatus humedasae;*
– Salicion albae: *Apatura ilia;*
– Querco-Carpinetum boreoitalicum: *Limenitis camilla;*
– Molinietum: *Coenonympha oedippus,* (Fig. 52, 53).

Fig. 52. Molinietum bordered by woodland–a typical habitat of *Coenonympha oedippus* (cf. fig. 53) in northern Italy: Piedmont: Novara district). Photo O. KUDRNA, 1983).

- Quercetalia pubescentis-petreae: *Arethusana arethusa*;
- Seslerio-Xerobromenion apenninum: *Polyommatus galloi*;
- Xerobromenion: *Polyommatus virgilius*;
- Cladonio-Ericetum: *Lycaeides corsica*;
- Quercetum ilicis galloprovinciale: *Hipparchia aristaeus, Maniola nurag, Aricia cramera, Charaxes jasius;*
- Quercetum ilicis mediterranae-montanum: *Papilio hospiton;*
- Brachypodion pheonicoidis: *Melanargia occitanica.*

It must be remembered that the existence of the relevant vegetational formation is an important precondition for the occurrence of all butterfly species, but that there are also other limiting factors which can be decisive in some cases; for instance *Erebia euryale* inhabits Rhododendro-Vaccinion only if it is associated with *Larix decidua*.

Terminology concerning butterfly habitats has been the cause of much confusion in many European languages owing to specific ecological terms used almost at random by lepidopterists (e. g. "heath" or German "Heide" is used for almost any kind of rather dry and more or less open habitat), and for the use of simple but meaningless terms to denote specific habitats

Fig. 53. *Coenonympha oedippus*, often accompanied by *Minois dryas* and *Lasiommata achine*, prefers to roost in thick undergrowth sheltered by trees (rather than in its typical open habitats). It may be one of the reasons why this species inhabits Molinietum especially if bordered by thick woodland. Here shown a part of the habitat of the species: N. Italy: Piedmont: Novara district). (Photo O. KUDRNA, 1983).

(e. g. open country, scrub, etc.). HEATH (1976) although apparently unaware of this deficiency produced a simple classification of Lepidoptera habitats of Great Britain, and although his units are quite broadly defined, they are useful at least for the time being. The classification of European butterfly habitats is important because:

– it can facilitate precise communication among lepidopterists, ecologists, etc.,
– nominal butterfly species confined to the same habitat type are exposed to similar, or identical, anthropogenic pressures (the vulnerability of its habitats is most significant for the survival of any stenotopic nominal species).

The development of a classification of European butterfly habitats is an important urgent task of ecological lepidopterology. The task is quite difficult and complicated because its classification units must be (1) unequivocally defined, (2) easy to recognize in nature (without special knowledge of advanced plant sociology, or other), (3) adequately broad, yet (4) species-group specific. It seems that certain units of physiognomic-phytosociological plant formations (ELLENBERG & MUELLER-DOMBOIS 1967) may be employed with advantage for this purpose.

It should be mentioned that an ecological classification of butterflies, a classification of their habitats, and the structure of butterfly communities are three different aspects of butterfly ecology. Whereas the ecological classification of butterflies is based on an analysis and comparison of their ecological requirements, the habitats are compared and described according to their properties. If certain butterfly communities prove to be closely related to certain phytosociological units, it will not indicate that they are one and the same thing.

Habitat management is usually understood as a means of propagating a certain nominal species: the habitat is transformed and/or maintained in such a way that it offers optimal conditions for its long term survival. Any transformation of the habitat means drastic changes which are very likely to damage the ecological balance and probably effect disadvantages for the rest of the community. At such a point the conservation of nature comes to an end, and is replaced by something similar to a "safari park". Should a habitat require regular management, it must be the task of the ecologist to develop forms of minimal neutral management, which while maintaining its continued identity will not affect the internal balance of the habitat's biocenosis.

# 6 Outline of a European comprehensive conservation programme for indigenous butterflies

A comprehensive conservation programme – a term introduced here for the first time – is an applied scientific concept aimed at the safeguarding from adverse anthropogenic pressures for an indefinite period of a taxonomic group indicated. The primary task of any one comprehensive conservation programme must be to preserve a natural evolution of the taxonomic group concerned in a territory defined either free of, or by application of, neutral anthropogenic pressures. Whereas the usual conservation efforts take care of the so-called threatened species only, the comprehensive conservation programme concentrates on the full ecological and taxonomic diversity, free of regional (local) bias, using so far as possible preventive measures aimed rather at the conservation of the whole communities than at the protection of single nominal species.

## 6.1 Definition of principles and priorities

The basic principle of the comprehensive conservation programme for European butterflies is the employment of extensive preventive conservation measures in strong contrast to the approach of intensive protection of single nominal species. The stress placed here upon the term "conservation" rather than "protection" is a very important one. All conservation measures must be concentrated on the prevention of anthropogenically caused damage rather than on correcting it afterwards, and causing perhaps by possibly not entirely suitable means further damage and destruction to nature. The "preventive conservation" is, incidentally, also by far the easiest and most economical (i. e. the cheapest and at the same time most reliable) method.

It is precisely the principle of preventive conservation that makes full use of the exceptional bioindicator value of butterflies as a whole, which is at its best in ecologically balanced natural communities and deteriorates progressively in degraded habitats and areas.

Also in secondary habitats which have evolved historically owing to certain human agencies, such as traditional meadows, pastures or "seminatural" woodland edges, inhabited by valuable communities of mainly mesophilous species, the forms of management must remain moderate and moderating to maintain the natural continuity. Only in very rare cases have some recently created secondary habitats been successfully invaded by highly specialized stenotopic species at the time common and widespread in their vicinity; such species and their habitats deserve full protection and may contribute to the safeguarding of such nominal species in Europe, as is the case with the endangered species *Lycaena dispar* living along main irrigation canals in rice fields in northern Italy (cf. figs. 18, 19 p. 70, 71), even if these habitats lack conditions for a natural community of butterfly species. Nevertheless, such extreme cases are always exceptionally rare.

Resources available for conservation projects–even in the case of hypothetical generous governments–are not unlimited. Their efficient application depends upon the clear definition of priorities, taking into account above all the urgency and the necessity of the undertaking, judged from the European point of view, and if necessary regardless of some national or local wishes, which may be relevant to European needs (cf.: protection of *Maculinea arion* in Great Britain).

It has been shown that the destruction of habitats, whatever its form and causes may be, is the main factor causing the overwhelming proportion of the decline of butterflies in Europe. The simple, logical and, indeed, perfectly obvious countermeasure is, therefore, an effective conservation of valuable habitats of diverse communities. This can be realized only if the sites and their exact location are known, their individual value is fully recognized, and the relevant information regarding these sites made available to all bodies concerned, regardless of country or region. Consequently it is necessary to set up a

● European register of valuable butterfly sites (v. 6.2).

The total stocks of all European butterfly species have been declining, some have diminished so far that the extinction in Europe of the nominal indigenous species concerned is only a question of time should the adverse causal factors continue to determine the trend of the stocks' development. As a countermeasure it is necessary to prepare a

● Programme for the conservation/protection of species acutely threatened by extinction in Europe (v. 6.3).

A number of butterfly species are exclusive to Europe and some of these endemic species are peculiar to small parts of Europe only, many of them confined to one or a few known sites only, their stocks being correspondingly low. These species, although not necessarily directly threatened by human agencies, are always very sensitive and have no natural reserves to enable them to survive a long term slow decline. Their survival depends upon setting up a

● Programme for the conservation of rare endemic species (v. 6.4).

A number of common and widespread butterfly species, particularly in central Europe, have been losing ground because of adverse changes inflicted upon their habitats by various forms of rationalisation of agriculture and forestry practices, which have made their former sites uninhabitable and even caused extensive regional extinction of some of them. Before these species become rare and isolated beyond the possibility of future expansion, it is necessary to set up for them a

● Programme for the conservation of eurychoric species (v. 6.5).

Some stenotopic butterfly species inhabit in certain areas unusual (extreme, relict) habitats, forming habitat specific ecotypes and representing possibly evolutionary units of new incipient species. Their sensitivity is comparable to that of rare endemic species and their long term survival depends on a

● Programme for the conservation of incipient species (v. 6.6).

Collecting for commercial purposes, overcollecting of certain species or populations, and trade in butterflies have been responsible for the decline and local extinction of many panoramic species. To combat these and similar threats it is necessary to draw up

● Guidelines for the collecting of and trade in European butterflies (v. 6.7).

Last but not least considerations must be given to the forms of administration, implementation and further development of this programme (v. 6.8).

## 6.2 European register of butterfly sites

The overwhelming proportion of the decline of butterflies in Europe is due to the destruction of their biotopes, whatever form this may take. It has been shown that extraction of a single vital ecoelement may lead to the extinction of a nominal species over the whole territory affected and is bound to contribute to some further changes in the composition of the community, which are likely to be deleterious. Obviously, the destruction of the whole habitat has the same result but the end comes more suddenly and usually affects the whole community at once. The exceptional value of butterflies in the conservation of nature is above all in their properties as bioindicators; this value must decrease with the increasing artificiality of the community. (All single nominal species protection programmes must lead inevitably to the devaluation of the indicating value of that species. Consequently, one of the first steps in the conservation of butterflies must be the

● Conservation (protection) of butterfly sites*.

There are two principle criteria for the protection of any site in Europe: (1) the diversity of (richness in) nominal species, and (2) the presence of exceptionally highly valued species (i. e. rare endemic species and/or species acutely threatened with extinction in Europe). The first criterion can particularly well be judged by the implementation of the biogeographical disposition of individual nominal species of the community present (i. e. the utilization of the chorological index). The second criterion can be judged by the implementation of the list of rare endemic species and acutely threatened species included elsewhere in this work. It must be remembered that relatively few sites will satisfy more than one criterion, and that overlapping of criteria is not a condition for the inclusion of the site concerned in the register, or for its protection. In choice of sites, general preference is to be given to climax biome habitats, and to habitats left to proceed through seral stages, because these require no special management.

It is impossible to repair sites which have suffered more than very slight damage, and even fairly slight damage may prove irreparable in some cases owing to the technical difficulties involved in any such undertaking. The safeguarding of all sites depends, therefore, entirely on effective

● Preventive measures.

Preventive measures can be possible only if the existence of the site, and its value, is known to the authorities concerned, that is if the site is defined, described, recorded (and perhaps named), and the data concerning the site are accessible at short notice. This urgently requires the setting up of a

● European butterfly site register,

---

* Note. Owing to the exceptional value of butterflies as bioindicators it may be convenient to use the term "invertebrate site" rather than "butterfly site" as a better expression of its significance. This is, however, a technical matter beyond the scope of this work.

perhaps as the first part of the future computer aided data bank on European butterflies.

All national, regional and local authorities granting planning permissions would have to be made aware of the presence of valuable habitats in the areas of their competence; they would have to ask advice before they granted any kind of permit to make alterations to the site (habitat). Also land owners, forestry commissions and farmers would have to be made aware of all valuable sites in their ownership or under their management or supervision.

The necessity and urgency of the above proposed measures is easy to exemplify. *Erebia christi* is one of the rarest European endemic butterfly species, confined to a few small localities in southern Switzerland, where it lives usually in small colonies and suffering in some places additionally from overcollecting, and recently found also across the border in northern Italy (LEIGHEB 1976). HEATH (1981) misinterpreted the distribution of the species: Simplon is in southern Switzerland (not in Italy, as he stated) and there seem to be no reliable records from the Val Formazza (if there are any at all) and confused thus an important issue. One of the best sites of the species is (was?) in the Laquintal, in size not much larger than 1 ha. Widening and straightening of a narrow dirt track cum footpath leading through the valley led to the destruction of much of the species' site, which was in the way of making two sharp bends easier for cars used apparently only by the commuters to a few small chalets a short way further up the valley. Now it is too late to attempt anything more than hoping for the best. Prevention at the right time would have saved the site and the colony of *E. christi*, without preventing the access to the valley.

All registered sites must be mapped. For the mapping, maps 1 : 25.000 are probably the most convenient compromise so far as they are available; good substitute maps would be 1 : 50.000 or the nearest possible equivalent, maps over 1 : 200.000 are useless. It is rather important to remember that a buffer zone protecting the site should be included, particularly so in case of all sites which could be destroyed by sinking of water tables in the area. The basic data concerning each site must comprise its photos and a list of all species recorded, with quantitative notes on their populations, and a brief description of the site with notes regarding the land use. The inclusion of further data subject to its becoming available could be reserved for the future reports.

The sites should be regularly monitored and annual reports compiled on the species observed, and filed for future use. Regular inspection of certain sites by rangers may be worth the effort, for instance to prevent unscrupulous collectors taking commercial advantage of rich butterfly colonies. The legal status of (at least the most important) sites must also be settled.

## 6.3 Conservation (protection) of species acutely threatened by extinction in Europe

The decisive factor determining the degree of relative resistance of a nominal butterfly species is the proportion of its stocks located safely away from all harmful anthropogenic pressures. All butterfly species acutely threatened in Europe are ecological specialists. Because the stocks (i. e. the number of colonies) of all acutely threatened species have been depleated to what may be now called a critical minimum, the aim of the conservation programme must be, in the first place, to stop their further decline by excluding the negative (and usually species specific) anthropogenic pressures from the existing colonies. As the reasons responsible for the decline of these species has usually been the loss of habitat and sites, the first step must be safeguarding of their remaining vital colonies. This can be exemplified by the most seriously threatened European butterfly species:

*Coenonympha oedippus* is doubtless the most seriously threatened butterfly species. It inhabits natural lowland sheltered fens covered with *Molinia caerulea* at altitudes ranging from sea level to over 400 m, and cannot withstand any form of cultivation, apparently including hay cutting (BISCHOF 1968). This type of habitat has become increasingly rare owing to draining often for rice cultivation. The survival of the species in Europe depends therefore on effective protection of its remaining European colonies, above all those in northern Italy (e. g. Piemonte) and in western France (e. g. along the Atlantic coast). The significance of the above mentioned colonies, particularly those in northern Italy, is that they are still quite rich in stocks of the species and that they are not immediately threatened at present (the land is of secondary interest in short term planning, at least in some localities). Any further loss of sites is likely to bring about the extinction of the species also here (it has already become extinct in some European countries), as its habitat is naturally restricted and highly threatened.

Fairly similar but perhaps not quite as critical is the situation of *Coenonympha hero* which still has some relatively rich colonies in Scandinavia. This species is also a hygrophil inhabiting *Carex* sp. covered grassland in woodlands.

*Lycaena dispar* is the only ecological specialist among the threatened species apparently capable of coping with a certain amount of anthropogenic pressure and of colonizing successfully in certain circumstances even secondary habitats, so far as they are within the limited dispersal potential of the species, apart from offering a free ecological niche. *L. dispar* was formerly common and widespread in the marshes along the river Po and some of its tributaries in northern Italy (e. g. in Piemonte). After their drainage and subsequent cultivation chiefly for rice fields, the species having lost over a period of several years its natural habitat invaded the newly created ecological niche and became well established along the main irrigation canals so long as they were not methodically treated with herbicides or cut regularly over long stretches (for the same reasons the species is unable to establish permanent colonies along the smaller secondary canals and ditches with similar conditions). North Italian colonies of *L. dispar* belong to the best in Europe, and can be conveniently maintained despite the intensive cultivation of the area (BALLETTO, TOSO & BARBERIS 1982). A special area specific ecological programme for this species must additionally include agreements with farmers and land owners where necessary.

The following steps must form a part of the conservation (protection) programme for any acutely threatened nominal species:

- Detailed mapping of all viable sites inhabited by the species (including a buffer zone wherever applicable); the viability of any site is enhanced by the lesser sensitivity of the area to anthropogenic pressures.
- Recording of the past and present management of the site and further relevant documentation (e. g. photos, list of other species, specific threats, etc.).
- An exhaustive ecological study of the species to provide information for specific forms of management, should these become necessary in the future.
- Monitoring of the species in selected sites, taking into account possible annual fluctuations.
- If necessary full legal protection of some sites, with restrictions on collecting should these become necessary (weak populations and species with small total stocks likely to be subject to overcollecting).

A list of acutely threatened species is found elsewhere. Since loss of habitat is generally the most important factor responsible for the species decline, a compilation of a preliminary record on each species, providing basic data regarding its distribution, biology and ecology could be most useful.

## 6.4  Conservation of rare endemic species

Over one third of the 446 indigenous butterfly species known from Europe are endemic species. Nearly two thirds of them are peculiar to a rather small territory, such as an island, a peninsula, or a mountain range; some 23 of these 93 endemic species are confined to very small areas ranging from the type-locality to several known colonies at the most. These are the true rare endemic species. The remaining 70 endemic species are somewhat more "widespread" and often abundant in the localities they inhabit. Although natural rarity of a nominal species is not necessarily a cause for con-

Fig. 54. A habitat of a rare endemic European species *Erebia christi* which is confined to a few restricted localities in southern Switerland and northern Italy, here being destroyed by a widening of a small secondary road leading to a few weekend chalets further up in the valley. Switzerland: Wallis: Laggintal. (Photo O. Kudrna, 1983).

cern of the species' survival, the rare endemic species (chorological index 13 or 14) are particularly sensitive to anthropogenic pressures because:

- Their long term survival depends upon the safeguarding of a particular, often very small, territory, in some cases of a single known site, where they live.
- Their small total stock offers no "reserves" and therefore very low resistance to anthropogenic pressures, particularly for instance during successive unfavourable years (and even regardless of anthropogenic influences).
- Their potential to disperse and colonize new sites is at present negligible or even non-existent, as they are apparently unable to adapt to ecological conditions outside their own locality.

European rare endemic species (sensu stricto), arranged alphabetically, with family name abbreviated in parenthesis, and countries they inhabit:

Fig. 55. *Erebia flavofasciata* is one of European rare endemic species confined to a few localities in southern Switzerland and northen Italy. Here a locality in the Val Formazza (N. Italy: Piedmont: Novara distr.) at ca. 2200 m. (Photo O. KUDRNA, 1983).

*Aglais ichnusa* (NY) – France: Corsica; Italy: Sardinia
*Agriades zullichi* (LY) – Spain: Sierra Nevada
*Apatura metis* (NY) – Hungary: Yugoslavia
*Colias balcanica* (PI) – Yugoslavia
*Cupido carswelli* (LY) – Spain: Prov. Murcia and Malaga
*Erebia christi* (SA) – Switzerland: Wallis; Italy: Piemonte (Fig. 54)
*Erebia flavofasciata* (SA) – S. Switzerland; N. Italy (Fig. 55)
*Euphydryas wolfensbergeri* (NY) – Austria; N. Italy; Switzerland
*Gonepteryx maderensis* (PI) – Portugal: Madeira
*Hipparchia bacchus* (SA) – Spain: Canary Is.: Hiero
*Hipparchia ballettoi* (SA) – Italy: Napoli: Mt. Faito
*Hipparchia gomera* (SA) – Spain: Canary Is.: Gomera
*Hipparchia malickyi* (SA) – Greece: Lesbos
*Kretania psylorita* (LY) – Greece: Crete
*Melanargia pherusa* (SA) – Italy: Sicily
*Melitaea asteria* (NY) – Austria; Italy; Switzerland
*Melitaea neglecta* (NY) – Germany: "DDR"; Czechoslovakia (?)
*Polyommatus ainsae* (LY) – Spain: Pyrenees (s. l.)

Fig. 56. A site of rare European endemic species *Polyommatus golgus* in an advanced stage of destruction, being "utilized" for the expansion of a nearby winter sports centre. *P. golgus* inhabits somewhat moist grassy slopes in the Sierra Nevada and is very local, although there are probably some "undiscovered" colonies in less accessible parts of the Sierra Nevada, above 2000 m. The locality shown (now presumed destroyed) was situated on the outskirts of the tourist centre 'Sol y Nieve' in the western Sierra Nevada (S. Spain: Prov. Granada) at about 2000 m. (Photo O. KUDRNA, 1976).

*Polyommatus galloi* (LY) – Italy: Mt. Pollino
*Polyommatus golgus* (LY) – Spain: Sierra Nevada (Fig. 56)
*Polyommatus humedasae* (LY) – Italy: Piemonte
*Polyommatus violetae* (LY) – Spain: Prov. Malaga
*Pseudochazara amymone* (SA) – Greece: Macedonia
*Pseudochazara cingovskii* (SA) – Yugoslavia: Macedonia
*Pseudochazara euxina* (SA) – U.S.S.R.: Krym
*Pseudochazara orestes* (SA) – Greece: Macedonia

A number of other endemic species are confined to a restricted range similar to the one of the species listed above, yet they are known to be abundant in their localities (e. g. *Hipparchia leighebi, H. sbordonii,* etc.): these species are excluded from the list as they are not really rare, and/or inhabit areas relatively free of anthropogenic pressures. Their exclusion is also the result of the necessity to draw priorities, however subjective they may be.

As these species do not live (or have not yet been recorded) outside Europe, the European countries where they live carry the full responsibility for their survival. Since these species usually belong to the less well known taxa, the individual conservation programmes must be based on a good proportion of original research: a special ecological study of every species should be commissioned as a matter of some urgency. Uniform comprehensive treatment of every species would be of some advantage and could well serve as a topic for doctoral theses for graduate students. A preliminary report on every species would also be useful. The individual projects must be based upon the compilation and evaluation of all published papers and other available sources of information. The resulting pro gramme must include the following aspects:

- Detailed mapping of species' site/s (including a buffer zone wherever necessary) using 1:25.000 maps (or nearest equivalent available).
- Record of the present and past site management and further relevant documentation (e. g. photos, list of other species, specific threats, etc.).
- An exhaustive ecological study of the species to provide information for specific forms of management, should these become necessary in the future.
- Monitoring of the species' trend, taking into account possible annual fluctuations.
- If necessary full legal protection of the species or site, with restrictions on collecting and inspections of site/s by rangers should this become necessary.

As some of the rare endemic species are also taxonomically rather poorly known, their status must be studied and this may also require collecting of material for morphological and other comparative investigations; this must be done with all due respect to the limited stocks of the species concerned.

There are probably still possibilities to discover hitherto unknown colonies of rare endemic species; every opportunity must therefore be taken to visit potential sites in the zone of their occurrence, and search for them. The recent discoveries in northern Italy of *Erebia christi* and *E. flavofasciata* (LEIGHEB 1976) show that it can be done.

The further about 70 endemic species listed below are also fairly localized, and will have to be investigated in a similar manner to the rare endemic species (as outlined above), but perhaps with less strict conservation measures. Unless they are specifically threatened their safeguarding is not quite as urgent. Also some panoramic species (marked with asterisk) may urgently need protection from overcollecting for commercial ends.

Fig. 57. A typical habitat of *Erebia hispania* near Panticosa (at about 1600 m) in central Pyrenees (N. Spain: Prov. Huesca), one of European endemic satyrids. (Photo O. KUDRNA, 1973).

**Papilionidae:** *Papilio hospiton\*, Zerynthia cretica\*;*

**Pieridae:** *Gonepteryx cleobule\*, Gonepteryx palmae, Pieris balcana, P. cheiranthi;*

**Lycaenidae:** *Agriades dardanus, Agriades pyrenaicus, Aricia anteros, Cyclirius webbianus, Glaucopsyche paphos, Lycaeides corsica, L. nevadensis, Plebejus hesperica, P. lycidas, Polyommatus aroaniensis, P. caelestissima, P. dolus, P. fabressei, P. menelaos, P. nephohiptamenos, P. philippi, P. virgilius, Pseudophilotes barbagiae, P. panoptes, Ultraaricia anteros, U. orpheus;*

**Satyridae:** *Coenonympha corinna, C. elbana, C. thyrsis, Erebia aethiopella, E. boreomontanum, E. calcaria, E. claudina, E. epistygne, E. eriphyle, E. gorgone, E. hispania, E. lefebvrei, E. melas, E. nivalis, E. orientalis, E. palarica\*, E. rhodopensis, E. scipio, E. sthennyo, E. zapateri, Hipparchia aristaeus, H. azorina, H. blachieri, H. caldeirense, H. christenseni, H. cretica, H. cypriensis, H. leighebi, H. maderensis, H.*

*miguelensis, H. neomiris, H. sbordonii, H. wyssii, Lasiommata tigelius, Maniola cypricola, M. nurag, Melanargia arge, Pararge xiphia, P. xiphioides, Pseudochazara graeca; (Fig. 57);*

**Nymphalidae:** *Argynnis elisa\*, Boloria graeca, Euphydryas beckeri, E. cynthia, E. glaciegenita, Melitaea varia.*

## 6.5 Conservation of eurychoric species

The general decline of eurychoric species which has been taking place over the last two or three decades particularly in most of central Europe has been caused in the first place by the changes in land use practice. The two main causers (BLAB & KUDRNA 1982) are

- agriculture: meliorations on a large scale, land consolidation, introduction of high production resistant forage grass varieties, use of artificial fertilizers, destruction of permanent grassland, weed and pest control, etc., and
- Forestry: abandonment of coppicing, extracting of weed trees, exclusion of grassland/woodland ecotone and transitional zones, increased growing of coniferous trees, loss of permanent grassland (meadows, pastures) in woodland, weed control and pest control, etc.;

all these measures amount to intensification and rationalization of production practices. A detailed analysis and classification of all causal factors relevant to central Europe and evidenced by examples from the Federal Republic of Germany was published (BLAB & KUDRNA) 1982.

The species affected (cf.) are essentially not threatened because their remaining stocks are adequate and their decline has always been chiefly regional, although there often pronounced. For example the apparent disappearance of *Papilio machaon* after extensive land consolidation and melioration schemes happened suddenly in various parts of Germany and Czechoslovakia, while in other parts of those countries, which have been spared, the species is still quite as abundant as before. Bearing in mind that the majority of data on the distribution of butterflies are supplied by collectors (as a byproduct of their activities), and that eurychoric species are not very attractive to a collector, it is not suprising that the decline is usually observed too late, after the species has disappeared from the region. (Irregular annual fluctuation of abundance of some species is also a complementary factor). Our contemporary (particularly central European) countryside probably contains barriers impassable even to most of the eurychoric species, which means that regionally extinct species cannot reestablish their colonies by natural reinvasion should their former site become inhabitable again, an extensive conservation programme for eurychoric species is necessary and urgent especially in central Europe. The basic principle of this programme is the safeguarding of existing and the creation of new ecological cells in the countryside (KLOFT 1978). The programme has two aspects:

- Safeguarding of selected sites inhabited by butterfly communities rich in species, both in meadowland and woodland ecosystems.
- Creation of substitute habitats in suitable areas, outside agricultural land and intensively managed forests, within the natural dispersal of potentially invading species.

For both these purposes nature parks also aimed at human recreation should be ideal, so far as they fulfil the conditions mentioned above. The programme requires the reestablishment of natural traditionally managed meadows and/or pastures (to replace the usually sickly looking grass monoculture called an English lawn) rich in indigenous grass and plant species. It should also be possible to create, perhaps over a longer period, natural grassland/woodland ecotones in suitable places in wooded areas. Methods for the creation of substitute habitats have never been adequately scientifically investigated, and there is a good opportunity for cooperation among universities, nature conservation authorities, regional planning authorities, and entomologists. Basic guidelines regarding selection and management of such habitats have been set out by BLAB & KUDRNA (1982).

The safeguarding of selected sites depends of their exact mapping, recording of species and planning of suitable forms of management. Unless they are to be purchased to become nature reserves, which is probably mostly unnecessary, an agreement between nature conservation authorities and their owners must be drawn up as to their future management. Indirect financial incentives should be made available to farmers and land owners leaving valuable sites traditionally managed where they are inhabited by rich and diverse colonies of mesophilous butterfly species. The forestry authorities should be requested to consider traditional forms of management for woodlands rich in butterflies. It must be the responsibility of regional nature conservation authorities to pay attention to such sites and provide the necessary guidance as to their correct management. Good opportunities to find new sites should be in environments where all cultivation is being withdrawn. Eurychoric, essentially mesophilous, butterfly species are an inseparable part of our environment; it would be very sad if human neglect made our–and their!–countryside uninhabitable for them so that it became necessary to create nature reserves to secure their survival.

## 6.6 Conservation of incipient species

Incipient species are groups or single populations of a nominal species differing in some for the evolution of this taxonomic unit significant exclusive hereditary features from the rest of the nominal species. This here introduced definition can be elucidated by the following examples:

*Papilio machaon* is essentially a mesophil inhabiting open grassland (with heliophilous preferences), but its English populations confined to the Broads in Norfolk constitute an entirely different ecotype. They are (hyper)hygrophils inhabiting fens flooded for most of the year and their larva feed as monophags on *Peucedanum palustre,* a hostplant not normally used by the species' larvae elsewhere in Europe. The adults differ only very slightly in morphological features and are not easy to tell from the first generation of central Europe. The populations of the Norfolk Broads are monovoltine (as against essentially multivoltine Continental populations) and probably differ also in their behaviour.

*Minois dryas* (cf. note no. 59) inhabits in Bavaria fens and watermeadows ("Streuwiesen") and differs in this respect from the rest of populations of the species, its larva feeds as a monophag on *Molinia coerulea.* Although constant taxonomic differences have not been established, this ecotype differs biologically in some significant hereditary characters from the rest of the species. *Colias palaeno* and *Vacciniina optilete* are boreo-alpine species inhabiting in central Europe lowland peat bogs. Although they apparently do not differ in taxonomically significant characters from other European populations of the species, the lowland populations represent a highly specialized heriditary ecotype adapted to their peculiar environment.

There are numerous other (groups of) populations of relict origin peculiar to certain specialized habitats and differing biologically (not necessarily also morphologically) from the rest of the species. Each of them represents a singular unit of evolution and – given time and conditions – could evolve to become a distinct nominal species. Protection (conservation) of these populations from adverse anthropogenic pressures amounts to allowing the natural evolution to take its course. Also certain recurrent natural hybrids, such as *Polyommatus coerulescens* (cf. note 89) represent from the evolutionary point of view similar, and in their significance comparable, entities.

All these forms are generally very incompletely, often even poorly, known, unless they happen to be panoramic species and have been given a subspecific rank, which alone does not necessarily mean that they are taxonomically distinct. The hereditary ecological properties of these populations are usually unknown and it is hardly surprising, that their list cannot be compiled at present. The compilation of data for the preparation of their list must, therefore, form the first step in their conservation, to be followed by the compilation of their sites (register and mapping). The protection of their sites and habitats is the most important step because their distribution is usually restricted, their stocks often low, their dispersal potential negligible and, above all, because they form a part of a unique ecological and evolutionary development, from which they are inseparable. It is unlikely that the indefinite survival of incipient species can be secured outside nature reserves and similar protected sites; also overcollecting can threaten their existence.

Protection of incipient species is essentially a task to be carried out by regional conservation programmes, although their status can be decided better outside that region.

## 6.7 Guidelines for collecting of and trade in European butterflies

The significance of collecting as both a method of study of European butterflies and as a potential harmful factor has been discussed at some length elsewhere and attention has been drawn to the possible and actual adverse effects on butterfly populations. It is fully justified to state that:

● Collecting of butterflies for any other purpose than legitimate research, educational and conservation purposes is unnecessary and not morally justified.

● Trade in wild caught butterflies–sales of pure research material to museums and similar public or private research institutions excepted–is most deplorable.

Nonetheless, there are many immoral and most deplorable things we must live with because they cannot be changed at present. It might be relatively easy to draft new or amend the present legislation limiting or excluding the trade in butterflies within the European Community, and it may become possible to persuade some other western countries to introduce similar legislation (cf. "Convention of International Trade in Endangered Species" of 1975, usually abbreviated "CITES", which included also one European species, *Parnassius apollo,* and to which several European countries are signatories). To some, a total ban on all trade in butterflies including their import/export between countries might appear the ideal answer. It is, however, quite unlikely that such legislation would be generally and universally accepted by most of European countries, that it could be enforced and, above all, that its side effects would not harm lepidopterological research, and in the end also the conservation of butterflies in Europe. It is, therefore, necessary to consider other, more practical, possibilities.

The main stream of trade in butterflies (and, indeed, all Lepidoptera and other insects) passes through two principal channels:

● Insektenbörsen organized in major German cities (e. g. Frankfurt a. M., München, Düsseldorf, etc.), in Switzerland (e. g. Basel) and hidden behind a much nicer "exhibition" in England (London), or in smaller measures also in other countries (e. g. spring and autumn "Exchange Day" in Czechoslovakia: Prague).

● Journal/supplement "Insektenbörse" appearing twice a month free to all subscribers of the Entomologische Zeitschrift (i. e. Ent. Z., Frankf. a. M.), published by the Kernen Verlag (Stuttgart) and edited from the Senckenberg Museum (Frankfurt a. M.).

The individual insect sale days are usually organized by local entomological societies as a reliable fund raising exercise. It would be surprising if a commercial publisher kept going, and indeed kept steadily expanding, a loss making journal, particularly if its sales were depending on the attractiveness of its supplement. Taking these financial aspects into consideration, the following two proposals would surely be a welcome voluntary contribution towards the conservation of European butterflies by those who commercialize them:

● The organizers of insect sale days (whatever they are called) should all agree to impose a certain levy on every specimen offered for sale, paid prior to the sale and not refundable for specimens not sold; it may be convenient to accept one Swiss Franc (i. e. Sfr. 1,—) or an equivalent in the national currency as a standard charge everywhere in Europe. This levy would be separate from the other usual charges made to traders by the organizers. Additionally, every visitor should be charged over and above the price of every ticket (if entrance fee is charged) Sfr. 1,— or equivalent in national currency. Both levies would be paid by the organizers to a specific research fund, to be called perhaps "Fund for the Conservation of European Butterflies" (v. further below).

● The publishers of journals and supplements like the "Insektenbörse" should voluntarily agree to pass at least 50% of their before tax profit gained by the publication of the journal/s concerned (or journals to the subscribers to which the "free" supplement is made available). Also this should be paid into the same "Fund for the Conservation of European Butterflies"; the publishers could additionally enjoy the tax relief usually available on such donations.

The establishment of such a fund, under the management of trustees, would hardly present any obstacles, and either the "Lepidoptera Research Foundation" or another reputable experienced research fund management (e. g. the "British Entomological and Natural History Society") would be suitable executors. The "Fund for the Conservation of European Butterflies" could provide financial support for research concerned with the conservation of butterflies in Europe, and possibly (on a money return basis) support the publication of certain conservation relevant scientific papers.

It is interesting to note, that the Association of British Entomological Suppliers has taken the initiative to restrict the trade in some threatened butterfly species. Their voluntary code is now 12 years old:

**Entomological Suppliers Association Code of Conservation Responsibility**
In November 1974 a Meeting of the main Entomological Suppliers was convened at the Royal Entomological Society to agree a code of Conservation Responsibility. The following points form the initial code:

1. A **"Red List"** of endangered species from overseas will be kept and any species on the list will not be bought by the Parties to the code or offered for sale. The list will be as brief as possible, and only species relevant to those which are likely to be imported will be included.
   The first three species are:
   *Troides aeacus kaguya*
   *Dilias hyparete peirene*
   *Delias aglaia*
   All from the island of Taiwan.

2. **Specimens of Protected or Endangered British Species** will not be collected for sale at all. Parties to the code wish to stress that sale of such specimens from old collections will continue, and it is by this means that collectors can continue to obtain rarities.
   **Species that will not be collected for sale as collectors' specimens**
   Large Blue *(Maculinea arion)*
   Chequered Skipper *(Carterocephalus palaemon)*
   Large Tortoiseshell *(Nymphalis polychloros)*
   Black Hairstreak *(Strymonidia pruni)* [= *Nordmannia pruni*]
   Brown Hairstreak *(Thecla betulae)*
   Heath Fritillary *(Mellicta athalia)* [= *Melitaea athalia*]

3. **Offered Series of wild-caught British Specimens** will be refused if they have been caught for the purposes of selling as a stock to suppliers. Genuine duplicates and "thinnings" from a collection are considered as

being quite distinct, but the Suppliers wish to make it clear that they will not go out themselves (or let any other person) and collect stocks of scarce or endangered butterflies, or in any way endanger our native fauna. Similarly livestock of endangered species will not be collected.

Note: The Parties to the code of Conservation Responsibility will regularly review the question of species for the Red List. The species will be confined to those whose need is critical, and in full agreement of those concerned. Moths will, of course, be included as necessary. The question has arisen over *Parnassius apollo* which is declining in some areas, yet is abundant in others. In this case the species may be restricted from defined areas.

The most complete analysis of world trade in Swallowtail butterflies (Papilionidae) was recently presented by COLLINS & MORRIS (1985). They recognized three different types of trade:

- Low value & high volume trade: Large numbers of common exotic species. Typical exporting country is Taiwan. Specimens are supplied in bulk to dealers, many sold as art objects.
- High value & low volume trade: Quality specimens usually with scientific data for collectors. Typical are supplies from Papua New Guinea (ranching and farming of butterflies).
- Livestock trade: Relatively low volume trade including both tropical and European species, the former mostly to breeders, the latter to collectors seeking perfect bred material.

COLLINS & MORRIS (1985) observed that massive collecting of butterflies in Taiwan (and possibly other countries) shows no apparent traces, such as depleted stocks. This is an interesting observation which should be further investigated.

The centre of world trade in butterflies is in Japan. At least some European prices are influenced by Japanese traders. There is extensive legislation to limit butterfly trade in Europe. *Parnassius apollo* is the only species listed by CITES. The reason for the protecting of *P. apollo* is probably only emotional as the species is widespread and locally abundant. COLLINS & MORRIS (1985) concluded their analysis of commercial collecting and trade in butterflies as follows: "Private collecting of butterflies can be an instructive hobby and is important for research into ecology, population dynamics, genetics and taxonomy. It brings a great deal of pleasure to many people and does not usually threaten butterfly species. However, in a small number of cases, irresponsible over-collection can cause a permanent decline. The latter is particularly true if the species has a very small range, has naturally low populations and low reproductive rate, or has already been severely reduced by other impacts. Commercial collecting can be an important source of income and should not be dismissed as necessarily harmful. If populations are harvested in a suitable manner, than both conservation and commercial interests can be satisfied. Habitat destruction is the main cause of decline in butterfly populations, but there is a danger that commercial collecting levels that were suitable in the past may become damaging in the ever-decreasing areas of suitable habitat." This is a very realistic assessment, except that the authors–both apparently lacking extensive practical knowledge of collecting–have overlooked that it is usually extremely difficult to overcollect a "rare" species (naturally low populations) because it is difficult to find and catch it. There are very few European species which might have naturally low reproductive rate, perhaps *Oeneis glacialis* is one of them. It would be very difficult to immagine that overcollecting could endanger it: it is hard to find and catch!

COLLINS & MORRIS (1985) closing their considerations stated: "Legislation against collecting and trade is unlikely to preserve a species unless parallel measures to protect its habitat are also enforced." How very true! The failure of German anti-collecting legislation to stop the decline of German Papilionidae-species proves their point; German legislation has never been accompanied by adequate protection of species' habitats. The conclusions arrived at by COLLINS & MORRIS (1985) differ considerably from the view expressed by EBERT, HESSELBARTH & KASY (1978) and PRETSCHER & SCHULT (1978).

With the exception of the assessment of world trade in papilionids made by COLLINS & MORRIS (1985), all critiques considering European and Palaearctic butterflies failed to note the composition of the market. Also in Europe, there is a high volume and low quality trade in exotic species, which is of no significance for the indigenous fauna, and the low volume and high quality trade in European butterflies. Those many thousands of butterflies, moths and other insects always found exhibited for sale at every Insektenbörse belong to the former category. All critiques have also overlooked that the high quality specimens of European butterflies are difficult to catch in nature as adults, and that their collecting would be so expensive, that the dealer could not compete in price with the material supplied by the breeders. This fact has commercial background:

– Collectors demand best quality specimens: only perfectly set fresh specimens can be sold at a good price.
– Such specimens are not easy to find in nature; it is much easier to catch a female and breed perhaps 50 or 100 fresh specimens from it.

- Surplus eggs, larvae or pupae can be reasonably well sold to other breeders and collectors.
- It is time consuming and expensive to stay long enough to get a series of specimens, but much easier to catch a female or two.
- The numbers of specimens offered are not high: otherwise a drammatic drop in price follows (ROSE 1985 and pers. comm.).
- Also slightly damaged specimens are not interesting as a commercial proposition: they are usually 50% cheaper than perfect ones.

Bearing in mind these facts, it is safe to conclude that a dealer does not present such a high threat to European butterflies, as for instance PRETSCHER & SCHULT (1978) or EBERT, HESSELBARTH & KASY (1978) claimed. Commercial collecting could possibly threaten some rare endemic species which cannot be successfully bred and can be collected as adults in good quantity and quality, so that the time and expenses "invested" by the dealer are likely to get him a good return.

Recent experience shows, that farming (breeding from parental stock held in captivity) or ranching (conceived by wild parental stock and reared in captivity) under licence or other controling mechanism is the answer to the problem of keeping the market under control. Nobody objects to sales of rare plants and one can purchase flowers everywhere. Why should some "conservationsts" object to sales of bred butterflies?

It may be useful to experiment with a selective ban imposed on the sale of certain endangered, panoramic and rare endemic species if all organizers (publishers) of insect sales agree on the selection; it may be more difficult to impose a ban on species from certain areas. All this would, however, require work intensive and time consuming inspections, and possibly disagreement in matters of identification. Ultimately, purpose bred specimens (i. e. from eggs oviposited in captivity by a captive female) are preferable to wild caught adults. It must be remembered that as long as there are customers, there will always be dealers. In such cases cooperation is usually much better than statutory measures.

## 6.8 Suggestions concerning the implementation of the Comprehensive Conservation Programme for European Butterflies

Outlining of a comprehensive conservation programme is the first rational step to be taken in the conservation of European butterflies. The implementation of proposals and suggestions contained therein is no longer the task for scientists alone. It requires decisions that must be taken above all by politicians.

Like any other project also the comprehensive conservation programme for European butterflies cannot be implemented without financial and administrative backing. This must be the responsibility of European governments, above all of the European Community because it is the largest and most important European political unit (particularly after the expected further growth of membership: Spain and Portugal) and some of the EC policies (e. g. the common agricultural policy) appear indirectly responsible for the decline of many butterfly species. No real effective support can be expected from the countries of the communist block.

To further and implement the comprehensive conservation programme for butterflies in the first place the

● Establishing of a research and coordination centre equiped with a computer aided data bank and other facilities, and adequately staffed.

It may be convenient to take advantage of some existing natural history museum or a university institute already equipped with a good library and reference material, preferably in a central position and certainly not in some corner poor in butterflies, on the outskirts of Europe. It may be advisable not to attach the institute (centre) too rigidly to the European Community administration. The institute would have to be kept free from direct government supervision in all essential matters of research and policy. The actual execution of the recommendations made by the institute would have to be carried out by the national (regional, local) nature conservation agencies and authorities with executive and legislative power; these would also have to oversee the implementation of prohibitions and orders provided by the institute (e. g. site protection by means of withholding of planning permissions). The essential information contained in the data bank would have to be made available to all member states of the European Community and other European countries joining the programme. It must be mentioned that HEATH (1981) made similar suggestions addressed to the Council of Europe, apparently without positive response.

The financing of the project outlined above can surely be found by savings on the common agricultural policy. In the meantime all government and private foundations supporting biological and relevant research should support generously applications for research grants to carry out projects concerned with the conservation of butterflies in Europe; they should consider also supporting applications placed by amateur entomologists (subsidies towards travel and, perhaps, equipment) so far as their projects contribute to the conservation of European butterflies. Amateur entomologists have contributed overwhelmingly to the research of European butterflies in the past and their experience, knowledge and enthusiasm is indispensible at present, and is likely to remain so in the future. Better coordination of their efforts, including scientific rationalization in some cases, would increase their potential in many ways. Amateur entomologists could contribute positively towards the realization of the comprehensive conservation programme for European butterflies particularly competently in the following tasks:

- research and compilation of faunistic reports including the preparation of faunistic monographs and faunistic synopsis;
- monitoring of selected sites and species, perhaps making use of techniques developed by DOUWES (1977) and POLLARD (1977);
- simple ecological studies of selected threatened or endemic species;
- compilation of reports on the distribution and dynamics of selected threatened or endemic species;
- studies of the biology of selected species, including their hostplants and the description of early stages.

Additionally, amateur entomologists should use every opportunity to improve public awareness of the importance of the conservation of butterflies, with all its political implications. The administrative centre of the comprehensive conservation programme will have to rely on their cooperation heavily, and it will need a special fund to back up their work.

Conservation of nature is a discipline the long term success of which depends on the active and willing cooperation of the equal interdependant partners:

● the scientists, whose scientific concepts are for the conservation of nature as indispensible as
● the politicians, who have the power bestowed upon them by the electorate, to implement them.

Unfortunately, in practice, the relationship of the two groups is not as equal as it should be: the politicians have additionally the power to, by and large, decide what the scientists may do by the providing, through the state agencies, the basic financial support for approved projects. As there is at present no major private (independant) research fund supporting primarily projects concerned with the conservation of nature, anywhere in western Europe, the upper hand of the politicians is quite powerful. The scientific concept presented here has been prepared without any official backing, financial or otherwise. The responsibility for its implementation and, indeed, for the survival of European butterflies (and other groups represented by their bioindicating properties) rests now solely with the politicians.

# 7 Bibliography

Although an extensive bibliography of European butterflies has recently become available (KUDRNA 1985, vol. 1 of this series) it is thought useful to list here apart from literature cited in the text also a selection of publications relevant to the conservation of butterflies in Europe; included are primarily scientific papers and books of "general" lepidopterology useful to the conservationist not particularly familiar with European butterflies. Papers dealing with regional faunistics have been excluded but are included in the above mentioned bibliography and easy to find by means of a subject index to key works forming a part of that publication. Further references to publications related to the conservation of butterflies with particular reference to central Europe are listed by BLAB & KUDRNA (1982), including faunistic papers concerning Germany and some adjacent countries. The general arrangement follows the principles laid down by KUDRNA (1985).

BAKER, R. R., 1978. The evolutionary ecology of animal migration. – 7 + 1012 pp., ill.; Hodder & STOUGHTON, LONDON.

BALFOUR-BROWNE, F., 1963. A code of entomological nomenclature. – Entomologist's Rec. J. Var. **75:** 209–214.

BALLETTO, E. & KUDRNA, O., 1985. Some aspects of the conservation of butterflies in Italy, with recommendations for a future strategy. – Boll. Soc. ent. ital. 117: 39–59.

BALLETTO, E. & TOSO, G. G., 1980. Electrophoretic techniques as a systematic research on Lepidoptera. – Nota lepid. **3:** 25–31.

BALLETTO, E., TOSO, G. G. & BARBERIS, G., 1982. La comunita di Lepidotteri Ropaloceri di alcuni ambienti relitti della Padania. – Struttura delle Zoocenosi Terrestri **4:** 45–67; Roma.

BATA, L., 1929. Versuch einer faunistischen Bearbeitung der Makrolepidopteren des südlichsten Böhmens. – Z. öst. EntVer. **14** (1929): 49–51, 62–64, 82–83, 91–92, 127–128; **15** (1930): 73–76, 83–84, 90–92, 122–123; **16** (1931): 6-7, 14–16.

BATA, L., 1930. Fauna motyli a flora jiznich Cech s hlediska biocenosy. – Roc. vlastived. Spol. jihocesk. **1** (1929): 92–110.

BAYNES, E. S. A., 1970. Supplement to a revised catalogue of Irish Macrolepidoptera. – 28 pp.; E. W. Classey, Hampton.

BAYNES, E. S. A., 1973. A revised catalogue of Irish Macrolepidoptera. (Ed. 2). – 3 + 110 pp.; E. W. Classey, Hampton.

BERGER, L., 1946. *Maculinea rebeli* HIRSCHKE, bona species. – Lambillionea **46:** 95–110.

BERGER, L. A., 1948. A *Colias* new to Britain. – Entomologist **81:** 129–131.

BERGMANN, A., 1951. Die Gross-Schmetterlinge Mitteldeutschlands. 1. Die Natur Mitteldeutschlands und ihre Schmetterlingsgesellschaften. – 631 pp., ill.; Urania-Verlag; Jena.

BERGMANN, A., 1952. Die Gross-Schmetterlinge Mitteldeutschlands. 2. Tagfalter. – 495 pp., ill.; Urania-Verlag, Jena.

BERNARDI, G., 1980. Les categories taxonomiques de la systematique evolutive. – Mem. Soc. zool. Fr. **40:** 373–425.

BERNARDI, G. & MELVILLE, R. V., 1979. Proposed addition to the species group of names for taxa differentiated by geographical criteria. – Bull. zool. Nomencl. **36:** 71–72.

BEURET, H., 1954. Dritter Beitrag zur Kenntnis von *Palaeochrysophanus candens* HERRICH-SCHÄFFER. – Mitt. ent. Ges. Basel **4:** 33–40.

BINDER, A., 1910. Macrolepidopteren von Gratzen (Südböhmen). – Int. ent. Z. **4:** 136–138, 141–142, 148–149, 160–161.

BISCHOF, A., 1968. *Coenonympha oedippus* FABRICIUS, eine kleine Chorographie. – Mitt. ent. Ges. Basel **18:** 41–64.

BLAB, J. & KUDRNA, O., 1982. Hilfsprogramm für Schmetterlinge. Ökologie und Schutz von Tagfaltern und Widderchen. – Natursch. aktuell **6:** 1–135.

BLAB, J., NOWAK, E., TRAUTMANN, W. & SUKOPP, H., 1977. Rote Liste der gefährdeten Tiere und Pflanzen in der Bundesrepublik Deutschland. – Natursch. aktuell **1:** 1–67.

BLASCHE, P., 1955. Raupenkalender für das mitteleuropäische Faunengebiet. – 149 pp., A. Kernen Verlag, Stuttgart.

BOWDEN, S. R., 1971. *Pieris* specimens for androconia: the end of the hybrid species? – Entomologist's Rec. J. Var. **83:** 369–371.

BRCAK, J., 1948. Biocenologicka studie Macrolepidopter na raselinisti SZ od Veseli n. Luz. v jiz. Cechach. – Ent. Listy **11:** 92–111.

BRETHERTON, R. F., 1966. A distribution list of the butterflies of western and southern Europe. – Trans. Soc. Br. Ent. **17:** 1–94.

BROWN, J., 1977. Subspeciation in the butterflies of the Peloponnesos with notes on adjacent parts of Greece. – Entomologist's Gaz. **28:** 141–174.

BRYK, F., 1940. Geographische Variabilität von *Melitaea didyma* (ESPER). – Folia zool. hydrobiol. **10:** 293–353.

BURESCH, I., 1915. Biology of *Doritis apollinus* HBST. and its distribution in the Balkan Peninsula. [In Bulgarian]. – Spis. bulg. Akad. Nauk. **12:** 15–36.

BURESCH, I. & TULESCHKOW, K., 1929. Die horizontale Verbreitung der Schmetterlinge in Bulgarien. [1]. [In Bulgarian]. – Izv. tsarsk. prirodonauch. Ins. Sof. **2:** 145–250.

CAIN, A. J., 1971. Animal species and their evolution. (Ed. 3). – 192 pp.; Hutchinson, London.

CHRISTENSEN, G., 1975. Wer rottet aus . . .? – Ent. Z., Frankf. a. M. **85:** 246–248.

COLLINS, N. M. & MORRIS, M. G., 1985. Threatened Swallowtail butterflies of the World. – 401 pp., 8 col. pls.; IUCN, Gland & Cambridge.

COOKE, B. H., 1928. An entomological motor tour in Spain in 1927. – Entomologist's Rec. J. Var. **61:** 154–159, 176–182, 197–202.

COX, C. B., HEALEY, I. N. & MOORE, P. D., 1973. Biogeography. – 8 + 184 pp., ill.; Blackwell, Oxford.

DABROWSKI, J. S. & KRZYWICKI, M., 1982. Ginace i zagrozone gatunki motyli w faunie Polski. – Studia nat. (B) **31:** 1–171.

DAVENPORT, D., 1941. The butterflies of the satyrid genus *Coenonympha*. – Bull. Mus. comp. Zool. Harv. **87:** 215–349.

DEMPSTER, J. P. & HALL, M. L., 1980. An attempt at re-establishing the Swallowtail butterfly at Wicken Fen. – Ecol. Ent. **5:** 327–334.

DENNIS, R. L. H., 1977. The British butterflies. – 14 + 318 pp., ill.; E. W. Classey, Faringdon.

DESCIMON, H., 1980. *Heodes tityrus tityrus* PODA et *H. tityrus subalpina* SPREYER: un probleme de speciation en milieu alpin. – Nota lepid. **2** (1979): 123–125.

DOWDESWELL, W. H., 1981. The life of the Meadow Brown. – 8 + 165 pp., 19 pls., 29 figs.; Heinemann Educational Books, London.

DOUWES, P., 1975. Distribution of a population of the butterfly *Heodes virgaureae*. – Oikos **26:** 332–340.

DOUWES, P., 1975. Territorial behaviour in *Heodes virgaureae* L., with particular reference to visual stimuli. – Norw. J. Ent. **22:** 143–154.

DOUWES, P., 1977. An area census method for estimating butterfly population numbers. – J. Res. Lepid. **15** (1976): 146–152.

DUFFEY, E., 1977. The re-establishment of the Large Copper butterfly *Lycaena dispar batava* OBTH. on Woodwalton Fen national nature reserve, Cambridgeshire, England. – Biol. Conserv. **12:** 143–158.

EBERT, G., 1983. SEL gegen Handel mit Schmetterlingen. – Mitt. LÖLF **8:** 7.

EBERT, G. & FALKNER, H., 1978. Rote Liste der in Baden-Württemberg gefährdeten Schmetterlingsarten. – Beih. Veröff. Naturschutz. Landschaftspfl. Bad.-Württ. **21:** 35–47.

EBERT, G., HESSELBARTH, G. & KASY, F., 1978. Die Bedeutung der Roter Listen in der Lepidopterologie. – Nota lepid. **1:** 69–76.

ECKWEILER, W. & HOFMANN, P., 1980. Verzeichnis iranischer Tagfalter. – Nachr. ent. Ver. Apollo (Suppl.) **1:** 1–28.

EHRLICH, P. R. & EHRLICH, A. H., 1981. Extinction. The causes and consequences of the disappearance of species. – 305 pp., ill.; Random House, New York.

EHRLICH, P. R. & MURPHY, D. D., 1982. Butterfly nomenclature: a critique. – J. Res. Lepid. **20** (1981): 1–11.

ELLENBERG, H., 1978. Vegetation Mitteleuropas mit den Alpen in ökologischer Sicht. (Ed. 2). – 981 pp., ill.; Ulmer, Stuttgart.

ELLENBERG, H. & MUELLER-DOMBOIS, D., 1967. Tentative physiognomic-ecological classification of plant formations of the earth. – Ber. geobot. Inst. eidg. techn. Hochsch. Stift. Rübel **37**: 21–55.

FOLTIN, H., 1954. Die Macrolepidopterenfauna der Hochmoore Ober-österreichs. – Z. Wien. ent. Ges. **39**: 98–115.

FOLTIN, H., 1961. Die Macrolepidopterenfauna der Flachmoore Ober-österreichs. – Z. Wien. ent. Ges. **46**: 49–58.

FORD, E. B., 1962. Butterflies. (Ed. 3). – 368 pp., ill.; Collins, London.

FORD, E. B., 1975. Ecological genetics. (Ed. 4). – 20 + 442 pp.; 18 pls., ill.; Chapman & HALL, LONDON.

FORD, H. D. & FORD, E. B., 1930, Fluctuation in numbers and its influence on variation in *Melitaea aurinia*, ROTT. – Trans. ent. Soc. London. **78**: 345–351.

FORSTER, W., 1938. Das System der paläarktischen Polyommatini. – Mitt. Münch. ent. Ges. **28**: 97–118.

FORSTER, W. & WOHLFAHRT, T. A., 1952–54. Die Schmetterlinge Mitteleuropas. 1. Biologie der Schmetterlinge. – 12 + 202 pp., 147 figs.; Franckh'sche Verlagshandlung, Stuttgart.

FORSTER, W. & WOHLFAHRT, T. A., 1976. Die Schmetterlinge Mitteleuropas. 2. Tagfalter. (Ed. 2). – 180 pp., ill.; Franckh'sche Verlagshandlung, Stuttgart.

FROHAWK, F. W., 1934. The complete book of British butterflies. – 384 pp., 32 col. pls.; ill.; Ward, Lock & Co., LONDON.

GEIGER, H., 1975. Schmetterlingssammler und Naturschutz. – Ent. Z., Frankfurt a. M. **85**: 261–262.

GEIGER, H., 1977. Eine Freilandkopula zwischen *Maniola jurtina* und *Aphantopus hyperantus*. – Ent. Z., Frankfurt a. M. **87**: 93–95.

GEIGER, H., 1978. Die systematische Stellung von *Pieris napi bryoniae*: biochemisch-genetische Untersuchungsbefunde. – Ent. Z., Frankfurt a. M. **88**: 229–235.

GEIGER, H., 1981. Enzyme electrophoretic studies on the genetic relationships of pierid butterflies. I. European taxa. – J. Res. Lepid. **19** (1980): 181–195.

GEPP, J., 1981. Programmrahmen für einen umfassenden Lepidopterenschutz. – Beih. Veröff. Natursch. Landschaftspfl. Bad.-Württ. **21**: 191–216.

GERAEDTS, W. H. J. M., 1982. Handleiding voor het projet dagvlinders (Rhopalocera). – 20 pp.; Vakgroep Natuurbeheer Landbouwhogeschool, Wageningen.

GERBER, H., 1972. Speziation und Biologie von *Euphydryas aurinia aurinia* ROTT., *E. euphydryas debilis* OBERTH. und *E. aurinia debilis* f. *glaciegenita* VERITY. – Mitt. ent. Ges. Basel **22**: 73–87.

GOMEZ BUSTILLO, M. R. & FERNANDEZ-RUBIO, F., 1974. Mariposas de la peninsula Iberica. Ropaloceros. I, II. – 198 + 259 pp., ill.; ICONA, Madrid.

HABELER, H., 1972. Zur Kenntnis der Lebensräume von *Coenonympha oedippus* F. – NachrBl. bayer. Ent. **21**: 51–55.

HACKRAY, J. & SARLET, L. G., 1969–74. Catalogue des Macrolepidopteres de Belgique. – Lambillionea (Suppl.) **67** (1969): 1–16; **68** (1969): 17–48; **69** (1970): 49–64; **70** (1970): 65–80; **70** (1971): 81–112; **71** (1972): 113–160; **72/73** (1973): 161–192; **72/73** (1974): 193–208; **74** (1974): 193–208.

HANSON, W. R., 1967. Estimating the density of an animal population. – J. Res. Lepid. **6**: 203–247.

HANSON, W. R. & HOVANITZ, W., 1968. Trials of several density estimators on a butterfly population. – J. Res. Lepid. **7**: 35–49.

HAUPT, J., 1982. Rote Liste der gefährdeten Gross-Schmetterlinge von Berlin (West). – SchrReihe LandschEntwickl. tech. Univ. Berlin **11**: 211–224.

HEATH, J., 1969. The Lepidoptera distribution maps scheme. Progress report 1968. – Entomologist **102**: 12–16.

HEATH, J. (Ed.), 1970. Provisional atlas of the insects of the British Isles. 1. Lepidoptera Rhopalocera: Butterflies. – 57 pp., ill.; Biological Record Centre, Huntingdon.

HEATH, J., 1974 A century of change in the Lepidoptera. – Syst. Ass. spec. Vol. **6**: 275–292.

HEATH, J., 1976. Habitats. – Moths Butterfl. Gt. Br. Ire **1**: 92–106.

HEATH, J., 1981. Threatened Rhopalocera (butterflies) in Europe. – Nature Environ. Ser. **23**: 1–157.

HEATH, J. & LECLERCQ, J. (Ed.), 1981. Provisional atlas of the Invertebrates of Europe. Maps 1–27. – [65 pp.]; EIS & ICIS, Cambridge & GEMBLOUX.

HEATH, J., POLLARD, E. & THOMAS, J. A., 1984. Atlas of the butterflies in Great Britain and Ireland. – 158 pp., ill.; Viking, Harmondsworth.

HENRIKSEN, H. J. & KREUTZER, I., 1982. The butterflies of Scandinavia in nature. – 215 pp., col. ill.; Skandinavisk Bogforlag, Odense.

HIGGINS, L. G., 1941 An illustrated catalogue of the Palaearctic *Melitaea*. – Trans. R. ent. Soc. Lond. **91**: 175–365.

HIGGINS, L. G., 1950. A descriptive catalogue of the Palaearctic *Euphydryas*. – Trans. R. ent. Soc. Lond. **101**: 435–489.

HIGGINS, L. G., 1955 A descriptive catalogue of the genus *Mellicta* BILLBERG and its species, with supplementary notes on the genera *Melitaea* and *Euphydryas*. – Trans. R. ent. Soc. Lond. **106**: 1–131.

HIGGINS, L. G., 1976. The classification of European butterflies. – 320 pp., 402 figs.; Collins, London (1975).

HIGGINS, L. G., 1978. A revision of the genus *Euphydryas* SCUDDER. – Entomologist's Gaz. **29**: 109–115.

HIGGINS, L. G. & RILEY, N. D., 1970. A field guide to the butterflies of Britain and Europe. – 380 pp., 60 col. pls., ill.; Collins, London.

HIGGINS, L. G. & RILEY, N. D., 1973. A field guide to the butterflies of Britain and Europe. (Ed. 2). – 381 pp., 60 col. pls., ill.; Collins, London.

HIGGINS, L. G. & RILEY, N. D., 1980. A field guide to the butterflies of Britain and Europe. (Ed. 4). – 384 pp., 63 col. pls., ill.,; Collins, London.

HINTON, H. E., 1951. Myrmecophilous Lycaenidae and other Lepidoptera. – Proc. Trans. S. Lond. ent. nat. Hist. Soc. **1949/50**: 111–175.

HOLLOWAY, J. D. & ROBINSON, G. S., 1979. Comment on draft Article 58. In: Comments by zoologists on the draft Code Z. N. (S.) 2250. – Bull. zool. Nomencl. **36**: 15–16.

HOLMES, S. (Ed.), 1979. Henderson's dictionary of biological terms. (Ed. 9). – 11 + 510 pp.; Longman, London & NEW YORK.

HOWARTH, T. G., 1973. South's British butterflies. – 210 pp., 48 col. pls., ill.; F. Warne, London.

HRUBY, K., 1956. *Araschnia levana* L. v Ceskoslovensku. – Ochr. Prir., Praha **11**: 257–264.

HRUBY, K., 1964. Prodromus Lepidopter Slovenska. – 962 pp., ill.; Vydav. Slov. Akad. Vied., Bratislava.

JACHONTOV, A. A., 1935. Our butterflies. [In Russian]. – 160 pp., 50 figs.; GUPI, Moscow.

KAABER, S., 1964. Studies on *Maculinea alcon* (SCHIFF.) – *rebeli* (HIR.) with reference to the taxonomy, distribution and phylogeny of the group. – Ent. Meddr. **32**: 277–319.

KAISILA, J., 1961 The influence of culture on the Finnish butterfly and moth fauna. – Fennia **85**: 106–111.

KAISILA, J., 1962. Immigration and Expansion der Lepidopteren in Finnland in den Jahren 1869–1960. – Acta ent. fenn. **18**: 1–452.

KLOFT, W. J., 1978. Ökologie der Tiere. – 304 pp., 86 figs.; UTB Ulmer, Stuttgart.

KLOTS, A. B., 1933. A generic revision of the Pieridae. – Entomologica am. (N. S.) **12**: 139–242.

KLOTS, A. B., 1936. The relationship of the species of the genus *Lycaena* FABRICIUS. – Bull. Brooklyn ent. Soc. **31**: 154–171.

KOCAK, A. Ö., 1981. Critical check-list of European Papilionoidea. [1]. – Priamus **1**: 46–90.

KOCAK, A. Ö., 1982. Notes on *Archon apollinus* HERBST, 1798). – Priamus **2**: 44–64.

KOCAK, A. Ö., 1982. Critical check-list of European Papilionoidea. [2]. –
    Priamus **1** (1981): 155–167; **2** (1982): 69–92.
KOCAK, A. Ö., 1983. Critical check-list of European Papilionoidea. [3]. –
    Priamus **3**: 11–37.
KOCAK, A. Ö., 1983. On the nomenclature of *Papilio thersamon* ESPER,
    1784 from the west Palaearctic region. – Priamus **3**: 3–5.
KOUTSAFTIKIS, A., 1974. Systematic, ecological and zoogeographical study
    of the Rhopalocera of mainland Greece. [In Greek, English summary].
    – 154 pp., ill.; Athens.
KORSHUNOV, Y. P., 1972. Catalogue of diurnal butterflies of the fauna of
    the U.S.S.R. [In Russian]. – Ent. Obozr. **51**: 136–154, 352–368.
KOVACS, L., 1953. Die Gross-Schmetterlinge Ungarns und ihre Ver-
    breitung. – Folia ent. hung. **6**: 77–167.
KRALICEK, M. & POVOLNY, D., 1980. K sucasnemu stavu faunistiky
    moravskych dennich motylov. – Ent. Problemy **16**: 107–131.
KRZYWICKI, M., 1962. Bielinki–Pieridae, Motylowce–Papilionidae. –
    Klucze Oznacz. Owad. Pol. **27** (65/66): 1–45.
KUDRNA, O., 1957. K poznani motylu jiznich Cech. – Cas. csl. Spol. ent.
    **54**: 401.
KUDRNA, O., 1968. Denni motyli v okoli Vimperka. – Sb. jihoces. Mus.
    Ceskych Budejovicich Prir. Vedy **8**: 18–23.
KUDRNA, O., 1970–71. Butterflies of south Bohemia. – Entomologist's
    Rec. J. Var. **82** (1970): 323–330; **83** (1971): 53–67.
KUDRNA, O., 1973. On the status of *Pieris cheiranthi* HÜBNER. – En-
    tomologist's Gaz. **24**: 299–304.
KUDRNA, O., 1974. A distribution list of butterflies of Czechoslovakia. –
    Entomologist's Gaz. **25**: 161–177.
KUDRNA, O., 1975. A revision of the genus *Gonepteryx* LEACH. – En-
    tomologist's Gaz. **26**: 3–37.
KUDRNA, O., 1977. A revision of the genus *Hipparchia* FABRICIUS. –
    300 pp., 353 figs.; E. W. Classey, Faringdon.
KUDRNA, O., 1978. Chapter XII. Homonymy. Article 58. Variant spelling
    deemed to be identical. In: Draft third edition of the International Code
    of Zoological Nomenclature: Comments by zoologists S. Z. (S.) 2250. –
    Bull. zool. Nomencl. **35**: 82.
KUDRNA, O., 1983. An annotated catalogue of the butterflies named by
    Roger Verity. – J. Res. Lepid. **21** (1982): 1–106.
KUDRNA, O., 1984. On the taxonomy of the genus *Hipparchia* FABRICIUS,
    1807, with descriptions of two new species from Italy. – Fragm. ent. 7:
    229–243.
KUDRNA, O., 1985. Butterflies of Europe. 1. Concise bibliography. –
    448 pp.; Aula-Verlag, Wiesbaden.

KUDRNA, O., 1986. Grundlagen zu einem Artenschutzprogramm für die Tagschmetterlingsfauna in Bayern und Analyse der Schutzproblematik in der Bundesrepublik Deutschland. – Nachr. ent. Ver. Apollo (Suppl.) **6**: 1–90.

KURENTZOV, A. I., 1970. The butterflies of the Far East U.S.S.R. [In Russian]. – 163 pp., 14 col. pls., 104 figs.; Nauka, Leningrad.

LANGER, T. W. [1958]. Nordens dagsommerfugle. – 344 pp., 16 col. pls.; Munsgaard Forlag & SKANDINAVISK BOGFORLAG, ODENSE.

LASSO DE LA VEGA, R., 1978. Una nueva colonia de *Cupido minimus carswelli* (STEMPFFER, 1927). – Revta Lepid. **6**: 226, 234.

LATTIN, G. DE, 1949. Über die Artfrage in der *Hipparchia semele* L.-Gruppe. – Ent. Z., Frankfurt a. M. **59**: 113–118, 124–126, 131–132.

LATTIN, G. DE, 1967. Grundriss der Zoogeographie. – 602 pp., 170 figs.; G. Fischer, Jena.

LEDERER, G., [1941]. Die Naturgeschichte der Tagfalter. 2 vols. – 354 pp., ill.; O. R. Wrede, Frankfurt a. M.

LEMPKE, B. J., 1953. Catalogus de nederlandse Macrolepidoptera. (Erste supplement). – Tijdschr. Ent. **96**: 239–305.

LEMPKE, B. J., 1954. Catalogus de nederlandse Macrolepidoptera. (Tweede supplement). – Tijdschr. Ent. **97**: 301–345.

LEMPKE, B. J., 1956. Catalogus de nederlandse Macrolepidoptera. (Derde supplement). – Tijdschr. Ent. **98** (1955): 283–355.

LEMPKE, B. J., 1956. Catalogus de nederlandse Macrolepidoptera. (Vierde supplement). – Tijdschr. Ent. **99**: 155–216.

LEMPKE, B. J., 1957. Catalogus de nederlandse Macrolepidoptera. (Vijfde supplement). – Tijdschr. Ent. **100**: 427–487.

LESSE, H. DE, 1960. Speciation et variation chromosomique chez les Lepidopteres Rhopaloceres. – Annls. Sci. nat. (12) **2**: 1–223.

LORKOVIC, Z., 1955. Zavisnost varijabilnosti organa muskog genitalnog aparata kukaca njihovoj funkcionalnoj vrijednosti. – Biol. Glasn. **7**: 234–235.

LORKOVIC, Z., 1958. Die Merkmale der unvollständigen Speziationsstufe und die Frage der Einführung der Semispezies in die Systematik. – Uppsala Univ. Arsskr. **1958**: 159–168.

LORKOVIC, Z., 1979. Komentar popisu Rhopalocera Jugoslavije. – Acta ent. jugosl. **14**: 110–113.

LORKOVIC, Z. & JAKSIC, P., 1979. Ispravci alfabetskog popisa i komentara za karticu Rhopalocera Jugoslavije. – Acta ent. jugosl. **15**: 155–156.

MALICKY, H., 1968. Freilanduntersuchungen über eine ökologische Isolation zwischen *Maculinea teleius* BGSTR. und *M. nausithous* BGSTR. – Wiss. Arb. Burgenld. **40**: 65–68.

MALICKY, H., 1969. Uebersicht ueber Präimaginalstadien, Bionomie und

Ökologie der mitteleuropäischen Lycaenidae. – Mitt. ent. Ges. Basel **19**: 25–91.

MALICKY, H., 1970. New aspects on the association between lycaenid larvae and ants. – J. Lepid. Soc. **24**: 190–202.

MANLEY, W. B. L. & ALLCARD, H. G., 1970. A field guide to the butterflies and burnets of Spain. – 192 pp., 40 col. pls.; E. W. Classey, Hampton.

MARCUZZI, G., 1979. European ecosystems. – Biogeographica 15: 1–779.

MAYR, E., 1969. Principles of systematic zoology. – 428 pp., ill.; McGraw-Hill Book Co., New York.

MEYER, M. & PELLES, A., 1979. Rote Liste der Schmetterlinge Luxemburgs. – Paiperlek **1** (2): 1–9.

MEYER, M. & PELLES, A., 1981. Atlas provisoire des Insectes du Grand-Duche de Luxembourg. – Trav. scient. Mus. Hist. nat. Luxemb. **1**: 1–147.

MORRIS, M. G., 1976. Conservation and the collector. – Moths Butterfl. Gt. Br. Ire. **1**: 107–116.

MORRIS, M. G., 1981. Conservation of butterflies in the United Kingdom. – Beih. Veröff. Natursch. Landschaftspfl. Bad.-Württ. **21**: 35–47.

MUGGELTON, J., 1973. Some aspects of the history and ecology of blue butterflies in the Cotswolds. – Proc. Trans. Br. ent. nat. Hist. Soc. **6**: 77–84.

MUGGLETON, J. & BENHAM, B. R., 1975. Isolation and the decline of the large blue butterfly *(Maculinea arion)* in Great Britain. – Biol. Conserv. **7**: 119–128.

MÜLLER, L., 1933. *Pieris bryoniae* O. und *napi* L. – Int. ent. Z. 27: 93–99, 105–110, 141–145, 173–176, 181–183, 197–199, 233–244, 296–303.

MÜLLER, L. & KAUTZ, H., 1939. *Pieris bryoniae* O. und *Pieris napi* L. – 16 + 191 pp., 16 col. pls.; Oesterreichischer Entomologen-Verein, Wien.

NEKRUTENKO, Y. P., 1968. Phylogeny and geographical distribution of the genus *Gonepteryx*. [In Russian, English summary]. – 128 pp., 20 pls.; Naukova dumka, Kiev.

NICULESCU, E. V., 1961. Lepidoptera. Fam. Papilionidae (Fluturi). – Fauna Repub. pop. rom. **11** (5): 1–103.

NICULESCU, E. V., 1963. Lepidoptera. Fam. Pieridae (Fluturi). – Fauna Repub. pop. rom. **11** (6): 1–202.

NICULESCU, E. V., 1965. Familia Nymphalidae. – Fauna Repub. pop. rom. **11** (7): 1–361.

NIKUSCH, I., 1981. Die Zucht von *Parnassius apollo* LINNAEUS mit jährlich zwei Generationen als Möglichkeit zur Erhaltung bedrohter Populationen. – Beih. Veröff. Natursch. Landschaftspfl. Bad.-Württ. **21**: 175–176.

NORDSTRÖM, F., 1955. De Fenoskandiska dagfjärilarnas utbredning. – Acta Univ. lund. (N.F.) **66** (1): 1–176.

NOVAK, I. & SPITZER, K., 1982. Ohrozeny svet hmyzu. – 138 pp., 88 col. + 25 figs.; Academia, Praha.

OEHMIG, S., 1983. *Hipparchia azorina* (STRECKER, 1899): Biology, ecology and distribution on the Azores Islands. – J. Res. Lepid. **20** (1981): 136–160.

OLIVER, C. G., 1971. Genetic incompatibility between *Pararge aegeria* and *P. megera*. – Entomologist **104**: 316.

OWEN, D. F., 1975. Estimating the abundance and diversity of butterflies. – Biol. Conserv. **8**: 173–183.

PACLT, J., 1949. Nomenclator sive enumeratio critica Lepidopterorum Slovaciae. – Ent. Listy **12**: 140–155.

PACLT, J., 1952. Proposed suspension of the Regles for two nomina nuda of [Denis & SCHIFFERMÜLLER]. – ENT. BER., AMST. **14**: 91–92.

PALIK, E., 1980. The protection and reintroduction in Poland of *Parnassius apollo* LINNAEUS. – Nota lepid. **2** (1979): 163–164.

PARKER, R., 1983. The butterflies of Cyprus. – Entomologist's Gaz. **34**: 17–53.

PARKINSON, C. N., 1977. Parkinson's law or the pursuit of progress. – 109 pp., ill.; Penguin Books Ltd., London.

PARNASSE, A. P., 1980. Schmetterlinge weinen nicht! – Natur Landsch., Stuttgart **55**: 263.

PASSOS, C. F. DOS & GREY, L. P., 1945. A genitalic survey of Argynninae. – Am. Mus. Novit. **1296**: 1–29.

PERSSON, G. ET AL., 1982. Acidification today and tomorrow. – 231 pp., ill.; Swedish Ministry of Agriculture, Stockholm.

PETERSEN, W., 1904. Die Generationsorgane der Schmetterlinge und ihre Bedeutung für die Artbildung. – Zap. imp. Akad. Nauk. (8) **16** (8): 1–84.

POLLARD, E., 1977. A method for assessing changes in the abundance of butterflies. – Biol. Conserv. **12**: 115–134.

POLLARD, E., 1979. A national scheme for monitoring the abundance of butterflies: the first three years. – Proc. Trans. Br. ent. nat. Hist. Soc. **12**: 77–90.

POVOLNY, D., 1954. Individualni formy dennich motylu ve sbirkach Moravskeho Musea a jejich vyvojovy vyznam. – Cas. mor. Mus. Brne **39**: 146–163.

PRETSCHER, P., 1977. Rote Liste der in der Bundesrepublik Deutschland gefährdeten Tierarten. Teil II – Wirbelose; 4. Gross-Schmetterlinge, Macrolepidoptera s.l. (Insekten). (1. Fassung). – Natur Landsch., Stuttgart **52**: 164–168, 210–215.

PRETSCHER, P. & SCHULT, A., 1978. Die Gefährdung der Insektenfauna, insbesondere der Schmetterlinge, durch Fang und Handel. – Natur Landsch., Stuttgart **53**: 308–312.

PYLE, R., BENTZIEN, M. & OPLER, P., 1981. Insect conservation. – A. Rev. Ent. **26**: 233–258.

REBEL, H., 1903. Studien über die Lepidopterenfauna der Balkanländer. 1. Bulgarien und Ostrumelien. – Annln. naturh. Mus. Wien **18**: 123–347.

REBEL, H., 1904. Studien über die Lepidopterenfauna der Balkanländer. 2. Bosnien und Herzegowina. – Annln. naturh. Mus. Wien **19**: 97–377.

REBEL, H., 1911. Die Lepidopterenfauna von Herkulesbad und Orsova. – Annln. naturh. Mus. Wien **26**: 253–430.

REBEL, H., 1913. Studien über die Lepidopterenfauna der Balkanländer. 3. Sammelergebnisse aus Montenegro, Albanien, Mazedonien und Thracien. – Annln. naturh. Mus. Wien **27**: 281–334.

REBEL, H., 1916. Die Lepidopterenfauna Kretas. – Annln. naturh. Mus. Wien **30**: 66–171.

REBEL, H. & ZERNY, H., 1931. Die Lepidopterenfauna Albaniens. – Denkschr. Akad. Wiss. Wien **103**: 37–161.

REICHL, E. R. & GEPP, J., 1977. Computer-unterstützte lokalfaunistische Datenerfassung am Beispiel der Steiermark. – Mitt. naturw. Ver. Steiermark **107**: 207–215.

REICHHOLF, J., 1973. Die Bedeutung nicht bewirtschafteter Wiesen für unsere Tagfalter. – Natur Landsch., Stuttgart **48**: 80–81.

REINHARDT, R., 1982. Übersicht zur Tagfalterfauna der DDR. – Nota lepid. **5**: 177–190.

REISS, H. & TREMEWAN, W. G., 1967. A systematic catalogue of the genus *Zygaena* FABRICIUS. – Series ent. **2**: I–XVI, 1–329.

RILEY, D. & YOUNG, A., 1968. World vegetation. – 96 pp., 123 figs.; Cambridge University Press, London.

ROBERTSON, T. S., 1980. An estimate of the British population of *Apatura iris* (LINNAEUS). – Proc. Trans. Br. ent. nat. Hist. Soc. **13**: 89–94.

ROBINSON, R., 1971. Lepidoptera genetics. – 9 + 687 pp.; Pergamon Press, Oxford.

ROESLER, R.-U., 1980. Die gefährdeten Tagfalter der Pfalz und ihre Biotope. – Pfälzer Heimat **31**: 134–147.

RÜHL, F. & HEYNE, A., 1892–95. Die palaearktischen Grossschmetterlinge und ihre Naturgeschichte. – 857 pp.; Heyne, Leipzig.

SCHACK, E., 1936. Mein erster *Argynnis pandora* SCHIFF. – Ent. Z., Frankfurt a. M. **50**: 125–128.

SCHMIDT-KOEHL, W., 1971. Lepidoptera Rhopalocera et Grypocera de la Sarre (Saarland). In: EIS, Atlas provisoires hors-series. – 7 pp., 5 + 100 maps.; Fac. Sci. Agron., Zool. Gen. Faun., Gembloux.

SCHREIBER, H., 1976. Arealveränderungen von Lepidopteren in der Bun-

desrepublik Deutschland und Vorschläge für den Naturschutz. –
SchrReihe Vegetationskde. **10:** 341–357.

SCHWARZ, R., 1948. Motyli. 1. – 14 + 42 pp., 291 figs.; Vesmir, Praha.

SCHWARZ, R., 1949. Motyli. 2. – 10 + 69 pp., 505 figs.; Vesmir, Praha.

SHIELDS, O., 1974. Toward a theory of butterfly migration. – J. Res. Lepid.
**13:** 217–238.

SKELTON, M. J. & HEATH, J., 1975. Insect distribution maps scheme.
Lepidoptera Rhopalocera. Butterflies. Provisional distribution maps. –
[64 pp.]; Biological Record Centre, [Huntingdon].

SLABY, O., 1951. O vlivu klimatickych cyklu na migraci motyly a na motyli
zvirenu Cech. – Cas. csl. Spol. ent. **48:** 242–253.

STERNECK, J. VON, 1929. Prodromus der Schmetterlingsfauna Böhmens.
297 pp., ill.; publ. by author, Karlsbad.

STUBBS, A. E., 1985. Is there a future for butterfly collecting in Britain? –
Proc. Trans. Br. ent. nat. Hist. Soc. 18: 65–73.

STÜBINGER, R. & GLITZ, D., 1981. Rote Liste. Schmetterlinge. 1. Tagfalter.
– 36 pp., ill.; Behörde für Naturschutz, Hamburg.

STÜBINGER, R., 1983. Schutzprogramm für Tagfalter und Widderchen in
Hamburg. – SchrReihe Behörde Bezirksangel. Natursch. Umweltge-
stalt. **7:** 1–103.

THOMAS, J., 1980. Why did the Large Blue become extinct in Britain? –
Oryx **15:** 243–247.

THOMAS, J., 1982. Why did the Large Blue butterfly become extinct in
Britain. – Atala **7** (1979): 50–52.

THOMAS, J. A. & SIMCOX, D. J., 1982. A quick method for estimating larval
populations of *Melitaea cinxia* L. during surveys. – Biol. Conserv. **22:**
315–322.

THOMAS, J. & WEBB, N., 1984. Butterflies of Dorset. – 128 pp., 56 col.
figs., ill.; Dorset nat. Hist. & Archaeol. Soc., Dorchester.

THOMSON, G., 1973. Geographical variation of *Maniola jurtina* (L.). –
Tijdschr. Ent. **116:** 185–227.

THOMSON, G., 1980. The butterflies of Scotland. A natural history. –
267 pp., 39 pls. (8 col.), 97 figs.; Croom Helm Ltd.; London.

TULESCHKOW, K., 1958. The Lepidoptera of Bulgaria. [In Bulgarien]. –
343 pp., 543 figs.; Nauka i Iskutstvo, Sofia.

VERITY, R., 1905–11. Rhopalocera palaearctica. [1.] Papilionidae et
Pieridae. – 86 + 368 pp., 2 + 12 + 72 pls. (some col.); R. Verity, Firenze.

VERSTRAETEN, C., 1970. Enquete pour etablir la repartition des Macrolepidopteres de Belgique et du Grand-duche de Luxembourg.
[Papilionidae, Pieridae]. **In:** Atlas provisoire des Insectes de Belgique. –
2 pp., 14 maps.; Gembloux.

VERSTRAETEN, C., 1971. Enquete pour etablir la repartition des Macrolepidopteres Satyrides et Nemeobiides de Belgique et du Grand-duche de Luxembourg. **In:** Atlas provisoire des Insectes de Belgique. – 3 pp., 24 maps.; Gembloux.

VERSTRAETEN, C., 1971. Enquete pour etablir la repartition des Macrolepidopters Nymphalides et Sphingides de Belgique et du Grand-duche de Luxembourg. **In:** Atlas provisoires des Insectes de Belgique. – 4 pp., 52 maps.; Gembloux.

VERSTRAETEN, C. & PRINS, W. DE, 1976. Enquete pour etablir la repartition des Lepidopteres de Belgique et du Grand-duche de Luxembourg. Lycaenidae. **In:** Atlas provisoires des Insectes de Belgique. – 8 pp., 36 maps.; Gembloux.

VIEDMA, M. G. DE & GOMEZ BUSTILLO, M. R., 1976. Libro rojo de los Lepidopteros ibericos. – 117 pp., ill.; ICONA, Madrid.

WAGENER, S., KINKLER, H. & REHNELT, K., 1977. „Rote Liste" der in Nordrhein-Westfalen gefährdeten Schmetterlingsarten. – Mitt. ArbGem. rhein.-westf. Lepid. **1:** 15–36.

WAGNER-ROLLINGER, C., 1980. Les biotopes de nos papillons diurnes. – 64 pp.; [Selbsverlag], Luxembourg.

WARNECKE, G., 1935–36. *Chrysophanus (Heodes) dispar* HAW., ein gefährdeter Tagfalter. – Ent. Z., Frankfurt a. M. **49** (1935): 137–140; (1936): 439–443, 453–456.

WARNECKE, G., 1961. Rezente Arealvergrösserungen bei Makrolepidopteren in Mittel- und Nordeuropa. – Bonn. zool. Beitr. **12:** 113–141.

WARREN, B. C. S., 1936. Monograph of the genus *Erebia*. – 407 pp., 104 pls.; British Museum (Natural History), London.

WARREN, B. C. S., 1944. Review of the classification of the Argynnidi: with a systematic revision of the genus *Boloria*. – Trans. R. ent. Soc. Lond. **94:** 1–101.

WARREN, B. C. S., 1947. Some principles of classification in Lepidoptera, with special reference to the butterflies. – Entomologist **80:** 208–217, 235–241, 262–268, 280–282.

WARREN, B. C. S., 1953. Problems of speciation in the genus *Erebia*. – Entomologist's Rec. J. Var. (Suppl.) **65:** (1–6).

WARREN, B. C. S., 1959. On *Erebia aquitania* FRUHSTORFER: with a note on the value of anatomical characters in this and related species. – Entomologist's Rec. J. Var. **71:** 184–190.

WARREN, B. C. S., 1970. On three North African species of the genus *Pieris: P. maura* VTY., *P. atlantica* ROTHSCH., *P. segonzaci* LE CERF. – Entomologist's Rec. J. Var. **82:** 221–230.

WARREN, B. C. S., 1981. Supplement to monograph of the genus *Erebia*. – 17 pp., ill.; E. W. Classey, Faringdon.

WEISS, D., 1967. Perletovec *Proclossiana eunomia* ESPER, 1797, (*C.*

*aphirape* HÜBNER, 1799) v Ceskoslovensku. – Cas. narod. Mus. **136:** 195–200.

WIKLUND, C., 1973. Host plant suitability and the mechanism of host selection in larvae of *Papilio machaon*. – Entomologia exp. appl. **16:** 232–242.

WIKLUND, C., 1974. Oviposition preferences in *Papilio machaon* in relation to the host plants of the larvae. – Entomologia exp. appl **17:** 189–198.

WIKLUND, C., 1975. The evolutionary relationship between adult oviposition preferences and larval host plant range in *Papilio machaon* L. – Oecologia **18:** 185–197.

WIKLUND, C., 1977. Oviposition, feeding and spatial separation of breeding and foraging habitats in a population of *Leptidea sinapis*. – Oikos **28:** 56–58.

WILKINSON, C., 1981. Modern biosystematics. – Entomologist's Gaz. **32:** 205–215.

WILLEMSE, L., 1977. *Kirinia climene* (ESPER, 1786), new to Greece. – Ent. Ber., Amst. **37:** 148–151.

WILTSHIRE, E. P., 1957. The Lepidoptera of Iraq. – 162 pp., 17 pls. (2 col.); Nicolas Kaye, London.

WOLDSTEDT, P., 1954. Das Eiszeitalter. 1. Die allgemeinen Erscheinungen des Eiszeitalters. – 7 + 374 pp., 136 figs.; P. Enke, Stuttgart.

WOLDSTEDT, P., 1958. Das Eiszeitalter. 2. Europa, Vorderasien und Nordafrika im Eiszeitalter. – 438 pp., 125 figs., 24 tabs.; P. Enke, Stuttgart.

ZINNERT, K. D., 1966. Quantitative Untersuchungen nach der Lincoln-Index-Methode an einer Population von *Lysandra coridon* PODA im zentralen Kaiserstuhl. – Mitt. bad. Landesver. Naturkde. (N.F.) **9:** 75–83.

ZINNERT, K. D., 1966. Beitrag zur Faunistik und Ökologie der in der Oberrheinebene und im Südwestschwarzwald vorkommenden Satyriden und Lycaeniden. – Ber. naturf. Ges. Freiburg i. B. **77:** 77–141.